Pro/MECHANICA Structure Tutorial
Release 2000i^2 - Independent Mode

Preface

In his excellent text <u>Finite Element Procedures</u>, K.J. Bathe identifies two possible and different objectives for studying Finite Element Analysis (FEA) and methods: to learn the proper use of the method to solve complex problems (the practitioner's goal), and to understand the methods themselves in depth so as to pursue further development of the theory (the researcher's goal). This tutorial was created with the former objective in mind, recognizing that this is a formidable task and not one that can be totally accomplished in a single, short volume. Thus, the primary purpose of the tutorial is to introduce new users to Pro/MECHANICA® (Parametric Technology Corporation, Waltham, MA) and see how it can be used to analyze a variety of problems.

The tutorial lessons cover most of the major concepts and frequently used commands required to progress from a novice to an intermediate user level. The commands are presented in a click-by-click manner using simple examples and exercises that illustrate a broad range of the most common analysis types that can be performed. In addition to showing/illustrating the command usage, the text will explain why certain commands are being used and, where appropriate, the relation of commands to the overall FEA philosophy. Moreover, since error analysis is an important skill, considerable time is spent exploring the created models (in fact, sometimes intentionally inducing some errors), so that users will become comfortable with the "debugging" phase of model creation.

In this 4th edition, the tutorial has been updated to Release 2000i^2. **This tutorial deals almost exclusively with operation in independent mode**, that is, without the use of Pro/ENGINEER® as the geometry engine front-end. However, a rather lengthy final chapter in this tutorial introduces the use of integrated mode. Use of Pro/E and Pro/M in integrated mode is covered in a companion book from SDC. Independent mode allows full access to all MECHANICA commands and features (some of which are not available in integrated mode). Most of these are covered in this tutorial. The new capability (as of Release 2000i) to handle large deformation problems, that is problems involving geometric non-linearity, has not been covered due to space restraints. In any case, this functionality is of a significantly more advanced level than what is required (perhaps) in an introductory tutorial.

Students with a broad range of backgrounds should be able to use this book. The approach taken in the manual is meant to allow accessability to persons of all levels. These lessons, therefore, were written for new users with no previous experience with FEA, although some familiarity with computers and elementary strength of materials is assumed.

This book is **NOT** a complete reference manual for Pro/MECHANICA. There are several thousand pages of reference manuals available on-line with the Pro/MECHANICA installation, with good search tools and cross-referencing to allow users to find relevant material quickly.

It continues to be a challenge to decide what to include and what to exclude in this introduction in terms of the command set within Pro/MECHANICA. The author can only hope that the presented material will be found useful, and in the right dose! It has also been interesting to design suitable demonstration problems that are interesting, feasible with the state of learning of the user, physically meaningful, and illustrate a broad set of Pro/MECHANICA functionality - all within the space of 200 or so pages. It is hoped that at least some of these goals have been satisfied.

Although every effort has been made in proofreading the text, it is inevitable that errors will appear. The author takes full responsibility for these and hopes they will not impede your progress through the tutorial. Any comments, criticisms, and/or suggestions will be gratefully received and acknowledged. You can reach the author by email at the address *procaden@telusplanet.net*.

Notes to Instructors:

Each of these tutorial chapters will take between 1-1/2 to 3 hours to complete depending on the ability and background of the student. Moreover, additional time would be beneficial for experimentation and additional exploration of the program. Most of the material can be done by the student on their own, however there are a few "tricky" bits in some of the lessons. Therefore, it is important to have experienced and knowledgeable teaching assistants available (preferably right in the computer lab) who can answer special questions and especially bail out students who get into trouble. Most common causes of confusion are due to not completing the lessons or digesting the material. This is not surprising given the volume of new information or the lack of time in students' schedules. However, I have found that most student questions are answered within the lessons.

In addition to the tutorials, it is presumed that some class time over the duration of a course will be used for discussion of some of the broader issues of FEA, such as the treatment of constraints. It is vitally important for students to compare their FEA results with other possible solutions. This can be accomplished using simple problems for which either analytical solutions or experimental data exist. An extended discussion and exploration of modeling of boundary conditions would be very beneficial. It takes a while for students to realize that just creating the model and producing pretty pictures is not sufficient for design work, and the notions of accuracy and convergence need careful treatment and discussion.

It should be expected that most students, after having gone through a lesson only once, will not have absorbed all the material. My experience is that many students execute the commands without reading or studying the accompanying text explaining *why*. The second pass through the lesson usually results in considerably more retention and understanding. Each lesson concludes with a number of review questions and simple exercises that can be completed using new commands taught in that lesson. Where possible, students should be given additional problems that can be verified independently by experiment or analytical methods. Students really don't feel comfortable or confident until they can make models from scratch on their own.

That having been said, I am continually amazed at how quickly many students can get up the learning curve on both Pro/ENGINEER and Pro/MECHANICA. Any instructor introducing this software to a class of capable students should be prepared to move very quickly to stay ahead of the class!

Acknowledgment

Some of the models used in these tutorials are based on the treatment in **The Finite Element Method in Mechanical Design** (PWS-Kent, 1993) by Charles E. Knight. This is a clearly written and informative book.

Thanks are due to Stephen Schroff at Schroff Development Corporation for his efforts in taking this work to a wider audience and for his tolerance of the delays in its arrival!

Finally, once again I must express special thanks to my wife, Elaine, for her unflagging support and tolerance of the many hours and days spent on this project, and to our daughters Jenny and Kate for their patience when Daddy was preoccupied with this work. And, as always, thanks are due to our good friends, Jayne and Rowan.

To users of this material, I hope you enjoy the lessons. I apologize beforehand for any omissions and errors that may have appeared and I would appreciate any comments, criticisms, and suggestions for the improvement of this manual.

RWT
Edmonton, Alberta
26 August 2000

DISCLAIMER

The discussion, examples, and exercises in this tutorial are meant only to demonstrate the functionality of the program and are not to be construed as fully engineered design solutions for any particular problem. Use of the methods and procedures described herein are for instructional purposes only and are not warranted or guaranteed to provide satisfactory solutions in any specific application. The author and publisher assume no responsibility or liability for any errors or inaccuracies contained in the tutorial, or for any results or solutions obtained using the methods and procedures described herein.

Organization and Synopsis of the Tutorials

A brief synopsis of the ten lessons in this series is given below. Each lesson should take at least 1.5 to 3 hours to complete - if you go through the lessons too quickly or thoughtlessly, you may not understand or remember the material. For best results, it is suggested that you scan/browse through the lesson completely before going through it in detail. You will then have a sense of where the lesson is going, and not be tempted to just follow the commands blindly. You need to have a sense of the forest when examining each individual tree!

Chapter 1 - Introduction to MECHANICA

An introduction to finite element analysis, with some cautions about its use and misuse; examples of problems solved with MECHANICA; organization of the tutorials; tips and tricks for using MECHANICA

Chapter 2 - Finite Element Modeling with MECHANICA

Background information on FEA. The concept of modeling. Particular attention is directed at concerns of accuracy and convergence of solutions, and the differences between h-code and p-code FEA. Overview of MECHANICA operations and nomenclature

Chapter 3 - Plane Stress Analysis of a Thin Plate (Part 1)

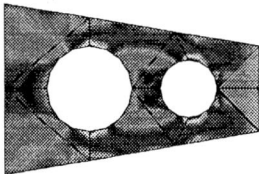

A simple model is created using the built-in geometry tools in Pro/MECHANICA. The complete sequence of steps required for a static analysis will be outlined, and basic result display options presented.

Chapter 4 - Plane Stress Analysis of a Thin Plate (Part 2)

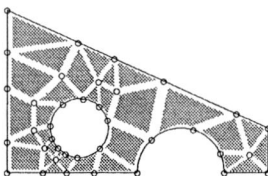

Using symmetry in the model. More Geometry commands. Creating surfaces. Automatic mesh generation using *AutoGEM*. Diabolical cases (point loads and constraints, reentrant corners).

Chapter 5 - Axisymmetric Models; Sensitivity Studies

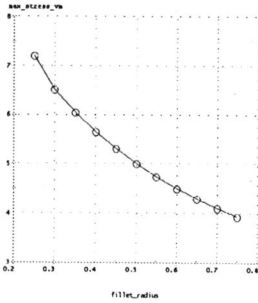

More geometry commands; axisymmetric models using solid and shell elements; pressure and centrifugal loads; sensitivity studies

Chapter 6 - Optimization

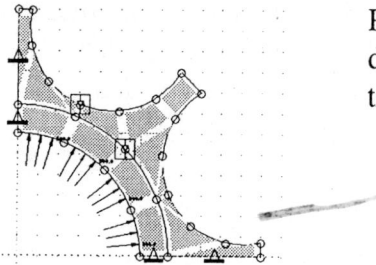

Plane strain models; setting up design variables and optimization design studies; more geometry commands (translate, rotate, copy, trim); plane strain analysis; applying temperature loads

Chapter 7 - Plates and Shells

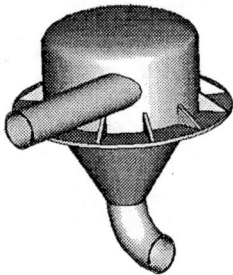

Creating shell models in 3D; a cantilevered C-channel beam; shell creation using AutoGEM; geometry commands for creating and manipulating surfaces in 3D; extruding and revolving curves to create elements

Chapter 8 - Beams and Frames

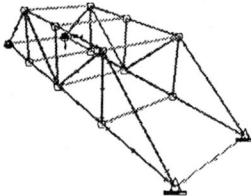

Beam elements in 1D, 2D, and 3D problems; beam coordinate systems, sections, and orientation; distributed loads; beam releases; shear and bending moment diagrams; trusses and frames; gravity load; groups of entities

Chapter 9 - Solid Models

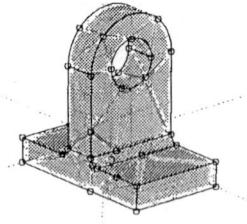

Creating solid models using manual, semi-automatic, and fully automatic methods; solid element types; extruding surfaces containing shell elements; extruding multiple curves simultaneously; setting up new coordinate systems

Chapter 10 - Integrated Mode with Pro/ENGINEER

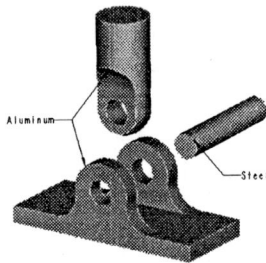

Analysis of models created with Pro/E. Setting up design variables for sensitivity studies and optimization. Treatment of 2D models. Cyclic symmetry. Shell elements as idealizations of thin-walled solids. Treatment of beams, point masses, springs. Analysis of Pro/E assemblies with contact regions.

As you go through these lessons, take the time to explore the options available and experiment with the commands. You will learn the material the best when you try to apply it on your own ("flying solo"), perhaps trying to create some of the models shown in the exercises at the end of each lesson.

TABLE OF CONTENTS

Chapter 1 : Introduction

Chapter 2 : Finite Element Modeling with MECHANICA

Chapter 3 : Plane Stress Analysis of a Thin Plate (Part 1)

Chapter 4 : Plane Stress Analysis of a Thin Plate (Part 2)

Chapter 5 : Axisymmetric Models and Sensitivity Studies

Chapter 6 : Optimization

Chapter 7 : Plates and Shells

Chapter 8 : Beams and Frames

Chapter 9 : Solid Models

Chapter 10 : Integrated Mode with Pro/ENGINEER

Chapter 1 :

Introduction to the Tutorials

Synopsis

An introduction to finite element analysis, with some cautions about its use and misuse; examples of problems solved with MECHANICA; organization of the tutorials; tips and tricks for using MECHANICA

Overview of this Lesson

♦   general comments about using Finite Element Analysis (FEA)
♦   examples of problems solved using Pro/MECHANICA Structure
♦   layout of the tutorials
♦   how the tutorial will present command sequences
♦   tips and tricks for using MECHANICA

Finite Element Analysis

Finite Element Analysis (FEA), also known as the Finite Element Method (FEM), is probably the most important tool added to the mechanical design engineer's toolkit this century. The development of FEA has been driven by the desire for more accurate design computations in more complex situations, allowing improvements in both the design procedure and products. The growing use of FEA has been made possible by the creation of computation engines that are capable of handling the immense volume of calculations necessary to carry out an analysis and easily display the results for interpretation. With the advent of very powerful desktop workstations, FEA is now available at a practical cost to virtually all engineers and designers.

The Pro/MECHANICA software described in this introductory tutorial is only one of many commercial systems that are available. All of these systems share many common capabilities. In this tutorial, we will try to present both the commands for using MECHANICA and the reasons behind those commands, so that the general procedures can be transferred to other FEA packages. Notwithstanding this desire, it should be realized that Pro/M is unique in many ways among packages currently available. Therefore, numerous topics treated will be specific to Pro/M.

Pro/MECHANICA (or Pro/M as we will call it) is actually a suite of three programs: *Structure*, *Thermal*, and *Motion*. The first of these, *Structure*, is able to perform the following:

♦   linear static stress analysis
♦   modal analysis (mode shapes and natural frequencies)
♦   buckling analysis
♦   large deformation analysis

and others. This manual will be concerned only with the first these analyses. The remaining types of problems are beyond the scope of an introductory manual. Once having finished this manual, however, interested users should not find the other topics too difficult. The other two programs (*Thermal* and *Motion*) are used for thermal analysis and dynamic analysis of mechanical systems, respectively. These are planned to be the topics of further tutorials in the Click-by-Click series. In this book, the use of Pro/M is meant to imply *Structure* only.

Pro/M offers much more than simply an FEA engine. We will see that Pro/M is really a design tool since it will allow parametric studies as well as design optimization to be set up quite easily. Moreover, unlike many other commercial FEM programs where determining accuracy can be difficult or time consuming, Pro/M will be able to compute results with some certainty as to the accuracy[1].

Pro/M does not currently have the ability to handle non-linear problems, for example a stress analysis problem involving a non-linearly elastic material like rubber. New capability introduced in Release 2000*i*, however, allows problems involving very large geometric deflections to be treated, as long as the stresses remain within the linearly elastic range for the material.

In this tutorial, we will concentrate on the main concepts and procedures for using the software and focus on topics that seem to be most useful for new users and/or students doing design projects and other course work. We assume that readers do not know anything about the software. A short overview of the FEA theoretical background has been included, but it should be emphasized that this is very limited in scope. Our attention here is on the use and capabilities of the software, not providing a complete course on using FEA, its theoretical origins, or the "art" of FEA modeling strategies. For further study of these subjects, see the reference list at the end of the second chapter.

Examples of Problems Solved using MECHANICA

To give you a taste of what is to come, here are three examples of what you will be able to do with MECHANICA on completion of these tutorials. The examples are a simple analysis, a parametric design study called a sensitivity analysis, and a design optimization. In

---

[1]This refers to the problem of "convergence" whereby the FEA results must be verified or tested so that they can be trusted. We will discuss convergence at some length later on and refer to it continually throughout the manual.

MECHANICA's language, these are called *design studies*.

Example #1 : Analysis

This is the "bread and butter" type of problem for
MECHANICA. A model is defined by some geometry (in
2D or 3D), material properties are specified, loads and
constraints are applied, and one of several different types
of analysis can be run on the model. In the figure at the
right, a model of a somewhat crude connecting rod is
shown. This part is modeled using 3D solid elements. The
hole at the large end is fixed and a lateral bearing load is
applied to the inside surface of the hole at the other end.
The primary results are shown in Figures 2 and 3. These
are contours of the Von Mises stress[2] on the part, shown in
a *fringe* plot (these are, of course, in color on the computer

Figure 1 Solid model of a part

screen), and a wireframe view of the total (exaggerated)
deformation of the part (this can be shown as an animation). Here, we are usually interested in
the value and location of the maximum Von Mises stress in the part, and the magnitude and
direction of deformation of the part.

Figure 2 Von Mises stress fringe plot

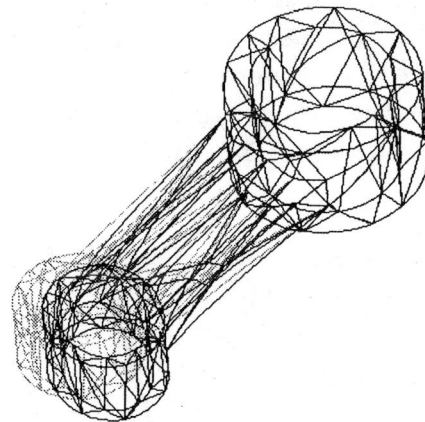

Figure 3 Deformation of the part

Example #2 : Sensitivity Study

Often you need to find out the overall effect of varying one or more design parameters, such as

---

[2] The Von Mises stress is obtained by combining all the stress components at a point in a
way which produces a single value that can be compared to the yield strength of the material.
This is the most common way of examining the computed stress in a part.

dimensions. You could do this by performing a number of similar analyses, and changing the geometry of the model between each analysis. MECHANICA has an automated routine which allows you to specify the parameter to be varied, and the overall range. It then automatically performs all the modifications to the model, and computes results for the intermediate values of the design parameters.

The example shown in Figure 4 is a quarter-model (to take advantage of symmetry) of a transition between two thin-walled cylinders. The transition is modeled using shell elements.

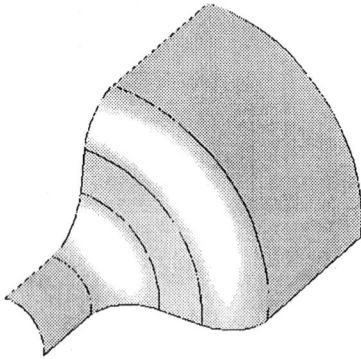

Figure 4 3D Shell quarter-model of transition between cylinders

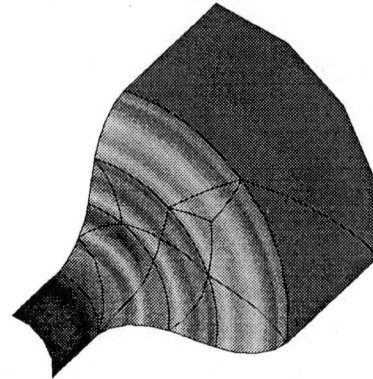

Figure 5 Von Mises stress in shell model

Figure 5 shows the contours of the Von Mises stress on the part. The maximum stress occurs at the edge of the fillet on the smaller cylinder just where it meets the intermediate flat portion. The design parameter to be varied is the radius of this fillet, between the minimum and maximum shapes shown in Figures 6 and 7.

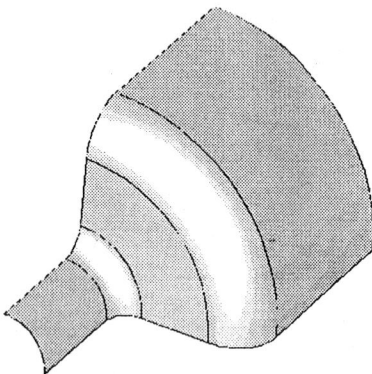

Figure 6 Minimum radius fillet

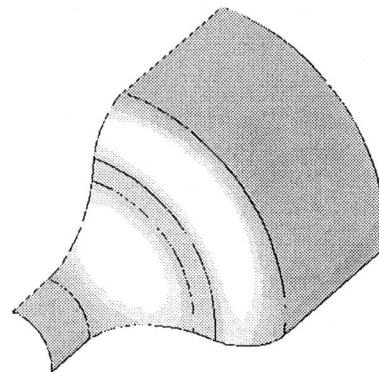

Figure 7 Maximum radius fillet

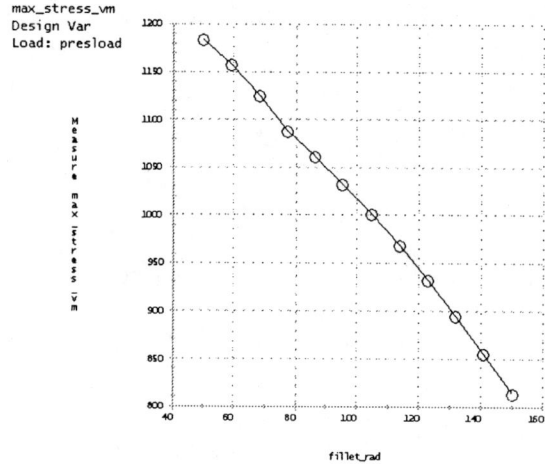

Figure 8 Variation of Von Mises stress with fillet radius in shell model

Figure 8 shows the variation in the maximum Von Mises stress in the model as a function of radius of the fillet. Other information about the model, such as total mass, or maximum deflection is also readily available.

Example #3 : Design Optimization

This capability of MECHANICA is really astounding! When a model is created, some of the geometric parameters can be designated as design variables. Then MECHANICA is turned loose to find the combination of values of these design variables that will minimize some objective function (like the total mass of the model) subject to some design constraints (like the allowed maximum stress and/or deflection). Pro/M searches through the design space (for specified ranges of the design variables) and will find the optimum set of design variables automatically!

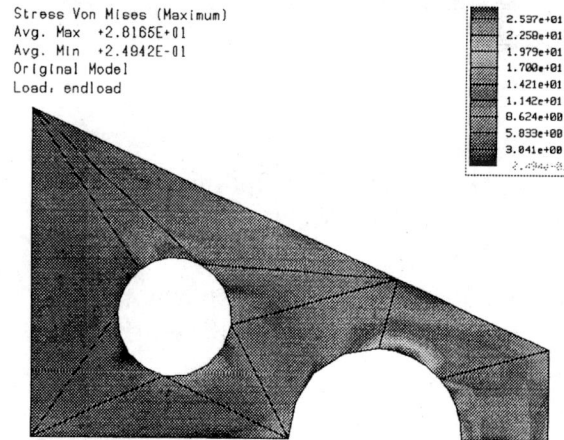

Figure 9 Initial Von Mises stress distribution in plate before optimization

The example shown is of a plane stress model of a thin, symmetrical, tapered plate under tension. The plate is fixed at the left edge, while the lower edge is along the plane of symmetry. A uniform tensile load is applied to the vertical edge on the right end. The Von Mises stress contours for the initial design are shown in Figure 9. The maximum stress, which exceeds a design tolerance, has occurred at the large hole located on the plate centerline, at about the 12:30 position. The stress level around the smaller hole is considerably less, and we could probably increase the diameter of this hole in order to reduce mass. The question is: how much?

The selected design variables are the radii of the two holes. Minimum and maximum values for these variables are indicated in the Figures 10 and 11. The objective of the optimization is to minimize the total mass of the plate, while not exceeding a specified maximum stress.

Figure 10 Minimum values of design variables

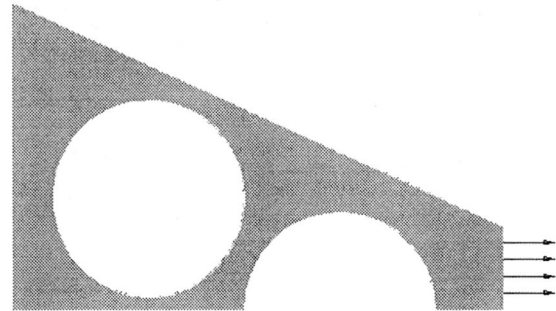

Figure 11 Maximum values of design variables

Figure 12 shows a history of the design optimization computations. The figure on the left shows the maximum Von Mises stress in the part - note that this initially exceeds the allowed maximum stress, but Pro/M very quickly adjusts the geometry to produce a design within the allowed stress. The figure on the right shows the mass of the part. As the optimization proceeds, this is slowly reduced until a minimum value is obtained (approximately 20% less than the original). Pro/M allows you to view the shape change occurring at each iteration.

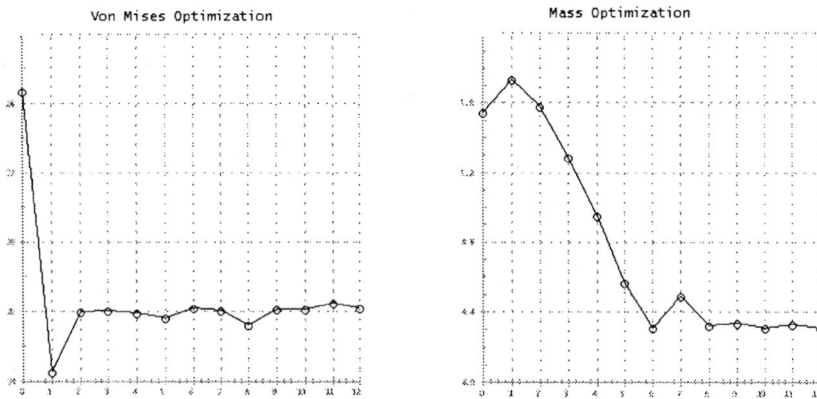

Figure 12 Optimization history: Von Mises stress (left) and total mass (right)

The final optimized design is shown in Figure 13. Notice the increased size of the interior hole, and the more efficient use of material. The design limit stress now occurs on both holes.

```
Stress Von Mises (Maximum)
Avg. Max  +2.5037E+01
Avg. Min  +1.0193E+00
Original Model
Load: endload
```

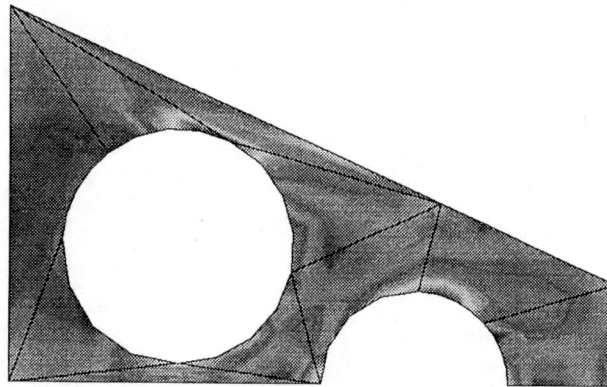

Figure 13 Von Mises stress distribution in optimized plate

FEA User Beware!

Users of this (or any other FEA) software should be cautioned that, as in other areas of computer applications, the GIGO ("Garbage In = Garbage Out") principle applies. Users can easily be misled into blind acceptance of the answers produced by the programs. **Do not confuse pretty graphs and pictures with correct modeling practice and accurate results**.

A skilled practitioner of FEA must have a considerable amount of knowledge and experience. The current state of sophistication of CAD and FEA software may lead non-wary users to dangerous and/or disastrous conclusions. Users might take note of the fine print that accompanies all FEA software licenses, which usually contains some text along these lines: "The supplier of the software will take no responsibility for the results obtained . . ." and so on. Clearly, the onus is on the user to bear the burden of responsibility for any conclusions that might be reached from the FEA.

We might plot the situation something like Figure 14 on the next page. In order to intelligently (and safely) use FEA, it is necessary to acquire some knowledge of the theory behind the method, some facility with the available software, and a great deal of modeling experience. In this manual, we assume that the reader's level of knowledge and experience with FEA initially places them at the origin of the figure. The tutorial (particularly Chapter 2) will extend your knowledge a little bit in the "theory" direction, at least so that we can know what the software requires for input data, and how it computes the results. The step-by-step tutorials and exercises will extend your knowledge in the "experience" direction. Primarily, however, this tutorial is meant to extend your knowledge in the "FEA software" direction, as it applies to using Pro/MECHANICA. Readers who have already moved out along the "theory" or "experience" axes will have to bear with us - at least this manual should assist you in discovering the capabilities of the MECHANICA software package.

modeling experience

knowledge of
FEA theory

knowledge of
FEA software

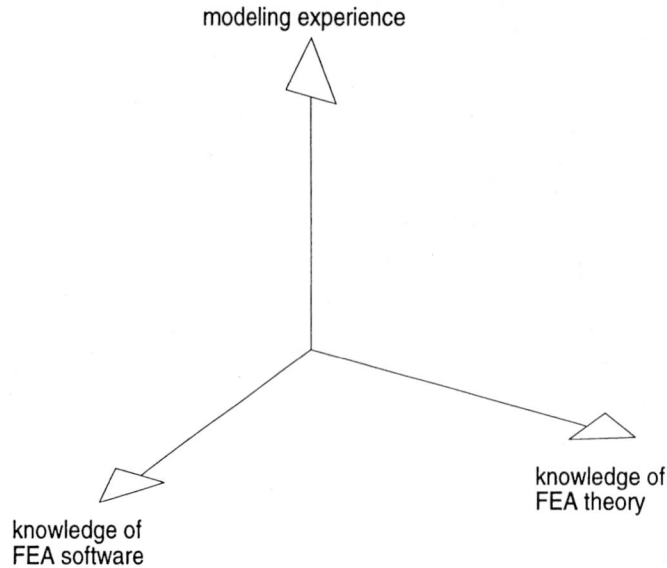

Figure 14   Knowledge, skill, and experience requirements for FEA users

In summary, some quotes from speakers at an FEA panel at a recent ASME Computers in Engineering conference should be kept in mind:

"Don't confuse convenience with intelligence."

In other words, as more powerful functions (such as automatic mesh generation) get built in to FEA packages, do not assume that these will be suitable for every modeling situation, or that they will always produce trustworthy results. If an option has defaults, be aware of what they are and their significance to the model and the results obtained. Above all, remember that just because it is easy, it is not necessarily right!

"Don't confuse speed with accuracy."

Computers are getting faster and faster. This also means that they can compute an inaccurate model faster than before - a wrong answer in half the time is hardly an improvement!

and finally, the most important:

"FEA makes a good engineer better and a poor engineer dangerous."

As our engineering tools get more sophisticated, there is a tendency to rely on them more and more, sometimes to dangerous extremes. Relying solely on FEA for design verification might be dangerous. Don't forget your intuition, and remember that a lot of very significant engineering design work has occurred over the years on the back of an envelope. Let FEA become a tool that extends your design capability, not define it.

Layout of this Manual

Running the Pro/MECHANICA software is not a trivial operation. However, with a little practice, and learning only a fraction of the capabilities of the program, you can perform FEA of reasonably complex problems. This manual is meant to guide you through the major features of the software and how to use it. The manual is not meant to be a complete guide to either the software or FEA modeling - consider it the elementary school of practical FEA!

Chapter 2 of the tutorial will present an overview of the theory and mathematics behind how FEA is implemented in MECHANICA. In particular, the origin and differences between h-code analysis and the p-code method in MECHANICA are discussed. The primary purpose of this chapter is to outline the main capabilities of MECHANICA as they apply to the design and analysis of mechanical parts. These include simple analyses, sensitivity studies, and parameter optimization. This chapter will basically introduce you to the terminology used in the program, and give you an overview of its operation.

Chapters 3 and 4 will present some commands for creating 2D geometry, and performing a simple analysis of a plane stress problem. Common methods of displaying results are shown. Some issues of modeling are discussed, such as symmetry. Several modeling pitfalls, which also occur in other model types (axisymmetric and 3D, for example) are investigated, and solutions proposed. The automatic mesh generator, AutoGEM, is introduced in Chapter 4.

Chapter 5 will introduce you to sensitivity studies in Pro/M and the definition of design variables. The context will be that of axisymmetric models using solid and shell elements. Some new geometry commands will be introduced as well.

Chapter 6 is devoted to setting up an optimization. Here, the context will be simple plane stress and plane strain models. The use of a temperature load is introduced.

Our first major foray into 3D modeling comes in Chapter 7 where we will have a look at more geometry commands and models that utilize shell elements. Beams and frames are treated in Chapter 8, including distributed loads, shear and moment diagrams, and beam releases. Finally, solid models will be the topic of Chapter 9 where we will use three different models of the same part, created using different command variations.

Chapter 10 is devoted to the use of Pro/MECHANICA in integrated mode with Pro/E. We will treat solid models, shell models, 2D idealizations, cyclic symmetry, and a simple assembly with contact analysis.

At the end of each of these chapters, a number of additional exercises are presented. You should try to do as many of these as you can in order to build up your knowledge and repertoire of modeling scenarios.

Tips for using MECHANICA

In the tutorial examples that follow, you will be lead through a number of simple problems keystroke by keystroke. Each command will be explained in depth so that you will know the "why" as well as the "what" and "how". Resist the temptation to just follow the keystrokes - you must think hard about what is going on in order to learn it. You should go through the tutorials while working on a computer so that you experience the results of each command as it is entered. Not much information will sink in if you just read the material. We have tried to capture exactly the key-stroke, menu selection, or mouse click sequences to perform each analysis. These actions are indicated in ***bold face italic type***. Characters entered from the keyboard are shown in simple **bold type**. When more than one command is given in a sequence, they are separated by the symbol ">". When several commands are entered on a single menu or window, they are separated by the pipe symbol " | ". An option from a pull-down list will be indicated with the list title and selected option in parantheses. So, for example, you might see command sequences similar to the following:

> ***Materials > Assign > Part >* STEEL_IPS *| Accept***
> ***Analysis (QuickCheck)***
> ***Results > Create >* VonMises *| Accept***

At the end of each chapter in the manual, we have included some Questions for Review and some simple Exercises which you should do. These have been designed to illustrate additional capabilities of the software, some simple modeling concepts, and sometimes allow a comparison with either analytical solutions or with alternative modeling methods. The more of these exercises you do, the more confident you can be in setting up and solving your own problems.

Finally, here a few hints about using the software. Menu items and/or graphics entities on the screen are selected by clicking on them with the *left mouse button*. We will often refer to this as a 'left click' or simply as a 'click'. The *middle mouse button* ('middle click') can be used (generally) whenever ***Accept, Enter, Close*** or ***Done*** is required. The dynamic view controls are obtained by holding down the *Ctrl* key and dragging with a mouse button (left = zoom, middle = spin, right = pan). Users of Pro/ENGINEER will be quite comfortable with these mouse controls. Any menu commands grayed out are unavailable for the current context. Otherwise, any menu item is available for use. You can, for example, jump from the design menus to the pulldown menus at any time.

So, with all that out of the way, let's get started. The next chapter will give you an overview of FEA theory, and how MECHANICA is different from other commercial packages.

Questions for Review

1.   In MECHANICA-ese, what is a design study?
2.   What are the three types of design study that can be performed by Pro/M?
3.   What is the Von Mises stress? From a strength of materials textbook, find out how this is computed and its relation to yield strength. Also, for what types of materials is this a useful computation?
4.   Can Pro/M treat non-linear problems?
5.   What does GIGO mean?
6.   What three areas of expertise are required to be a skilled FEA practitioner?

Exercises

1.   Find some examples of cases where seemingly minor and insignificant computer-related errors have resulted in disastrous consequences.

(This page left blank.)

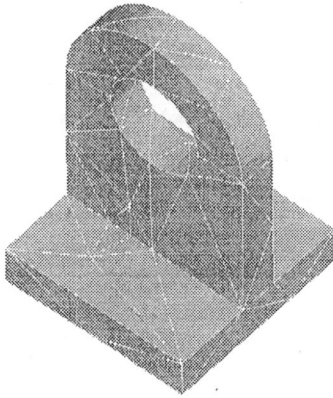

Chapter 2 :

Finite Element Modeling with MECHANICA

Synopsis

Background information on FEA. The concept of modeling. Particular attention is directed at concerns of accuracy and convergence of solutions, and the differences between h-code and p-code FEA. Overview of MECHANICA.

Overview of this Lesson

This chapter presents an overall view of FEA in general, and discusses a number of ideas and issues involved. The major differences between Pro/M, which uses a p-code method, and other packages, which typically use h-code, are presented. The topics of accuracy and convergence are discussed. The major sections in this chapter are:

- ♦   overview and origins of FEA
- ♦   discussion of the concept of the "model"
- ♦   general procedure for FEA solutions
- ♦   FEA models versus CAD models
- ♦   p-elements and h-elements
- ♦   convergence and accuracy
- ♦   sources of error
- ♦   overview of MECHANICA

Although you are probably anxious to get started with the software, your understanding of the material presented here is very important. We will get to the program soon enough!

Finite Element Analysis : An Introduction

In this section, we will try to present the essence of FEA without going into a lot of mathematical detail. This is primarily to set up the discussion of the important issues of accuracy and convergence later in the chapter. Some of the statements made here are generalizations and oversimplifications, but we hope that this will not be too misleading. Interested users can consult a number of text and reference books (some are listed at the end of this chapter) which describe the theoretical underpinnings of FEA in considerably greater detail.

In the following, the ideas are illustrated using a planar (2D) solution region, but of course these ideas extend also to 3D. Let's suppose that we are faced with the following problem: We are given a connected region (or volume) R with a boundary B as shown in Figure 1(a). Some continuous physical variable, e.g. temperature T, is governed by a physical law within the region R and subjected to known conditions on the boundary B. In a finite element solution, the geometry of the region is typically generated by a CAD program, such as Pro/ENGINEER.

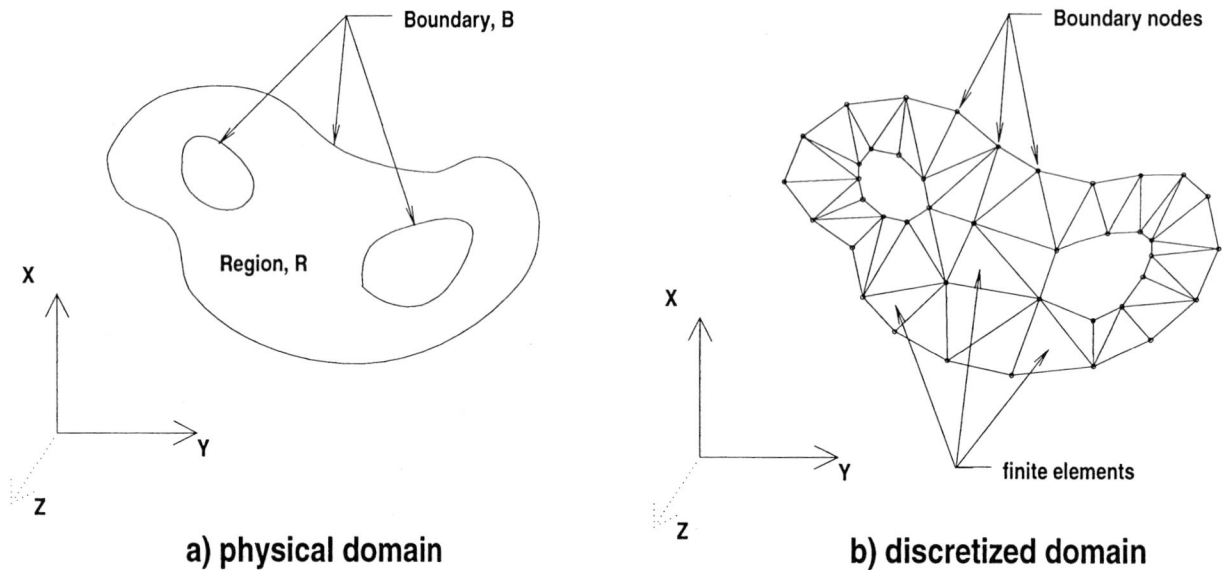

a) physical domain   b) discretized domain

Figure 1   The problem to be solved is specified in a) the physical domain and b) the discretized domain used by FEA

For a two dimensional problem, the governing physical law or principle might be expressed by a partial differential equation (PDE), for example[1]:

$$\frac{\partial^2 T}{\partial x^2} + \frac{\partial^2 T}{\partial y^2} = 0$$

that is valid in the interior of the region R. The solution to the problem must satisfy some boundary conditions or *constraints*, for example T = T(x,y), prescribed on the boundary B. Both interior and exterior boundaries might be present and can be arbitrarily shaped. Note that this governing PDE may be (and usually is!) the result of simplifying assumptions made about the

---

[1] The PDE given represents the temperature within a solid body which is governed by the conduction of heat within the body. There are no heat sources, and temperature on the boundary of the body is known.

physical system, such as the material being homogeneous and isotropic, with constant linear properties, and so on.

In order to analyze this problem, the region R is *discretized* into individual *finite elements* that collectively approximate the shape of the region, as shown in Figure 1(b). This discretization is accomplished by locating *nodes* along the boundary and in the interior of the region. The nodes are then joined by lines to create the finite elements. In 2D problems, these can be triangles or quadrilaterals; in 3D problems, the elements can be tetrahedra or 8-node "bricks". In some FEA software, other higher order types of elements are also possible (e.g. hexagonal prisms). Some higher order elements also have additional nodes along their edges. Collectively, the set of all the elements is called a *finite element mesh*. In the early days of FEM, a great deal of effort was required to set up the mesh. Recently, automatic meshing routines have been developed in order to do most, if not all, of this tedious task.

In the FEA solution, values of the dependent variable (T, in our example) are computed only at the nodes. The variation of the variable within each element is computed from the nodal values so as to approximately satisfy the governing PDE. One way of doing this is by using interpolating polynomials. In order for the PDE to be satisfied, the nodal values of each element must satisfy a set of conditions represented by several linear algebraic equations.

The boundary conditions are implemented by specifying the values of the variables on the boundary nodes. There is no guarantee that the true boundary conditions on the continuous boundary B are satisfied between the nodes on the discretized boundary.

When all the individual elements in the mesh are combined, the discretization and interpolation procedures result in a conversion of the problem from the solution of a continuous differential equation into a very large set of simultaneous linear algebraic equations. This system can typically have many thousands of equations in it. The solution of this algebraic system, which requires special and efficient numerical algorithms, represents an *approximation* to the continuous solution of the initial PDE. An important issue, then, is the accuracy of this approximation. In classical FEM solutions, the approximation becomes more accurate as the mesh is refined with smaller elements. In the limit of zero mesh size, requiring an infinite number of equations, the FEM solution to the PDE would be exact. This is, of course, not achievable. So, a major issue revolves around the question "How fine a mesh is required to produce answers of acceptable accuracy?" and the practical question is "Is it feasible to compute this solution?" We will see a bit later how Pro/M solves these problems.

IMPORTANT POINT: In FEA stress analysis problems, the dependent variable in the governing PDE's is the displacement from the reference (usually unloaded) position. The material strain (displacement per unit length) is then computed from the displacement by taking the derivative with respect to position. Finally, the stress components at any point in the material are computed from the strain at that point. Thus, if the interpolating polynomial for the spatial variation of the displacement field is linear within an element, then the strain and stress will be constant within that element, since the derivative of a linear function is a constant. This will be illustrated a bit later in this lesson.

The FEA Model and General Processing Steps

Throughout this manual, we will be using the term "model" extensively. We need to have a clear idea of what we mean by the FEA model.

To get from the "real world" physical problem to the approximate FEA solution, we must go through a number of simplifying steps. At each step, it is necessary to make decisions about what assumptions or simplifications will be required in order to reach a final workable model. By "workable", we mean that the FEA model must allow us to compute those features of interest (for example, the maximum stress in the material) with sufficient accuracy and with available time and resources. It is no good building a model that is over-simplified to the point where it cannot produce the results with sufficient accuracy. It is also no good producing a model that is "perfect" but will not yield useful computational results for several weeks!

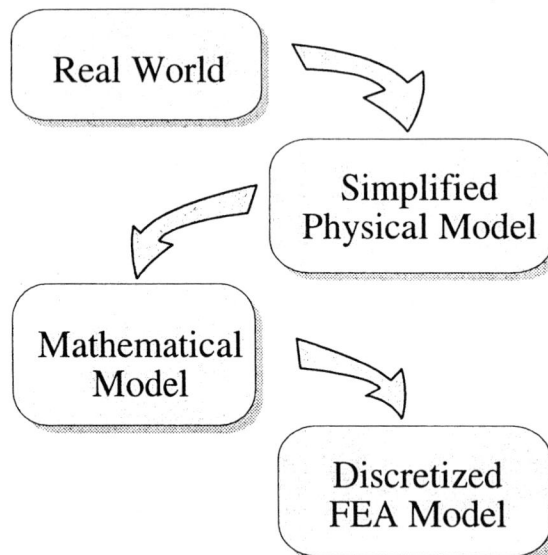

Figure 2 Developing a Model for Finite Element Analysis

To arrive at a model suitable for FEA, we must go through a number of simplifying steps, shown in Figure 2, as follows:

Real World → Simplified Physical Model

This simplification step involves making assumptions about physical properties or the physical layout and geometry of the problem. For example, we usually assume that materials are homogeneous and isotropic and free of internal defects or flaws. It is also common to ignore aspects of the geometry that will have no (anticipated) effect on the results, such as the chamfered and filleted edges on the bracket shown in Figure 3, and perhaps even the mounting holes themselves. Ignoring these "cosmetic" features, as shown in Figure 4, is often necessary in order to reduce the geometric complexity so that the resulting FEA model is practical.

Figure 3 The "Real World" Object

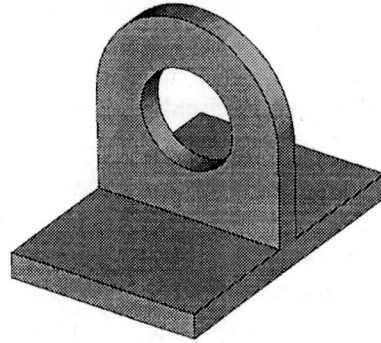

Figure 4 The idealized physical model

Simple Physical Model ➜ Mathematical Model

To arrive at the mathematical model, we make assumptions like linearity of material properties, idealization of loading conditions, and so on, in order to apply our mathematical formulas to complex problems. We often assume that loading is steady, that fixed points are perfectly fixed, beams are long and slender, and so on. As discussed above, the mathematical model usually consists of one or more differential equations that describe the variation of the variable of interest within the boundaries of the model.

Mathematical Model ➜ FEA Model

The simplified geometry of the model is discretized (see Figure 5), so that the governing differential equations can be rewritten as a (large) number of simultaneous linear equations representing the assembly of elements in the model.

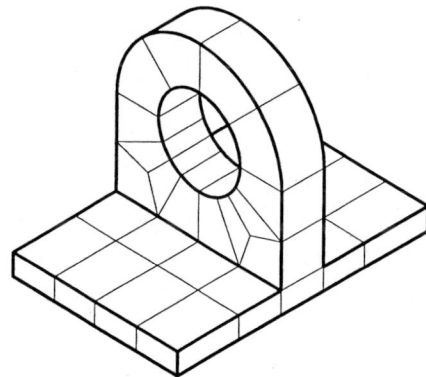

Figure 5 A mesh of solid brick elements

In the operation of FEA software, the three modeling steps described above often appear to be merged. In fact, most of it occurs below the surface (you will never see the governing PDE, for example) or is inherent in the software itself. For example, Pro/M automatically assumes that materials are homogeneous, isotropic, and linear. However, it is useful to remind yourself about these separate aspects of modeling from time to time, because each is a potential source of error or inaccuracy in the results.

Steps in Preparing an FEA Model for Solution

Starting from the simplified geometric model (which can be created in Pro/M or imported from another source), there are generally five steps to be followed in preparing the model for solution. These are:

1.   discretize the geometry to produce a finite element mesh
2.   identify the material properties, constraints, and loads
3.   solve the system of linear equations
4.   compute items of interest from the solution variables
5.   critically review results and, if necessary, repeat the analysis

The overall procedure is illustrated in Figure 6. Some additional detail on each of these steps is given below. The major steps must be executed in order, and each must be done correctly before proceeding to the next step. When a problem is to be re-analyzed (for example, if a stress analysis is to be performed for the same geometry but different loads), it will not usually be necessary to return all the way to the beginning. The available re-entry points will become clear as you move through these tutorials.

The five steps shown in the figure are:

1.   The geometric model of the part/system is created using either MECHANICA, Pro/ENGINEER, or another CAD package. Creation of the finite element mesh from the geometric model can be done either manually, automatically, or semi-automatically with Pro/M. **This model creation step will typically take over 80% of the effort in performing the overall analysis.**

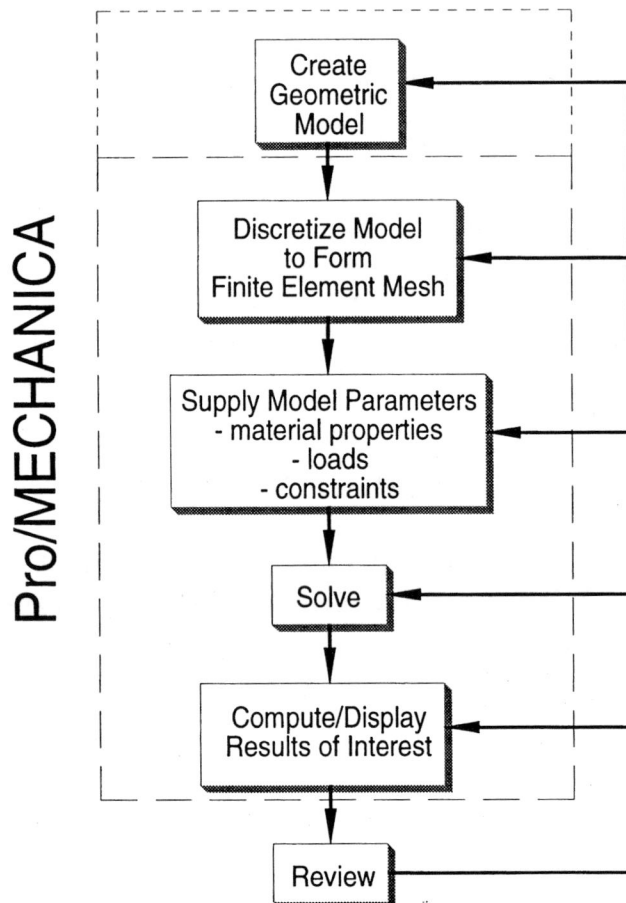

Figure 6 Overall Steps in FEA Solution

2.   A)   Specify material properties for all elements in the mesh (Pro/M has some useful shortcuts for this). It is not necessary that all the elements have the same properties. For stress analysis the required properties are Young's modulus and Poisson's ratio. Most FEA packages contain built-in libraries containing properties of common materials (steel, iron, aluminum, etc.).

     B)   Identify the constraints on the solution. In stress analysis, these could be fixed points,

points of specified displacement, or points free to move in specified directions only.
C)   Specify the loads on the model (point loads, uniform edge loads, pressure on surfaces, etc.).

3.   Once you are satisfied with your model, you set up and run a processor that actually performs the solution to the posed FEA problem. As far as the user is concerned, this is a one-step job. Pro/M will trap some modeling errors here. The processor will produce a summary file of output messages which can be consulted if something goes wrong - for example, a model that is not sufficiently constrained by boundary conditions.

4.   FEA produces immense volumes of output data. The only feasible way of examining this is graphically. MECHANICA has very powerful graphics capabilities to not only create the model but also to examine the results of the FEA - displaced shape, stress distributions, mode shapes, etc. Hard copy of the results file and screen display is easy to obtain.

5.   Finally, the results must be reviewed critically. In the first instance, the results should agree with our modeling intent. For example, if we look at an animated view of the deformation, we can easily see if our boundary constraints have been implemented properly. The results should also satisfy our intuition about the solution (stress concentration around a hole, for example.). If there is any cause for concern, it may be advisable to revisit some aspects of the model and perform the analysis again.

P-Elements versus H-Elements

Not all discretized finite elements are created equal! Here is where a major difference arises between MECHANICA and other FEA programs.

Convergence of H-elements (the "classic" approach)

Following the classic approach, other programs often use low order interpolating polynomials in each element. This has significant ramifications, especially in stress analysis. As mentioned above, in stress analysis the primary solution variables are the displacements of the nodes. The interpolating functions are typically linear (first order) within each element. Strain is obtained by taking the derivatives of the displacement field and the stress is computed from the material strain. For a first order interpolating polynomial within the element, this means that the strain and therefore the stress components within the element are constant everywhere. The situation is depicted in Figure 7, which shows the computed Von Mises stress in each of the elements surrounding a hole in a thin plate under tension. Such discontinuity in the stress field between elements is, of course, unrealistic and will lead to inaccurate values for the maximum stress. Low order elements lead to the greatest inaccuracy precisely in the regions of greatest interest, typically where there are large gradients within the real object.

An even more disastrous situation is shown in Figure 8. This is a solid cantilever beam with a uniform transverse load modeled using solid brick elements. With only a single first-order

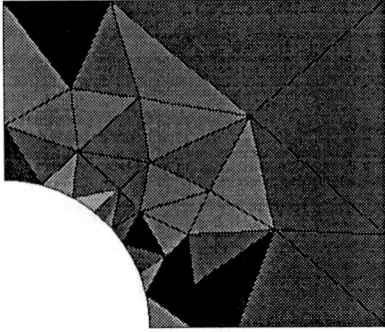

Figure 7 Von Mises stress in 1/4 model of thin plate under tension using first order elements

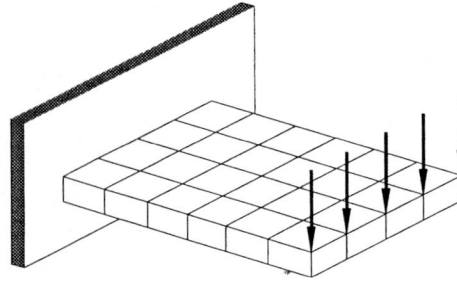

Figure 8 A disaster waiting to happen using first order elements

element through the thickness, the computed stress will be the same on the top and bottom of the beam. This is clearly wrong, yet the FEA literature and product demonstrations abound with examples similar to this.

This situation is often masked by the post-processing capabilities of the software being used, which will sometimes average or interpolate contour values within the mesh or perform other "smoothing" functions strictly for visual appearance. This is strictly a post-processing step, and may bear no resemblance at all to what is actually going on in the model or the real object.

Using first order elements, then, in order to get a more accurate estimate of the stress, it is necessary to use much smaller elements, a process called *mesh refinement*. It may not always be possible to easily identify regions where mesh refinement is required, and quite often the entire mesh is modified. The process of mesh refinement continues until further mesh division and refinement does not lead to significant changes in the obtained solution. The process of continued mesh refinement leading to a "good" solution is called *convergence analysis*. Of course, in the process of mesh refinement, the size of the computational problem becomes larger and larger and we may reach a limit for practical problems (due to time and/or memory limits) before we have successfully converged to an acceptable solution.

The use of mesh refinement for convergence analysis leads to the *h-element* class of FEA methods. This "h" is borrowed from the field of numerical analysis, where it denotes the fact that convergence and accuracy are related (sometimes proportional to) the step size used in the solution, usually denoted by *h*. In FEA, the *h* refers to the size of the elements. The elements, always of low order, are referred to as h-elements, and the mesh refinement procedure is called *h-convergence*. This situation is depicted in parts (a) and (b) of Figure 9, where a series of constant-height steps is used to approximate a smooth continuous function. The narrower the steps, the more closely we can approximate the smooth function. Note also that where the gradient of the function is large (such as near the left edge of the figure), then mesh refinement will always produce increasingly higher maximum values.

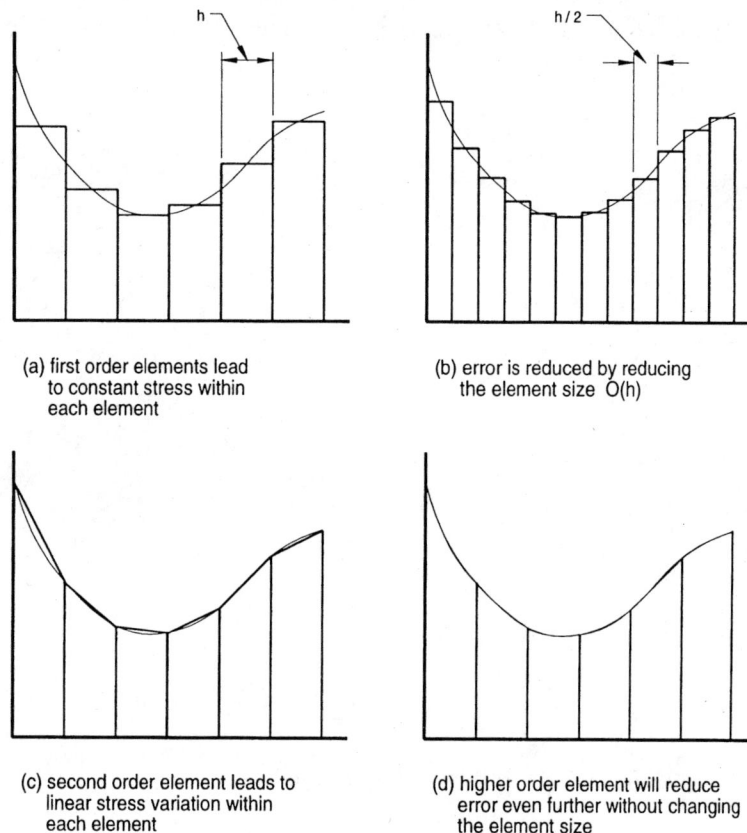

(a) first order elements lead to constant stress within each element

(b) error is reduced by reducing the element size O(h)

(c) second order element leads to linear stress variation within each element

(d) higher order element will reduce error even further without changing the element size

Figure 9 Approximation of stress function in a model

The major outcome of using h-elements is the need for meshes of relatively small elements. Furthermore, h-elements are not very tolerant of shape extremes in terms of skewness, rapid size variation through the mesh, large aspect ratio, and so on. This further increases the number of elements required for an acceptable mesh, and this, of course, greatly increases the computational cost of the solution.

Convergence of P-elements (the Pro/MECHANICA approach)

Now, the major difference incorporated in MECHANICA is the following: instead of constantly refining and recreating finer and finer meshes, convergence is obtained by *increasing the order of the interpolating polynomials on each element*. The mesh stays the same for every iteration, called a *p-loop pass*. The use of higher order interpolating polynomials for convergence analysis leads to the *p-element* class of FEA methods, where the "p" denotes polynomial. This method is depicted in parts (c) and (d) of the Figure 9. Only elements in regions of high gradients are bumped up to higher order polynomials. Furthermore, by examining the effects of going to higher order polynomials, MECHANICA can monitor the expected error in the solution, and automatically increase the polynomial order only on those elements were it is required. Thus, the convergence analysis is performed quite automatically, with the solution proceeding until an accuracy limit (set by the user) has been satisfied. With MECHANICA, the limit for the polynomial order is 9. In theory, it would be possible to go to higher orders than this, but the computational cost starts to rise too quickly. If the solution cannot converge even with these 9th order polynomials, it may be necessary to recreate the mesh at a slightly higher density so that lower order polynomials will be sufficient. This is a very rare occurrence.

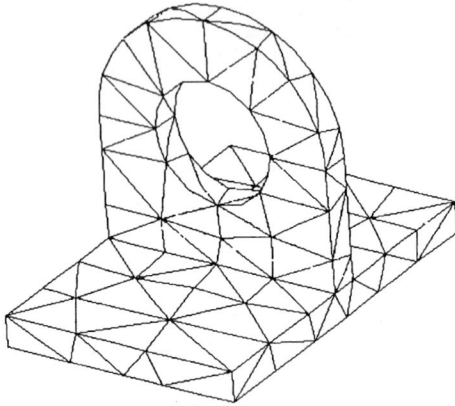

Figure 10 A mesh of solid tetrahedral (4 node) h-elements

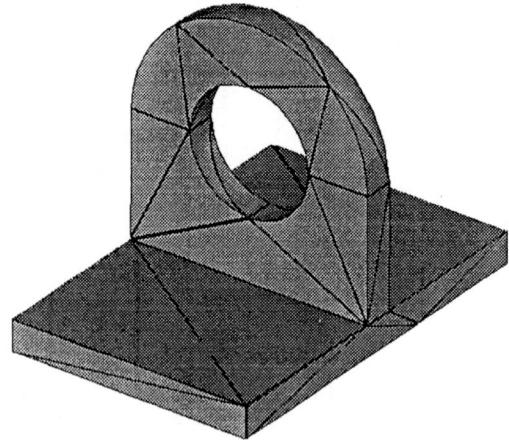

Figure 11 A mesh of tetrahedral p-elements produced by MECHANICA.

The use of p-elements has a number of features/advantages:

▸ The same mesh can be used throughout the convergence analysis, rather than recreating meshes or local mesh refinement required by h-codes.

▸ The mesh is virtually always more coarse and contains fewer elements than h-codes. Compare the meshes in Figures 10 and 11, and note that the mesh of h-elements in Figure 10 would probably not produce very good results, depending on the loads and constraints applied. The reduced number of elements in Pro/M (which can be a couple of orders of magnitude smaller) initially reduces the computational load, but as the order of the polynomials gets higher, this advantage is somewhat diminished.

▸ The restrictions on element size and shape are not nearly as stringent for p-elements as they are for h-elements (where concerns of aspect ratio, skewness, and so on often arise).

▸ Automatic mesh generators, which can produce very poor meshes for h-elements, are much more effective with p-elements, due to the reduced requirements and limitations on mesh geometry.

▸ Since the same mesh is used throughout the analysis, this mesh can be tied directly to the geometry. This is the key reason why MECHANICA is able to perform sensitivity and optimization studies during which the geometric parameters of a body can change, but the program does not need to be constantly re-meshing the part.

Convergence and Accuracy in the Solution

It should be apparent that, due to the number of simplifying assumptions necessary to obtain results with FEA, we should be quite cautious about the results obtained. No FEA solution should be accepted unless the convergence properties have been examined.

For h-elements, this generally means doing the problem several times with successively smaller elements and monitoring the change in the solutions. When decreasing the element size results in a negligible (or acceptably small) change in the solution, then we are generally satisfied that the FEA has wrung all the information out of the model that it can.

As mentioned above, with p-elements, the convergence analysis is built in to the program. Since the geometry of the mesh does not change, no remeshing is required. Rather, each successive solution (called a *p-loop pass*) is performed with increasing orders of polynomials (only on elements where this is required) until the change between iterations is "small enough". Figure 12 shows the convergence behavior of two common measures used to monitor convergence in MECHANICA. These are the maximum Von Mises stress and the total strain energy. Note that the Von Mises stress will generally always increase during the convergence test, but can behave quite erratically as we will see later. Because Von Mises stress is a local measure, the strain energy is probably a better measure to use to control convergence.

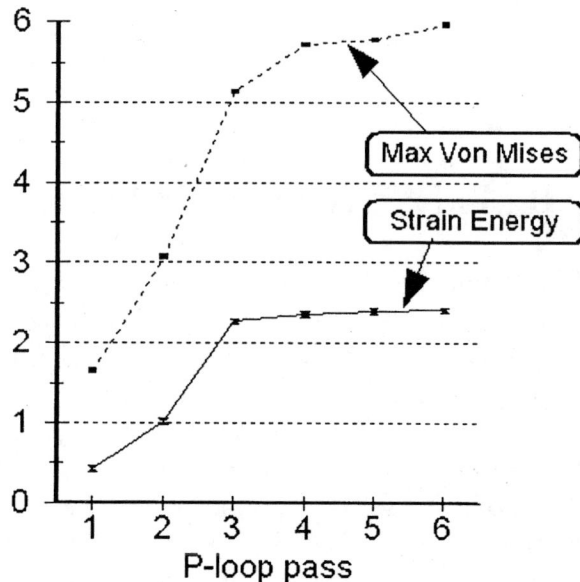

Figure 12 Two common convergence measures using p-elements.

Sources of Error

Error enters into the FEA process in a number of ways:

♦   **errors in problem definition** - are the geometry, loads, and constraints known and implemented accurately? Is the correct analysis being performed? Are the material properties correct and/or appropriate?

♦   **errors in creating the physical model** - can we really use symmetry? Is the material isotropic and homogeneous, as assumed? Are the physical constants known? Does the material behave linearly?

♦   **errors in creating the mathematical model** - is the model complete enough to capture the effects we wish to observe? Is the model overly complex? Does the mathematical model correctly express the physics of the problem?

♦   **errors in discretization** - is the mesh too coarse or too fine? Have we left accidental "holes" in the model? If using shell elements, are there tears or rips (free edges) between elements where there shouldn't be?

♦   **errors in the numerical solution** - when dealing with very large computational problems, we must always be concerned about the effects of accumulated round-off error. Can this error be estimated? How trustworthy is the answer going to be?

♦   **errors in interpretation of the results** - are we looking at the results in the right way to see what we want and need to see? Are the limitations of the program understood[2]? Has the possible misuse of a purely graphical or display tool obscured or hidden a critical result?

You will be able to answer most of these questions by the time you complete this tutorial. The answers to others will be problem dependent and will require some experience and further exposure before you are a confident and competent FEA user.

A CAD Model is *NOT* an FEA Model!

One of the common misconceptions within the engineering community is the equivalence of a CAD solid model with a model used for FEA. These are, in fact, not the same despite proclamations of the CAD vendors that their solid models can be "seamlessly" ported to one or another FEA program. In fact, this is probably quite undesirable! It should not be surprising that CAD and FEA models are different, since the two models are developed for different purposes.

The CAD model is usually developed to provide a data base for manufacturing. Thus, dimensions must be fully specified (including tolerances), all minor features (such as fillets, rounds, holes) must be included, processing steps and surface finishes are indicated, threads are specified, and so on. Figure 13 shows a CAD solid model of a hypothetical piping component, complete with bolt holes, flanges, o-ring grooves, chamfered edges, and carrying lugs. Not visible in the figure are the dimensions, tolerances, and welding instructions for fabrication which are all part of the CAD model.

FEA is usually directed at finding out other information about a proposed design. To do this *efficiently*, the FEA model can (and often needs to) be quite different from the CAD model. A simple example of this is that the

Figure 13 A hypothetical 3D solid model of a piping junction

symmetry of an object is often exploited in the preparation of the FEA model. In one of the exercises we will do later, we will model a thin tapered plate with a couple of large holes. The plate has a plane of symmetry so that we only need to do FEA of one-half of the plate. It is also

---

[2] The author once had a student who was rightly concerned about the very large deflections in a truss computed using a simple FEM program. It turned out that the program was performing a linear analysis, and was computing stresses in some members several orders of magnitude higher than the yield strength of the material. It took some time to explain that the FEM software knew nothing about failure of the material. It turned out that a simple data entry error had reduced the cross sectional area of the members in the truss.

quite common in FEA to ignore minor features like rounds, fillets, chamfers, holes, minor changes in surface profile, and other cosmetic features unless these features will have a large effect on the measures of interest in the model. Most frequently, they do not, and can be ignored.

Figure 14 shows an FEA model of the piping component created to determine the maximum Von Mises stress in the vicinity of the filleted connection between the two pipes. The differences between the two models shown in Figures 13 and 14 are immediately obvious. Figures 15 and 16 show the mesh of shell elements created from the surface, and the computed Von Mises stress.

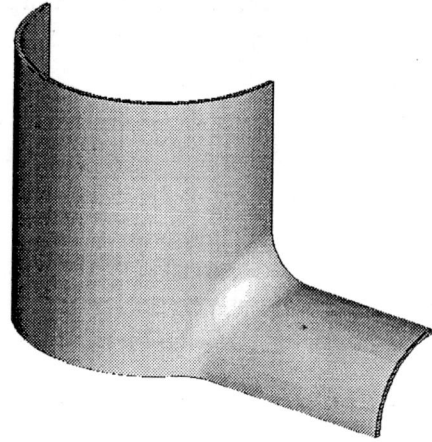

Figure 14 The 3D solid model of pipe junction

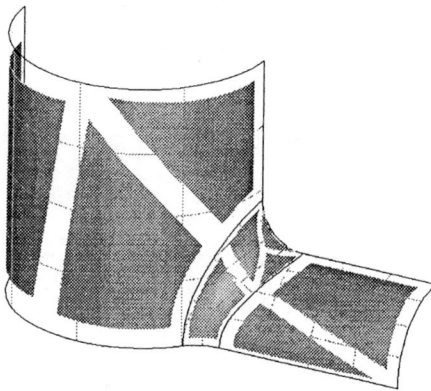

Figure 15 Shell elements of specified thickness created from 3D model

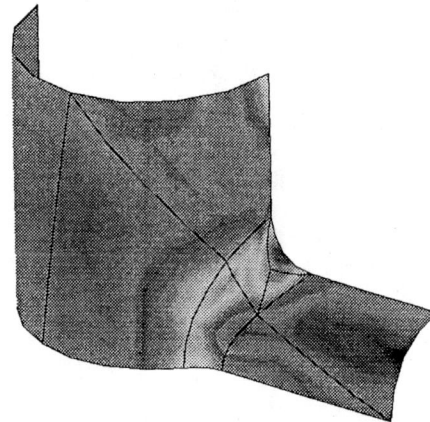

Figure 16 Von Mises stress in the FEA model

In summary, the stated goal of FEA (the "Golden Rule", if you like) might be expressed as:

Use the simplest model possible that will yield sufficiently reliable results of interest at the lowest computational cost.

You can easily see how this might be at odds with the requirements of a CAD model. For further discussion of this, see the excellent book **Building Better Products with Finite Element Analysis** by Vince Adams and Abraham Askenazi, Onword Press, 1998.

Overview of Pro/MECHANICA Structure

Basic Operation

We are going to start using Pro/M in the next chapter. Before we dive in, it will be useful to have an overall look at the function and organization of the software. This will help to explain some of the Pro/M terminology and see how the program relates to the ideas presented in this chapter's overview of FEA.

We can divide the operation and functionality of Pro/M Structure according to the rows in Table I below. These entries are further elaborated in the next few pages. In the process of setting up and running a solution, you will basically need to pick one option from each row in the table. The top-down organization of the table is roughly in the order that these decisions must be made. Other issues such as creation of the model geometry and post-processing and display of final results will be left to subsequent chapters.

TABLE I - An Overall View of Pro/M Capability and Function

	MECHANICA Options	Description
Mode of Operation	Independent Integrated	how Pro/M is operated with respect to Pro/ENGINEER
Type of Model	3D Plane Stress Plane Strain Axisymmetric	basic structure of the model
Type of Elements	Shell Beam Solid Spring Mass	element types that can be used in a model
Analysis Methods	Static Modal Buckling Pre-stress modal Pre-stress buckling	the fundamental solution being sought for the model
Convergence Methods	Quick Check Single Pass Adaptive Multi-Pass Adaptive	method of monitoring convergence in the solution
Design Studies	Standard Sensitivity Optimization	high level methods to organize essentially repetitive computations

Modes of Operation

A discussion of the full details of operating modes gets pretty confusing, so only the main points are presented here. These are:

1.   Pro/M can operate in two modes[3], in relation to its cousin application Pro/ENGINEER. These are: **independent** and **integrated**. A special license is required to run the independent version. In the student and educational editions, only integrated mode is possible.

2.   The user interface is determined by the mode:
     ♦   integrated mode - Pro/ENGINEER interface
     ♦   independent mode - Pro/MECHANICA interface

3.   If you start out in Pro/ENGINEER to create the part (or assembly) geometry and call up MECHANICA, you will initially be running in integrated mode. You can then switch to independent mode if desired (and if your license allows it), as illustrated here (note that the arrows are one-way transfers):

Integrated ➡ Independent
Mode   Mode

4.   If you switch to independent mode, the connection with Pro/ENGINEER will be severed. Any changes in design parameters (for example following an optimization) must be manually transferred back into the Pro/E model.

5.   In integrated mode, a few Pro/M commands and result displays are not available. However the tight integration with Pro/E makes it very easy to perform design modification and quick FEA.

6.   In integrated mode, the user interface is the same as Pro/E. Only one set of controls to learn! The independent mode user interface is quite different.

7.   The full set of Pro/M commands and functions are available in independent mode (for example: display of some types of results such as element p-levels).

8.   Although independent mode gives access to the complete range of MECHANICA functionality, the benefits of feature-based geometry creation/modification are lost.

A condensed comparison of these operating modes is shown in Table II on the next page. As mentioned above, all the tutorials in this manual are meant to be run in integrated mode.

---

[3] A third mode, called *linked*, was available up until Release 2000*i*, but has been removed.

TABLE II - Pro/MECHANICA Modes of Operation

Integrated Mode	Independent Mode
Pro/E interface	Pro/M interface
all analyses available	all analyses available
2D and 3D models	2D and 3D models
some measures of results not available	all measures available
some analysis options not available (eg excluding elements)	all options available
all elements generated automatically	element creation manual or automatic
sensitivity and optimization using Pro/E parameters only	sensitivity and optimization uses Pro/M variables

Types of Models

This is fairly self-explanatory. In addition to 3D solid, shell, and beam models, Pro/M in both modes can treat 2D models (plane stress, plane strain, or axisymmetric). Note that all geometry and model entities (loads and constraints) for all 2D model types must be defined in the XY plane of a selected coordinate system. Also, a very thin plate might be modeled as a 2D shell, but if it is loaded with any force components normal to the plate, then it becomes a 3D problem.

Independent Pro/M contains a good set of tools to create both 2D and 3D geometry. Complicated 3D geometry of parts would be easier to make in Pro/E or some other CAD package, and brought into Pro/M in integrated mode. The model geometry is generally created entirely in Pro/E. It is possible to create some (non-solid) simulation features while in Pro/M, such as datum points and curves.

Types of Elements

The various types of elements that can be used in Pro/M are listed in Table I. It is possible to use different types of elements in the same model (e.g. combining solid + beam + spring elements), but we will discuss only a couple of models of this degree of complexity in these tutorials. At first glance, this seems like a limited list of element types. H-element programs typically have large libraries of different element types, but these are often necessary to overcome the limitations of low order simple h-elements. In Pro/M, we do not have this problem and you can do practically anything with the elements available.

Analysis Methods

For a given model, several different analysis types are possible. For example, the *static* analysis will compute the stresses and deformations within the model, while the *modal* analysis will compute the mode shapes and natural frequencies. *Buckling* analysis will compute the buckling loads on the body, and so. Other analysis methods are available but in this manual, we will only look at static stress and modal analysis.

Convergence Methods

As discussed above, using the p-code method allows Pro/M to monitor the solution and modify the polynomial edge order until a solution has been achieved to a specified accuracy. This is implemented with three options:

- **Quick Check** - This actually isn't a convergence method since the model is run only for a single fixed (low, usually 3) polynomial order. **The results should never be trusted.** What a Quick Check is for is to quickly run the model through the solver in order to pick up any errors that may have been made, for example in the constraints. A quick review of the results will also indicate whether any gross modeling errors have been made and possibly to point out potential problem areas in the model.

- **Single Pass Adaptive** - More than a Quick Check, but less than a complete convergence run, the single pass adaptive method performs one pass at a low polynomial order, assesses the accuracy of the solution, modifies the p-level of "problem elements", and does a final pass with some elements raised to an order that should provide reasonable results. Unless the model is very computationally intensive and/or is very well behaved and known, avoid this method. The Single Pass Adaptive analysis is available for most model types.

- **Multi-Pass Adaptive** - The ultimate in convergence analysis. Multiple "p-loop" passes are made through the solver, with edge orders of "problem elements" being increased with each pass. This iterative approach continues until either the solution converges to a specified accuracy or the maximum specified edge order (default 6, maximum 9) is reached. At the conclusion of the run, the convergence measures may be examined. These are typically the Von Mises stress and the total strain energy, as shown in Figure 12. Unless you have a very good reason not to, always base your final conclusions on the results obtained using this convergence method.

Design Studies

A Design Study is a problem or set of problems that you define for a particular model. When you ultimately press the **Run** button on Pro/M, what will execute is a design study - it is the top-most level of organization in Pro/M. There are three types of design studies:

- A **Standard** design study is the most basic and simple. It will include at least one but possibly several analyses (for example a static analysis plus a modal analysis). For this study, you need to specify the geometry, create the elements, assign material properties, set up loads and constraints, determine the analysis and convergence types, and then display and review the final results. The Standard design study is what most people would consider "Finite Element Analysis."

■   A **sensitivity** design study can be set up so that results are computed for several different values of designated design variables or material properties. In addition to the standard model, you need to designate the design variables and the range over which you want them to vary. You can use a sensitivity study to determine, for example, which design variables will have the most effect on a particular measure of performance of the design like the maximum stress or total mass.

■   Finally, the most powerful design study is an **optimization**. For this, you start with a basic FEA model. You then specify a desired goal (such as minimum mass of the body), geometric constraints (such as dimensions or locations of geometric entities), material constraints (such as maximum allowed stress) and one or more design variables which can vary over specified ranges. Pro/M will then search through the space of the design variables and determine the best design that satisfies your constraints. Amazing!

A Brief Note about Units

It is crucial to use a consistent set of units throughout your Pro/M activities. The program itself has no default set of units, and only uses the numerical values provided by you. Thus, if your geometry is created with a particular linear unit like mm or inches in mind, you must make sure that any other data supplied, such as loads (force, pressure) and material properties (density, Young's modulus, and so on) are defined consistently. The built-in material libraries offer properties for common materials in four sets of units (all at room temperature):

> inch - pound - second
> foot - pound - second
> meter - Newton - second
> millimeter - Newton - second

Note that the weight of the material is obtained by multiplying the mass density property by the acceleration of gravity expressed in the appropriate unit system.

If you require or wish to use a different system of units, you can enter your own material properties, but must look after consistency yourself. Table III outlines the common units in the various systems including how some common results will be reported by MECHANICA. For further information on units, consult the on-line help page "Unit Conversion Tables."

TABLE III - Common unit systems in Pro/MECHANICA

Quantity	System and Units			
	SI MNS	Metric mm-N-s	English FPS ft-lb-sec	English IPS in-lb-sec
length	m	mm	ft	in
time	s	s	sec	sec
mass	kg	tonne (1000 kg)	slug	lbf-sec^2 / in
density	kg/m^3	tonne/mm^3	slug/ft^3	lbf-sec^2 / in^4
gravity, g	9.81 m/s^2	9810 mm/s^2	32.2 ft/sec^2	386.4 in/sec^2
force	N	N	lbf	lbf
stress, pressure, Young's modulus	N/m^2 = Pa	N/mm^2 = MPa	lbf/ft^2	lbf/in^2 = psi

Files and Directories Produced by Pro/MECHANICA

Pro/M produces a bewildering array of files and directories. Unless you specify otherwise (or specified in your default system configuration), all of these will be created in the Pro/M start-up or working directory. It is therefore wise to create a new subdirectory for each model, make it your working directory, and store the part file there. Locations for temporary and output files can be changed at appropriate points in the program. For example, when you set up to run a design study, you can designate the location for the subdirectory which Pro/M will create for the output files.

The important files and directories are indicated in the Table IV. In the table, the symbol ① represents the directory specified in the *Run > Settings* dialog box for output files, and ② represents the directory specified in the same dialog box for temporary files. Unless the run terminates abnormally, all temporary files are deleted on completion of a run. The names *model*, *study*, and *filename* are supplied by you during execution of the program. Note that many of these files are stored in a binary format and are not readable by normal file editors.

Table IV - Some Files Produced by Pro/MECHANICA

File Type	File/Directory Name	Comments
Model Files	*model*.**mdb** *model*.**mbk**	the **mdb** file contains the last-saved model database. **mbk** is a backup that can be used if the **mdb** file is lost or corrupted
Engine Files	①/*study*/*study*.**mdb**	contains the entire model database at the time a design study is started
	①/*study*/*study*.**cnv** ①/*study*/*study*.**hst** ①/*study*/*study*.**res** ①/*study*/*study*.**rpt**	Engine output files: - convergence information - model updates during optimization - measures at each pass - output report for a design study (also accessible with the ***Run > Summary*** command)
Exchange Files	*filename*.**dxf** *filename*.**igs**	file formats used for import/export of geometry information
Temporary Files	②/*study*.**tmp**/*.**tmp** ②/*study*.**tmp**/*.**bas**	should delete automatically on completion of design study
Results Files	*filename*.**rwd**	result window definitions stored with Save in the Result Windows dialog box
AutoGEM Files	*model*.**agm**	information about the most recent AutoGEM operation. If the model has not yet been named, this file is **untitled.agm**
Miscellaneous Files	**mechevnt**	a complete history of the most recent Pro/M session (every command, mouse click, and data entry). Automatically overwritten with next session.

On-line Documentation

For further details on any of these functions or operating commands, consult the on-line documentation available with MECHANICA. See your local system administrator for information on how to access these files.

Summary

This chapter has introduced the background to FEA. In particular, the difference between h-code and p-code methods have been discussed. The general procedure involved in performing an analysis was described. Finally, an overview of MECHANICA has been presented to give you a view of the forest before we start looking at the individual trees!

You are strongly urged to have a look at the articles written by Dr. Paul Kurowski that are listed in the References at the end of this chapter. These offer an in-depth look at common errors made in FEA, the concept of convergence, a comparison of h- and p-elements, and more comments on the difference between CAD and FEA.

In the next Chapter, we will start to look at the basic tools within MECHANICA. We will start with the simplest type of model - a 2D plane stress model of a flat plate - and go through the process of setting up a standard design study for static analysis. We will also take a first look at the methods for viewing the results of the analysis.

References

"Avoiding Pitfalls in FEA," Paul Kurowski, *Machine Design*, November 1994.

"When good engineers deliver bad FEA," Paul Kurowski, *Machine Design*, November, 1995.

"Good Solid Modeling, Bad FEA," Paul Kurowski, *Machine Design*, November, 1996.

Finite Element Methods for Engineers, Roger T. Fenner, Macmillan, 1975.

Building Better Products with Finite Element Analysis, Vince Adams and Abraham Askenazi, Onword Press, 1998.

The Finite Element Method in Mechanical Design, Charles E. Knight, Jr., PWS-Kent, 1993.

CAD/CAM Theory and Practice, Ibrahim Zeid, McGraw-Hill, 1991.

The Finite Element Method, T.J.R. Hughes, Prentice Hall, 1987.

Computer-Assisted Mechanical Design, J.Ed Akin, Prentice Hall, 1990.

Questions for Review

1. What is the purpose of interpolating polynomials in FEA?
2. What is a "model?" What are some different types of models and how do these relate to the real world?
3. Is it ever possible for a FEM solution to be "exact?" Why or why not?
4. What is the primary source of error when using first-order h-elements for stress analysis?
5. Give an outline of the necessary steps in performing FEA.
6. Why is it probably not a good idea to use a CAD model directly in an FEA solution?
7. What is the "Golden Rule" of FEA?
8. How is convergence of the solution obtained using h-code and p-code methods?
9. Does mesh refinement always yield higher maximum stresses?
10. What is the maximum edge order available in Pro/M? In the (unlikely) event that the solution will not converge, what needs to be done?
11. What measures are typically used in Pro/M to monitor convergence?
12. How will error enter into an FEA?
13. What is a *design study*? What types are available in Pro/M?
14. What are the three methods of convergence analysis? When would each be appropriate?
15. What types of 2D models can be created? In what operating modes? What restrictions are there on 2D models?
16. What types of analyses can be performed on a model?
17. How can you gain access to the on-line help on your system?
18. Compare the advantages and disadvantages of *integrated* and *independent* modes of operation.
19. What is the maximum edge order available in Pro/M? In the (unlikely) event that the solution will not converge, what needs to be done?
20. What measures are typically used in Pro/M to monitor convergence?
21. What are the steps required to perform a complete FEA with Pro/MECHANICA?
22. Where and how do you set up the units for the Mechanica model?

Exercises

1. Consult a numerical methods textbook and find out what algorithms are used to solve very large linear systems. What effect does round-off error have, and can this be quantified? Are some methods more susceptible to round-off than others?

2. Locate some product brochures for FEM software, and look for the kind of modeling errors discussed in this chapter. Compare the models to the "real thing" and comment on any differences you notice.

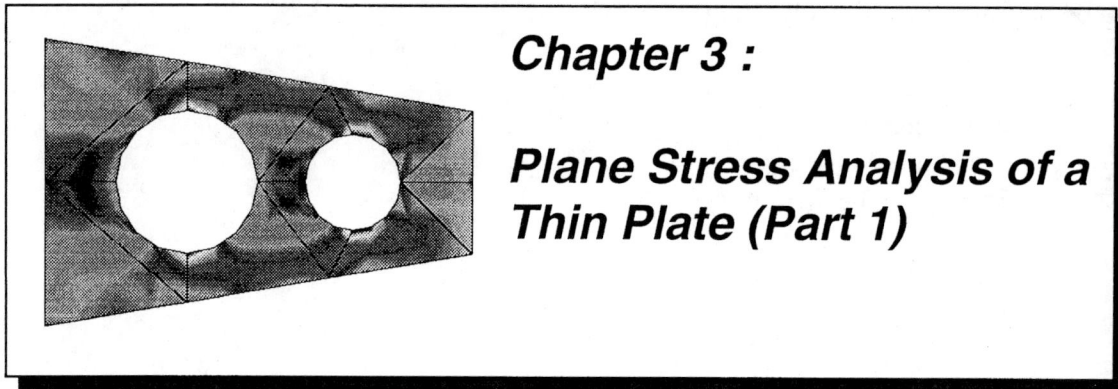

Chapter 3 :

Plane Stress Analysis of a Thin Plate (Part 1)

Synopsis:

A simple model is created using the built-in geometry tools in Pro/MECHANICA. The complete sequence of steps required for a static analysis will be outlined, and basic result display options presented.

Overview of this Lesson

Running Pro/MECHANICA in independent mode, we will create a model of a thin plate loaded in tension. The plate (see Figure 1) has two holes and is fixed at the wide end and loaded on the narrow end. As long as the plate thickness is small compared to its length/width and the load stays in the plane of the plate, we can treat this as a plane stress problem. This geometry will be used to illustrate some simple construction tools in Pro/M and allow us to go through an entire analysis to find the stresses acting in the plate and its deformation.

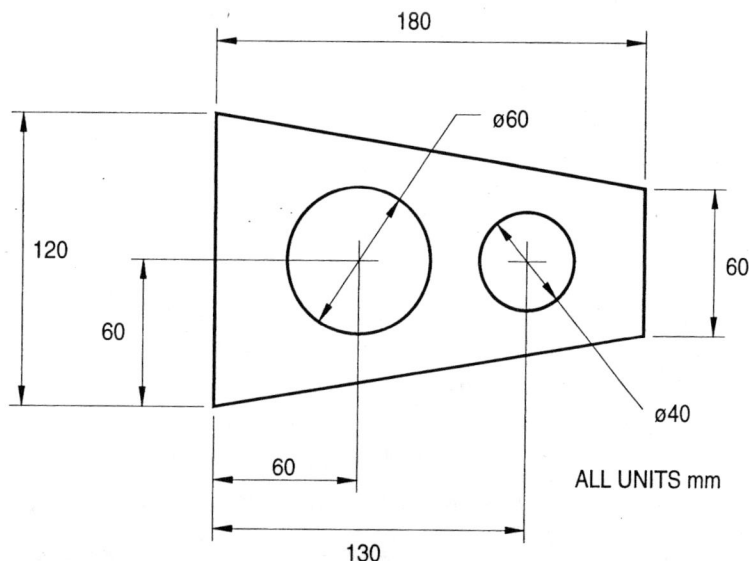

Figure 1   The thin plate

The steps to be performed are the following:

1. Create the geometry
2. Create the elements
3. Set the material properties
4. Apply loads and constraints
5. Set up the design study
6. Run the analysis
7. View the results.

You will quickly get in the habit of performing these steps automatically.

There will be lots to do here. It is ALL important, so go slowly. If necessary, you might have to come back and redo the lesson.

Let's get started...

Starting Pro/MECHANICA

Start up Pro/MECHANICA on your system. Details on how to do this will vary from system to system. If it is not clear how to do this, see your system administrator. On Windows systems, the command sequence will be something like:

> *Start*
> *Programs*
> *Pro/MECHANICA*
> *Structure*

or your system may be set up with a shortcut to launch Pro/M directly from the desktop.

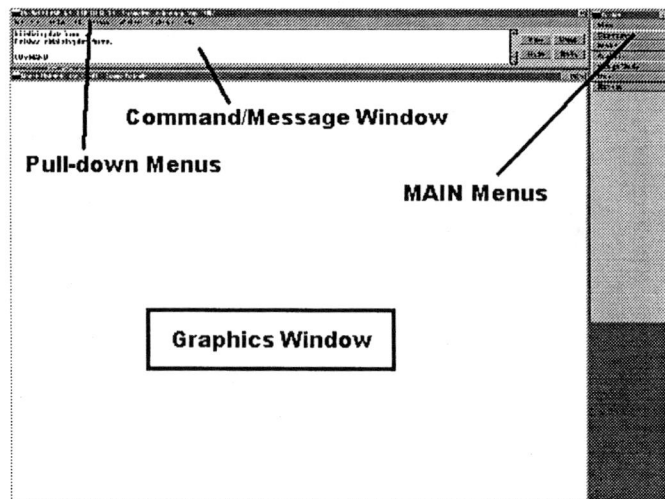

Figure 2 The main screen in Pro/MECHANICA

After a few seconds the main screen will appear as shown in Figure 2. This includes the main graphics window, the command/message window (with pull-down menus), and the Main menu. The *graphics window* will be were you will view your model and analysis results. The *main menu* leads to the major Pro/M command sub-menus. The *pull-down menus* at the top contain many of the utility tools and controls for the screen display and editing tasks. The *command/message window* will be where Pro/M tells you of its progress and prompts you for required data. This data can be entered either by typing in values or selecting graphical elements in the graphics window.

You will have to get used to watching the three critical areas on the screen at the same time: the main menu on the right, the graphics window, and the command/message window.

Let's have a look at the Main menu buttons (Figure 3):

Geometry - leads to sub-menus used to create the geometric
structure of the model by drawing points, curves, surfaces,
volumes, and so on

Model - this brings up commands for specifying the model based
on the geometry. This includes creating elements,
specifying material properties, adding loads and
constraints.

Analysis - here is where we specify the type of analysis to be
performed on the model (static, modal, ...)

Figure 3 Main menu options

Design Study - allows you to choose the type of design study (standard, sensitivity,
optimization) and set appropriate parameters

Run - after the model is fully specified, this leads to a menu to set the run parameters and
perform the model analysis

Results - lets you set up window definitions and view the results for the model (stresses,
deformations, strains, modal shapes, and so on)

As you go through the modeling steps, the flow of your work will be from the top to the bottom
on this menu.

Before we start creating anything, we should set up the graphics display. In the pull-down menus
select:

Display > Master Visibilities > All On | Accept

That is, turn everything on except the grid. Note that we have separate visibility control over
many different kinds of entities: geometry, elements, model, and miscellaneous. Turning
everything on will make sure that we will see everything as it is created.

Finally, notice the coordinate system icon in the lower corner of the graphics window. This
shows us that our default drawing or working plane is the XY plane (the two red axes), with Z
coming out of the screen.

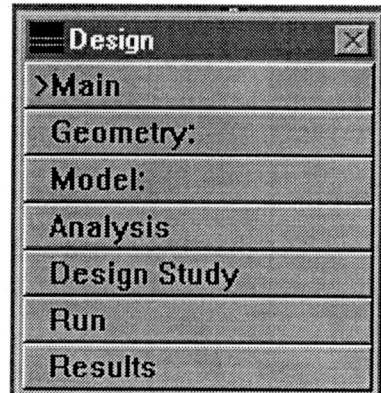

Creating the Geometry

We will create the geometry by entering coordinates of key points on the model from the keyboard. It is possible to import the geometry either from IGES files or directly from Pro/ENGINEER. As required, we will use other built-in tools. Start with the four corners of the plate:

> ***Main > Geometry***
> ***Point > Single Points***
> ***Snap(Point)***

The Snap menu (Figure 4) will be very important. Scan down the list of snap options. The message window prompts you

"Select a point or enter coordinates:"

Type in the coordinates of the lower left corner of the plate as

> **0, 0**

A small yellow circle will appear in the center of your screen. Note that we did not have to enter a value for Z; if omitted, it is assumed to be 0. Type in some more sets of coordinates for the other corners (our dimensions are mm):

> **0 120**
> **180 30**
> **180 90**

Note we didn't need a comma, just a space, to separate the numbers. Finally, press the ***Enter*** key on a blank input line to close out the command, or click the middle mouse button. **The middle mouse button will always be interpreted by Pro/M as if you had pressed the Enter key.**

It may be that nothing shows up on your screen. At the right end of the command window, select

> ***View > Fit | Done***

The View menu (Figure 5) presents controls for the graphical display. For now, just scan the list of commands on this menu. The Fit command will refit the current view so that all defined entities are visible in the graphics window. Continue entering coordinates as follows (these are the circle centers):

> ***Single Points > Snap(Point)***
> **60, 60**
> **130, 60**

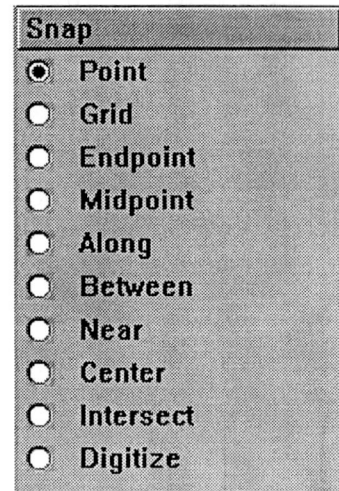

Figure 4 The Snap menu

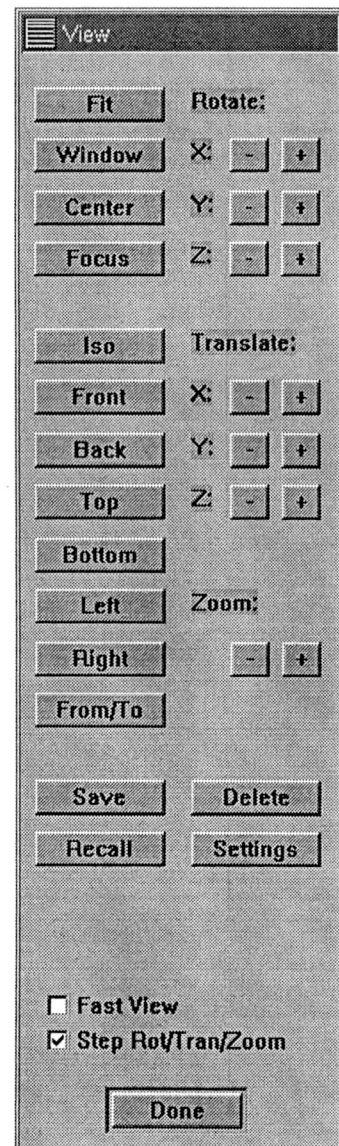

Figure 5 The View menu

If you make a data entry error and put a point at the wrong place, you can delete it with

Edit > Delete > Entity > Points

and click on the wrong point, then middle click twice.

Here's another useful hint: **You can zoom in or out on your model using CTRL-left**, that is hold down the CTRL key on the keyboard and click and drag with the left mouse button. Users of Pro/Engineer will be quite familiar with this, and will correctly anticipate that CTRL-middle will spin the model, and CTRL-right will pan. If you spin the model, return to the original orientation with *View > Front | Done*.

Now we will connect the four corner points with edges. Select

Geometry > Curve > Line > Point Chain > Snap(Point)

Left click on each of the four corner points in sequence around the plate. Middle click when the last side is closed.

We'll add the circular holes. Keep your eye on the command/message window while you do this, since the mouse will be used for short-cuts here. Select

Geometry > Curve > Circle > Radius-Center

For the larger hole, enter a radius of **30** and left click on the appropriate center point. Then middle click once to back up one level in the command. Enter the radius of the smaller hole as **20**. Left click on the other center point and middle click twice to completely exit the circle command. Your geometry should now look like the figure below.

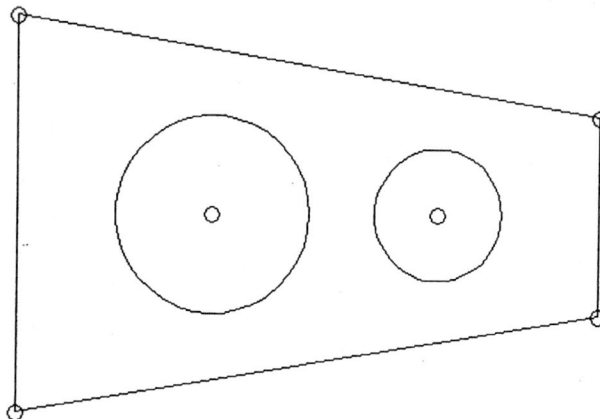

Figure 6 All edges of the plate defined

We will now use these edges to create more points that will be used to set up the elements. Select

Geometry > Point > Along Curve

Click on the left edge of the plate. Read the message window and enter the number of points to create **1**. Do the same for the right edge. When prompted for the number of points, note the default <1>. Middle click to accept. Now click on the upper edge and create **2** new points. Do the same for the lower edge. Finally, middle click to exit the command. Note the default for *Along Curve* is equally spaced points.

For the next step (adding points to the circles), we will need a construction line. This is not an edge of the model, but just a convenience. Select

Geometry > Curve > Construction Geom > Horizontal > Snap(Point)

and click on the point in the center of the large circle.

Now we'll create points on the circles. Note that we are backing out of a command by selecting a higher level menu. Select

Geometry > Point > Along Curve

Select the big circle and enter the number of points to insert as **4**. For a closed curve, we need to specify where the first point is; the rest will be equally spaced around the curve. This is why we needed the construction line. Select

Snap(Intersect)

and click first on the large circle and then on the construction line at about the 3 o'clock position on the circle. Four points should appear on the circle. Everything is all set up for the second circle so we only need a few mouse clicks to do the job:

> click on the smaller circle,
> middle click to accept the default number of points as 4,
> click on the circle again,
> click on the construction line at the 3 o'clock position,
> and finally, middle click to exit the command.

Your model should now look like Figure 7.

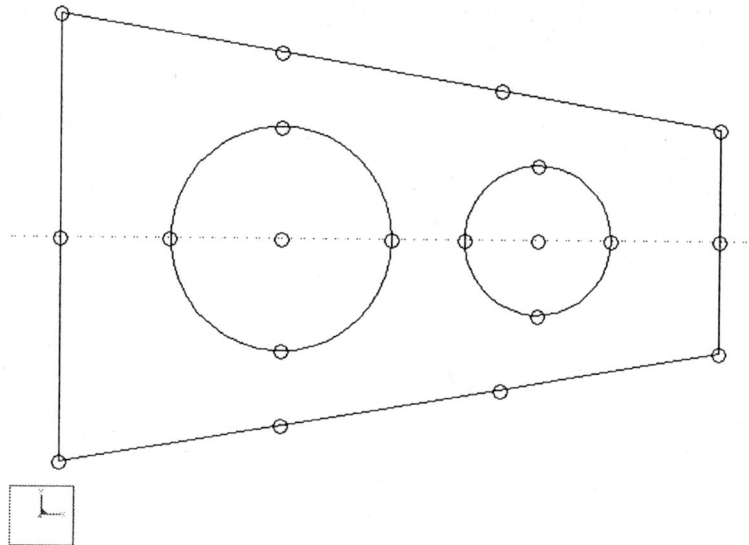

Figure 7 All points constructed

All the geometry for this model is now defined. On to the next step - creating the finite elements.

Creating the Elements

Select

Main > Model

Since this is the first time into the model menu, we are faced with the Model Type window shown in Figure 8. This shows the four types of models that Pro/M can treat. Click on *Plane Stress > Accept*.

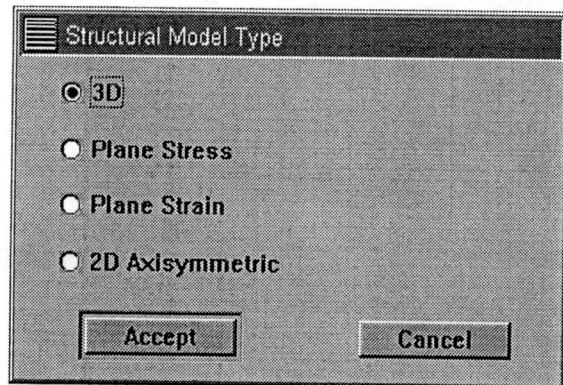

Figure 8 The Model Types window

We will now proceed to define aspects of the model, going down the list presented in the menu at the right on the screen (Elements, Properties, Constraints, and so on)..

First, we need to construct the elements. We will use a mix of 3- and 4-sided elements (triangles and quads). Select

Elements > 2D Plate > Quad | Point

Have a look at Figure 9 below to identify the quad elements (there are eight). These are set up by clicking on the four vertices that make up the corners of each element. **IMPORTANT:** Use a symmetric layout of the elements here. We will come back to this point in the next lesson and create an asymmetric layout to see if this affects the results.

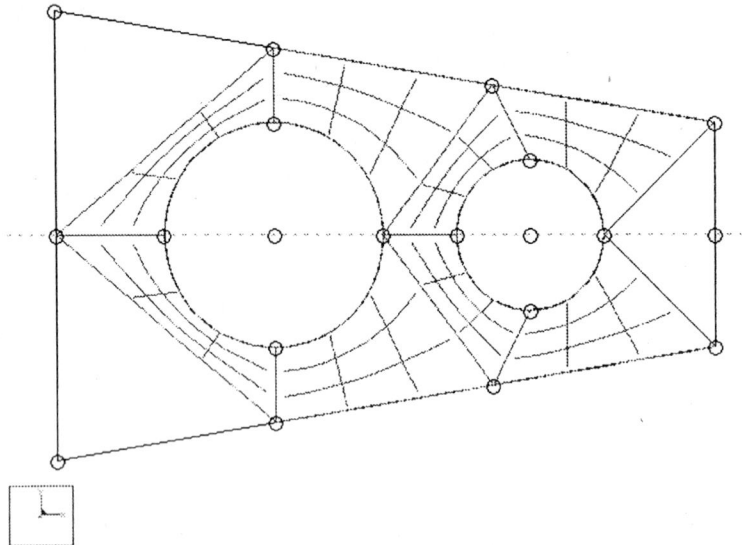

Figure 9 Quad elements defined

If you make a mistake selecting vertices for an element, you can get rid of the element with

Edit > Delete > Entity > 2D Plates

and click on the element to be deleted. Middle click twice to return to the Elements menu.

Now select

Tri | Point

and click on the vertices of the triangular elements at each end. Click the middle button when all the elements have been defined.

To help distinguish between the geometry (edges and curves of the model) and the elements, we can adjust the display using (in the pull-down menus)

Display > Settings > Shrink All Elements > Accept

Some installations may have this set by default and should result in the display of the model shown in Figure 10.

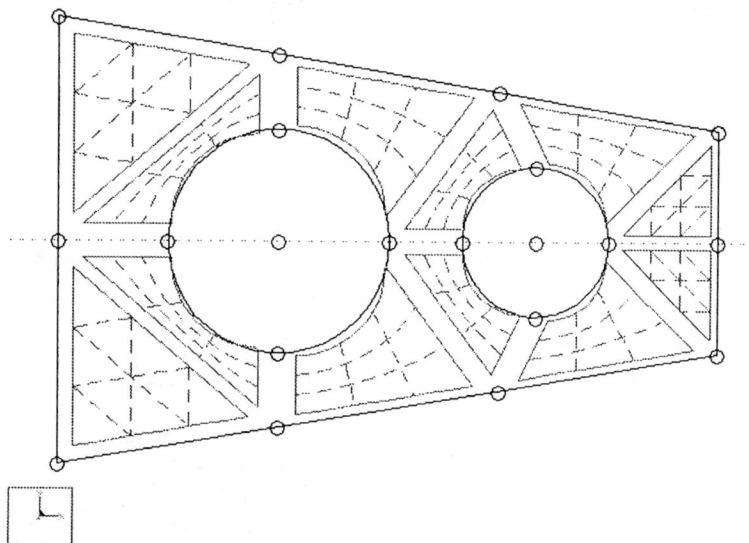

Figure 10 Elements shrunk

In the **Display > Settings** menu, you can experiment with different marking schemes for the 2D plate elements and the points. You might also like to shade the elements (the default is wireframe). This will make it quite obvious when elements are missing.

Assigning Properties

We have to define material properties and specify the thickness of the plate. First, the material properties - select:

Model > Properties > Material

This opens the Materials dialog window (Figure 11). This lists all the materials contained in the Pro/M library with the physical properties defined in various systems of units. We will not need to add new materials to this list in these lessons. For now, since our length units are millimeters, select **AL2014_mmNS** in the left column and transfer it to the right pane using the **>>>** button. Now select

Assign > 2D Plate > All

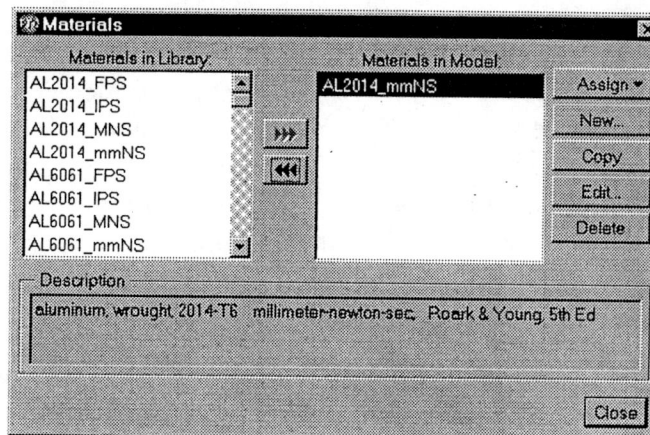

Figure 11 The Materials dialog window

The elements will be highlighted in red. Click the middle button to accept the selection.

To see the material properties, select **Edit**. The properties window comes up showing the values of Young's modulus, Poisson's ratio and other constants for the material. Accept this box with no changes. In the Materials window, select **Close**.

Now we specify the plate thickness. Select

Properties > Shell Property > 2D Plate > All

Once again the elements highlight in red. Accept with the middle button and the Shell Properties window comes up. Enter **thick2** in the top box, a description in the middle box, and finally a thickness of **2**. The complete box should look like Figure 12. **Accept** the window.

We are now finished defining the element and model properties. On to the next step...

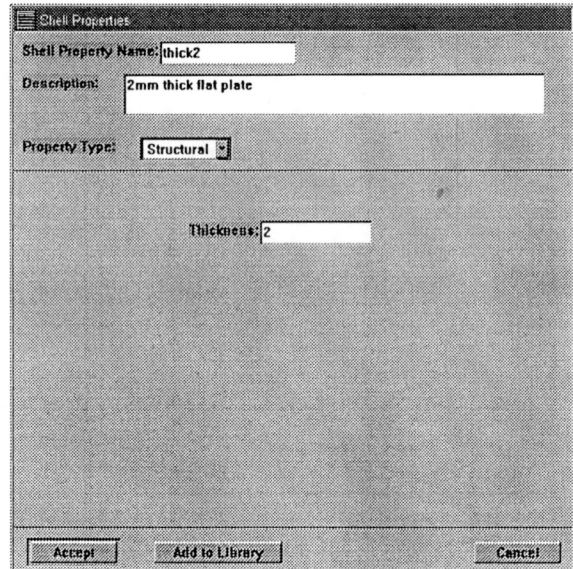

Figure 12 Entering the plate thickness

Defining the Constraints

At a minimum, all models must be constrained against rigid body motion (translation or rotation). In our case, the plate will be fixed at the left end. This means no translation will be allowed in any direction for points along the edges of the elements on the left end.

VERY IMPORTANT POINT: We will define the constraint using the GEOMETRY rather than the ELEMENTS! Why do this? First, the elements are *associated* with the geometry through the points we specified. This means that the constraint defined on the geometry will be passed on to the elements automatically. Secondly, if we define the constraints on the elements themselves and decide later to delete, rearrange, or modify the elements, the defined constraints will be lost and we would have to create them again. This is only mildly annoying for a simple model, but when we get to optimization we will want the geometry to be constrained and not the elements themselves because in the course of the calculations the elements may be rearranged automatically.

Select

Model > Constraints > Curve

This brings up the Constraint dialog window (Figure 13). Each constraint (and load) that we create in a model has a name and is assigned to a particular constraint (or load) set. For simple models you can probably live with the default names. But when your models become more complex, you will want to use more descriptive names.

For our model, enter the constraint name **fixededge**, and leave the default **ConstraintSet1** as is. Select the button under Curves and pick on the left vertical edge. This is another advantage of the shrunken elements, since this edge is easy to pick out. When the desired edge highlights, click the middle button. Note the default coordinate system is the WCS, as shown in the graphics window.

At the bottom of the Constraint window are the allowed degrees of freedom. This area will change depending on your model type. For plane stress, only translations in the X and Y directions can be specified. Leave both of these Fixed using the center button. The other buttons are for Free and Prescribed translations. Finally, accept the dialog with OK.

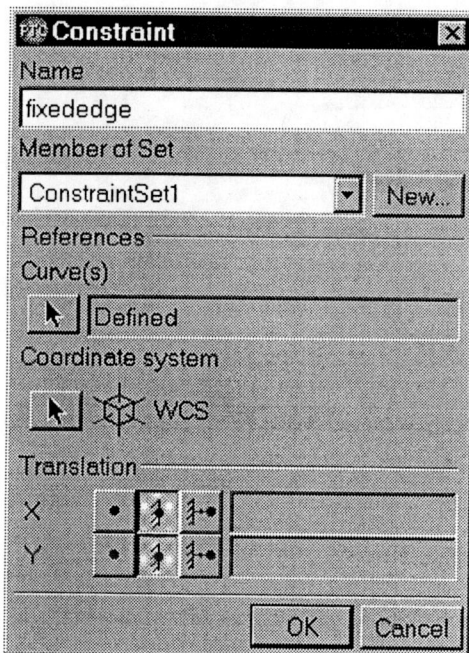

Figure 13 Specifying the constraint

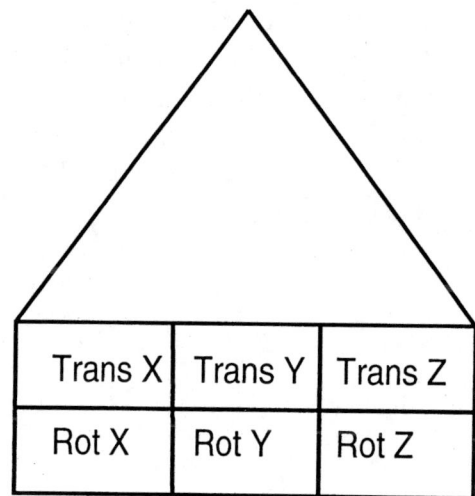

Figure 14 The Constraint symbol

A constraint symbol will appear on the left edge. This symbol is coded as shown in Figure 14. Any degree of freedom that is fixed is color filled in the boxes at the bottom of the symbol. An empty box indicates that degree of freedom is free or unconstrained.

We have now constrained the plate, and can get on with specifying the load on the other end.

Specifying the Load

We will set a uniformly distributed load on the narrow end of the plate, putting the plate in tension. Once again, we apply the load to the geometry rather than directly to the elements, for the same reasons as for the constraints described above. Select

Model > Loads > Curve

This opens the Force/Moment dialog window (Figure 15). As for constraints, loads are given names and contained within load sets. A model can have many load sets, each containing one or more loads. We will discuss multiple load sets a bit later in the lessons. Enter a load name **xhoriz** and leave the default set **LoadSet1**. Select the button under Curves and click on the right edge. It will highlight. Middle click. Make sure that **Total Load** and **Uniform** are selected in the pull-down lists, and enter the force components (in Newtons) X = **1000** and Y = **0**. When all the data is entered, you can select *Preview* to see load arrows applied. This is useful to check directions before accepting the dialog. Accept the dialog box with *OK* (or middle click).

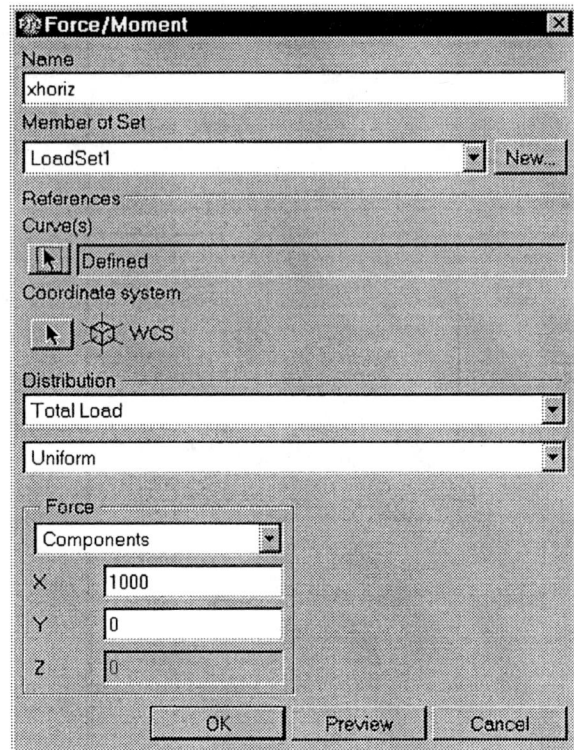

Figure 15 Specifying the load

Shrink the display a bit with CTRL-left, then select

Display > Settings > Display Load Magnitudes | Precision(1)

This will put a label on the model, which should now look like Figure 16. This completes our definition of the model.

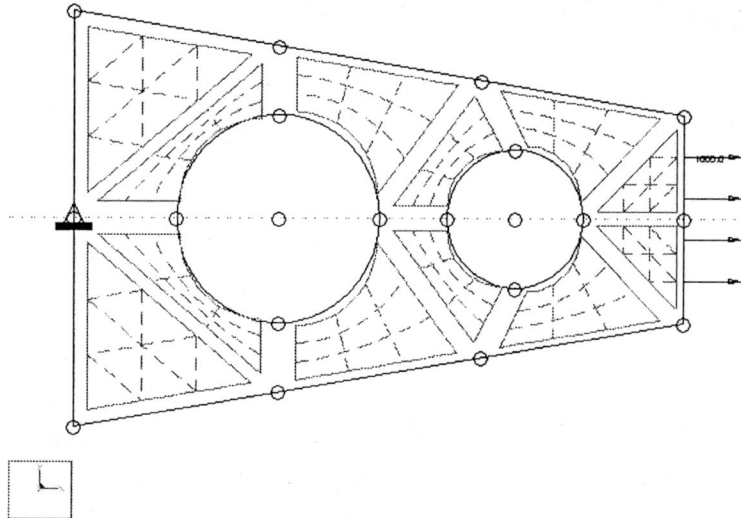

Figure 16 Completed model

Setting the Analysis

Now we specify the type of analysis we want Pro/M to perform. We generally always start out with a "quick and dirty" run through the computation to see if there are any gross errors in the model. This is called a *Quick Check*. Select:

Main > Analysis

In the Analyses window, open the pull-down list at the top to see the available analysis types. The default is Static. Now select

New

The Static Analysis Definition window opens (Figure 17). At the top, enter a unique analysis name such as **plate1**. Enter a description, like *"tapered plate with two hole"*. The only existing constraint and load sets should already be selected. Select *Quick Check* from the Convergence pull-down list. Finally, *Accept* the dialog.

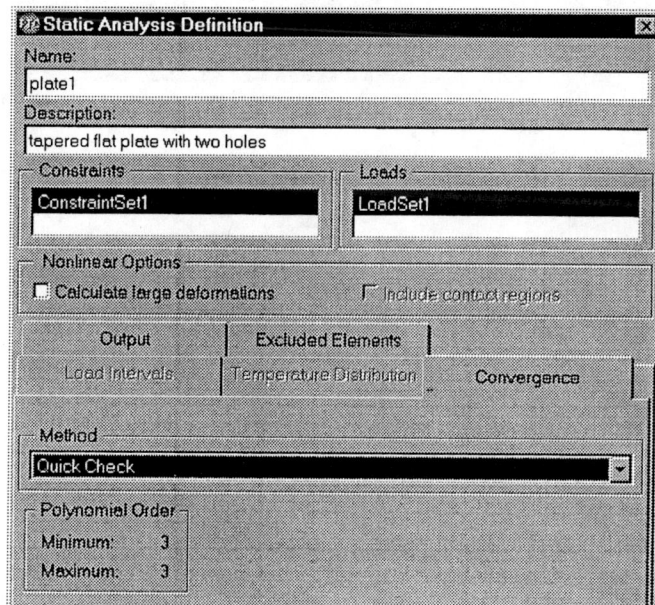

Figure 17 Defining a static analysis

Back in the Analyses window, all the currently defined analyses will be listed. So far, we only have one. When we come back to modify the analysis, we get at it through this window using the *Edit* button. For now, select *Done*.

Running the Analysis

We can now run the model. Select

> *Main > Run*

In the window that opens (Figure 18), *plate1* is shown as a Standard/Static analysis. Select

> *Settings*

and change temporary and output directories to *\temp*, or some other easy-to-identify place with lots of free disk space and that you won't bother about keeping later. IMPORTANT: Make a note of the location of the output directory. Then *Accept* the settings.

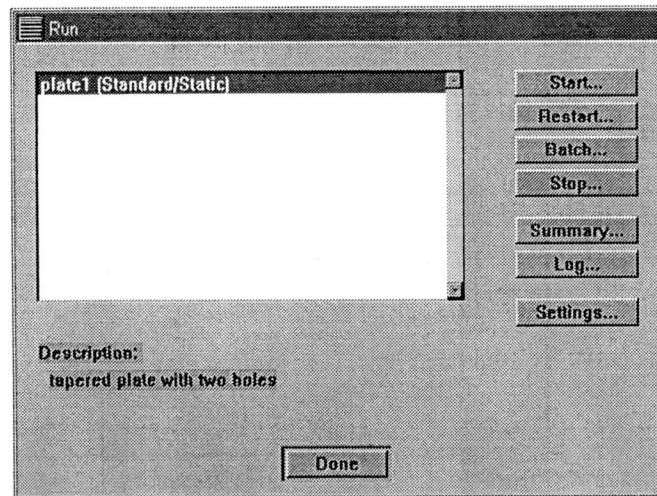

Figure 18 The Run window

Ready to go? Select

> *Start*

You will be asked if you want error detection. Answer *Yes*. You may be informed that the material assigned to the model does not contain failure data. This is used to plot contours of factor of safety. Ignore this for now by selecting *Continue*. If all goes well, Pro/M will process the model and report that there are no errors. If errors are found, follow the prompts and retrace your steps. Once the model has passed the error check, if you haven't done this already you will have to specify a file name in which to save the model. Save it as *plate1* in the current working directory (Pro/M will automatically add the mdb extension).

You will then see the message

"The design study has started."

up in the message window. The run should only take a few seconds for this simple model. In the

Run window, click on

Summary

A scrollable text window will open that reports data on the run. This includes: run settings, a model summary (number of geometry entities, number of elements), design study type, convergence method, convergence loop log, warnings and errors, some model properties, summary of primary measures, and CPU and memory utilization. In this window find the value of the measure **max_stress_vm** (maximum Von Mises Stress, should be about 24 MPa) and total CPU time (should be just a few seconds).

If everything went well with the Quick Check, that is, no warnings or errors were reported, we can go back and specify a more accurate analysis type. Select *Close* in the Summary text window and *Done* in the Run window. Select

Main > Analysis > Edit

and change Quick Check to **Multi-Pass Adaptive**, use **Lcl Disp & Lcl SE & Glbl RMS Stress**, set the convergence limit to **5%** and set the polynomial (edge) order maximum to **9** as shown in Figure 19.

Accept the dialog box, return to the **Run** menu, and select **Start**. You will be notified that output files already exist. Answer **Yes** to remove them. We will not need error detection. The design study will start up. While it is running, you can select **Summary** to watch the progress of the run. The multi-pass run will go to loop 6, with a maximum edge order of 6 on convergence. Check out the measure **max_stress_vm** (it will have increased from before, to about 28 MPa) and the total CPU time (it will have roughly doubled from before). Close the text window and select **Done** in the Run window. Now we can have a look at the results. This might be a good time to take a little stretch break!

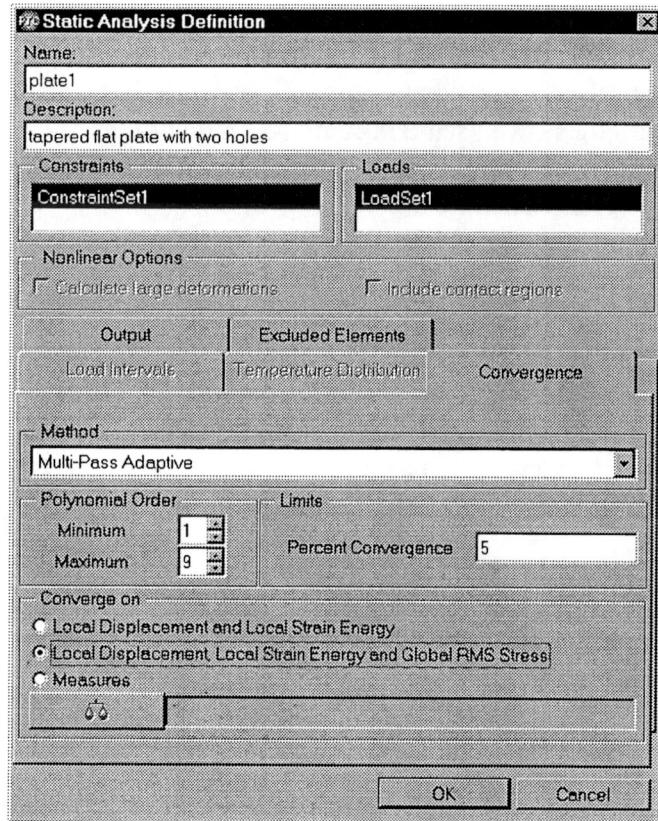

Figure 19 Setup for Multi-Pass Adaptive run

Viewing the Results

There are many ways that we can view the results of this run. Each view is identified with a unique window name that you supply. Then you specify what is to be plotted in the window. We will introduce a few of the most common window views here. Select

> *Main > Results > Create*

Displaying the Stress Contours

In the first window, we will create a fringe plot of the Von Mises stress[1] in the plate. In the small window that opens, enter the window name as *vm*, and *Accept* the dialog (don't forget you can do this either by clicking the Accept button, pressing the Enter key, or clicking the middle mouse button).

We now have to tell Pro/M where the data is that we want to plot. We do this by identifying the design study, for which we supplied a name back in Figure 17. This was "plate1". We also told Pro/M where to store all the output files (under Settings in the Run window). All we have to do is identify the location of those results[2]. Go to the directory that you designated to store the results files - we used **temp** above. In that directory, there should be a subdirectory called **plate1** that was the name of the analysis. Select this subdirectory (DO NOT OPEN IT) by a single click. The directory name will appear in the top box. *Accept* the dialog.

Now we define what we want to see in the result window. See Figure 20. Enter the following data or select from the pull-down lists (accept all other defaults):

Title	*"Von Mises Stress"*		
Quantity	*Stress*	*Total*	*Von Mises*
Display	*Fringe*		
Levels	*9*	*Continuous Tone* (deselect Average)	

and *Accept* the dialog box.

---

[1] The Von Mises stress is obtained by combining all the stress components at a point in a way which yields a single value that can be compared directly to the yield strength of the material.

[2] This seems a bit round-about at this time, since we just finished doing the analysis and all this information should be available to Pro/M already. However, it is possible to go directly to the Results command on entering Pro/M, in which case these locations would be unknown, or we might like to set up a result window from a totally different run. In either case, we have to provide the location of the results files.

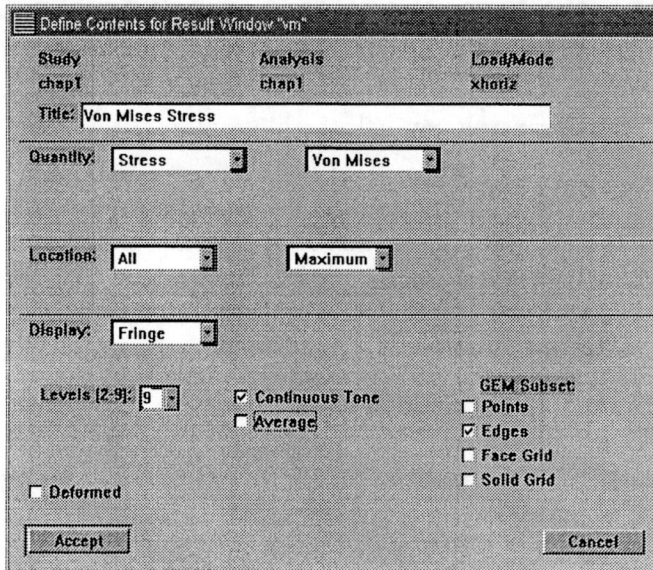

Figure 20 Defining the contents for the Result window

Now select

Show

The following image should come up on your screen. Your display will, of course, be in color.

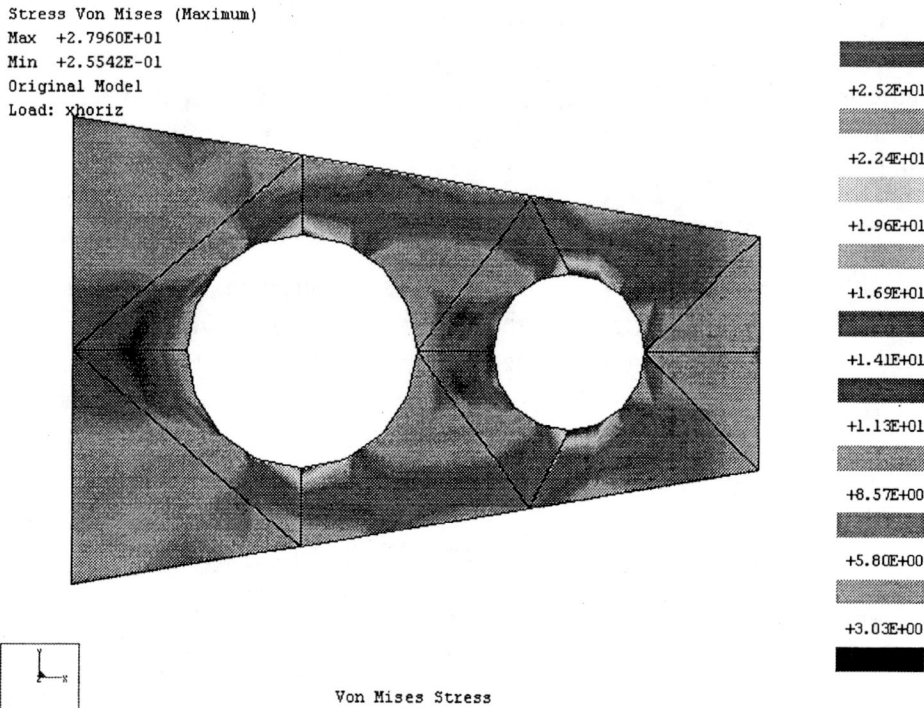

Figure 21 Fringe display of Von Mises stress

This shows that the maximum Von Mises stress is at the top and bottom of the two circular holes, as expected. We also note that the stress pattern is symmetrical about the horizontal line through the hole centers, again as expected. This leads us to think that we could solve this problem by analyzing only the upper or lower half the plate. We will do that in the next lesson.

For now, close out this result window (select **Done**). We will create a few more result windows containing different data. The easiest way to do this is by copying the current window (*vm*), supplying the copy with a new name, and changing its definition.

Displaying an Animated Deformation

Let's set up a window to show an animation of the deformation. Make sure *vm* is highlighted in the *Edit* column of the Results window and select:

> *Copy > [deform] > Review*

and enter the following definition (accept the defaults for other data fields)

Title	*"Deformed Shape"*	
Quantity	*Displacement*	*Magnitude*
Display	*Animation*	
Frames	*24*	*Reverse*
	Accept	

In the *Show* column of the Result window, make sure that only the window name **deform** is highlighted. Then select *Show*. A static image will appear showing the plate geometry in wireframe. Select the *Controls* button under the Main Menu, and then click on *Start*. The wireframe will animate to show you an exaggerated view of the deformation. Note the scale factor is indicated. See Figure 22.

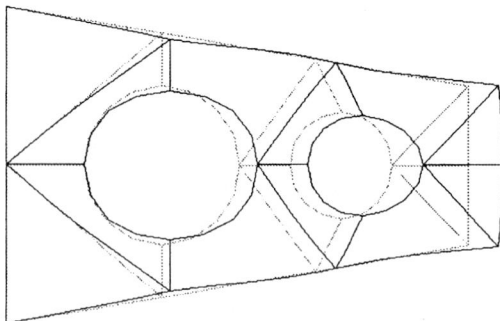

This animated view is most useful for checking whether the boundary constraints have been set properly, since the fixed edge of the plate should not move. It also will give you a more intuitive feel for the deformation within the part.

Select *Done* (twice) to return to the Result window.

Figure 22 The deformed plate

Examining the Convergence Behavior

Following the same procedure, make two more copies and modify the window contents to define the following result windows. Make sure the correct window name is highlighted in the right column (*Edit*) in the Result window.

Name	*convm*	
Title	*"Von Mises Convergence"*	
Quantity	*Measure*	Select: *Max_stress_vm*
	Accept	

Name	*constr*	
Title	*"Strain Energy Convergence"*	
Quantity	*Measure*	Select: *Strain_energy*
	Accept	

With only the titles **convm** and **constr** highlighted in the Show column of the Result window, select *Show*. Both windows will appear on the screen showing graphs of the two quantities as a function of the loop pass. See Figure 23.

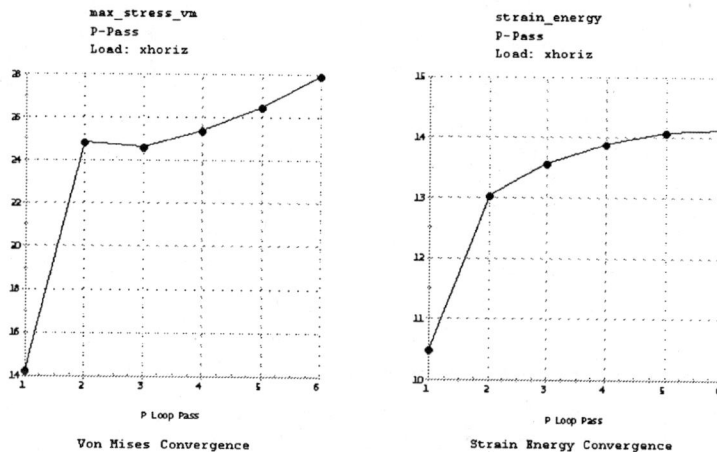

Figure 23 Convergence behavior - Von Mises and strain energy

Notice that the Von Mises stress increases with each pass, while the strain energy steadily approaches a limiting value. This is one reason why we NEVER use the Von Mises stress to monitor convergence. The strain energy will always converge monotonically. Also notice that if we had done this analysis with first order (linear) elements, the maximum Von Mises stress would be wrong by a factor of 2 from the converged value.

Examining the Model Edge Order

During the multi-pass solution, some element edges within the model required higher and higher order polynomials in order to ensure an accurate solution. In our case, the maximum edge order was 6. To see where this occurred, and what the other edges were doing, we can plot the model with the edge order data.

Make another copy of a result window and modify the definition as follows:

Name	*plevel*
Title	*"Element Edge Polynomial Order"*
Quantity	*P-level*
Display	*Fringe*
	Accept

Now, **Show** this window. You will see a colored plot similar to Figure 24. This indicates the polynomial order on each edge - note the maximum and minimum values. This information is useful since if the model is having difficulty converging, or requires very high polynomial orders (up to 9), we will know by examining this plot where we need to make modifications to the element mesh.

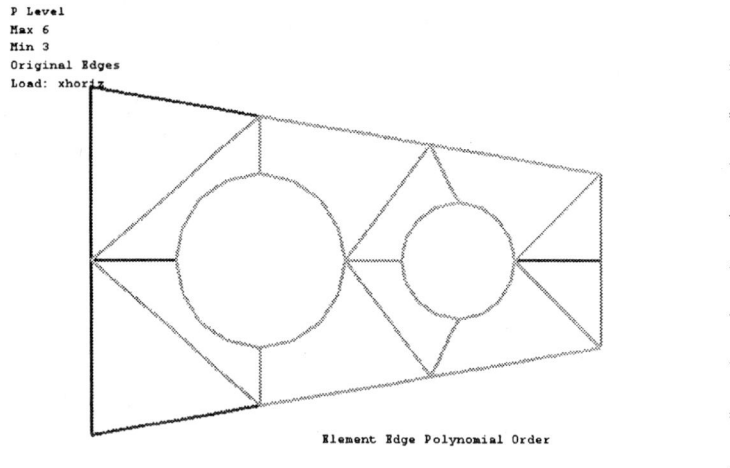

P Level
Max 6
Min 3
Original Edges
Load: xhoriz

Element Edge Polynomial Order

Figure 24 Edge order in converged solution

Summary

This concludes our first look at the basic functionality in Pro/MECHANICA. We have analyzed a very simple model, but you have seen all the major steps involved in doing a standard static analysis, probably the most common FEA problem.

In the next lesson, we will return to this model and explore some issues in modeling (such as the use of symmetry), more geometry commands, how to get the element mesh to generate automatically, and more view and display controls.

Meanwhile, you are encouraged to explore what we have covered. You will only become more proficient with the software by continued practice. Some exercises are given below, but feel free to make up your own problems.

Questions for Review

See how many of these you can answer without referring to the text.

1.   What are the seven steps required to perform a complete FEA with Pro/MECHANICA?
2.   What functions/commands are performed or available with the following buttons on the **Main** menu:
    Geometry
    Run
    Design Study
    Results
    Model
    Analysis
3.   Which of the buttons in the last question did we not use in this lesson?
4.   In what order are the commands/functions listed in question #2 executed?
5.   Suppose your display is showing all the geometry, elements, loads, and constraints in the model. How do you:
    i.   shrink the elements
    ii.   show only the geometry
    iii.   show only the elements
    iv.   show the elements in shaded mode
    v.   zoom in on a small area of the display
    vi.   zoom out so that all visible entities are within the display
6.   What are five of the **Snap** options?
7.   What function is performed by the middle mouse button?
8.   What are three different ways to create a circle?
9.   When creating new points using *Along Curve*, what is the difference between open and closed curves? How are the new points distributed?
10.   How do you create a construction line?
11.   What are the two element types available for plane stress analysis?
12.   How do you specify the thickness of a plate?
13.   How do you tell Pro/M what the part being studied is made of?
14.   Why do we apply loads and constraints to geometry instead of elements?
15.   Sketch the constraint symbol and identify the six boxes.
16.   The first analysis usually performed is simply to determine if there are any errors in the model. This is called a _____. How is this set up?
17.   What is the purpose of a multi-pass adaptive analysis?
18.   How do you set up a window to view the results of an analysis?
19.   What is the main benefit of seeing an animated deformation?
20.   What is meant by "convergence"? How is this set up? What are two ways of examining the convergence behavior?
21.   How can you find out the edge order of each element in the model? Why is this information significant?

Exercises

Perform an FEA of the following problems. All are thin plates with a thickness of 2mm. All dimensions in millimeters. Produce plots of Von Mises stress, deformation, P-level, and convergence behavior.

Exercise #1: This is the same plate we used in this lesson, but with the load containing a component in the Y direction.

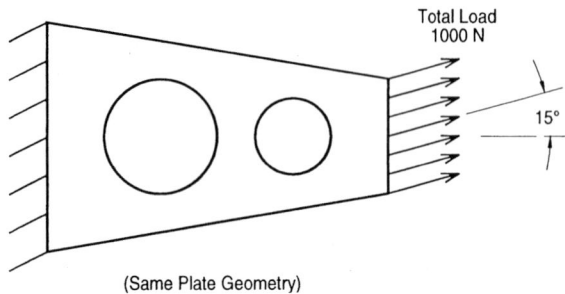

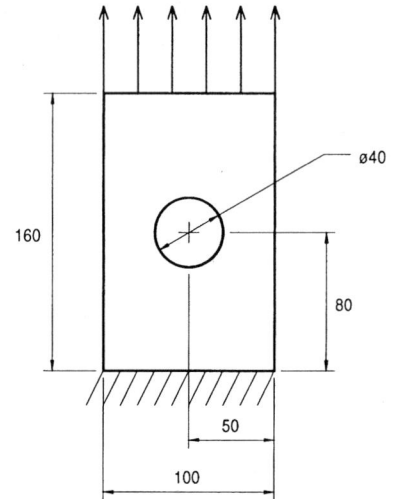

Exercise #1

Exercise #2: This is the "classic" hole-in-a-plate problem. You can compare the results you obtain to analytically obtained solutions, or to tabulated values for the stress concentration around the hole. What effect does the length of the plate have? An analytical solution will likely assume an infinitely long plate.

Exercise #2

Exercise #3: This problem should give you lots of practice with the geometry commands covered in this lesson. Think carefully about how you might like to arrange the elements, and therefore where you want to create points.

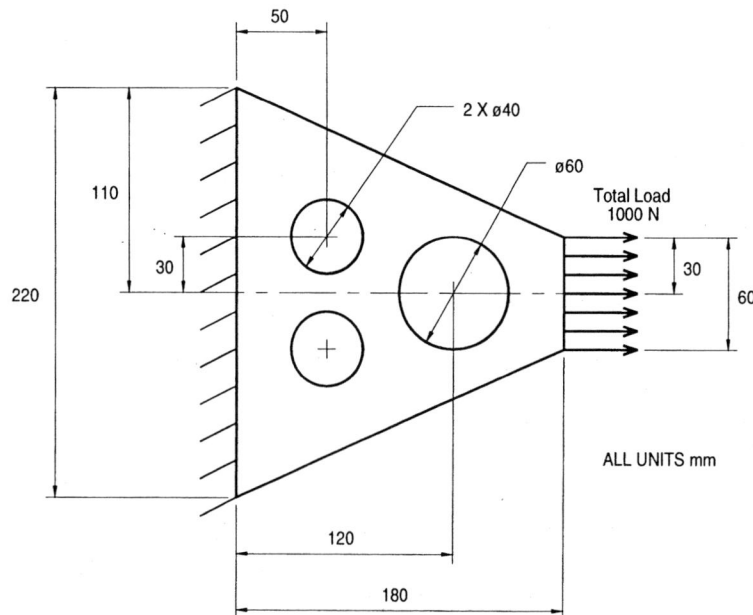

Exercise #3

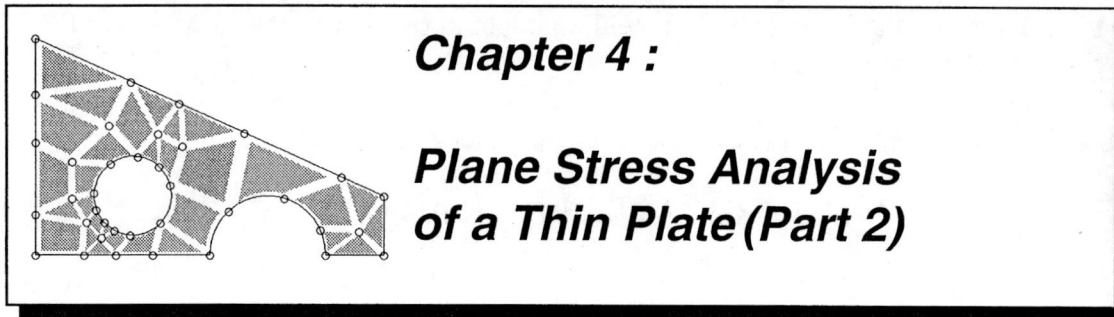

Chapter 4 :

**Plane Stress Analysis
of a Thin Plate (Part 2)**

Synopsis:

Using symmetry in the model. More Geometry commands. Creating surfaces. Automatic mesh
generation using *AutoGEM*. Diabolical cases (point loads and constraints, reentrant corners).

Overview of this Lesson

We will continue our examination of the basic operations in Pro/M using the plane stress model
of the thin tapered plate with two holes started in the previous lesson. Here, we will examine the
effect of using an asymmetrical mesh on the solution, and then show how we can exploit
symmetry in the model to reduce computational requirements and time. Along the way, we will
discover some more commands for creating and editing the geometry of the model. We will
introduce a new problem and see how to automatically generate the mesh of 2D elements,
including a short cut for assigning element properties. Some new commands for setting up the
Results display will be introduced. Finally, we will look at some simple cases, called
"diabolical", where naive modeling errors can have a major effect on the solution.

Exploring Symmetry

Effect of Asymmetric Elements

Start Pro/MECHANICA as usual and bring in the model from the last lesson:

> *File > Open > [plate1] > Accept*

Your display may be showing just elements and nodes. Turn everything on (except the grid) with

> *Display > Master Visibilities > All On | Accept*

Delete all elements on the bottom half of the model:

> *Edit > Delete > Entity > 2D Plates > Select*

Pick on the six elements on the lower half. They will highlight in red and disappear when you middle click. Middle click again to exit Edit mode.

Now create four new quad elements and two new triangular elements (see Figure 1) using:

> *Main > Model > Elements > 2D Plate > Quad | Point*

and

> *Tri | Point*

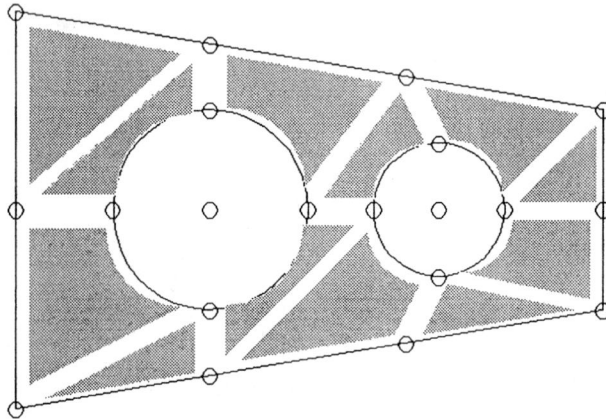

Figure 1 Asymmetric element layout on thin plate

Save the model as **plate2**

> *File > Save As > [plate2]*

Assign material properties and thickness to the new elements:

> *Main > Model > Properties > Material > Assign > 2D Plate > All*

With all elements highlighted, middle click, then *Close* the dialog. Now specify the thickness:

> *Properties > Shell Property > 2D Plate > All*

Again all elements will highlight, middle click. You will be asked if you want to change the properties of the top six elements again, select *Yes*. In the Material Property Sets window, select *thick2* (which we defined in the previous lesson) in the right column and *Accept*. Accept the next window.

Now do a Quick Check.

> *Main > Analyses > Edit*

Change the name of the analysis to **plate2**. Modify the description to something like "plate with asym elements". Make sure that the constraint and load sets are selected. Change the

Convergence Method back to **Quick Check** and accept the dialog box with *OK*. Then select *Close* in the Analyses window. It's time to run the model:

> *Main > Run > Settings*

to make sure the directories are set correctly for temporary and output files. Then exit this window and select

> *Start > Yes* (to error detection)

You will get a message about the failure index. Select **Continue**. There should be no errors found in the model. Bring up the **Summary** window. The analysis should execute with no errors with a maximum Von Mises stress of about 23 MPa. If so, we can reset the analysis convergence method:

> *Main > Analyses > [plate2] > Edit*

Change the Convergence Method to **Multi-Pass**, 5%, *Lcl Disp & Lcl SE and Glbl RMS Stress* with a maximum polynomial edge order of *9*. Accept the dialog, and select **Close.** We should be able to run the analysis immediately (no settings change in the Run window)

> *Run > Start*

Delete the existing output files, and open the **Summary** window. The analysis should converge on the 7th loop, with a maximum Von Mises stress of about 30 MPa. Note that this is significantly higher than the Quick Check result.

Create some result windows:

> *Main > Results > Create > [vm]*

Get the data from directory *\temp\plate2* (or wherever you instructed Pro/M to put the output data). Enter title **"Von Mises Stress"**, quantity: **stress, Von Mises, Fringe, 9 levels continuous** and **Accept** the window definition.

Copy this window and create the usual result windows and review their definitions (see pages 4-15 to 4-19): **deform** (deformed shape animation), **convm** (Von Mises convergence), **constr** (strain energy convergence), and **plevel** (P-level fringe plot)

Minor details in the Von Mises stress distribution are somewhat asymmetric as seen in Figure 2. The maximum stress is roughly the same as last time

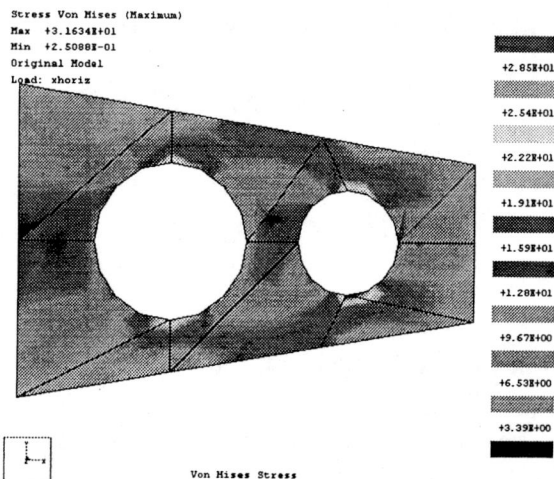

Stress Von Mises (Maximum)
Max +3.1634E+01
Min +2.5088E-01
Original Model
Load: xhoriz

+2.85E+01
+2.54E+01
+2.22E+01
+1.91E+01
+1.59E+01
+1.28E+01
+9.67E+00
+6.53E+00
+3.39E+00

Von Mises Stress

Figure 2 Von Mises stress on asymmetric elements model

and the overall pattern is more or less the same, but fine detail is asymmetric slightly. The difference may be due to a different convergence endpoint achieved with this mesh.

The deformation animation has the same configuration as the previous analysis, so there is nothing new here. The convergence plots, however, are quite different as shown below.

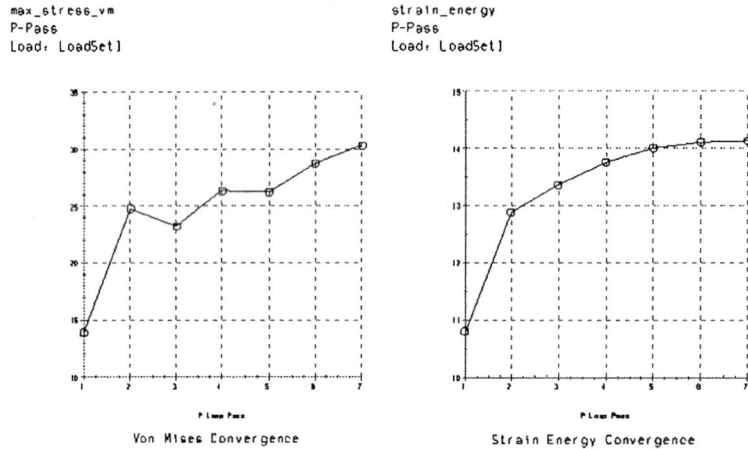

Figure 3 Convergence in asymmetric elements model

So, for this model, the asymmetric element layout had a minor effect on the solution. In this case the mesh is reasonably coarse. In order to get 5% convergence, the asymmetric model went one extra loop, resulting in a slightly higher stress level.

The Symmetric Half-Model

Whenever possible, we try to exploit symmetry in the model. This includes symmetry in all of the geometry, loads, constraints, and material properties. We will convert the previous model to a half-plate symmetric model and see how the results compare.

The first thing to do is delete elements across the bottom of the model. Then change the geometry and fill in the gaps along the line of symmetry.

Edit > Delete > Entity > 2D Plate > Select

Click on the six elements on the bottom half of the model. They will highlight in red. Middle click to delete them. Then select

Curves

and click on bottom edge; middle click.

Draw new lines across the bottom of half of the model:

Main > Geometry > Curve > Line > Two Points > Snap(Point)

Draw three short lines across the bottom of model on the construction line to close the gaps between the left and right sides and the circles. Middle click. Trim back the left and right edges:

Edit > Geometry > Trim Curve

Follow along in the message window for this: Click on the top half of the edge at the left of plate (to identify the curve to be trimmed). Click the point in the middle of the line, then click on the point at the bottom of the line. Do the same procedure for the edge at the right end.

Now trim back the circles

Edit > Geometry > Trim Curve

Click on the top half of the big circle. We can't directly remove the lower half of the circle by selecting at the left and right points because Pro/M will not know which half to trim (and the top half is associated with the existing elements. Instead, click the point at 9 o'clock, then the point at 6 o'clock. Select the upper half of the circle again, then click at 3 and 6 o'clock. Do the same for the small circle.

Delete the existing constraints and loads:

Edit > Delete > Entity > Constraints

Click on the constraint symbol; middle click. Select

Loads

Click on the load at the right end; middle click twice to return to the command line.

We will now recreate the constraints for the symmetric half-plate. We need two separate constraints for the left and lower edges. We'll put them both in the same constraint set.

Main > Model > Constraints > Curve

Enter a name for the first constraint **v_edge**. Beside the constraint set list, select New. Call the constraint set **symedge** and enter a description. Select the button under Curves and pick the left vertical edge of the plate. This time we'll let this edge move in the Y direction (remember Poisson's ratio). Thus, the translation constraints are *Free* for Y and *Fixed* for X. Accept the dialog. A new constraint symbol shows up; observe the indicators in the two rows of the constraint symbol. To set the constraint on the symmetry plane (bottom edge), select

Curve

Name this constraint **h_edge**. It should still be in the constraint set **symedge**. Select the button under Curves and click on all three line segments across the bottom of the model; middle click. For this constraint, set **X** translation **Free** and **Y** translation **Fixed**. Accept the dialog. A symbol will show up on each edge.

Now we need to apply the end load:

Main > Model > Loads > Curve

Create a *New* load set **endload**, and call the first (and only) load **endload** as well. Select the vertical edge on the right end and set the options to **Total Load, Uniform**, with components X = *500*, Y = *0* and accept the dialog. The new model should look like Figure 4.

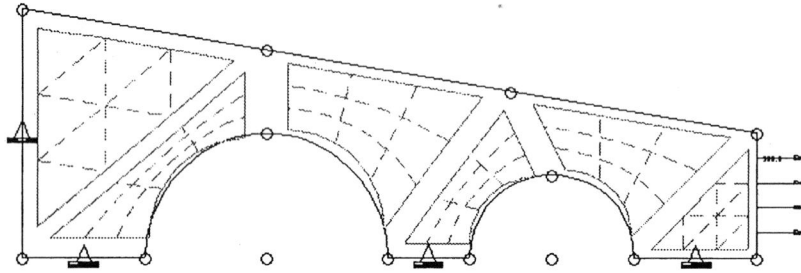

Figure 4 The symmetric half-plate model

Save this new model with a new name:

File > Save As > [plate3]

Go to *Analyses > Edit* and change the analysis name to **plate3**. Change the description to "symmetric half model" and make sure that the selected constraint set is **symedge** and the load set is **endload**. We will first do a **Quick Check**. When that has been set up, go to

Run > Settings

to check that these are all correct. Then *Start* the analysis with error detection. Go to the *Summary* window to see what happened (no errors or warnings, max_vm is about 24 MPa). Since that all went OK, we can change the analysis type:

Analyses > Edit

Change the convergence method to *Multi-Pass Adaptive*, with a *5%* convergence on *Lcl Disp & Lcl SE & Glbl RMS Stress*.

OK > Close > Run > Start

Delete the existing output files, no error detection. Open the *Summary* window.

The analysis should take 7 passes, resulting in a maximum edge order of 7, a maximum Von Mises stress of about 27 MPa.

Delete all of the current result windows for plate2 using

Results > Delete (the highlighted window in the **Edit** column is deleted)

Create the standard output windows (**vm, convm, constr, deform, plevel**) and display them. Note that you can display more than one window at once. These windows are shown below.

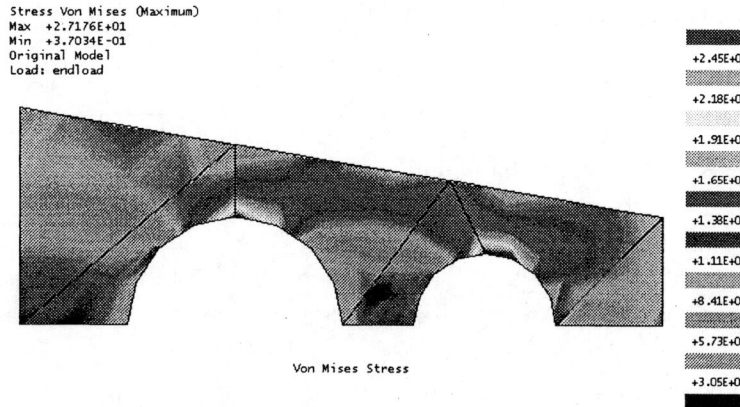

Figure 5 Von Mises stress in half-plate model

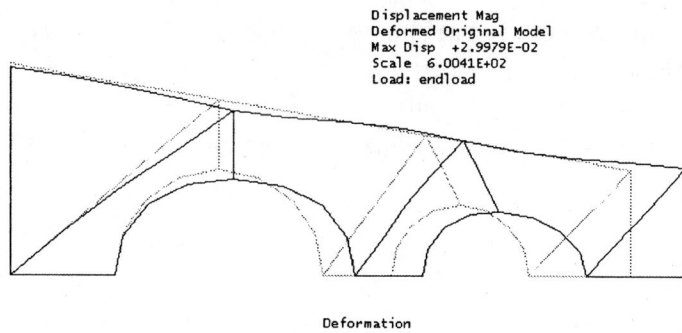

Figure 6 Deformation of half-plate model

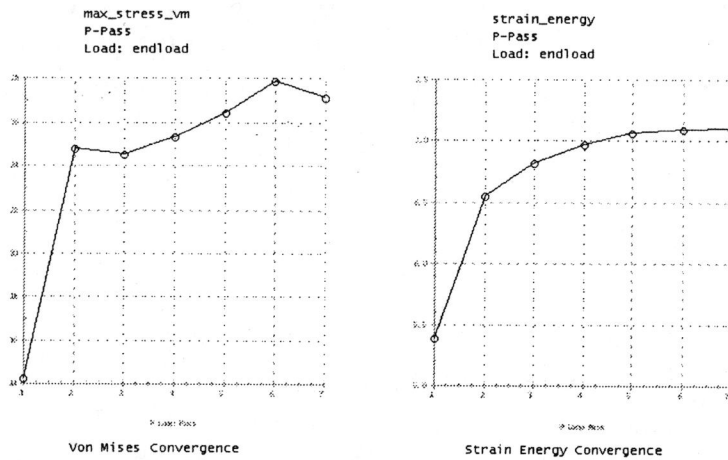

Figure 7 Convergence in half-plate model

```
Min 3
Original Edges
Load: endload                              P Level
                                           Max 7
                                           Min 3
                                           Original Edges
                                           Load: endload
```

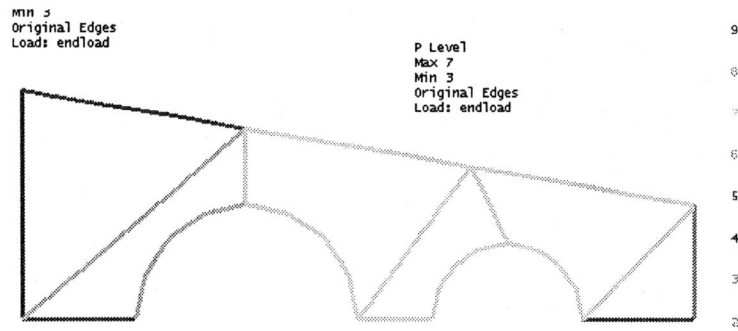

Figure 8 P-levels in half-plate model

You can compare these results with Figures 21 through 24 of Chapter 3 which were for the analysis of the full plate. The results are essentially in agreement.

The important thing to note is that the CPU time of the symmetric half-plate was about 25% less than that required for the full plate with no significant loss in accuracy. On a more complicated model (with possibly several hundred elements), this reduction would be much greater, since the computational requirements are a non-linear function of the number of elements. So, if you can, always use symmetry in the model, unless you have a very good reason not to, or are willing to put up with additional CPU time. You do have to be careful about how you are going to specify the constraints along the plane(s) of symmetry. Remember, too, that symmetry of the model involves geometry, constraints, and loads together. You could not use our model above if the load on the end was at an angle to the horizontal axis of the plate.

Automatic Mesh Generation

As you can imagine, manual mesh creation is a laborious task and for even moderately complex geometries will be prohibitive, particularly when we get to three dimensional models. In this section, along with some new geometry commands, we will introduce the automatic mesh generator called *AutoGEM*. We will analyze the plate presented as the last exercise in the previous lesson, taking advantage of the symmetry of the model.

Start up Pro/M or, if it is already is loaded, select

> *File > New*

Turn on the visibility of all entities except the grid:

> *Display > Master Visibilities > All On | Accept*

More Geometry Commands

We are going to create a symmetric half model of the plate in the last exercise in Chapter 3. For reference, the geometry is shown again in Figure 9 below. The origin of the model will be set at the lower left corner of the plate.

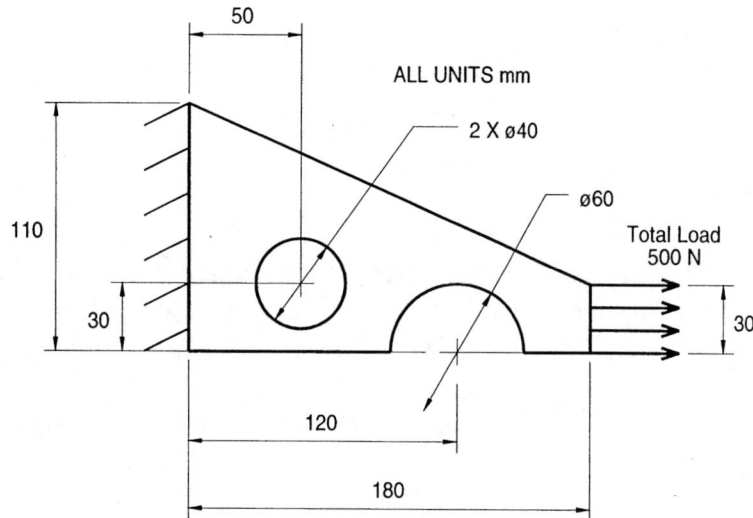

Figure 9 Half-plate model for automatic mesh generation

Our strategy for creating geometry will be slightly different from before. Instead of creating points and joining them with edges, we will go directly to creating the edges. Then, with the edges created, we will create a new geometry entity - a *surface*.

> *Main > Geometry > Curve*
> *Line > Point Chain > Snap(Point)*

and enter the following coordinates:

> *0   0*
> *0   110*
> *180   30*
> *View > Fit | Done*
> *180   0*
> *150   0*
> *90   0*
> *0   0*

Middle click twice to close out the command. Now we add the interior circle

> *Geometry > Curve > Circle > Radius-Center*

Set the radius *20* and locate the center at *50,30*. Middle click twice.

The arc of the big semi-circle is created using

Curve > Arc> Start - End - Radius > Snap(Point)

click the point at the 3:00 position on arc, and again at the 9:00 position. Enter a radius of **30** and middle click. Delete the line segment across diameter of circle

Edit > Delete > Entity > Curves

Click on the line segment, then middle click twice. All the edges/curves of the model are now defined. Note that we do not have to create any additional points along the top edge or around the circular curves.

Creating Surfaces

We will now create a surface that will be *associated* with the edges. An association means that if the edges move (for example during a sensitivity study or optimization), then the surface will change shape as well. This means that AutoGEM will be able to recreate elements automatically.

For 2D planar problems, a surface is defined using a single closed exterior loop edge and any number of interior loop edges. Select

Geometry > Surface > Planar

Read and follow the prompts in the message window: click on the exterior edge (the entire edge outlines in red), then click on the inside circle (highlight red). Middle click.

A gray hatch pattern will appear that indicates the new surface. Middle click to leave the surface command.

Now we can create elements on this surface using the automatic mesh generator. Before we do that, we will assign properties to the surface. These will be inherited by any elements made from the surface.

Main > Model > Plane Stress | Accept
Properties > Material
(Move the material **AL2014_mmNS** to the right pane)
Assign > Surface

and click on the surface hatch. It will highlight in red; middle click. *Close* the dialog. Then,

Properties > Shell Property > Surface

Click on the hatch pattern and set up definition for a 2mm thickness. If you are continuing from earlier in this lesson, the property set **thick2** may be available already.

Generating a Mesh with AutoGEM

AutoGEM is really quite easy to use:

Main > Model > Elements > AutoGEM > Surface

Pick on the hatch that represents the surface of the plate. It will highlight in red; middle click. AutoGEM will then create a mesh that covers the designated surface. Upon completion, a summary window appears as shown in the figure below.

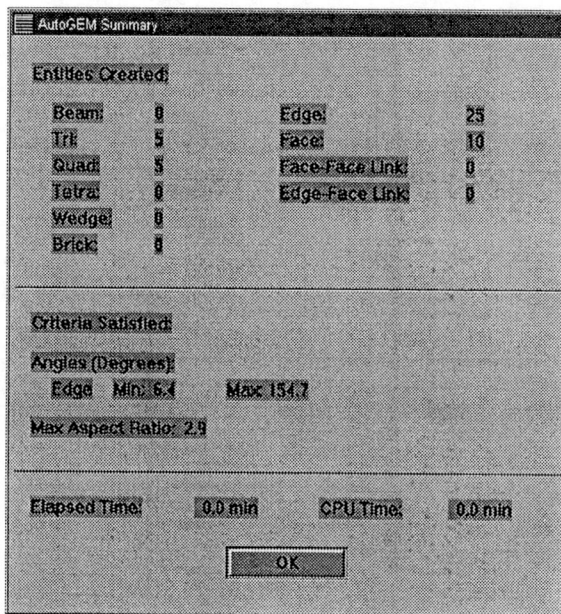

Figure 10 AutoGEM Summary window

This window shows the number of elements created of various types, and the minimum and maximum edge angles, and the maximum element aspect ratio for all elements in the mesh. The edge angles are measured between edges of each element meeting at a node. The aspect ratio is a measure of the ratio of length to width of the element. We will be discussing these some more a bit later in this lesson.

To have a better look at the elements:

Display > Settings > Display Type (Flat Shade)
Shade (Elements) > Shrink all Elements > Accept
Display > Master Visibilities > (turn Surfaces off)

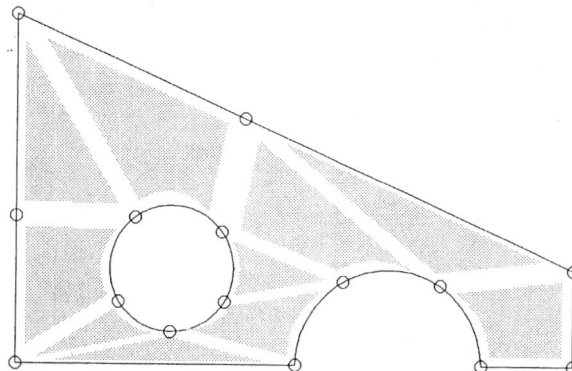

Figure 11 Mesh created with AutoGEM
(default settings); model: *plate4*

That's all there is to creating the mesh automatically. Note that AutoGEM created new points along the arcs. The next job is to assign the constraints. Remember that we are using symmetry here, and we are relying on associativity (constraints are defined on edges that are used to form a surface which is used to create elements).

Model > Constraints > Curve

Set up a *New* constraint set **symedge**, and name the first constraint **v_edge**, as before. Select the left vertical edge. Call the constraint set *symedge*, Set the X translation as **Fixed**, and the Y translation as **Free**. For the lower edge, select

Curve

Name this constraint **h_edge** (still in constraint set **symedge**). Pick the bottom two edges of plate and define the constraint **Fixed** in Y, **Free** in X.

Now add the load to the right end of the plate

Model > Loads > Curve

Create a *New* load set **endload**. Name the first load **endload**. Select the vertical edge on the right end and set *Total Load*, *Uniform*, Fx = *500*, Fy = *0*, *OK*.

The model is now complete, so now is a good time to save it:.

File > Save As > [plate4]

Running the Model

As we have done several times by now, we will first perform a Quick Check to see if there are any modeling errors. You should know the command sequence for this by now. Call the new analysis **plate4** and make sure that **symedge** and **endload** are specified for the constraint and load sets. Enter a description like "symmetric half model of tapered plate with 3 holes" and set the convergence method as *Quick Check*. Then go to

Run > Settings

Set output and temporary files to *\temp* or your preferred location.

Start

Accept error detection; no errors should be found in model. Call up the *Summary* window to find the maximum Von Mises stress was about 18 MPa.

Since everything seemed to work properly, change the analysis to multi-pass adaptive.

> *Analyses > Edit*

Change the convergence method to ***Multi-Pass Adaptive***, *5%*, ***Lcl Disp & Lcl SE & Glbl RMS Stress***, maximum polynomial order *9*. Now select

> ***Run > Start***

Delete the existing output files and turn off error detection. Open the ***Summary*** window. The analysis should converge on pass 8 with a maximum Von Mises stress of about 26 MPa.

Examining the Results

Create the standard result windows for Von Mises Stress, Measures: VM and Strain Energy Convergence, Deformation, P-Level. Some of these results are shown below.

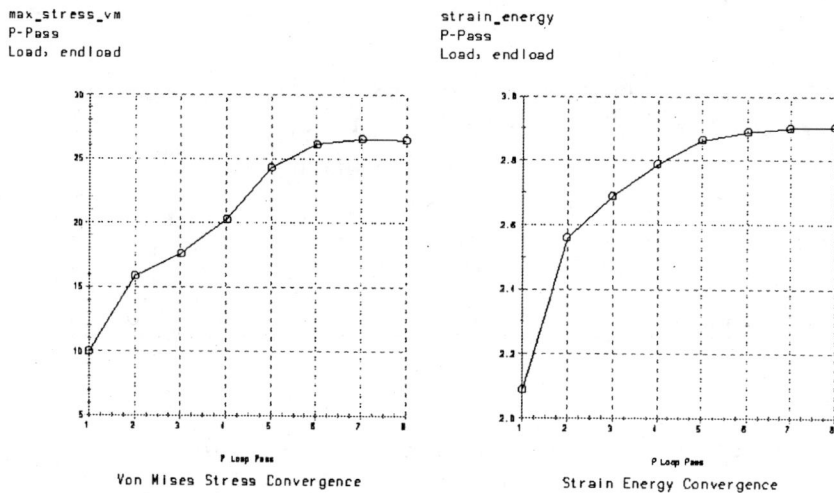

Figure 12 Convergence plots of *plate4* model

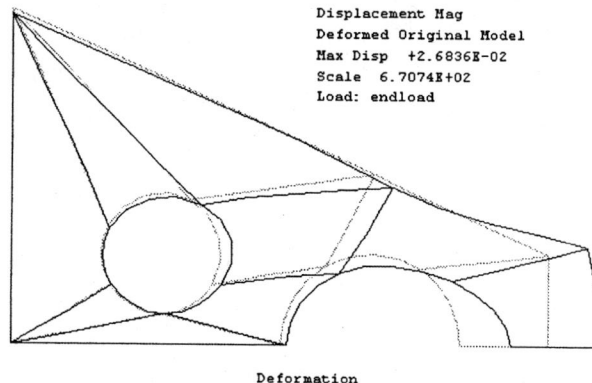

Figure 13 Deformation of *plate4* model

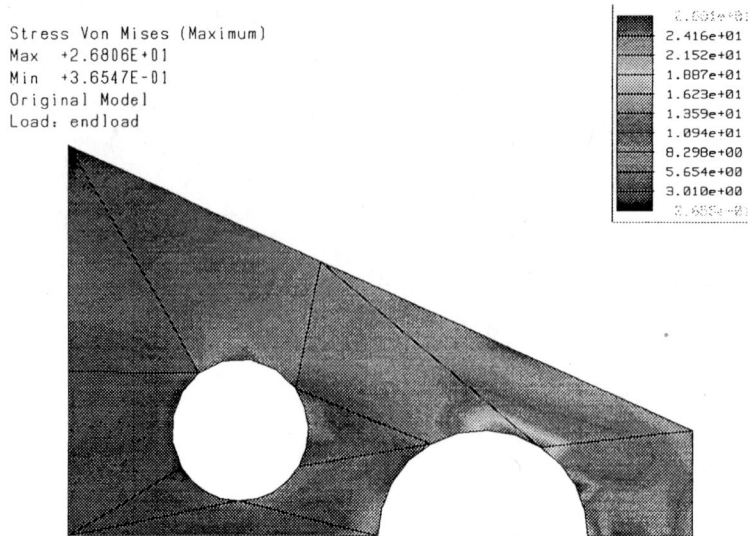

Stress Von Mises (Maximum)
Max +2.6806E+01
Min +3.6547E-01
Original Model
Load: endload

2.416e+01
2.152e+01
1.887e+01
1.623e+01
1.359e+01
1.094e+01
8.298e+00
5.654e+00
3.010e+00

Figure 14 Von Mises stress in *plate4* model

Note on the top corner of the left vertical edge there is some y displacement due to Poisson contraction. As an exercise, you might like to try the analysis again with fully fixed left edge. Do you think this will affect the maximum stress around the large hole significantly?

Dynamic Query of Results

Here are a few commands that may come in handy. Show the Von Mises stress window and select:

Dynamic Query > Show View Max > Show View Min

The location, and a label, will appear showing the maximum and minimum stresses in the current view of the model. Press *Clear All > Yes*. To find the stresses at any point on the model, select

Query

A small window opens up. Click and hold down the left mouse button. Drag it around on the part. The Query window will show the Von Mises stress at the cursor location on the part. Release the mouse button and select *Done* to leave the Query window, and *Done* again to leave the Dynamic Query Ctl menu.

Modifying the Legend

It may sometimes be useful to modify the contour levels in the fringe plot associated with the legend. Select

Controls > Edit Legend

Click on the second from the top number in the legend and type in new value *20*. In the message window, read the message, press *Y* (or enter or middle click). Select the second from the bottom number in the legend, change it to *4*. Accept the default to redistribute the levels linearly (they will be multiples of 2). Middle click to return.

Suppose that we want to find all regions in the model with a stress greater than 15 MPa. Edit the legend so that the maximum level is 15, and redistribute all levels. After a few seconds, the display will regenerate with all the desired regions shown in the top legend color (red).

You might like to check out the *Titles* and *Labels* buttons. When you are finished, back out of the Results windows.

Using AutoGEM

On very rare occasions, we may be required to deviate from the default mesh created by AutoGEM. In this section, we will investigate how the settings in AutoGEM can be used to change the overall mesh. Further customization is possible, but we will not get into that here. Another motivation for this is that users of FEM packages that utilize linear elements (h-codes) will be surprised by both the small number of elements used in Pro/M and their seemingly high distortion. As mentioned in the introductory chapters, h-codes typically require many, many small elements (especially in regions of high gradients) and the shape of these elements cannot deviate very much from simple squares and (equilateral) triangles. So, in this section, we will obtain some results that will hopefully convince these users that the Pro/M mesh and p-code is accurate.

First, delete the previous element mesh using

Edit > Delete > Entity > 2D Plates > All

Middle click. Now get rid of all the points on the geometry added by AutoGEM last time around. This is easy to do with (we're still in the *Delete > Entity* menu)

Points > All

Middle click. The corner points cannot be deleted since they are associated with the lines (and hence with the surface).

AutoGEM Settings

Before we invoke AutoGEM to create a new mesh, we will change some of the settings that control the size and number of elements. Select

Main > Model > Elements > AutoGEM > Settings

The AutoGEM Settings window will open as shown in Figure 15. This contains a checklist of options available.

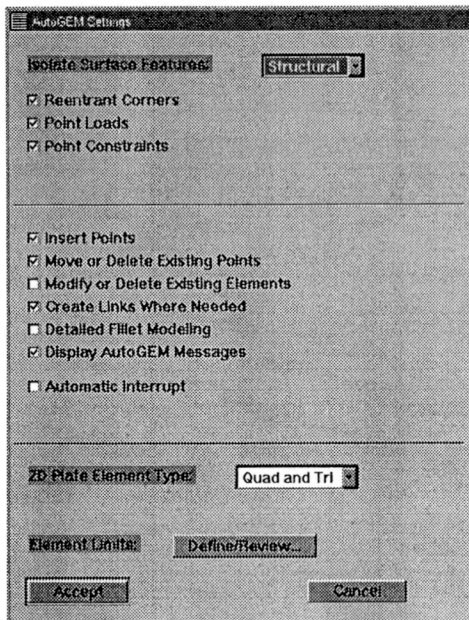

Figure 15 AutoGEM Settings
window

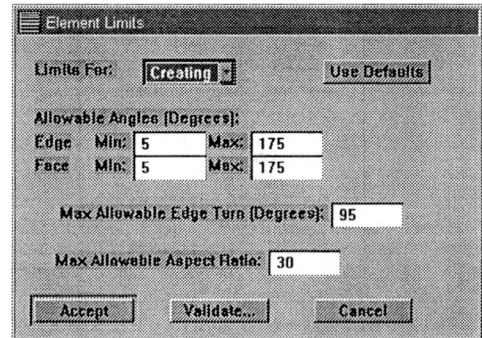

Figure 16 Element Limits window

The check boxes in the Settings window control the action taken by AutoGEM as follows:

Reentrant corners, Point Loads, Point Constraints - these allow AutoGEM to deal with the diabolical cases discussed in the next section. These options are almost always checked.

Insert Points, Move or Delete Existing Points - these give AutoGEM the freedom to place nodes at the most convenient locations on the surface. Otherwise, it will only use the node points you define in the geometry. Looking at Figure 11, you can see that AutoGEM inserted a number of new points into the geometry.

Modify or Delete Existing Elements - if some elements have been created manually, for some reason, then checking this box will allow AutoGEM to manipulate them. Since there must have been a good reason for creating them manually, this option is not checked by default.

Create Links Where Needed - used in 3D meshes to connect new elements to previously created ones

Detailed Fillet Modeling - used to automatically create a denser mesh on corner fillets

Display AutoGEM messages - in advanced modes of operation, AutoGEM may require input during mesh creation. Deselect this option to have AutoGEM take default action.

Automatic Interrupt - select this option to have AutoGEM stop when it has created a specified fraction of the mesh creation. This may be useful if you have a very large model and limited computer resources.

2D Plate Element Type - select Tri or mixed (Quad and Tri) mesh

At the bottom of this window, beside **Element Limits** select

Define/Review

The Element Limits window (Figure 16) opens. Note the defaults for edge angle min 5, max 175, and aspect ratio 30. These settings resulted in the mesh we had previously. Let's change these values to see the effect on the model. Change the min edge angle to **30**, and max edge angle to **150**, and max allowed aspect ratio to **2**. These are the extreme values allowed by Pro/M. The narrower these limits are, the more elements AutoGEM will have to create to satisfy them. *Accept* the dialog, and then the AutoGEM Settings dialog.

Now, recreate the elements using these new settings.

> *Surface*

and click on the surface of the model. (If the surface is not showing, use **Display > Master Visibilities** and make sure the Surfaces check box is selected). Middle click. AutoGEM will now create the new mesh as shown in Figure 17. Note the additional points inserted in the interior of the plate, and the number of Quad elements that have been split into two Tri elements in order to satisfy our element limits.

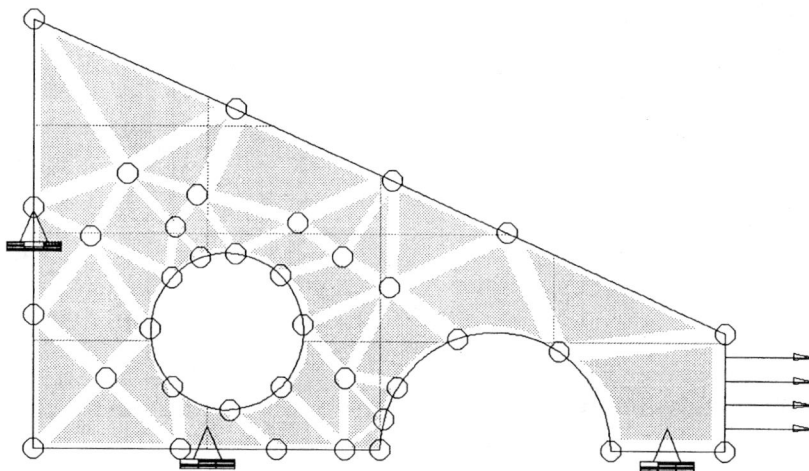

Figure 17 Custom mesh with new AutoGEM element limits

Even though these are new elements, you will not have to define Material Properties and Shell Property since these are inherited from the surface.

Run a multi-pass adaptive analysis. The results are shown in the table below, along with the results obtained using the default AutoGEM settings. It is observed that producing a finer mesh, with three times as many elements in this case, has not resulted in significantly different results at 5% convergence.[1] This will usually be the case, and it is very rare that the AutoGEM settings need to be changed. Create and show the result windows for the Von Mises stress, deformation, and convergence. Compare these to Figures 12, 13, and 14.

---

[1]If we had used a 1% convergence criterion, the results would be even closer together.

	Mesh #1 (Default) Figure 11	Mesh #2 (Custom) Figure 17
Settings		
Min Edge Angle	5	30
Max Edge Angle	175	150
Max Allowed Aspect Ratio	30	2
Mesh Results		
No. of elements	10	32
Min Edge Angle	6.4	30.1
Max Edge Angle	154.7	141.9
Max. Aspect Ratio	2.9	2.0
Run Results		
Loops	8	7
Max Von Mises Stress (MPa)	26.4	27.7
Max Displacement (mm)	0.0269	0.0269
Strain Energy	6.07	6.07
CPU time	1.31	1.75

However, we do note that with more elements, the number of convergence loops required has decreased. The CPU has increased only slightly. If we were to create a mesh with many more elements (especially in regions where the required polynomial edge order is high), it might be possible to reduce the number of convergence loops even further. Eventually, we would get so many elements that only a linear or 2nd order element would suffice for the same accuracy. However, the CPU time required would be difficult to determine because it depends on both the number of elements *and* their order. In some cases, it might be beneficial (in terms of CPU time) to have more elements of lower order.

Generally, we are satisfied with the default mesh. One symptom of problems with the mesh is if a large number of elements require the maximum available edge order (9). In this case, it is a good idea to increase the number of elements, using the element limits, so that the solution can be obtained with more elements of lower order (6 or 7). If the solution does not converge with the maximum edge order, then we may have other problems, as shown in the following sections.

Diabolical Models

Now is an appropriate time to point out some common modeling errors and problems. These arise from the basic nature of the analysis performed by Pro/M, that is, the p-code method. The two major difficulties we will look at involve the use of point loads and constraints, and reentrant corners. To do this, we will recall a model produced in the last lesson.

Select

> *File > Open*

and select *plate1.mdb* from the list.

Point Constraints and Loads

First, delete the constraint defined on the left edge of the plate:

> *Edit > Delete > Entity > Constraints*

and click on the constraint symbol. Then, middle click to delete the constraint.

The Problem

Set up new constraints using

> *Main > Model > Constraints > Point*

Create a *New* constraint set called **pointbc**, and name the constraint **pointbc**. Select the button under Points and pick the top and bottom points on the left edge and middle click. Set both X and Y translation to *Fixed*. All other settings are OK. The resulting model should look like the figure at the right. Note the constraint symbols on the two points.

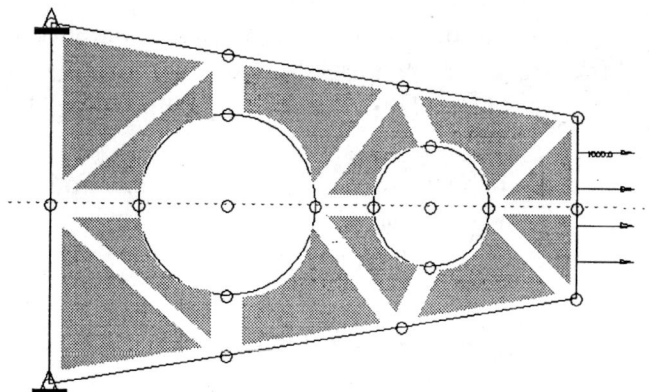

Figure 18 *plate1* with point constraints

Go to

> *Main > Analyses > Edit*

and make sure that **pointbc** is selected as the constraint set. The load set should still be the same as before. Accept this dialog with *OK*.

Check the settings for the analysis, and do the multi-pass adaptive run, deleting any files that already exist and accepting error detection. After you select **Start**, at some point the constraints will be highlighted and a message window will open. Read the message about "excluded elements". Click **OK** and in the next window, select **No**. The run will now proceed as usual. You are even informed that there are no errors in the model. Is this true? Check the **Summary** window and note that there is no convergence after 9 passes. The maximum Von Mises stress is a whopping 356 MPa. What is going on here? Even though convergence was not achieved, we can still look at the results of the analysis.

Set up the usual result windows for the Von Mises stress and the convergence plots. They should look like the figures below.

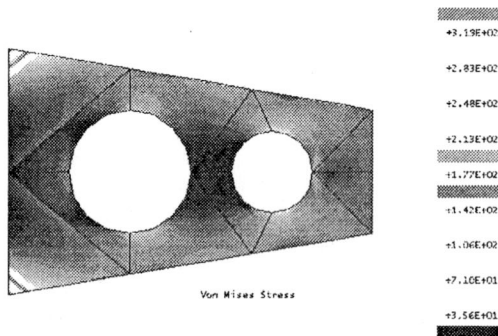

Figure 19 Von Mises stress with point constraints

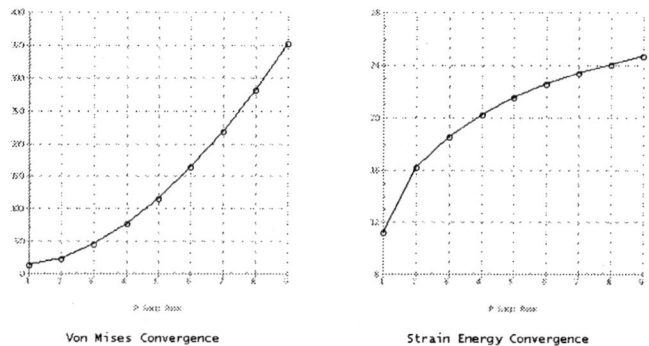

Figure 20 Convergence with point constraints

Note on the Von Mises fringe plot that the stresses near the constrained points are extremely high. Because the fringe legend is equally spaced, all the stress variation around the holes is hidden in the lowest fringe value. In the convergence plot, although the strain energy looks like it might be converging, the Von Mises stress is increasing steadily with each pass as the polynomial order increases. Modify the legend in the Von Mises stress plot so that the minimum value is 3 and the maximum value is 25 (these correspond roughly with what they were before). Note that far from the constraints, the stress contours are essentially the same as the previous model (Figure 21 in Chapter 3, Figure 6 in this chapter). So these stresses are accurate, and the problem with this model's convergence seems to be directly related to the point constraints.

Let's see what happens with point loads. Delete both the current constraints and load. Recreate the old edge constraint **edgebc** on the entire left edge, fixing the X and Y translation for the entire edge. For the point loads, select

Main > Model > Loads > Point

Create a **New** load set **pointloads**. Name the first load in this set **corner_loads**. Select the button under Points and click on the top and bottom points on the right end. Enter the values Fx = **250**, Fy = **0** and **Accept** the dialog. Now create another point load in the same load set named **mid_load**. Select the middle point on the right edge and

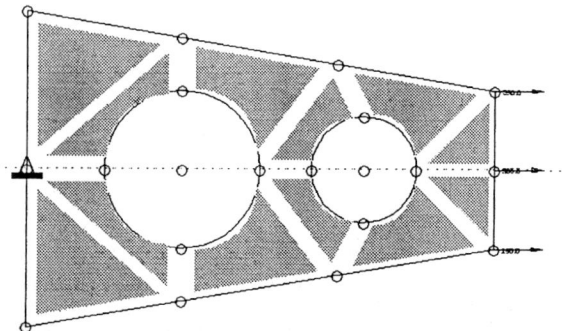

Figure 21 *plate1* with point loads

specify the load components Fx = *500*, Fy = *0*. This gives a total load of 1000 N, and approximates the effect of a uniform load along the edge. The model should look like the Figure 21.

Check the analysis settings using

Main > Analyses > Edit

Make sure **edgebc** and **pointloads** are selected for the constraint and load sets, respectively. Set up a multipass adaptive analysis.

Run the multipass adaptive analysis. There will be a message about excluded elements being required at the point loads. Click *OK* and then *No* in the next window to not create an group.

Open the *Summary* window. Once again, the analysis should not converge in 9 passes. The maximum Von Mises stress will be about 210 MPa.

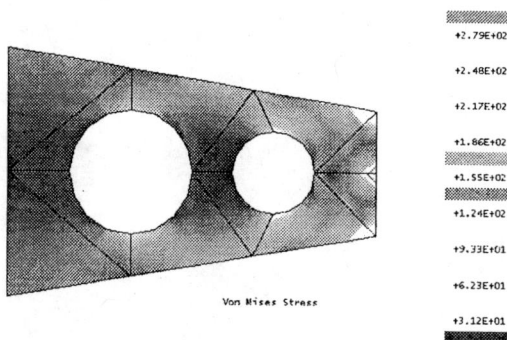

Figure 22 Von Mises stress in *plate1* with point loads

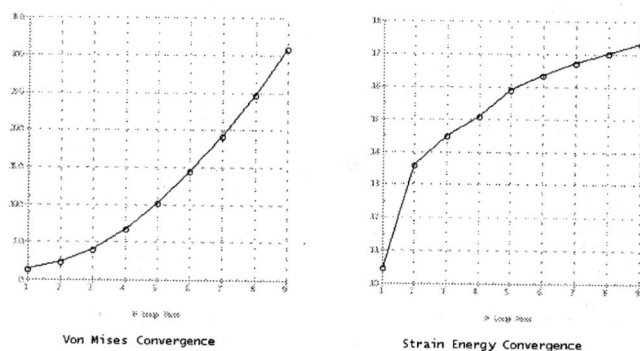

Figure 23 Convergence of *plate1* with point loads

Create Results windows for Von Mises stress and the usual convergence measures (Von Mises and strain energy). These are shown in Figures 22 and 23. Once again, we note that the stresses are very high close to the point loads. The convergence plot of the Von Mises stress also shows that it is continuing to increase as the polynomial order goes up with each loop. As before, change the legend on the Von Mises plot to see that, except in the immediately vicinity of the point loads, the stress in the plate is essentially the same as before.

The Solution

As we have seen, point loads and point constraints severely distort the results. This is because these cause *singularities* in the solution, that Pro/M can only try to match by steadily increasing the order of the polynomial edge as it tries to achieve convergence. It cannot converge with a finite maximum polynomial order because of the infinite gradients in the vicinity of these singular points. The solution is fairly obvious - **don't use point constraints or loads!** In 2D models, always apply constraints and loads to edges (of the geometry). If it is absolutely necessary to apply a point load or constraint, the methods described in the next section (using excluded elements) will come in handy.

The same result will hold true when we go to three dimensional models. There, we will find that edge constraints and loads will usually cause problems. In 3D, we always try to apply constraints and loads to surfaces instead of edges or points.

Now let's look at another modeling problem that is not quite so easy to avoid. This is a problem associated with the geometry itself.

Reentrant Corners

We will create a new model (Figure 25) using some new geometry commands. Select

> *File > New*
> *Geometry > Curve > Rectangle > Snap(Point)*

and enter the following coordinates to define a square and some construction lines:

> *0   0*
> *100   100* (Middle click)
> *View > Fit | Done*
> *Construction Geom > Vertical > Snap(Point)*
> *40   0*
> *Construction Geom > Horizontal > Snap(Point)*
> *0   40*
> *Curve > Line > Point Chain > Snap(Intersect)*

Select the following pairs of intersecting lines:

> top edge and vertical construction line
> both construction lines
> right edge and horizontal construction line

Middle click twice to back out of the command. To remove the unwanted parts of the square:

> *Edit > Geometry*
> *Trim Curve*

and use the picks shown in Figure 24 to convert the model to the L-shape. Pick first where indicated by the X, then pick the two points that bound the line segment to be removed.

You can delete the construction lines with

> *Edit > Delete > Entity*
> *Construction Geom > All*

and middle click.

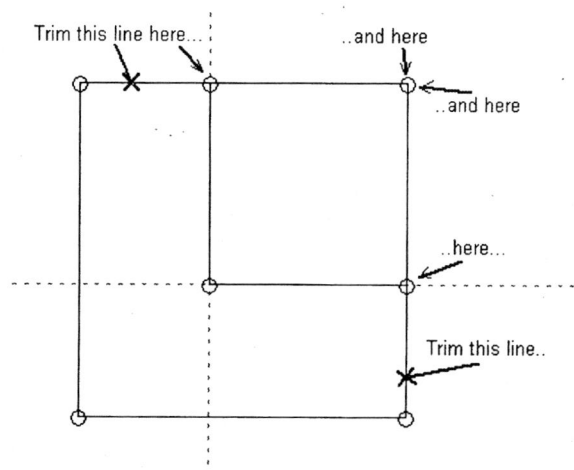

Figure 24 Editing the geometry to produce L-shaped plate

Now create the four triangular elements (*2D Plates*) shown in the figure below. When you first enter the *Model* menu, identify the model as *Plane Stress*.

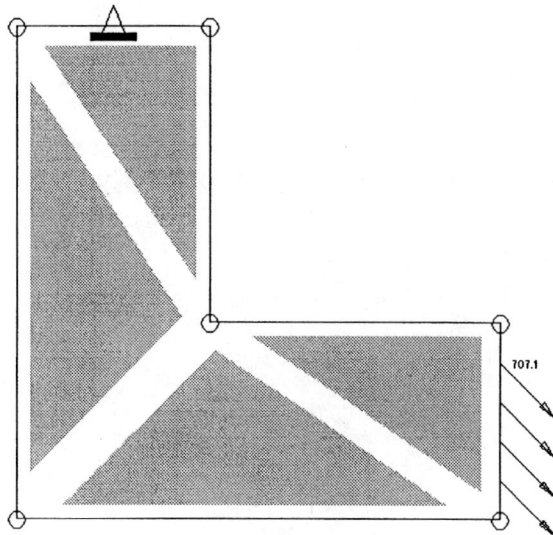

Set the usual material properties and thickness. Apply a fixed edge constraint at the top edge of the L. Apply a uniform edge load Fx = *500*, Fy = *-500* on the right vertical edge.

Save the model as **plate6**.

Figure 25 L-bracket with manual mesh

The Problem

Run a multi-pass adaptive analysis with the usual settings (5% convergence on Local Displacement, Local Strain Energy and Global RMS Stress). The analysis should not converge, even after 9 passes, and have a maximum Von Mises stress of 152 MPa. Some Result windows are shown below.

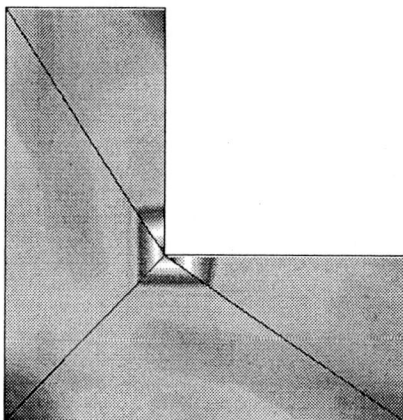

Von Mises Stress

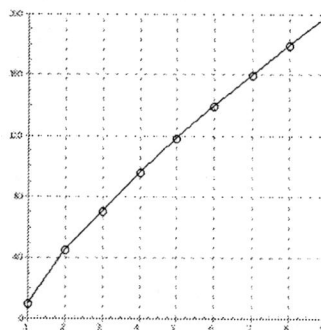

Figure 26 Von Mises stress in *plate6*

Von Mises Convergence

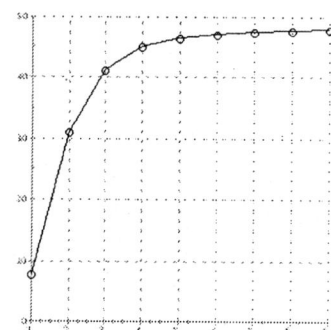

Von Mises Convergence

Figure 27 Convergence of model *plate6* (left: Von Mises; right: strain energy)

Note the very high stresses shown on the fringe plot near the inside corner, and the behavior of the Von Mises stress in the convergence plot. It increases steadily with each pass. The reentrant corner has caused a similar situation as the point constraints and loads. In this case, however, we don't have the same options in setting up the model to solve the problem, since the corner is part of the geometry itself.

The Solution

There are two possible solutions to this problem at the reentrant corner on the plate. The first involves changing the geometry by adding a small fillet to the corner. The second uses the original geometry, but we instruct Pro/M basically to ignore what is happening at the corner, using what are called *excluded elements*, when it is doing the convergence checks. Let's look at both of these solutions.

1. Put a small fillet at corner.

Delete the current elements. Create the fillet using

Main > Geometry > Curve > Fillet

Near the corner, select the vertical edge and the horizontal edge; enter a radius of **5.** *Accept* the default for trimming the curves back to the tangency points.

Now manually create the elements shown in Figure 28. Keep the same constraint on the top edge and the load on the right edge. Of course, since we deleted the previous elements, you will have to define the material and shell properties again.

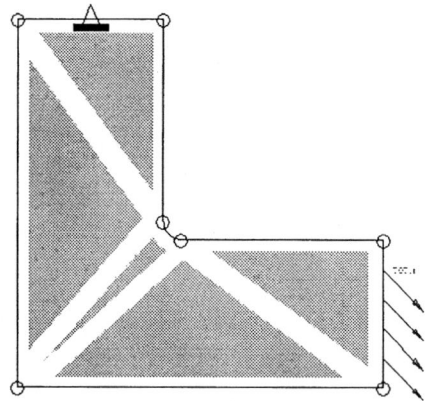

Figure 28 Fillet added at reentrant corner; manual mesh creation

        Run a multi-pass adaptive analysis with the usual settings. The results show convergence on the 9th loop with a maximum Von Mises stress of around 160 MPa. This is a slight improvement over the non-filleted case, although requiring 9 passes is cause for some alarm. Some results are shown in Figures 29 and 30. Note the difference between the Von Mises convergence shown in Figure 30 (with fillet) to that shown in Figure 27 (no fillet).

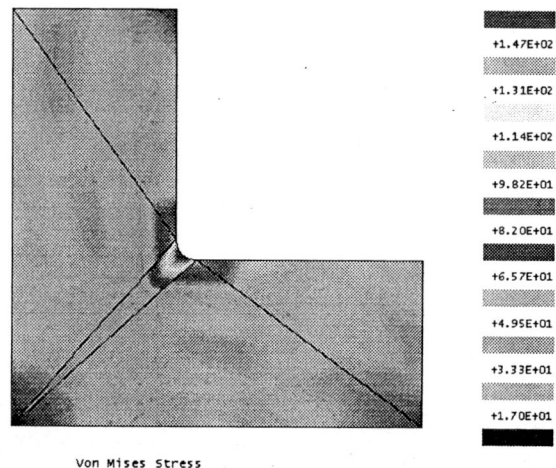

Von Mises Stress

```
+1.47E+02
+1.31E+02
+1.14E+02
+9.82E+01
+8.20E+01
+6.57E+01
+4.95E+01
+3.33E+01
+1.70E+01
```

Figure 29 Von Mises stress in *plate6* with fillet

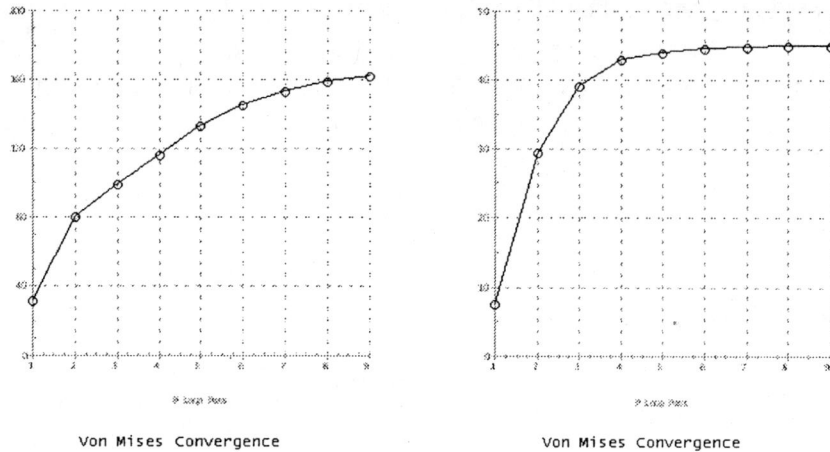

Figure 30 Convergence of *plate6* with fillet (manual mesh)

Let's see what happens with AutoGEM. Delete the current elements. Create a surface using the current edges using

Main > Geometry > Surfaces > Planar

Pick on the edge, then middle click (there are no interior loops). Assign material and shell properties to the surface so that they will be inherited by the elements. Use AutoGEM with the default settings to create the mesh automatically on the surface. It should create only 1 tri and 2 quad elements. Run a multipass adaptive analysis with 5% convergence. You will find that the model will not converge after 9 passes. The indicated maximum Von Mises stress at the end of the run is about 167 Mpa. Not much difference.

There is another option in AutoGEM to explore. Delete the current elements and select

Model > Elements > AutoGEM > Settings

Check the box beside **Detailed Fillet Modeling** and accept the dialog. Create the mesh by selecting the surface. AutoGEM will create 8 tri and 2 quad elements, with the triangular elements clustered at the fillet location as shown in Figure 31. Run a multipass adaptive analysis. This should converge on the 7th pass. Examine the Von Mises stress and P-level fringe plots. This solution is much better behaved than either of the previous ones. The maximum Von Mises stress is about 169 MPa, not much different from before. This was obtained with double the number of elements, however. Note the maximum p-level occurs away from the fillet, whose elements have orders of 4 and 5 only. This option may be useful for large models where you may have to use AutoGEM to

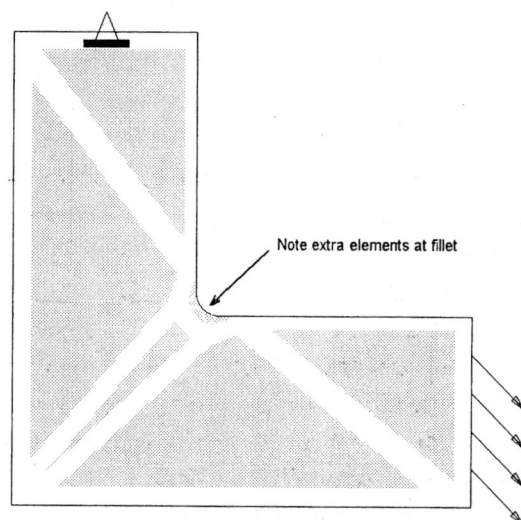

Note extra elements at fillet

Figure 31 AutoGEM with "Detailed Fillet Modeling" setting selected

mesh the model instead of doing it manually.

There is a second solution to this problem, which is of more general application than tweaking the geometry at the problem points. This is using excluded elements, discussed in the next section.

2. Excluding elements

Delete all the existing elements and the surface

> *Edit > Delete > Entity > 2D Plates > All* (middle click)
> *Surface > All* (middle click)

Also, we have to delete the fillet to recover the sharp corner.

> *Curves*

and pick on fillet, then middle click twice. We will have to extend the existing edges back to the corner:

> *Edit > Geometry > Extend*

select the vertical edge, then the point on the end of the horizontal edge. The vertical edge will extend to the corner point. Select the horizontal edge, then the lower vertex on the vertical line. The horizontal edge will also extend into the corner. We can delete all the extra points using

> *Edit > Delete > Entity > Points > All*

Some of the points will not be deleted. Why?

We are going to use AutoGEM, so we will need to create the surface again:

> *Main > Geometry > Surface > Planar*

select the edge of the plate. When the surface is created, assign the usual material and shell properties.

Now will get AutoGEM to create the mesh. It has special built-in procedures to treat reentrant corners:

> *Main > Model > Elements > AutoGEM > Settings*

Note that "Reentrant corners" is checked at the top by default, as are point loads and point constraints. AutoGEM would treat those in the same way it is going to deal with the corner. *Accept* the default settings. Now select

> *Surface*

Click on the surface, then middle click. The AutoGEM results window opens. Note the additional elements created by AutoGEM in the vicinity of the corner (Figure 32).

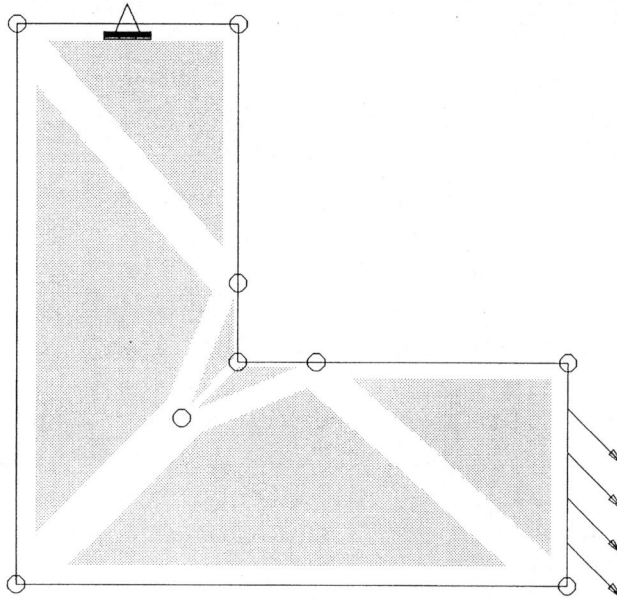

Figure 32 AutoGEM mesh with automatically added elements at reentrant corner

Run a multipass adaptive analysis of the new mesh, and open the **Summary** window. The analysis does not converge in 9 passes. The maximum Von Mises stress is almost 500 MPa. This seems rather excessive, so what happened? Create the Von Mises stress fringe plot and the usual Von Mises and Convergence plots. These will appear as shown in Figures 33 and 34. In the stress fringe plot, we can see the very localized effect of the singularity at the reentrant corner. The convergence plot again shows that the Von Mises stress increases steadily with each loop pass, although it appears that the strain energy reaches a steady value.

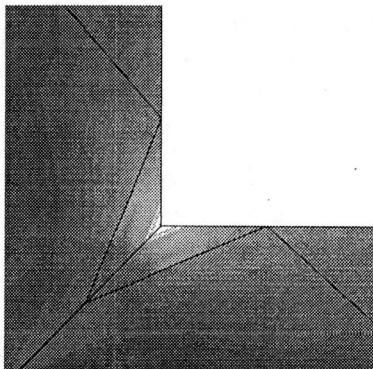

Figure 33 Von Mises stress at reentrant corner(close-up view)

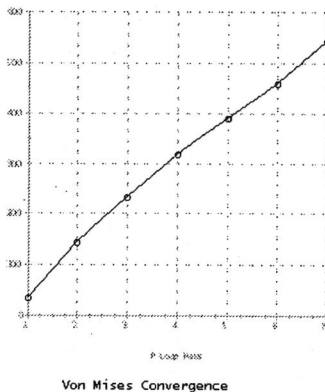

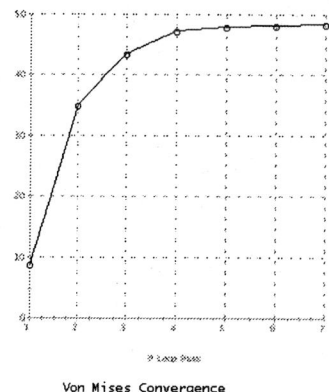

Figure 34 Convergence of model with reentrant corner (no excluded elements)

Pro/M offers a special tool to deal with this problem. We can tell Pro/M to ignore certain elements when it is evaluating convergence of the model. These are called *excluded elements*.

To set these up, select

>   *Analyses > Edit*

Check the **Excluded Elements** tab, then the **Exclude Elements** box. Click on the **Select** button. The elements added by AutoGEM at the corner are highlighted. AutoGEM has noted that this is a reentrant corner and has anticipated our desire to exclude these elements. We could also identify other excluded elements manually. Click *OK* to have these excluded from the convergence analysis. We don't want to exclude any others, so middle click. Set a convergence criterion of 10% and middle click to accept the dialog.

Run a multipass adaptive analysis of the model, deleting the old *plate6* files.

In the **Summary** window, note that the analysis converged on loop 7 with a reported maximum Von Mises stress of about 58 MPa. This does not include the excluded elements, which may still show much higher stresses, as shown in Figures 35. Note that the legend in the Von Mises fringe plot has been rescaled. Also note the somewhat erratic behavior of the Von Mises stress during convergence.

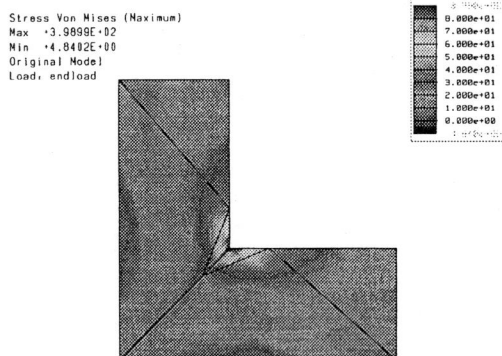

Figure 35 Von Mises stress in model with excluded elements

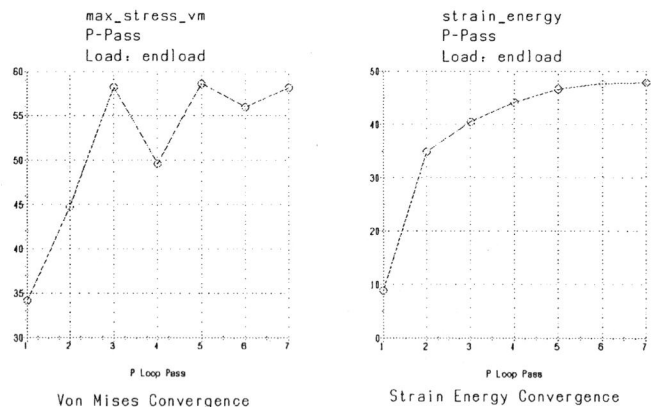

Figure 36 Convergence of model with excluded elements

Excluded elements can also be selected manually if you have reason to believe that they may be unduly influencing the convergence analysis of the model. These don't have to be generated by AutoGEM - they can be any elements in the model.

Summary

We have covered a lot of ground in this lesson. We have seen that for symmetric models, use of a half model will be beneficial in reducing the size, and hence the execution time, of the model. Some care must be taken in specifying the boundary constraints along the line of symmetry. The same will hold true for other model types, including three dimensional models.

We have also had a look at the automatic mesh generation procedures using AutoGEM. There are a number of customizing settings available with AutoGEM, but these will seldom be required. The default settings will usually be suitable.

Finally, we looked at several cases where, due to the underlying p-code and convergence analysis procedures in Pro/M, we must pay special attention to how constraints and loads are specified, and how reentrant corners in the geometry can be treated.

Most of the conclusions arrived at regarding performance and setup of the plane stress models treated here are also applicable to other model types, including 3D shell and solid models.

Questions for Review

1. What symmetry constraints (if any) would you use for the following models:

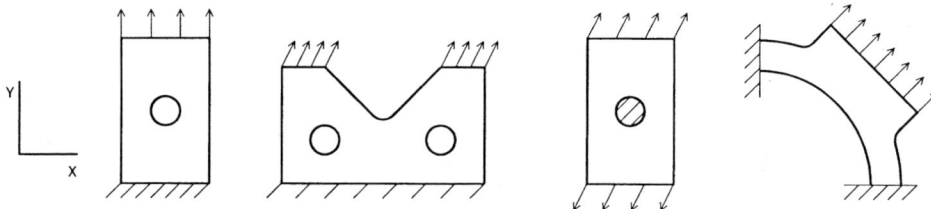

2. What are the advantages of exploiting symmetry in a model?
3. Symmetry in a model includes what entities/features?
4. How do you create a surface?
5. Does a surface inherit properties for the elements or the other way around?
6. How do you set up the graphics window to hide or show surfaces?
7. How can you get the stress fringe plot to display the magnitude and location of the maximum and minimum stresses?
8. How can you get the stress fringe plot to show stresses higher than a given value?
9. How can you customize the element mesh created with AutoGEM?
10. Elements to be ignored in the convergence analysis are called _____. How can you set these up: a) using AutoGEM, and b) manually?
11. What are the default element limits for 2D Plates used by AutoGEM?
12. By default, what will AutoGEM do with the following:
    a. existing points
    b. existing edges
    c. existing surfaces
    d. existing material property sets
    e. existing constraints and loads
13. What entities may AutoGEM add to the geometry of the model?
14. Describe the problem(s) that occur with point constraints and loads. What is the source of this problem? What is the solution?
15. Does the use of point constraints or loads automatically invalidate results throughout the model?

Exercises

1.   Find out how AutoGEM treats the following geometries with the following AutoGEM settings for the figures:

      a) all default settings   b) *Insert Points* ON and OFF

      c) *Reentrant Corners* ON and OFF   d) *Point Loads* ON and OFF

      For each mesh, obtain a display of a flat shaded view with shrunken elements.

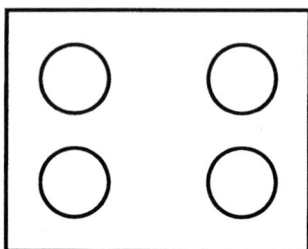

(a)

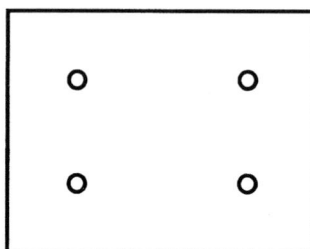

(b)

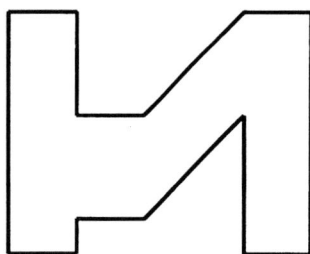

(c)

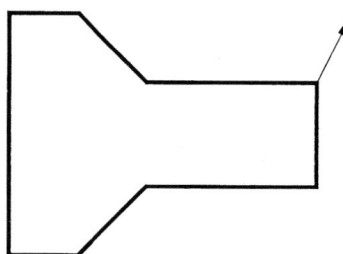

(d)

2. Perform a plane stress FEA of the following geometry and report the stress results, maximum deflection, p-level, and convergence data. The material is AL2014.

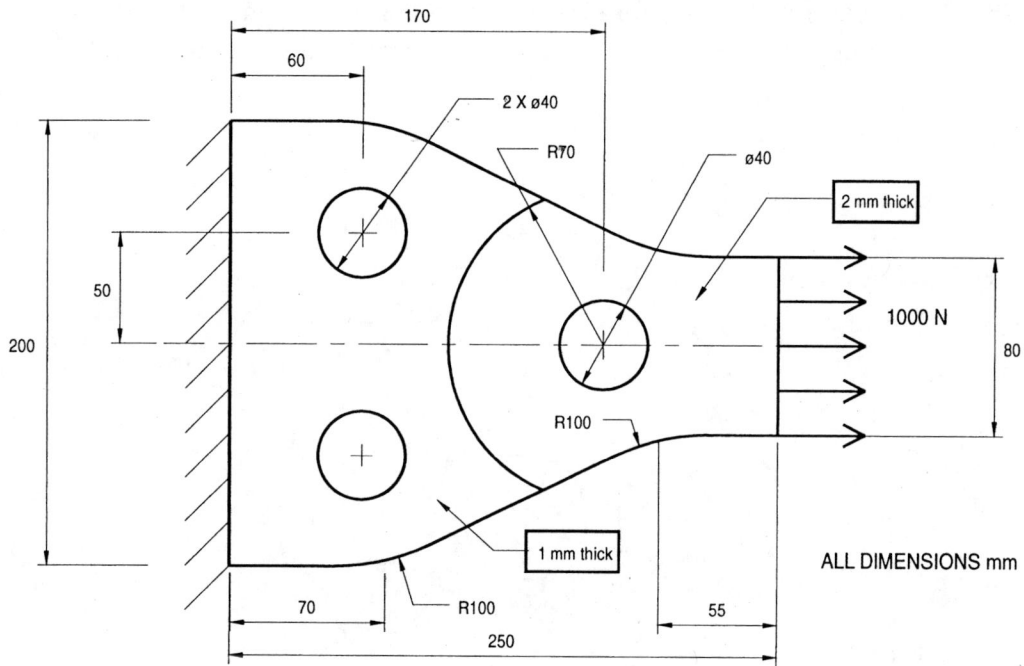

3.   Perform a plane stress FEA of the following geometry and report the stress results, maximum deflection, p-level, and convergence data. The material is AL2014.

      NOTE: This exercise is basically for geometry creation and dealing with a diabolical case. Do you think a plane stress analysis is appropriate for this problem? Why?

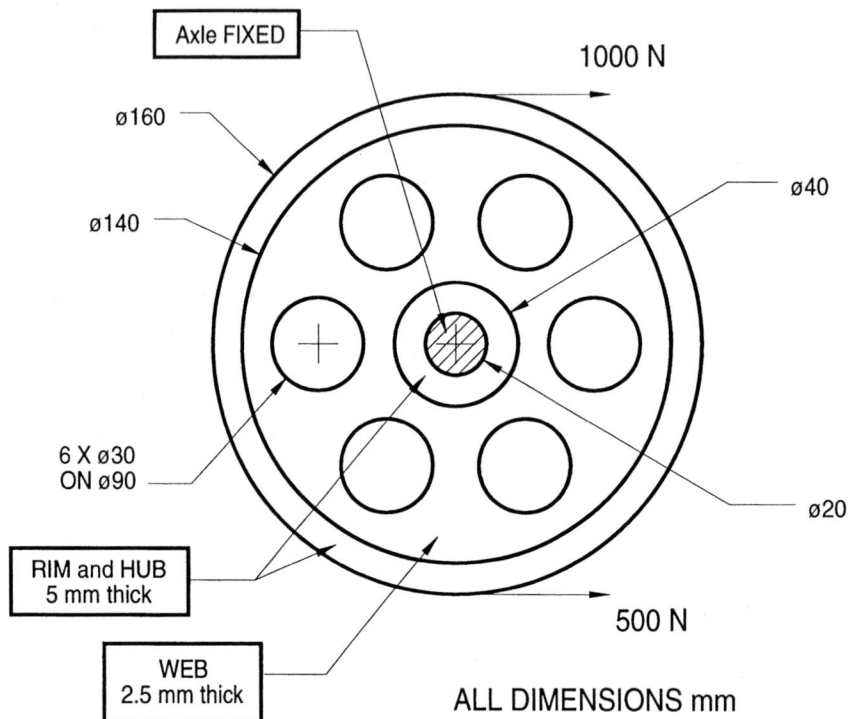

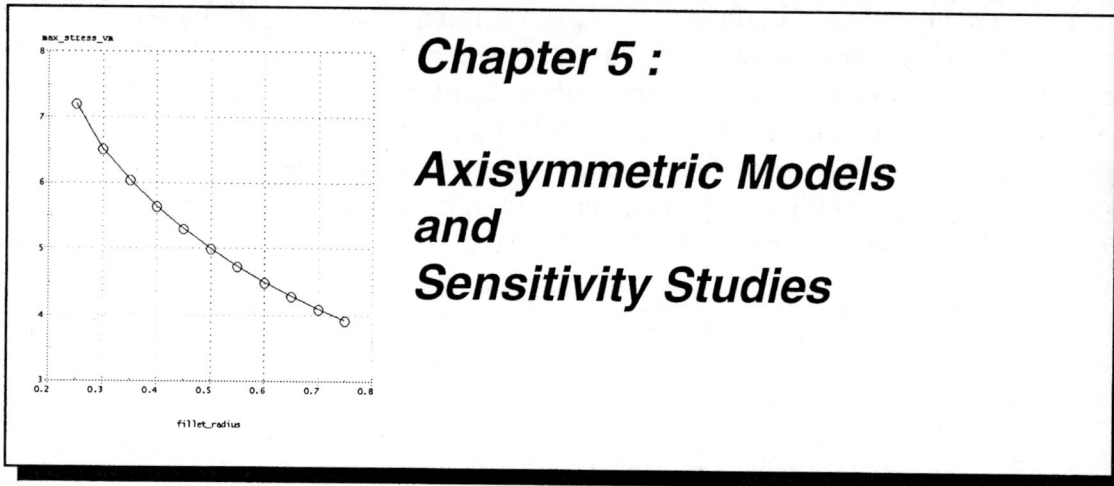

Chapter 5 :

Axisymmetric Models and Sensitivity Studies

Synopsis:

More geometry commands; axisymmetric models using solid and shell elements; pressure and centrifugal loads; sensitivity studies

Overview of this Lesson

The main objective of this chapter is to introduce you to another form of design study: the sensitivity study. To set a context for this, we will look at how an axisymmetric model is created using either solid or shell elements. Some new geometry commands, load types, and MECHANICA utilities will be introduced. Axisymmetric models will be used to demonstrate the procedure for designating design variables and performing a sensitivity study.

Sensitivity Studies

Suppose you want to find out how a particular dimension (size or location) or model property will affect the results of an analysis. In other words, you want to assess the sensitivity of the model to changes in this parameter. You could do this by manually editing the model (geometry or properties) and performing the analysis many times. The purpose of a sensitivity study is to automate this task.

The general procedure is to set up the model as usual - create the geometry, generate the elements, specify loads, constraints and material properties, and choose an analysis. Then, using commands in the *Design Variables* menu, pick the parameters you want to vary. You then specify the range over which the parameter should vary. A sensitivity study is then set up, identifying which design variable(s) you want to make active. The study is run and there you have it! Pro/M will automatically increment each specified design variable, manage the model (for example, remeshing if a change in geometry warrants it), and run a designated analysis on the model for each new configuration. You can then set up a results window to show the variation in some measure (like maximum Von Mises stress in the model) as a function of a designated design variable.

Although we used the word "automatic" in the previous paragraph, some subtle problems in setting up a sensitivity study may arise due to the changing geometry. Chief among these involves the automatic regeneration of the element mesh in the model. The design study can be set up to use the same elements, whose shape will change with the design variable, or to completely regenerate a new mesh with each new value of the design variable. You must be cautious about the possibility that certain combinations of design variables may result in impossible models. For example, if the design variables are the radii of two holes in a plate, then the locations of the holes and values of the radii must not allow the holes to intersect. Also, it may not be possible for AutoGEM to create a mesh (within the current element limit settings) for some combinations of design variables. Pro/M offers tools to check for these types of problems, and the solutions are often easy to obtain.

We will do a couple of examples of sensitivity studies, and at the same time introduce the methods used to model axisymmetric objects.

Axisymmetric Models

Objects with axisymmetry are quite common: pipes, shafts, wheels, drums, pulleys, and rotational machinery in general. The shape of the object is defined by a planar (2D) cross-section which is revolved around a central axis. The section does not necessarily need to include the axis. These are sometimes called revolved objects, with which users of 3D CAD programs such as Pro/ENGINEER will be familiar. The two figures below show cutaway views of typical examples of axisymmetric bodies.

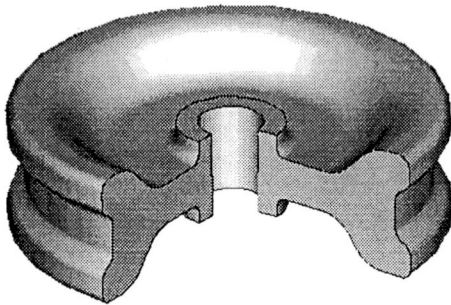

Figure 1 A solid flywheel that would be modeled with 2D Solid elements

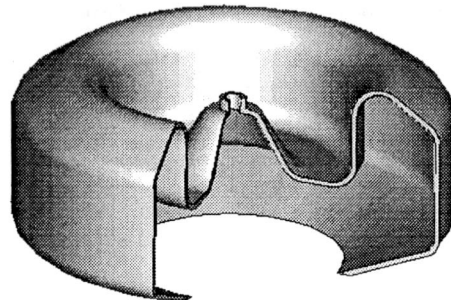

Figure 2 A hollow tank that would be modeled with 2D Shell elements

Elements

Two types of elements can be used with axisymmetric models: *2D Solid* or *2D Shell*. Both element types are defined on a single planar surface that intersects the axis of symmetry. The difference between objects for which these would be used is illustrated in the figures above. The figure on the left would use solid elements defined on a cross-sectional surface. The figure on the right would use shell elements that follow the cross sectional shape of the thin wall (midway between the inner and outer surfaces). In either case, only the two dimensional shape of the cross section needs to be defined.

Loads

A number of different loads can be applied to axisymmetric models. The major ones are:

- **Total Load** - If applied on a curve, edge, or shell represents the total load acting on the revolved surface obtained with the entity. If applied on a 2D Solid, represents the total load acting on the revolved volume. In either case, the total load stays the same when the geometry changes during sensitivity or optimization studies.
- **Force per Unit Area or Volume** - If applied on a curve, edge, or shell represents the load per unit area acting on the revolved surface obtained with the entity. If applied on a 2D Solid, represents the load per unit volume acting on the revolved volume. In either case, the total load will vary if the geometry changes during sensitivity or optimization studies.
- **Pressure** - Can be applied to free edges (only) of 2D Solids (ie edges between elements not allowed) or to 2D Shells. The pressure is applied uniformly around the circumference of the model, and is normal to the surface.

Other loads are available in axisymmetric models.

Note the significant departure in Pro/M from some other FEM packages, where axisymmetric loads are sometimes defined on a *per radian* of revolution basis.

Constraints

In an axisymmetric model, the axis of symmetry is fixed and is always the world Y axis. This automatically creates a constraint against rigid body motion in the radial (X) direction. The only other rigid body degree of freedom which must be constrained is translation in the Y direction. This will require an explicit constraint in the model. It is also often possible, and desirable, to use symmetry about the radial (or X) axis.

Restrictions

When setting up an axisymmetric model, some restrictions apply. Foremost among these is that the axis of symmetry must be the Y-axis of the default coordinate system, and all model elements must lie in the right half plane $X \geq 0$.

Example #1: A Thick-Walled Pressure Vessel

Our first axisymmetric model[1] is the thick-walled steel
pressure vessel shown in Figure 3. The inside of the tank
will be pressurized. Note that the upper and lower inside
corners of the tank have a fillet. It happens that the
maximum Von Mises stress that occurs in this tank is at
these filleted corners. After setting up the model, we will
perform a sensitivity study to see how the Von Mises
stress is affected by the fillet radius. Due to symmetry
about the horizontal mid-plane, we only need to model the
upper half of the vessel. We will model the cross section
using 2D Solid elements.

Creating the Model

Figure 3 Thick-walled pressure
vessel

Geometry

Before we create any geometry, it will be helpful to set up the Pro/M environment a bit:

> *Display > Master Visibilities > All On | Grid | Accept*
> *Display > Settings > Grid Spacing [0.5] | Points(Circle) | Accept*
> *Utility > Display Coordinates*

You may have to zoom out (***Ctrl-left*** mouse button) in order to see the grid mesh clearly. The
origin of the XY coordinate system is approximately in the center of the screen. The Coordinates
window shows where the cursor is in the graphics window.

We will create some construction lines for visual references. These will intersect at the origin of
the coordinate system.

> *Geometry > Curve*
> *Construction Geom > Horizontal > Snap(Point) > [0 0]*
> *Construction Geom > Vertical > Snap(Point) > [0 0]*

Reposition the screen so that you are looking at the upper right quadrant of the XY plane and can
obtain coordinates to X=3 and Y=4 at the upper right corner of the graphics window. We will
create the edge of the model as a chain of points, snapping to the grid and using the coordinate
display for location reference.

---

[1] See <u>The Finite Element Method in Mechanical Design</u>, Charles E. Knight, PWS-Kent,
1993, pp.165-168.

Curve > Line > Point Chain > Snap(Grid)

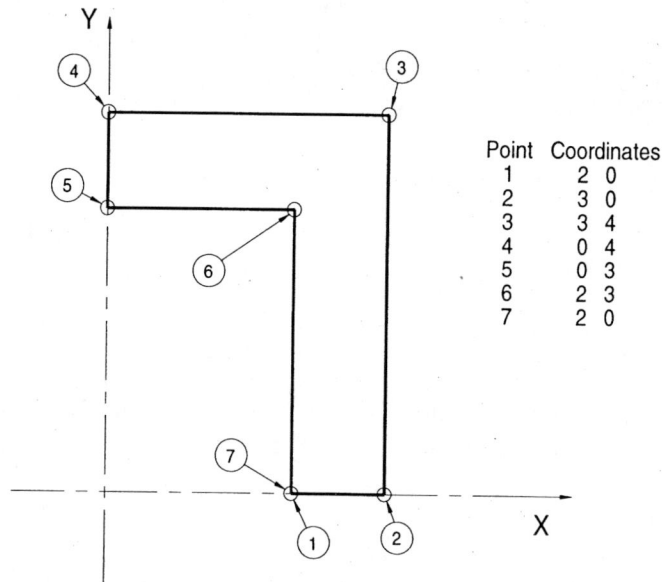

Point	Coordinates	
1	2	0
2	3	0
3	3	4
4	0	4
5	0	3
6	2	3
7	2	0

Figure 4 Creating the axisymmetric geometry

Click on the points 1 through 7 indicated in Figure 4. Our units are inches. Use the coordinate display to ensure the proper coordinates are entered. You do not need to be super accurate with your mouse clicks since the digitized points will snap to the grid at the intervals set above. When all points are entered, middle click.

Now, add a fillet using

Curve > Fillet

Pick on the two edges that intersect at the inside corner. In the command window, a prompt asks for radius, enter **0.5**. The prompt then asks if want to trim curves back; select the default *yes*. Middle click to exit.

We will create a surface so that assigned material properties will automatically be transferred to any elements made from the surface.

Geometry > Surface > Planar

Select any of the edges and then middle click (since there are no interior edges for this closed loop). The surface is created as shown in Figure 5. Middle click to exit.

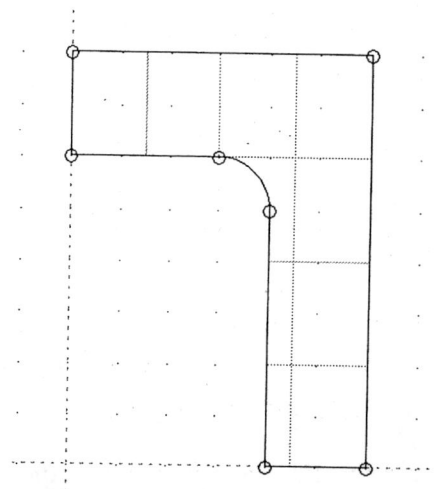

Figure 5 Geometry and surface completed

Model

With the geometry created, we can proceed to set up the model.

> *Main > Model > 2D Axisymmetric > Accept*
> *Properties > Material*

Move the material **STEEL_IPS** to the right pane. Then select

> *Assign > Surface*

and click on the surface. Middle click twice.

Only one constraint is required, to prevent rigid body translation in the Y direction. This constraint also occurs due to the top-bottom symmetry of the tank. To apply the constraint on the symmetry edge:

> *Model > Constraints > Curve*

Create a *New* constraint set **edges** and name the constraint **midtankedge**. Select the button under Curves and pick edge along the horizontal construction line (radial axis). *Free* the X translation but leave the Y translation *Fixed*. Note that, although it is given, the RotZ constraint is ignored for axisymmetric models. Accept the constraint with *OK*. The constraint symbol appears on the model.

Now we will create the elements using the automatic mesh generator.

> *Model > Elements > AutoGEM*

(We will use all the default settings, so if these have changed previously, go in to the *Settings* area in the AutoGEM menu and select *Element Limits > Default*.)

> *Surface*

Click on the surface (or select the *All* button), middle click. AutoGEM should create 1 tri and 2 quad elements. Modify the display using

> *Display > Settings*
> *[check the box for Shrink All Elements]*
> *Display Type(Flat Shade)*
> *Shade(Elements) > Accept*

The display should now look like the Figure 6.

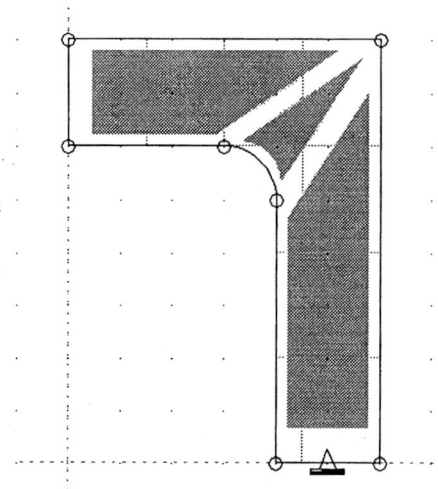

Figure 6 Elements created by AutoGEM; constraint on lower edge

We can now apply loads, in this case an internal pressure. Note that the procedure here deviates from our preferred practice of applying loads to geometry. With 2D Solid elements, we must apply the pressure load directly to the elements.

Model > Loads > Pressure > Edge

Create a *New* load set **presload** and name the load **pres1000**. Click on the three element edges on the inside of the tank where pressure is applied. Middle click. **Uniform** should already be selected, enter a value of *1000*, and *OK*. Middle click to leave the loads menu.

To change the appearance of the load arrows,

Display > Settings

Click on loads pulldown list to "*Heads Touching*", check the Display Load Magnitudes box, and change the Precision setting to *1* . The screen should now look like the Figure 7.

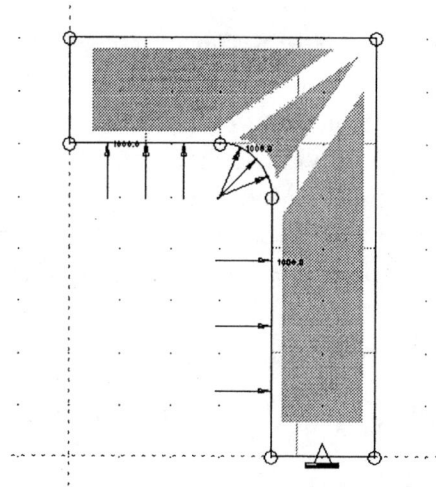

Figure 7 Axisymmetric model complete

Analysis

Our model is now complete. We should do a Quick Check before proceeding to see if any glaring errors are present in the model.

Main > Analyses

Create a New static analysis called **axitank1**, Enter a description. Select the constraint set **edges** and the load set **presload**. For Convergence, specify a *Quick Check* and leave the dialog. We are ready to run the analysis:

Run > Settings

Select the directories for output and temporary files, then *Accept* the Settings dialog.

Start > Error detection(Yes)

Since we have not yet saved the model, a dialog will come up asking for a model name. Save the model as **axitank1**. The design study starts up. Click on the *Summary* button and review the data. There should be no error messages. The maximum Von Mises stress is around 3876 psi, and the maximum deflections in the X and Y directions are 0.000181 in and 0.000217 in, respectively. Remember that these values don't mean very much with the Quick Check analysis since we have no idea about the convergence of this data.

Since there are no errors, we can change the analysis method to a multi-pass adaptive setting and rerun the study.

Analyses > Edit
Convergence Method(Multi-Pass Adaptive)
Convergence 5% on Lcl Disp & Lcl SE & Global RMS Stress
Polynomial order Max 9
OK > Close
Run > Start

Delete the previous output files and, just to be sure, accept error detection. Select the *Summary* button and review the run data. The run converges on pass 8 with a maximum edge order of 8. The maximum Von Mises stress has increased to 5075 psi, and the X and Y maximum deflections have changed to 0.000184 and 0.000264 inches, respectively[2]. You might note the total CPU time required, since an interesting result will occur shortly.

Results

Let's have a look at some results of the run.

Main > Results > Create > [vm]

Find the design study in the location you specified in the *Run > Settings* dialog. Set up windows for the Von Mises stress (fringe plot) and deformation (displacement magnitude, animation, 12 frames, Reverse). Once the first Result window has been set up, it is handy to use *Copy > Review* and change window parameters. The two windows should look like Figures 8 and 9.

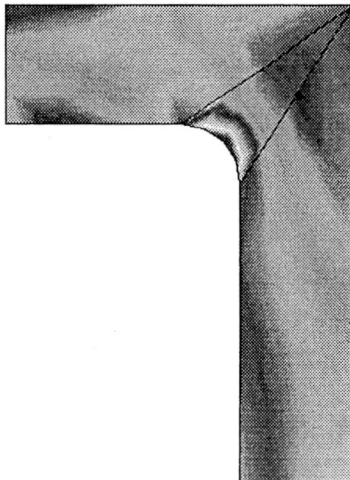

Von Mises Stress

Figure 8 Von Mises stress in original axisymmetric model (radius = 0.5)

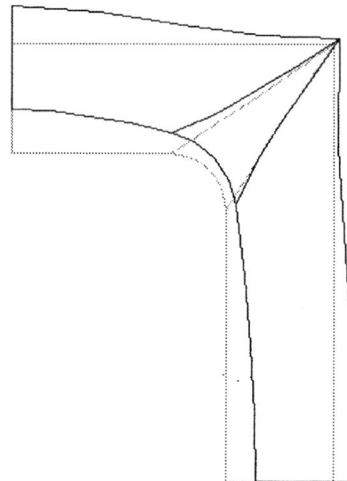

Deformation

Figure 9 Deformation of original axisymmetric model (radius = 0.5)

---

[2] The results obtained by Knight using an h-code analysis with 70 quad elements are: maximum Von Mises = 4021 psi, max deflection X = 0.000177, max deflection Y = 0.000255

Examine these results carefully. Things you should look for are: is the deformation what you would expect? Are the constrained edges behaving properly? Note that the edge on the vertical Y axis stays on the axis even though there is no explicit constraint there. Why? Do stress concentrations occur in the expected location(s)? You might like to set up result windows for the normal stresses in the X (radial), Y (axial), and Z (hoop) directions. On appropriate edges, the XX and YY normal stresses should show values of -1000 psi on the interior surface where pressure is applied, and 0 on the outer surface. The hoop stress on the interior surface can be computed theoretically if end effects are ignored, yielding a value of 2600 psi. What value do you get at the midplane of the model (furthest from the ends)? You can use a **Dynamic Query** in the fringe plots to review these values.

Using a Different Mesh

Before we proceed to the sensitivity study, we are going to re-mesh the model to produce additional elements. Why? There are two reasons. First, users of h-element codes will be surprised that only three elements were used in the previous model. An h-element model would require at least 40 or 50 times as many to obtain the same level of accuracy. So, to convince you of the accuracy of this solution, we will re-mesh with a denser mesh. Secondly, and more important for our purposes, we note that convergence of the previous multi-pass adaptive run required 8 passes. In a few minutes, we are going to set up the model so that the fillet radius will be reduced by half, to 0.25 inch. Using the same three element mesh, this is going to cause the pie-shaped triangular element to require an even higher edge order for convergence (if at all, within the limit of edge order 9). So, we will try to prevent that problem by creating a new mesh in advance that we hope will be able to handle all values of the fillet radius.

First, we have to delete all the existing elements

> *Edit > Delete > Entity > 2D Solids > All > middle click* (twice)

Note that the loads have also gone, because these were applied to element edges. Now create the new mesh:

> *Model > Elements > AutoGEM > Settings > Define/Review*

Set the min edge angle to *30*, max edge angle to *150*, and the max allowable aspect ratio to *2*. These are the extreme limits allowed by AutoGEM. Make sure that "Detailed Fillet Modeling" is turned off (unchecked). Accept the settings dialog. In the AutoGEM menu, select

> *Surface*

Click on the surface, then middle click. AutoGEM will create 7 tri and 4 quad elements (Figure10).

With a new set of elements, we need to reapply the pressure load:

> *Model > Loads > Pressure > Edge*

Create the load set as before. Select all the inside edges and set the magnitude to **1000**. The new mesh with loads applied is shown in the figure below.

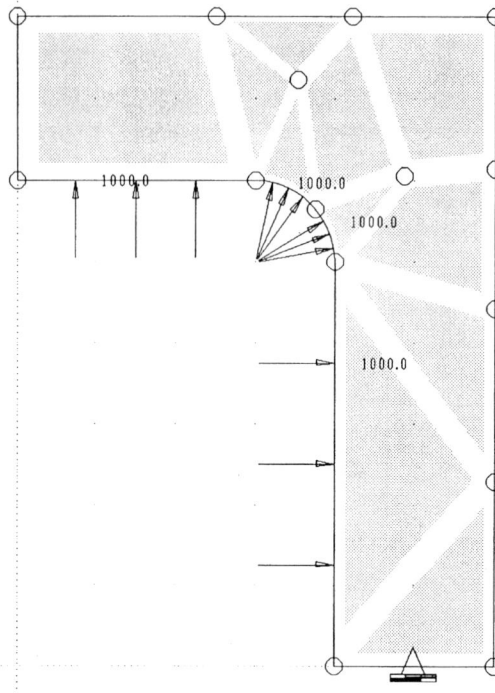

Figure 10 Model remeshed prior to
sensitivity study

Since we have been modifying the loading, check that the load set is still selected with:

> *Main > Analyses > Edit*

and make sure the **presload** load set is selected. Run the model:

> *Main > Run > (check Settings) > Start*

Delete the existing files. Look at the *Summary* file. The biggest change you will observe from the previous run is that the model has now converged on pass 4 instead of 8. This is expected since with a finer mesh, the adaptive analysis should converge at lower edge orders. This may even have decreased the total CPU time compared with the previous run on the original mesh. Although there are more elements, the total number of equations to be solved is reduced. The maximum Von Mises stress has changed slightly, from 5075 to 4861 psi (this may have been caused by a difference in the convergence obtained below the desired setting of 5%)[3]. The new deflections are 0.000183 and 0.000261 inches in the X and Y directions, essentially the same as before. Going from 3 to 11 elements has not significantly changed the results (except maybe the execution time). Plot the Von Mises and strain energy convergence graphs for this run.

---

[3] Try this run with a 1% convergence. The maximum Von Mises will increase to around 4906 psi.

We can use the existing results windows to look at the stresses and deformations. The Von Mises stress is shown in Figure 11. This shows essentially the same pattern as we had for the original 3-element mesh (Figure 8). The computed deformation using the new mesh is virtually identical to that shown in Figure 9.

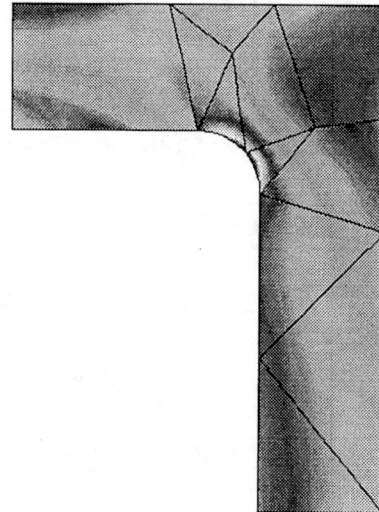

Von Mises Stress

Figure 11 Von Mises stress in model with new mesh

The Sensitivity Study

Creating Design Variables

We will now set up Pro/M to perform a series of analyses with the fillet radius varying between set limits. Select the following commands:

Model > Design Variables > Radius

and click on the geometry curve representing the fillet. Middle click. A dialog window will open as shown in the figure.

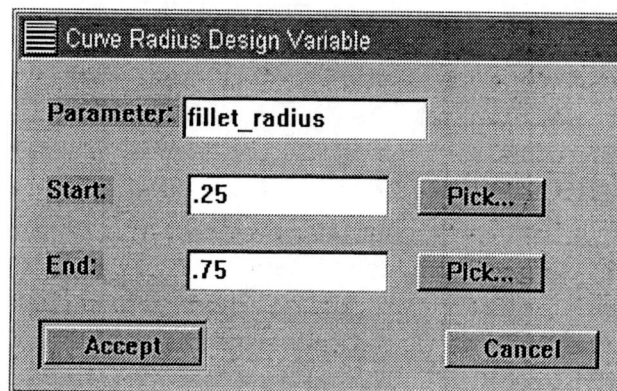

Figure 12 Specifying name and range of a design variable

Enter a parameter name *"fillet_radius"*, and set the Start and End values to 0.25 and 0.75, respectively. *Accept* the dialog and enter a description.

Before proceeding to run the analysis, it is a good idea to make sure that you have selected the correct geometric entity as a design variable, and especially that the designated range of values will not cause problems. In the Design Variables menu, select

Shape Review

The variable *fillet_radius* is checked with an initial setting of 0%, which corresponds to the start value entered in the dialog box above. Click on the *Review* button. The model geometry will be changed, and a new mesh generated as shown in Figure 13. Note the symbol on the fillet identifying it as associated with a design variable. Select *Return* and change the setting of the fillet radius to *100%* and click on *Review*. The model regenerates as shown in Figure 14

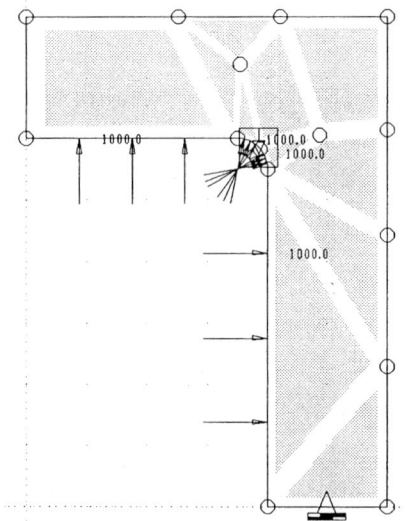

Figure 13 Shape review at minimum radius of fillet

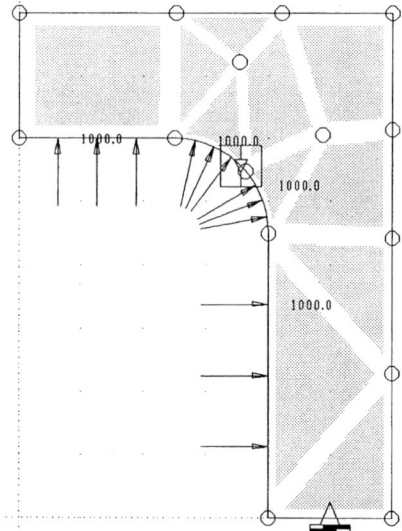

Figure 14 Shape review at maximum radius of fillet

Click *Return > Done.*

For another look at the range of geometry in the study, in the Design Variables menu, select

Shape Animate

In the dialog box that comes up note the Settings are from 0 to 100 % with 10 intervals. Click

Animate

to see the full range of geometry specified by the design variable. If there is going to be a problem with the mesh in the sensitivity study, it will be apparent here. Select *OK* to continue and then *Done*.

Setting Up The Design Study

With the design variable specified, we can set up the sensitivity design study.

> *Main > Design Study*

Enter a name for the study *"tankfillet"* and change the Type to ***Global Sensitivity***. Enter a short description. Note that the analysis we defined for this model (name *"axitank1"*, type static) is automatically selected. Check the box beside the parameter to be varied *"fillet_radius"*. Start and end values are indicated in the list boxes. Check these list boxes out to see what other options are available, making sure to leave them at ***Minimum*** and ***Maximum*** before you continue.

At the bottom of the dialog box, note that 10 intervals are automatically selected, and that ***regenerate elements*** is on by default. This option tells Pro/M to recreate the mesh for each new value of the design variable in the study. This new mesh will be generated using the current settings in AutoGEM. Since we are pretty sure that the current mesh will be satisfactory, we could turn this off. Do not do that at this point, since we are going to see what Pro/M does about this. Leave ***repeat P-convergence*** turned off. This will speed up the design study a bit, and is discussed below. ***Accept*** the dialog.

We can now run the design study:

> *Run > "tankfillet (Global Sensitivity)" > Start*

MECHANICA identifies elements associated with the pressure load. The program is telling us that these elements cannot be deleted if a mesh regeneration is necessary during the study. In another problem, this might mean that a new mesh could be created by AutoGEM that would have to violate its limit settings. Pro/M will let you do that, but it is warning you of this possibility now. This should not be required in this model, so select ***Continue***. Proceed with the design study and look at the ***Summary***.

In the summary file, we find that the first value of the fillet radius is set to the minimum, 0%. A multi-pass adaptive convergence is performed, and the run converges at pass 5 with edge order 5. This is higher than our previous run with this mesh which converged on pass 4, since the fillet radius is smaller. As anticipated, the smaller radius has required a higher edge order. This justifies our decision to remesh the model from our initial configuration of only three elements. Runs for all other values of *fillet_radius* are performed with the same p-levels as the first. (Recall that when we set up the design study, we specified NOT to repeat the p-convergence passes with each new value of radius).

Sensitivity Study Results

Let's see what results are available from the sensitivity design study. Select

> *Results > Create*

Create a new window called **filletsens**. Get the design study output directory **tankfillet**. Enter a title **Von Mises** for the window. Leave *Measure* in the Quantity list and select *max_stress_vm*, Below that in the dialog box, *Select* the design variable **fillet_radius**. Accept the dialog and *Show* the result window. This produces Figure 15, the primary result of the sensitivity study, showing the variation of the maximum Von Mises stress in the model as a function of the fillet radius. You could use this information, for example, to determine what the stress would be at an arbitrary fillet radius, or what radius would be required for a specific stress. Note that this curve is smooth enough that we could probably have done the sensitivity study with only 4 or 5 values instead of the default 10.

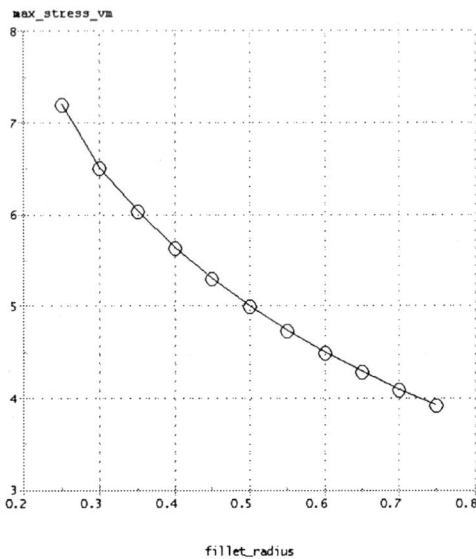

Figure 15 Variation of maximum Von Mises stress with fillet radius

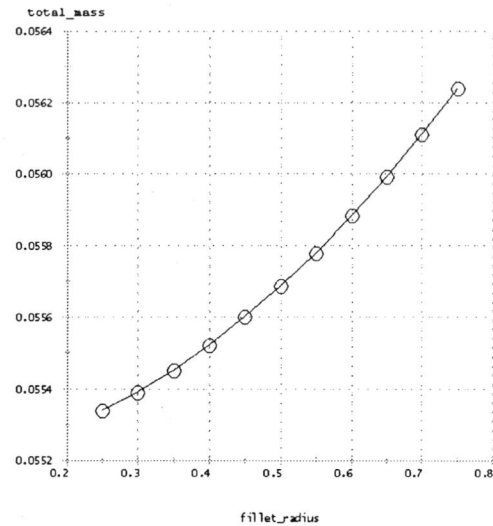

Figure 16 Variation of model total mass with fillet radius

You can also create a window to show the shape history, similar to the display obtained with the *Shape Review* command we used when we were setting up the design variable. You can also create a window that shows the variation of any other measure, for example *total_mass* with *Design Variable(fillet_radius)*, as shown in Figure 16.

Example #2 : The Centrifuge

This example will illustrate a number of Pro/M functions we haven't seen before: using 2D Shell elements, applying a centrifugal load, and two more kinds of design variables. The problem involves the analysis of the hollow axisymmetric object shown in Figure 17. The wall thickness is very small compared to the overall dimensions, so we will use shell elements. Loading on the part is due to a high speed rotation (50 rev/sec) about the symmetry axis. We are interested in finding out the stresses in the material, and how these are affected by the thickness of the shell and the location of the vertical interior cross brace.

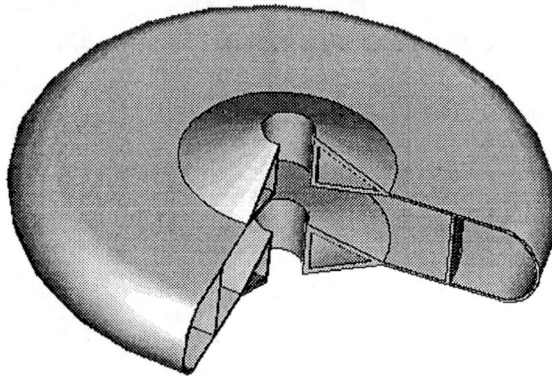

Figure 17 The centrifuge part - 400mm diameter, 50 revolutions per second

Creating the Model

The geometry of the model is shown in the figure below, minus the vertical brace.

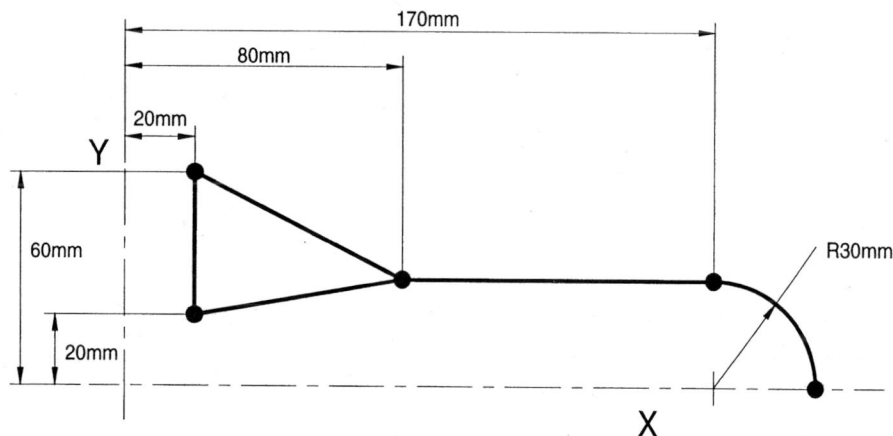

Figure 18 Dimensions for the axisymmetric half-model, without the vertical internal brace

Setting up MECHANICA

We will first set up Pro/M to make what is to follow a bit easier:

> *Display > Master Visibilities > All On | Grid | Accept*
> *Display > Settings |*
> *Grid Spacing [10] |*
> *Display Load Magnitude Precision [1] > Accept*
> *Utility > Display Coordinates*

Create some construction lines through the origin of the XY plane:

> *Geometry > Curve > Construction Geom > Horizontal > Snap(Point)*
> *[0 0]*
> *Construction Geom > Vertical > Snap(Point)*
> *[0 0]*

and middle click. Zoom in and pan until you see a 20 X 20 dot grid in the upper right quadrant of the XY plane.

Creating the Geometry

Create the geometry shown in Figure 18 above:

> *Curve > Line > Two Points > Snap(Grid)*

and click on the endpoints of each straight line segment in the figure. Middle click when complete. Now create the arc at the right end:

> *Curve > Arc > Start-Center-End > Snap(Grid)*

Pick on the grid at the start point (200, 0), center (170, 0), and endpoint (170, 30). Your geometry should now look like the figure below.

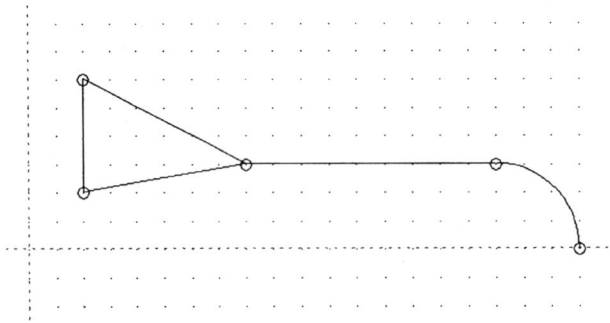

Figure 19 Geometry defined for the model

Setting Properties

We will assign material and shell properties to the underlying geometry. Any elements made using the geometry will then inherit the desired properties.

> *Main > Model > 2D Axisymmetric > Accept*
> *Properties > Material*

Select **AL2014_mmNS** and move it to the right pane. Then select

Assign > Curve > All

and middle click twice.

As mentioned above, we are going to use shell elements to define the model. In the model, a 2D Shell appears as a thick green line. The only property (in addition to material) that we have to specify is the thickness of the shell. We are going to set up the model with two different thicknesses in different areas. To specify the thickness of the shell elements,

Properties > Shell Property > Curve

select the horizontal line and quarter circle at the right end. Middle click and enter a shell property name as "*thick5*", a description, and a value of *5*. Accept the dialog. For the other shell elements, we will use a thicker shell:

Curve

and select the three lines that form the triangle at the left end of the model. Middle click and select *New Set*. Enter another property name "*thick8*", a description, and a value of *8*. Accept the dialog.

Creating Shell Elements

Now we can create the 2D shell elements:

Model > Elements > 2D Shell > Element Snap(Curve)

Click on all the geometry curves. They will highlight in green. Middle click.

Applying Constraints and Loads

We need to constrain the part against moving in the Y direction only. We will constrain the point on the horizontal centerline (due to symmetry, the vertical displacement of this point must be zero) and also the vertical element at the hub.

Model > Constraints > Point

Create a *New* constraint set **fixed** and name the constraint **center**. Select the button under Points and click on the point at the right end, middle click. Set the X translation **Free**, the Y translation **Fixed**, and the Z rotation **Fixed**. Accept the dialog. To constrain the shell element:

2D Shell

Call the constraint **hub** (it is still part of the constraint set **fixed**). Select the button under 2D Shell and click on vertical shell element at the left end, middle click. This will be completely constrained (fix all degrees of freedom),

To apply a centrifugal load is quite easy. The axis of rotation for 2D axisymmetric models is always the Y axis. All we need to specify is the speed of rotation in radians per second.

Model > Loads > Centrifugal

Create a *New* load set **centrif** and enter a load name **cent314.** Enter a value for the angular velocity of **314** rad/sec, which corresponds to 50 rev/sec. Accept the dialog. The completed model should look like Figure 20. Note the centrifugal load symbol at the lower left corner.

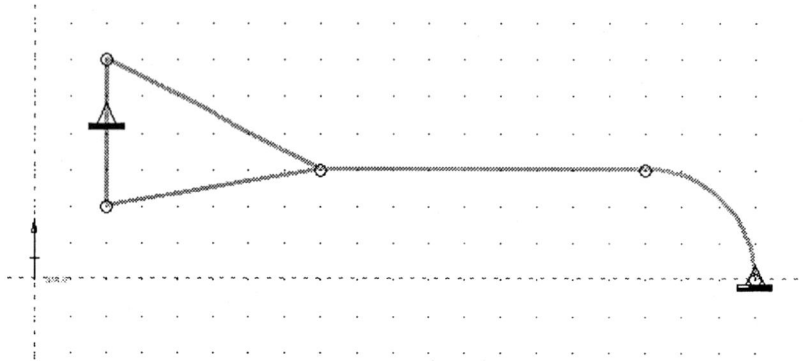

Figure 20 Model completed with elements, constraints, and centrifugal load

Performing the Analysis

As usual, the first time we run a model, we will perform a Quick Check to see if there are any serious modeling errors:

Main > Analyses

Create a *New* static analysis name **centrif**, check that the highlighted constraint set is **fixed** and the load set is **centrif**. Finally, select Quick Check and leave the dialog. Go to

Run > Settings

Select the desired directories for output and temporary files. Then leave the dialog and select

Start

Accept error detection. Pro/M will save the current model at the start of every design study. Since we have not specified a name for the model yet, you get a chance to do that here. Save it as *"centrifug"*. The design study starts. Check the Summary window for any reported errors or warnings. You might note that the maximum Von Mises stress is 9.37 MPa.

Since there are (or should be!) no errors, we can change the analysis:

Main > Analyses > Edit

Change to a multi-pass adaptive analysis with **5%** convergence on **Lcl Disp, Lcl S.E. & Global RMS Stress**, a maximum polynomial order of **9** and *OK*.

Run > Start

Delete the existing output files for the model. It is probably a good idea to always use error detection. Open the *Summary* window. The analysis converges on pass 3 with a maximum edge order 5. The maximum Von Mises stress has increased to 11.2 MPa; maximum X and Y deflections are 0.0185 and -0.0216, respectively.

View the Results

We will create a new kind of result window here.

Results > Create > [vm]

Get the output directory "*centrif*" from the location you specified under *Run > Settings*, enter a window title, set the quantity as **Stress (Von Mises)**. Under **Display type** select *Query* and set digits to *3*. *Accept* the dialog. *Copy* the window definition to a second window called **deform**, select *Review* and modify the definition to set up a deformation animation.

With the result name *vm* highlighted in the *Show* part of the window, select

Show > Controls > Query

Click at various places on the model. A label is placed on the model to show stress at that location as illustrated below.

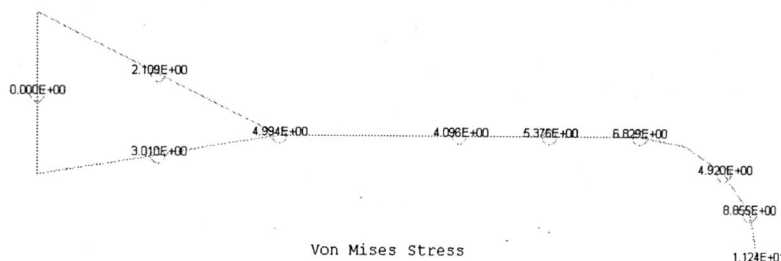

Figure 21 Von Mises stress at points on the model

Note that the maximum Von Mises stress occurs on the centerline axis at the right end of the model. Figure 22 shows the (exaggerated) deformed shape.

Deformation

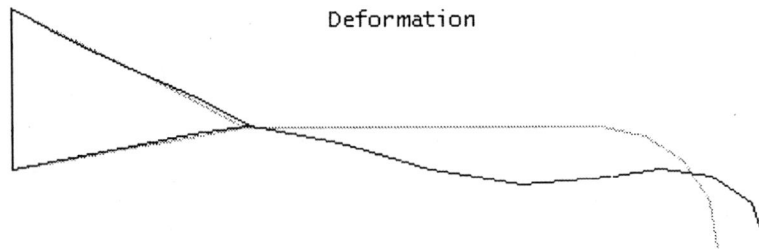

Figure 22 Deformation of un-braced model

From the deformation we see that due to the high centrifugal load, the wall of the shell collapses inwards.

Modifying the Model

We will add a vertical brace inside the shell to stiffen it in the transverse (Y) direction.

Geometry > Curve > Line > Two Points > Snap(Grid)

Create a vertical line at x = 130 between the horizontal construction line and the horizontal element. Apply properties to this new geometry item:

Main > Model > Properties > Material > Assign > Curve

Click on the new curve and select the material *AL2014* already defined in the model. In the question window, select *No*, and *Close* the Material window. Then pick

Shell Property > Curve

and click the new curve. Assign the existing shell property *thick8* to the curve.

The horizontal green line in the model contains only a single element. We need to delete it and create two new shell elements that join at the stiffener.

Edit > Delete > Entity > 2D Shells

click on the long horizontal element, then middle click. Now create two new ones:

Model > Elements > 2D Shell > Element Snap(Point)

Add two new elements between the points on the horizontal line. Middle click. Then select

Element Snap(Curve)

and click on the new vertical brace. Middle click.

We need to add a symmetry constraint on the lower point on the brace:

Model > Constraints > Point

Enter a constraint name **brace** (still in constraint set **fixed**). Pick the new point and middle click. Set the X translation **Free**, the Y translation **Fixed**, and the Z rotation **Fixed**. Accept. The new model should look like Figure 23.

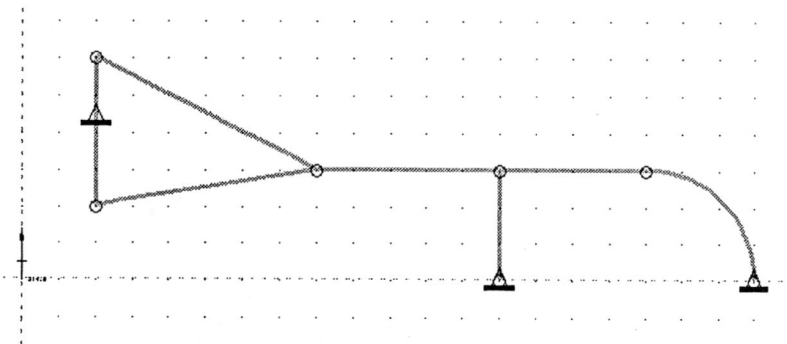

Figure 23 Complete model with vertical interior brace added

Somewhere in the last few commands we have made a couple of errors. Can you figure out what they were? We will see how Pro/M identifies them for us.

Some Pro/M Utilities

Let's take a moment here to explore some of the utility functions in Pro/M. First, in the pull down menus at the top select

Review > Model Summary

This gives an information window showing the number of bodies, number of curves, elements, and so on, and the type of model. Close this window and select

Edit > Property > Shell Property > 2D Shell

and click on the arc element at the right end. Pro/M should tell you that the property has been inherited from the curve. Select *No* and middle click. Click on *Curve* instead and pick the same arc. The thickness property assigned to the underlying curve is shown. This shows once again that properties can be attached to the geometry and not directly to the elements (at least in this case).

Running the Modified Model

We shouldn't have to make any changes to the analysis type, so we can go directly to

Main > Run > Start

Delete the existing output files and accept error detection. Hmmm.. we seem to have a problem: two elements do not have a thickness property. Why? Terminate the run with

Cancel > No > OK > Done

Let's turn off the display of the elements and examine the properties of the geometry:

Display > Master Visibilities > (uncheck) 2D Shells | Accept
Edit > Property > Shell Property > Curve

Click on the horizontal line. Pro/M shows that the property *thick5* has been assigned to this geometry. This is what we intended. *Cancel*. Turn the element display back on and examine the properties of the shells:

Display > Master Visibilities > 2D Shells | Accept
Edit > Property > Shell Property > 2D Shell

Click on the horizontal elements, and indeed no property has been assigned to these elements. What is going on? Recall that we created these two elements point to point, that is, not using or associating them with the geometry curve underneath. Although these elements lie on top of the geometry, they are not associated with it. We will have to specify their properties independently. Middle click a couple of times to back out of the current command, then select:

Model > Properties > Shell Property > 2D Shell

Select the two offending elements, middle click, and set the shell property to *thick5*. Accept.

Let's try again:

Main > Run > Start

Delete the output files and accept error detection. Once again an error is reported: we haven't specified the material property either for these elements not associated with the geometry underneath. Go to

Main > Model > Properties > Material > Assign > 2D Shell

and pick on the two elements to assign the correct material.

The Final Run

This time, the run should succeed. Select

> ### Run > Start

Open the **Summary** window. The run converges in 3 passes with a maximum edge order of 5. The maximum Von Mises stress is reduced from the previous value of 11.2 down to 8.99 MPa. The deflections are now 0.0146 mm and -0.0097 mm in the X and Y directions, respectively.

The same result windows will still be defined. Open the window showing the Von Mises stress and use **Query** to have a look at some values. Results should be as shown in Figure 24.

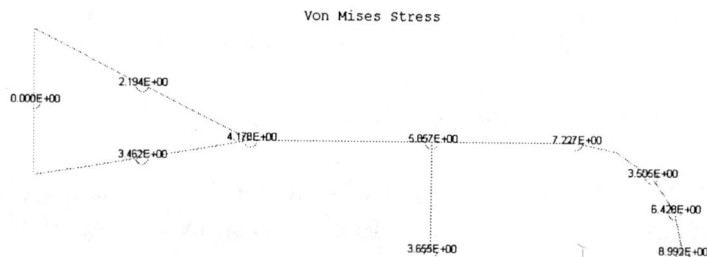

Von Mises Stress

Figure 24 Von Mises stress in completed model

The deformation of the model is shown in Figure 25. The vertical brace has prevented the collapse of the side wall, as intended, and served to reduce the maximum stress in the model.

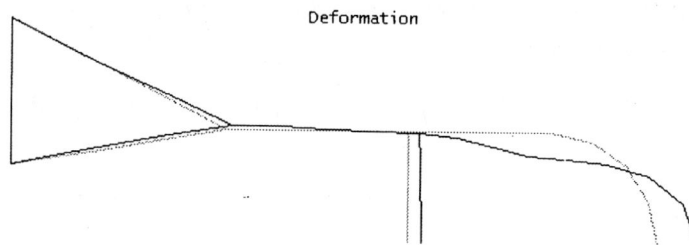

Deformation

Figure 25 Deformation of completed model

The Sensitivity Study

We want to find out the effect of the thickness of the elements in the *thick5* group, and also the effect of the location of the interior brace. This calls for a sensitivity study. The interesting thing to note here is that a design variable can be something other than a geometric dimension (in the previous lesson we used the radius of a curve). You could, for example, choose to examine several different materials. Secondly, if you use a geometric variable as a design variable, then Pro/M is quite clever about adjusting the geometry of any connected entities.

First set up the design variable for the shell thickness (a property variable):

Model > Design Variables > Property Vars > 2D Shell > thick5 > Accept

Enter a name of the parameter **thickness** and set start *3* and end *8*. Accept. Enter a description. Note the design variable symbol on the screen.

Now set up a design variable for the horizontal location of the brace:

Design Variables > Translate > Curve

Remembering that the brace element is associated with the curve underneath it (that's how it was created), click on the element. Middle click. A dialog box as shown below will open up:

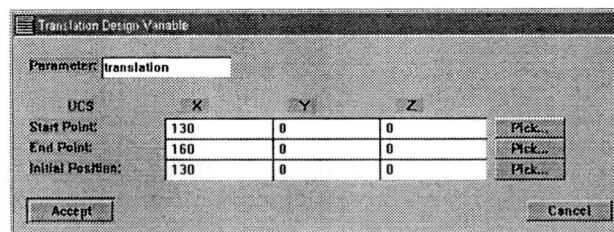

Figure 26 Specifying parameters for a *Translate* design variable

Enter a parameter name "*translation*". We now specify a vector that defines the translation (using a start and end point), and the initial position. Specify the *Start* point using

Pick > Snap(Grid)

and pick on the lower end of line (the location is 130 0 0). For the End point pick on (160 0 0) and set the initial position at (130 0). Accept the dialog and enter a description.

It is a good idea to make sure we have set this up correctly. Select

Design Variables > Shape Animate > Translation > Animate

The curve and the associated element will move to the right as shown in Figure 27. Not so apparent in that figure is that the two horizontal elements have changed length automatically in order to stay connected to the point on the top of the brace.

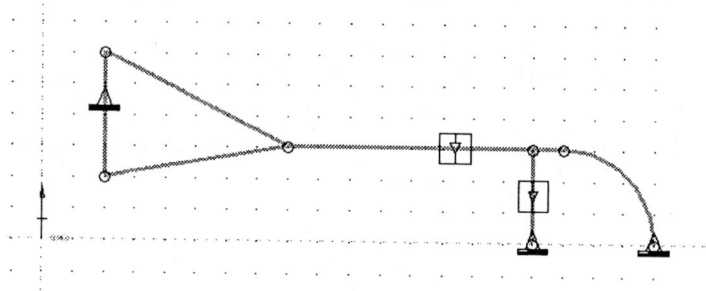

Figure 27 Extreme position of the vertical brace

Now we will set up a couple of design studies to determine the independent effects of these two parameters:

Main > Design Study

Enter a study name **sensthick**, select *Global Sensitivity*, check the variable **thickness** and set the range for min to max. Since the same elements will be used throughout, turn off *regenerate elements* and *smoothing*. Note the analysis to be used is **centrif**. Accept the dialog.

Now set up another study for the other design variable. This is not strictly necessary but if we include both variables in the same study, they will be varied simultaneously, which we don't want to do here. The easiest way to create the second design study is to:

Copy

Enter a new name "*senslocate*" and select *Review*. Turn off the *thickness* parameter and turn on the *translation* parameter, note that Global Sensitivity is already selected, and *Accept* the dialog.

Run the two design studies. For the first one, select

Run > senslocate > Start

Confirm error detection and the design study will start. Open the *Summary* window. Browse through the file looking for error or warning messages. When you are finished, back in the Run window select

sensthick > Start

and review the *Summary* window as before.

Viewing the Sensitivity Results

Create a couple of result windows for the two design variables.

> *Results > Create > [sensthick]*

Get the results from directory *sensthick*. Plot the Von Mises stress versus the design variable **thickness**. Create another window called **senslocate** and plot Von Mises stress versus the design variable **translation**

Highlight the two result window titles in the **Show** window and click on *Show*. The two graphs will be displayed side by side on the screen as shown in Figure 28.

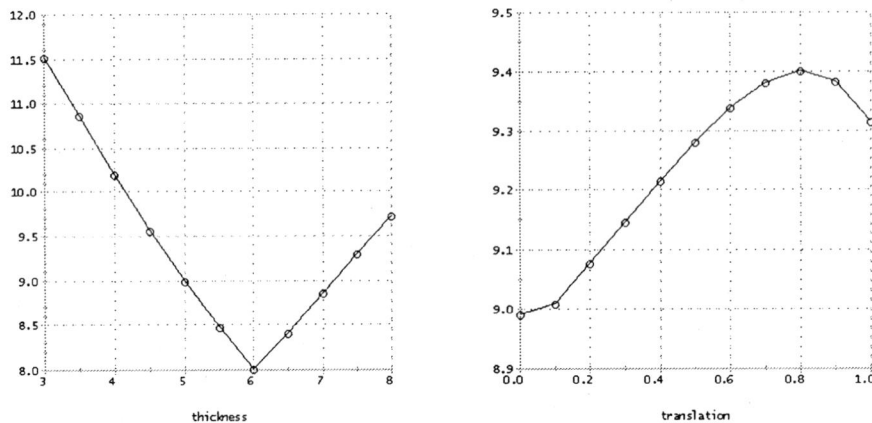

Figure 28 Sensitivity of the Von Mises stress in the model to shell thickness (left) and position of the brace (right)

This is a very interesting result in the Von Mises versus thickness graph on the left. The minimum stress occurs at a thickness of 6 mm and then increases again. We will explore this result below. In the other graph we see that the stress increases as the brace is moved outward, reaching a maximum just before the final position. Note that the vertical scales of these two graphs are different. The results would be easier to interpret if they had the same scale. Pro/M gives us an easy way to do this - called *tieing*. Select

> *Controls*

Read the message prompt, and click on translation (right) graph. Then select

> *Tie Qty*

and click on the thickness graph. The two graphs now have the same vertical scales (Figure 29). It is now very apparent that the thickness has much bigger effect on stress than the location of the brace.

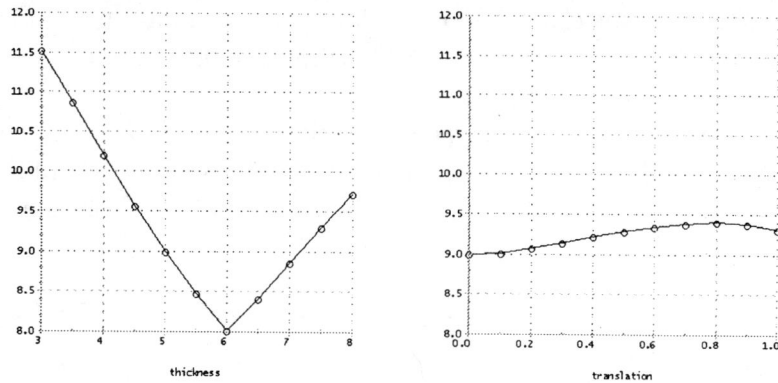

Figure 29 Sensitivity of Von Mises stress to thickness and location
of brace (with the same vertical scale)

Now, as for the curious effect of thickness, set up a single multi-pass adaptive run with a thickness of 7mm. This is easiest to do by modifying the shell property for ***thick5*** and changing the numerical value to *7*. What happens? At 7mm, the maximum Von Mises stress is 8.8 MPa. Open the result window ***vm*** to display the stress using ***Controls > Show Maximum***. The maximum stress in the model no longer occurs at the tip, but at the hub, as shown in Figure 30. This is the kind of unexpected effect you should look for when you see a discontinuity in a sensitivity plot.

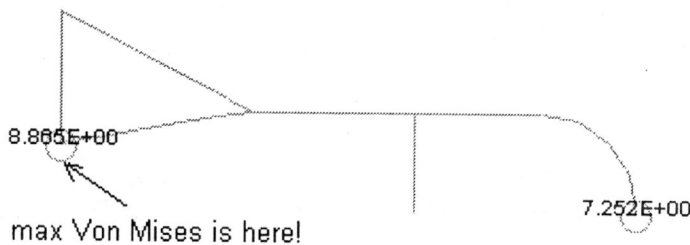

Figure 30 Von Mises stress for thickness 7mm

Summary

Axisymmetric models are quite common, and you should be familiar with both solid and shell elements. Fortunately, these are easy to set up and the computational load is very light, so the models will execute quickly. You should try to do some of the exercises below to get more practice at creating and interpreting these models.

Sensitivity studies are very useful if you wish to explore design options to try to determine what modifications to a design might be most beneficial. Some caution is required when setting up a sensitivity study to make sure that the element mesh will survive the changes in parameters specified. Pro/M offers useful tools (*Shape Review* and *Shape Animate*) to examine the effects of changing geometry. We will see another use for these tools in the next chapter.

In the next chapter, we will look at the final type of design study: optimization. This uses the concept of design variables introduced here, and adds a powerful search algorithm that will determine the set of design variables to produce the best possible design for your stated objectives.

Questions for Review

1.   On what plane do you have to create an axisymmetric model? Where is the axis of symmetry?
2.   What types of elements are available for axisymmetric models? Make some quick sketches or describe typical shapes appropriate for each element type.
3.   What are the three main load types available for axisymmetric models? How is the Pro/M definition different from standard FEM package definitions?
4.   What is the minimum constraint required in an axisymmetric model?
5.   Is it possible to have a model whose geometry crosses the Y-axis? (Trick question!)
6.   Is it possible to have a model which, under load, will deform such that it crosses the Y-axis?
7.   What is the command to produce a "live" numerical readout of the geometric cursor location on the screen?
8.   For which of the following geometric entity pairs can you create a fillet:
        i)   line and arc
        ii) line and line
        iii) arc and arc
        Can you find out what restrictions (if any) apply to these constructions?
9.   At what point in the model creation do you identify it as a 2D axisymmetric model?
10.   Where can you apply a pressure to a model composed only of 2D Solid elements?
11.   What will generally happen to the convergence behavior when you produce a finer mesh in Pro/M? Why?
12.   When setting up the design variables, there are two ways that you can determine the geometric effect of changes in a single variable. What are they, and where are these commands available?
13.   When running a sensitivity study, what does the "*repeat p-loop convergence*" option do? Under what circumstances would or wouldn't you use this?
14.   Another option in a sensitivity study is "*regenerate elements*". What does this refer to, and under what circumstances would or wouldn't you use this option?
15.   What results from a sensitivity study can you plot?
16.   What do we mean by "associativity?" Give an example. Is associativity automatic for entities located at the same place in a model?
17.   Is it possible to create 2D Solid elements that overlap? What about 2D Shell elements? First, do you think this is a reasonable thing to be able to do, and second, find out how Pro/M will respond if you do this.

18. Find out if it is possible to create shell elements of varying thickness along an individual element. If not, how would you approach modeling this?
19. What is the *lowest* edge order used in a multi-pass adaptive analysis of a 2D Shell model?
20. What happens if you run a sensitivity study with all defined design variables selected at once?

Exercises

1. Consider a 3" diameter circular steel rod with a circumferential semi-circular groove under an axial tension load.
   (a) Assuming that the load is 100 lb, find the maximum axial stress in the rod if R=0.25".
   (b) Do a sensitivity study for values of R ranging from 0.10" to 0.50" in order to find the variation in the maximum axial stress as a function of R. Plot these results in terms of a stress concentration factor, with the axial stress normalized with a nominal stress based on the minimum rod diameter. Compare this factor with published values (you'll find these in mechanical design textbooks). Justify your choice for the dimension L. HINT: You may have to play around with the mesh to get reliable results. Comment on the use of FEA for obtaining stress concentration factors.

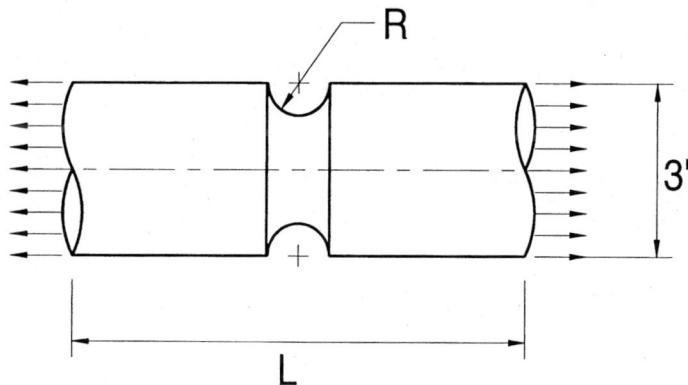

2. The figures on the next page show a combustion chamber in a jet engine (some artistic license here!). Assuming an internal pressure of 100 psi (approximately 0.70 MPa), find the maximum Von Mises stress and radial deflection if the wall thickness of the chamber is 2.0mm. The material is a titanium alloy (5AL 2.5Sn, with a yield stress of 860 MPa). Find the variation of the maximum Von Mises stress with wall thickness in the range of 1.0mm to 3.0mm. Assume the endpoints of the chamber are fixed.

   HINT: When you apply the pressure load, you may find that the pressure is initially set up acting inward instead of outward. To get the correct direction, you have to redefine the direction of the surface normal(s) as follows:

   > *Edit > Normals > 2D Shell > Flip*

   and select the elements that need to be switched.

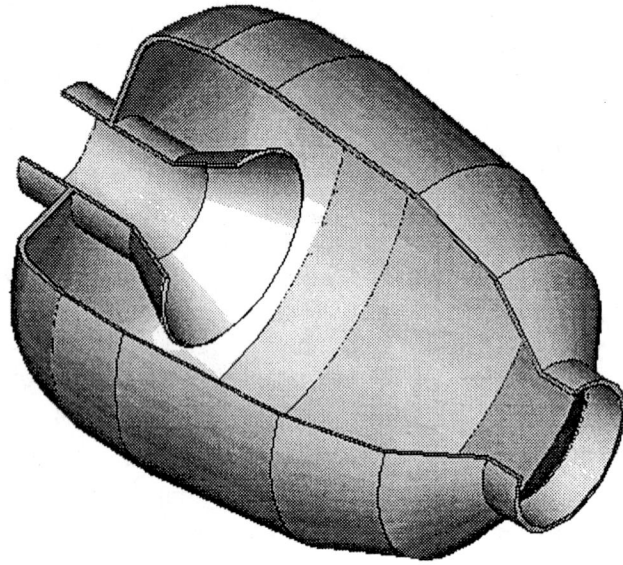

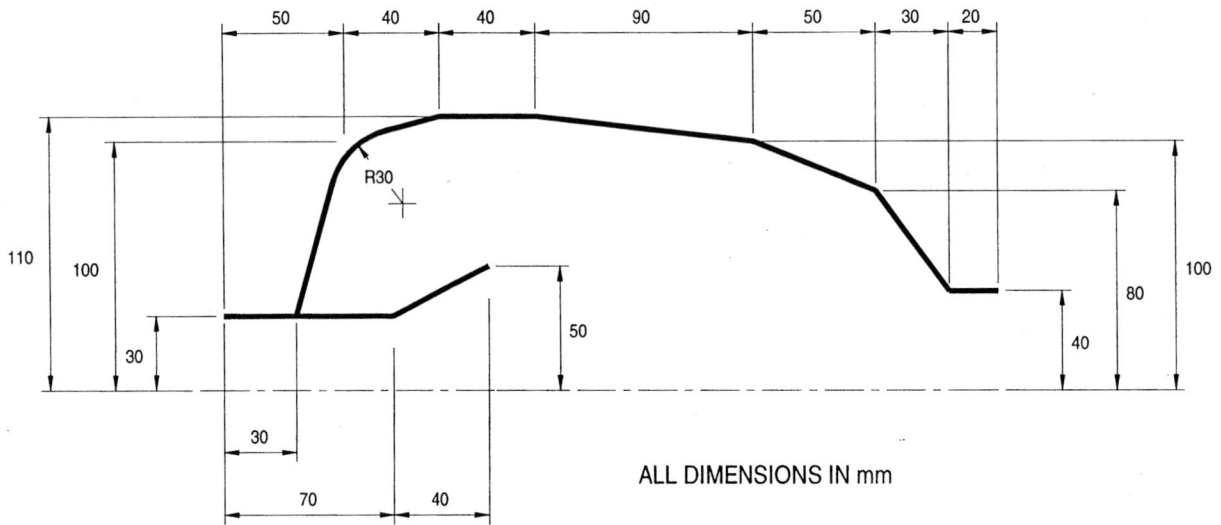

ALL DIMENSIONS IN mm

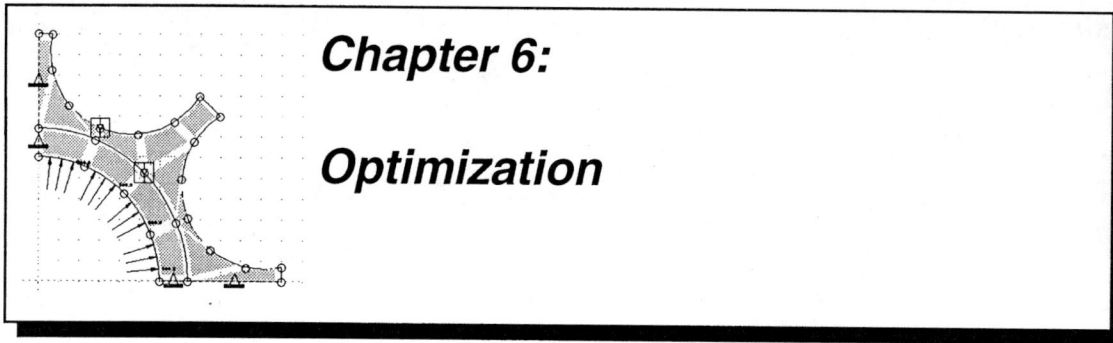

Chapter 6:

Optimization

Synopsis:

Setting up design variables and optimization design studies; plane strain models; more geometry commands (translate, rotate, copy, trim); applying temperature loads

Overview of this Lesson

This lesson will present the third and last of the three types of design studies: optimization. This is easily the most powerful and fascinating of the capabilities of Pro/MECHANICA. The lesson will use two examples to illustrate the major features of an optimization problem. A model is constructed as usual by specifying geometry, material properties, constraints, loads, and an analysis. Design variables are identified just as for performing a sensitivity study. The set of design variables and their range of values define a search space. To find the "best" or optimized set of variables, Pro/M conducts a search through this space. To do this, we set up a new type of design study which will contain a goal, such as obtaining the minimum mass, and one or more constraints, like not exceeding a specified stress or deflection. Pro/M then iteratively moves through the search space seeking the best solution. At the end of the run, we can see how the geometry changed throughout this process, and we can, of course, save the best final solution. This is truly a designer's dream!

Optimization requires considerable computing resources and considerably longer execution times than simple analyses or even sensitivity studies. Therefore, in this chapter we will explore only the basic functionality of optimization using very simple models. Some simple optimization problems are suggested at the end of the chapter for you to try on your own.

Example #1 - Optimization of a Thin Plate

The Model

This first example will use a geometry we have seen before - the tapered thin plate used in Chapter 4. This is a plane stress model of a symmetric aluminum plate with three interior holes, loaded axially with a uniform load on the free end. You can use the model file (*plate4.mdb*) created previously, or recreate the geometry using the figure below for reference.

Initial Geometry

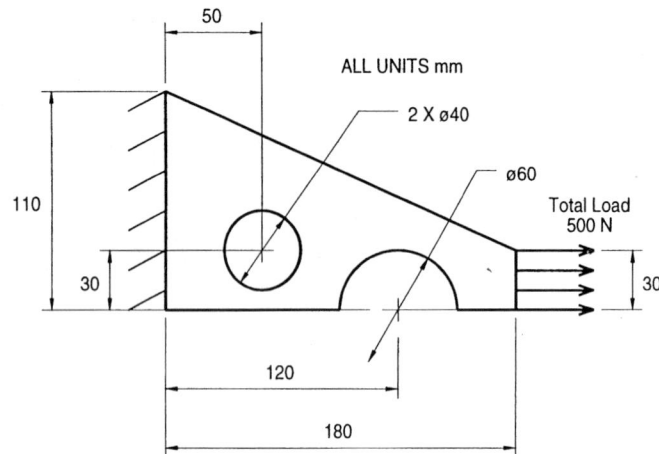

Figure 1 Geometry of thin plate *plate4*

If you have the previous file available (as we left it at the end of Chapter 4), use the following commands to bring it into Pro/M. The file should be in your default directory:

File > Open > plate4

This is a plane stress model containing 2D Plate elements, with constraints on the symmetric edge and the fixed left edge, and a uniform axial load on the right edge. When you bring in the model, it should look something the figure below. If your mesh is not the same as this, don't worry since we will be deleting it shortly.

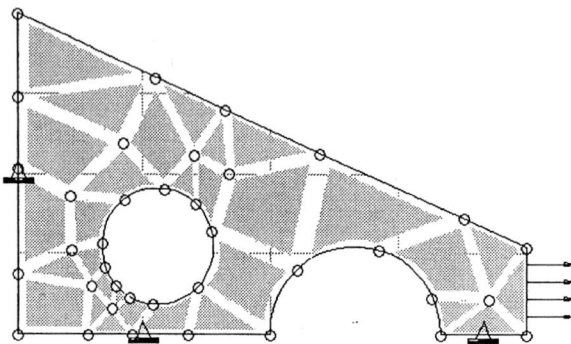

Figure 2 The thin plate model *plate4*

Some Pro/M Utilities

Reviewing the Model

Here are some handy commands to use when you bring in a model you have forgotten or with which you are unfamiliar. Start with the following:

>> *Review > Entity > Curve*

Pick on the interior hole on the left. A window opens up telling us the curve type, length, and so on. Notice that the radius is given as 20. Close this window, middle click to back out of the command, and select

>> *Surface*

If you click on the surface you will get the total surface area. Close this window, middle click, and select

>> *Edit > Property > Material*

The Materials window comes up showing the materials assigned in the model (in this case only one). Middle click to back out of this command. Now select

>> *Edit > Load*

and click on the load at the right end. The Force/Moment window opens showing you the name of the load, its type and components, and so on. Close this window and go back to a previous command

>> *Review > Entity > 2D Plate*

Click on one of the elements. It highlights in red and shows the associated surface in red underneath the element.

Deleting Elements and Points

For a couple of reasons, we want to remesh the model. First, meshing with fewer elements will speed up the optimization without significantly affecting the analysis accuracy, as shown in a previous chapter. More importantly, when the geometry changes during optimization the mesh must be able to change its shape with the geometry and still function without errors. Pro/M will try to accomplish this by changing as few elements as possible, in the region closest to the geometry that has changed. If we have too many small elements here, then Pro/M may run into difficulty creating a legal mesh. We will worry about these concerns later. For now, we are after some additional speed, so get rid of the existing elements and extra points:

>> *Edit > Delete > Entity > 2D Plates > All > middle click*
>> *Points > All > middle click*

Pro/M will indicate that 6 points (these are highlighted) can't be deleted because the geometry depends on them. Select *OK*.

Translating Geometry

Before we proceed with the optimization, we'll move the interior hole upwards. Select

Edit > Translate > Curves

Click on the circle and then middle click. Translation involves specifying a reference point (that doesn't have to be on the geometry) and then giving the new position of this point. The initial position is called the start point - we will use the center of the circle. Select

Snap(Center)

and click on the circle. An X marks the circle center and its location is given in the message window. Enter the end location using

Snap(Point)

and enter the coordinates of the new center at *50, 40*. The circle moves and the surface is automatically modified for the new geometry as shown in Figure 3. Middle click.

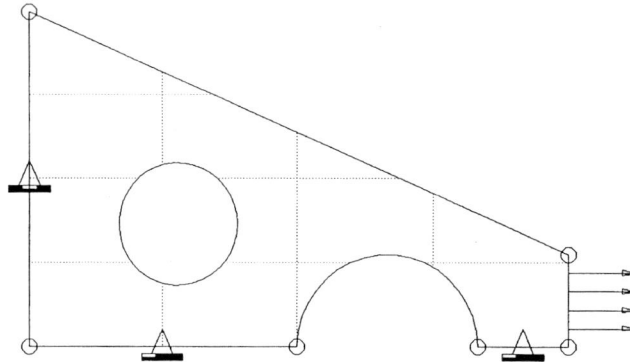

Figure 3 Thin plate after translating hole

Creating the New Mesh

Now we can generate a new mesh with AutoGEM:

> *Model > Elements > AutoGEM*
> *Settings > Define/Review > Use Defaults*

and accept twice. Select

Surface

click on the surface. Middle click. AutoGEM will create 6 tri and 4 quad elements.

Defining the Design Variables

We are going to optimize the geometry of the plate so that the plate has the minimum possible mass without exceeding a specified maximum stress. We will accomplish this by determining the required radii of the two holes. These radii are called the *design variables*, and we set them up in the same way as if we were doing a sensitivity study:

Model > Design Variables > Radius

Click on the interior hole (on the left). Middle click. Give a parameter name *radius1*, and enter the start *10* and end *35* values. Press *Accept* and enter a description like *"radius of interior hole"*. Then again select

Radius

Click on the other circular arc; middle click. Enter a name for the parameter *radius2*, and start and end values of *10* and *35*. Accept the dialog and enter a description *"radius of mid-plane hole"*.

As always when you set up design variables, you should do a shape review to make sure the mesh will survive throughout the range. Select

Shape Review

Check both parameters *radius1* and *radius2*. Set both to 0 and select *Review*. The geometry and mesh should appear as shown in Figure 4 below. Select *Return* and change both parameters to 100% and select *Review* again. The model should appear as shown in Figure 5. Select

Return > Done

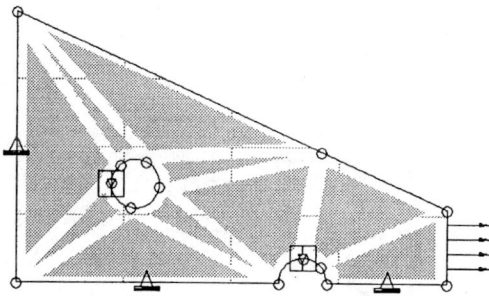

Figure 4 Design variables set to *minimum*

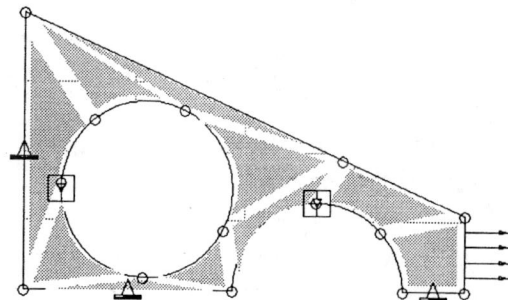

Figure 5 Design variables set to *maximum*

You might like to set one parameter at its minimum value and the other at its maximum value. You might also like to try *Shape Animate* here as well. Check both variables and select *Animate*. Of course, when the optimization occurs, these radii will not change simultaneously as shown in the animation. What we are trying to do is determine if there are any combinations of radius values that might cause the mesh to fail.

Results for the Initial Design

To get a baseline for our optimization, let's check the previous analysis:

Main > Analyses > plate4 > Edit

Note the constraint set **symedge**, load set **endload**, convergence method **5% Multi-pass Adaptive**, and maximum polynomial order **9**.

Run the analysis now to recall the stresses.

Run > Settings

These should be the same as last time.

Start

If you haven't already, your may have to delete previous files. Accept error detection - there should be no errors. The run should converge in 7 passes, with a maximum Von Mises stress of around 28 MPa.   Note that the total mass is 5.55e-05 tonne (55.5 grams).

Defining the Optimization Design Study

Now we can set up the optimization design study. There are four critical elements: the design study type (ie optimization), the optimization goal, the design variables, and design constraints. To define these, select:

Main > Design Study

Enter a study name *plat4opt*, select Type *Optimization*. The layout of the design study definition window will change as shown in Figure 6. Enter a description "plate optimization example #1". The default goal is to *Minimize* the total mass. Other optimization goals are also possible, such as minimizing the deflection or cost (assuming the material property definition contains a cost figure - this might be useful if the model contains more than one

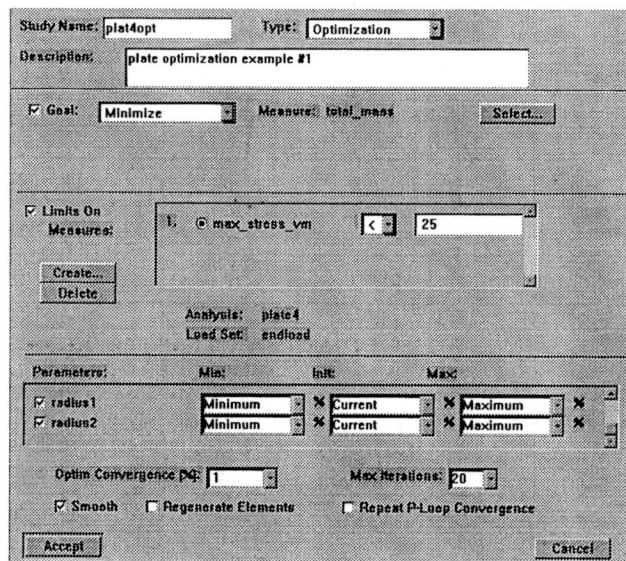

Figure 6 Setting up the optimization design study

material)[1]. We want to set a limit on the maximum Von Mises stress. In the Limits on Measures area select

Create

and in the measures list, select *max_stress_vm*. In the box to the right of the "<" symbol, enter the value *25*. Note that the initial design violates this constraint.

Check both boxes beside the parameters to optimize *radius1* and *radius2*. The three columns of pull-down lists indicate the range of values to search. Leave all these at their indicated default values. Set the **Optim Convergence** to **2%**. This basically means that the optimization iterations will terminate when the goal measure changes by less than 2% between successive iterations. Turn off the check boxes beside *Regenerate Elements* and *Repeat P-loop Convergence*. These functions should not be necessary for this model and we will speed up the computation a bit by turning them off. The first option causes AutoGEM to regenerate the mesh each time a new geometry is created. We have seen that the existing mesh should be able to handle all the variations in geometry in the model. The second option tells Pro/M to repeat the entire multi-pass adaptive analysis with each new run during the iterative solution. By turning this off, we will use whatever element orders are determined during a first analysis for each of the following iterations. As long as the mesh doesn't change drastically, this should be sufficient. *Accept* the design study definition and select *Done* in the Design Studies window.

Running the Optimization Design Study

We are now ready to run the optimization:

Main > Run

Select **plat4opt** (the name of the optimization study). Check the **Settings** - these should all be the same as for the *plate4* multi-pass adaptive analysis. Accept the settings.

Start

and accept error detection. Open the **Summary** window. A lot of information goes scrolling by. When the run is finished you can come back and browse through this output, watching out for warning messages. Meanwhile, while the design study is running (this will take a few minutes), here is a brief explanation about how it optimizes.

According to the documentation, you can select from two optimization algorithms: the sequential quadratic programming (SQP) algorithm and the gradient projection (GDP) algorithm. If the initial design point is feasible (that is, no constraints are violated), GDP operates like a normal steepest descent algorithm until/unless a constraint boundary is met in the search space. Then it

---

[1] Note that cost is based purely on the amount of material (mass) and does not include factors such as manufacturing cost.

moves in a direction tangent to the constraint surface, all the while seeking out the minimum value of the objective function. If the initial design point is infeasible, then an first correction step is taken to reach the constraint set. The GDP has the advantage that it tends to produce a series of intermediate designs that are always feasible, even if it is unable to locate the global optimum design (either due to the objective function or limits set by you). In contrast, the SQP algorithm does not guarantee that intermediate designs are feasible but only that the optimum (if found) is feasible. The advantage of SQP is its generally increased speed over GDP. For further information on these algorithms, and optimization in general, consult the excellent text Introduction to Optimum Design by J.S. Arora (McGraw-Hill, 1989), Chapter 6.

Getting back to our design study now, in the **Summary** window, we can see headers identifying the model, analysis, names of parameters, initial values of parameters (*radius1* = 40%, *radius2* = 80%), initial value of the goal and so on. The iterations then proceed. In the first iteration, the Von Mises stress violates the stress limit. A search is conducted to remove the violation. Pro/M finds a new feasible point where the stress limit is satisfied. It then starts to search along the boundary in the search space, keeping the stress as close as it can to the maximum allowed, and decreasing the mass by changing the hole radii. It will take several iterations to do this. The best design has a value for *radius1* 100% of range, and *radius2* is 68.4% of its range. The value of the goal (total mass) on completion is 4.25e-05 tonne (425 grams), so the reduction in weight is about 23% from the original.

Optimization Results

A number of new result windows are available for optimization. The most interesting of these shows the sequence of geometry changes that were made during the optimization run, and is called the *shape history*.

Results > Create > [shaphist]

Find the output directory *plat4opt*. Enter a window title like "**Shape History**". Select **Quantity(Shape History)**. Leave the check box beside Save Model unchecked for now. Accept this dialog.

We will create a couple more windows to show optimization results. These will show how various measures behaved with each optimization iteration. Select

Copy

and create another window called **vmhist**. **Review** this window definition and change the title to "Von Mises History". Select **Quantity(Measure)** and select **max_stress_vm**. Accept all the other defaults.

Copy the **vmhist** window to another called **mass**. **Review** the definition of this window, changing the title to "Total Mass", and selecting the measure **total_mass**. Accept the other defaults.

Now that all our result windows are defined, let's have a look at them. In the *Show* part of the result window, highlight *shaphist* (only) and click on *Show*. Under the **Show** menu, select

Controls > Step

An sequence of views of the model will then appear, some of which are shown below. Continue pressing Step. Eventually you will get to the end of the sequence (Figure 10) (see the message window) showing the final optimized design. Select *Done* twice.

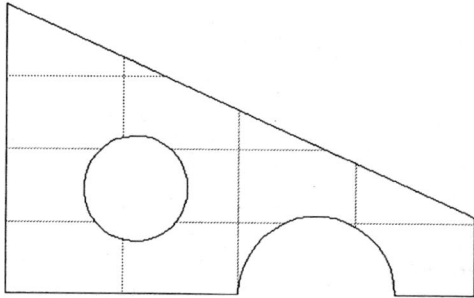

Figure 7 Optimization shape history - initial values

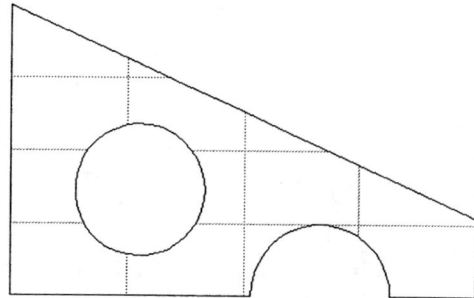

Figure 8 Shape history - intermediate

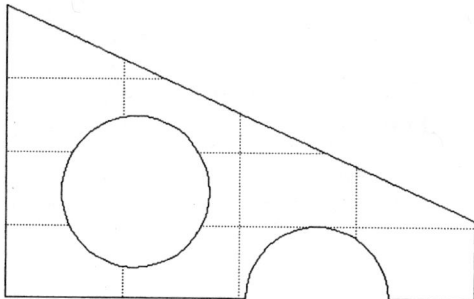

Figure 9 Shape history - intermediate

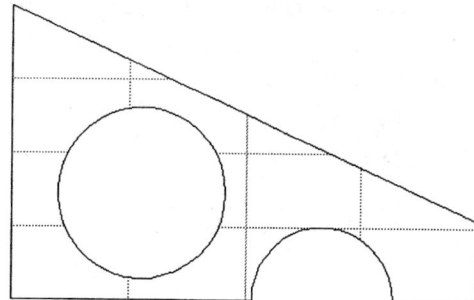

Figure 10 Shape history - final design

Now go back to the result window, turn off **shaphist**, and turn on **mass** and **vmhist** in the Show list box. Select *Show*. This will plot both windows side by side as shown in Figure 11. Observe the behavior of the graphs.

max_stress_vm
Optimize Pass
Load: endload

total_mass
Optimize Pass
Load: endload

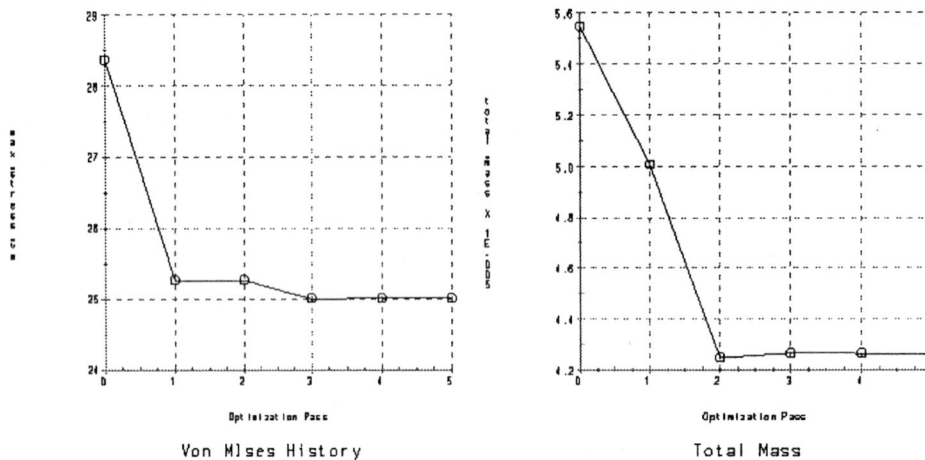

Von Mises History

Total Mass

Figure 11 Optimization measures (Von Mises and total mass)

Note that the initially high value of the Von Mises stress was lowered fairly quickly to a feasible value approaching our desired stress limit. Then, geometric changes were made to reduce the mass while maintaining the maximum stress at this limit (more or less!). When further geometric changes failed to produce further reductions in mass, Pro/M quit searching.

Go back to the definition of the shape history window. *Review* this, check the box beside *Save Model* and click on *Select*. Enter a new name for the optimized plate (note the directory where this is going) **plate4bst**. Display this window again with

Show > Controls > Start

This time, when you press *Done* (twice), a message shows that the final model has been saved in the output directory. You may want to move this file (*plate4bst.mbd*) to another directory at a later time.

Now, we'll have a look at the stresses. Create (or copy) a windows called vm and def to show the Von Mises stress and a deformation animation. See Figures 12 and 13. The maximum Von Mises stress is a little over our required minimum but within the 2% tolerance we accepted for optimization. Note that the stress is now high on both holes in the model, instead of just the central hole in the original design. When displaying the Von Mises fringe plot, if you use

Dynamic Query > Show Model Max

you will see that the maximum stress still occurs on the hole on the right.

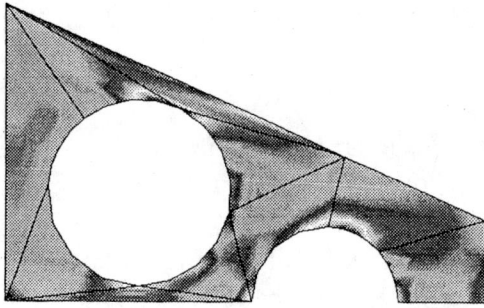

Figure 12 Von Mises stress in optimized model

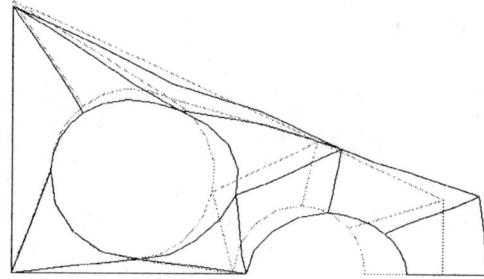

Figure 13 Deformation in optimized model

Get the final model using:

File > Open > plate4bst

The model will be brought in as shown in Figure 14.

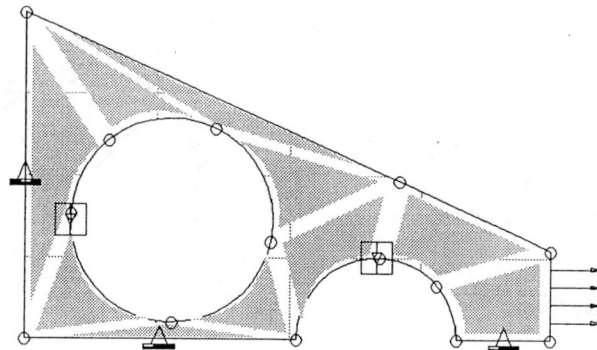

Figure 14 Optimized model

Use *Review > Radius* to find out the numerical values of the radii of the two arcs in the final design.

That completes our first optimization example. It is surprisingly easy, in principle, to do. We will find out that in more complicated problems, some things can go wrong with the simple approach we took here. Fortunately, Pro/M contains ample tools and options to deal with these difficult cases. Before we do any of those, here is a second relatively simple example that will also introduce a new type of 2D model.

Example #2: Heat Exchanger

The Model

In addition to performing another optimization design study, this example will be used to illustrate a number of new capabilities and functions in Pro/M that we haven't used before. These include setting up a model for plane strain analysis, some new geometry commands, using different materials in the same model, applying a temperature load, and using a single design variable to control multiple entities. In order to set up this example, a number of practical (ie. "Real Life") concerns have been neglected[2]. The scenario is the design of a long heat exchanger element that consists of an inner core like a pipe made of magnesium alloy, and an outer jacket with longitudinal fins made of aluminum. The inner pipe is pressurized to 500 psi and the entire model is elevated to a temperature 100° above the reference temperature. The objective is to find the radius at the interface between the inner magnesium core and the outer aluminum jacket, and the radius of the fin cut-outs in the jacket. The design goal is to minimize the mass without exceeding a specified maximum stress. The geometry of the model is shown in Figures 15 and 16.

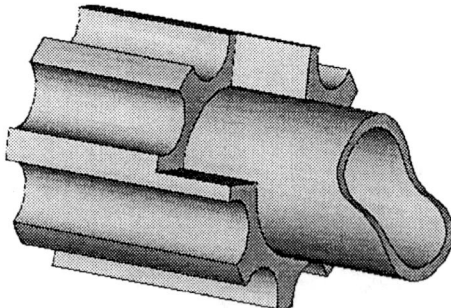

Figure 15 Cutaway shaded view of segment of heat exchanger

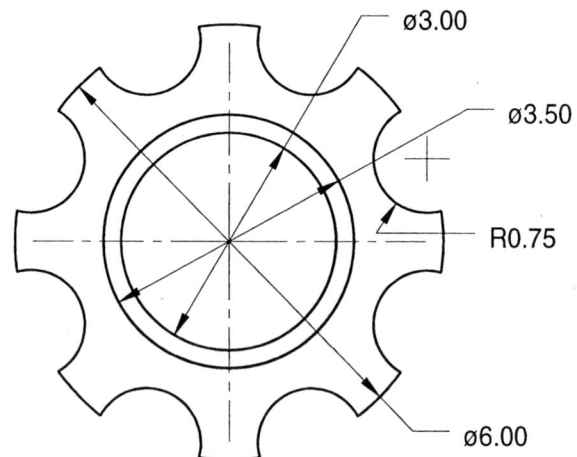

Figure 16 Dimensions of the heat exchanger cross section (inches)

Geometry

Our first task is to create the model geometry. This will be simplified since we can use symmetry about the horizontal and vertical planes in the cross section. We'll set up the Pro/M environment and create some reference construction lines:

> *Display > Master Visibilities > All On | Grid | Accept*
> *Display > Settings > Grid Spacing(0.25) | Accept*
> *Utility > Display Coordinates*

---

[2] In the words of a colleague, this is a solution in search of a problem!

Main > Geometry > Curve
Construction Geom > Horizontal > Snap(Point) > [0 0]
Construction Geom > Vertical > Snap(Point) > [0 0]

Pan and zoom until you have the upper right quadrant out to at least x = 3 and y=3.

Create the three concentric arcs, starting from the inside:

Curve > Arc > Start-Center-End > Snap(Grid)

Pick approximately on the location (*1.5, 0*). You do not have to be precise with this since snap is turned on. Verify your coordinates with the coordinate display. Then pick on the origin (*0, 0*) for the arc center, then at (*0, 1.5*) for the end of the arc. Create the next two arcs using the same procedure, with radii of *1.75* and *3.0*. Then middle click.

We will create the fin cutouts using a circle, and then trimming it back to the outer arc (another way of doing this is illustrated in the next lesson).

Curve > Circle > Radius-Center > [0.75] > Snap(Point)

Pick on the existing arc end point at (*3, 0*). Middle click twice.

Using *Rotate* (no copy)

Now we want to rotate the circle 22.5 degrees.

Edit > Rotate > Curves

Click on the circle and middle click. Read the prompt. Select *Snap(Grid)* and click on the origin. This defines the start point of the rotation axis. Middle click to accept the default axis, which is perpendicular to the screen in this case, and enter the angle of rotation *22.5*. The model should now look like Figure 17. Middle click.

Trimming Curves

Now we want to trim the circle back to the outside radius. The operation of the trim command when applied to a closed curve is to remove the shortest length of the curve between the two trim points. In this case, that would be inside the large outer arc, which we don't want. So, we will have to trim the circle in two steps: first to break

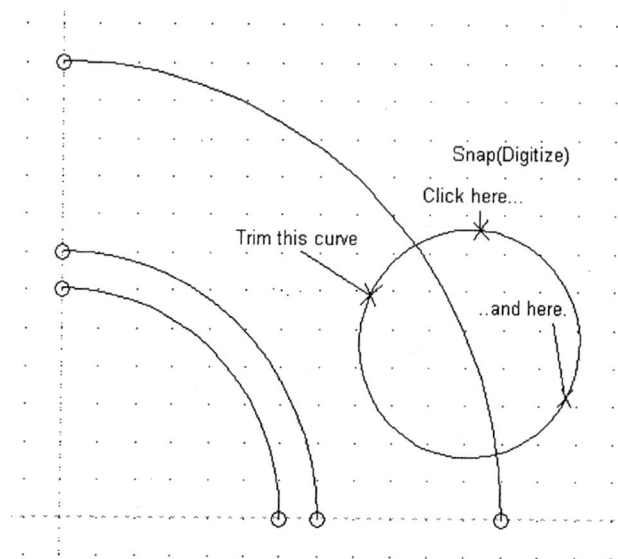

Figure 17 Creating the geometry - arcs and fin circle

it into an open arc, and then to trim the arc back to the outer curve of the heat exchanger. Select

Edit > Geometry > Trim Curve

Pick on the circle. We need to create two arbitrary trim points on the outside portion of the circle. Select *Split Snap(Digitize)* and click a point as shown in Figure 17. Repeat for the second trim point shown in the figure. This will remove a portion of the circle as shown in Figure 18.

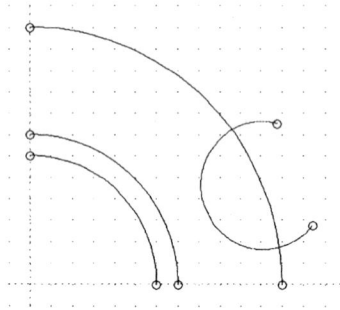

Figure 18 Circle trimmed

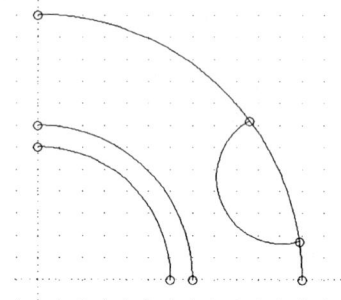

Figure 19 Arc trimmed to outer arc

Now click on the trimmed circle. The first trim point is a free end so select this using *Snap(Point).* The second trim point is at the intersection with the outer arc, so select *Snap(Intersect),* read the prompt, and click on the outside arc. Do the same for the other end of the arc to be trimmed. The result should look like Figure 19.

We can remove part of the outer arc. We are still in trim curves mode, so just click on the arc. Select *Snap(Point)* and click on the two points at the ends of the small arc. Middle click. See Figure 20.

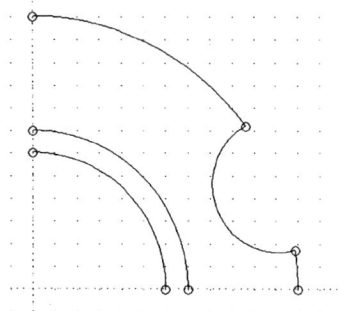

Figure 20 Outer arc trimmed

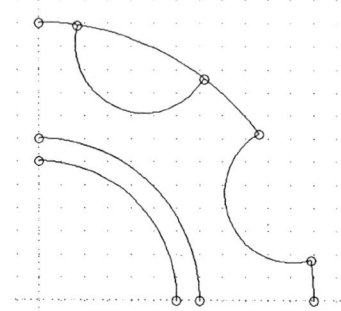

Figure 21 Rotated copy of fin arc

Using *Rotate* (with copy)

We can now do a rotated copy of the small arc.

Edit > Rotate > check the Copy box > Curves

pick on the cut arc, middle click. Set up the rotation axis start point using *Snap(Center)* and click on any of the concentric arcs. The rotation axis is normal to our drawing plane so (read the prompt) middle click and enter degrees of copy as *45*, number of copies is *1*. Middle click. A second arc will appear as shown in Figure 21.

Trim away the outer arc using the procedures described above:

Edit > Geometry > Trim Curve

click on the outer arc, select *Snap(Point)* and click on the ends of the copied arc. Middle click.

Close the geometry with lines on the bottom and vertical sides:

Geometry > Curve > Line
Two Points > Snap(Point)

IMPORTANT: make *two* line segments on each of the bottom and left vertical edges, since we need a node at the interior radius. Our edge geometry is now complete and should look like Figure 22. Middle click.

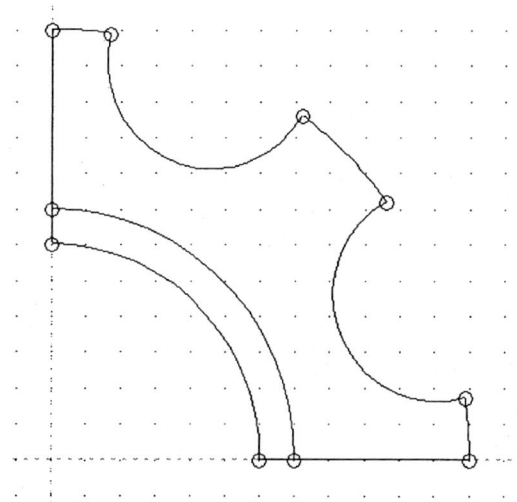

Figure 22 Geometry completed

Creating Surfaces

We will create two surfaces using the curves defined above. Each surface will have different material properties assigned to it. During the optimization, as the geometry changes, the new mesh elements will get their material properties from the associated surfaces. First, we'll do the inner surface, corresponding to the magnesium pipe.

Geometry > Surface > Planar

Click on the innermost arc. It highlights in red, and the edge of the surface follows the edge clockwise around the loop until it reaches a junction with another edge. See Figure 23.

At the junction, possible continuation edges are shown in magenta. Read the prompt. We have to tell Pro/M which direction to continue the loop. Click on the outer arc of the pipe. Another junction occurs at the bottom edge. Click on the

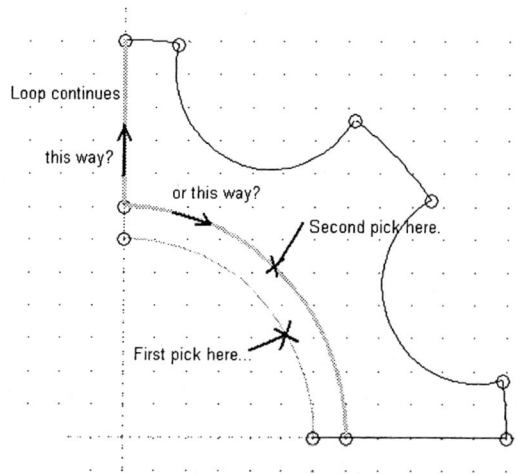

Figure 23 Creating the inner surface

short edge to close the surface. There are no interior edges for this surface, so middle click. The surface is now defined as shown in Figure 24.

The second surface is created in the same way. Pick on one of the outside edges. Where a junction is encountered, click the direction you want the loop to go. Proceed until the surface loop is defined, then middle click. This completes the surface definitions, and the model should appear as shown in Figure 25. Middle click to exit the command.

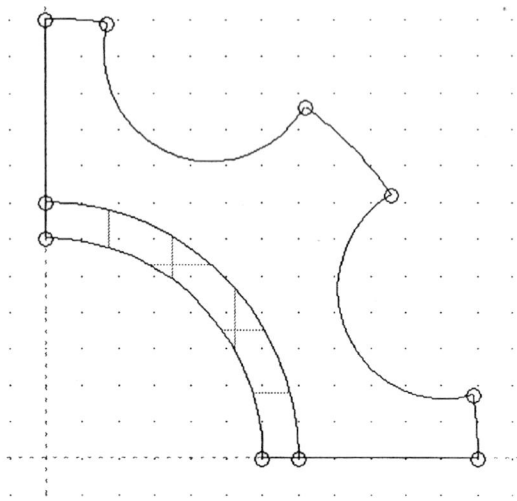

Figure 24 Inner surface created

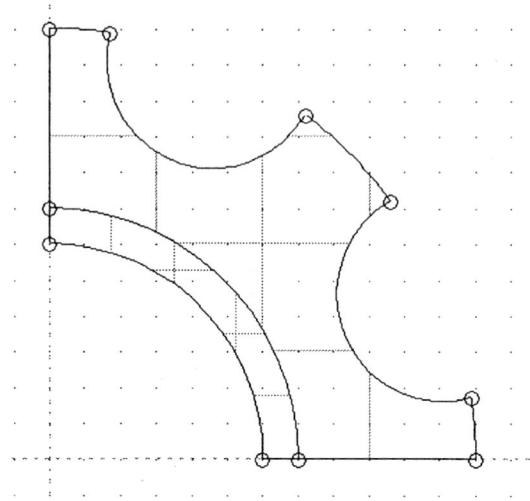

Figure 25 Outer surface created

Model Properties and Constraints

We can now set up all the remaining parameters for the model. We will use a *plane strain* analysis, which is common for long slender models that are transversely loaded. This model assumes that the strain in the direction normal to the section we have defined is zero. This might occur, for example, if the two ends of the heat exchanger were rigidly clamped. Set up the model as follows:

> *Main > Model > Plane Strain | Accept*
> *Properties > Material*

Select the material **MG_IPS** and move it to the right pane. Also select **AL2014_IPS**. Now highlight MG_IPS in the model list and select

> *Assign > Surface*

Pick on the hatch for the inner surface. Depending on your zoom extents, you may get a menu for selecting from two possible choices at the pick point, make sure the one you want is highlighted and Accept. Now highlight AL2014 in the model list and select

> *Surface*

and click on the other surface. Middle click and *Done*.

Since this is a plane strain model, there is no shell thickness, so we are finished with properties. Let's move on to the constraints:

Model > Constraints > Curve

Create a *New* constraint set **symedges**. The first constraint, call it **xedges**, is the two lower edges of the model. Set the constraints to X translation **Free** and the others **Fixed**. Accept with *OK*. Select

Curve

Name the next constraint **yedges** (still in constraint set **symedges**). Pick on the two vertical edges. Set the Y translation **Free**, and others **Fixed**. The constraints should show up as in Figure 26.

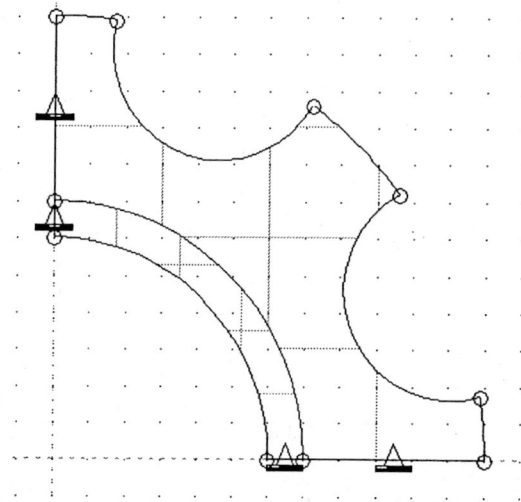

Figure 26 Symmetry constraints specified

To apply the pressure load we have to generate the elements (recall that pressure on 2D models can only be applied to element edges).

Main > Model > Elements > AutoGEM > Settings > Define/Review

The maximum allowable edge turn default is 95 degrees. This is the maximum length around an arc that can form a single element edge. If we used this default, AutoGEM would create a single element on the inner surface - not what we need as we'll see in a moment. Enter a new value of **22.5** here, so that we will have several elements in the quadrant of the inner pipe. *Accept* the AutoGEM settings then select.

Surface

Click on the inner surface. Middle click. See Figure 27.

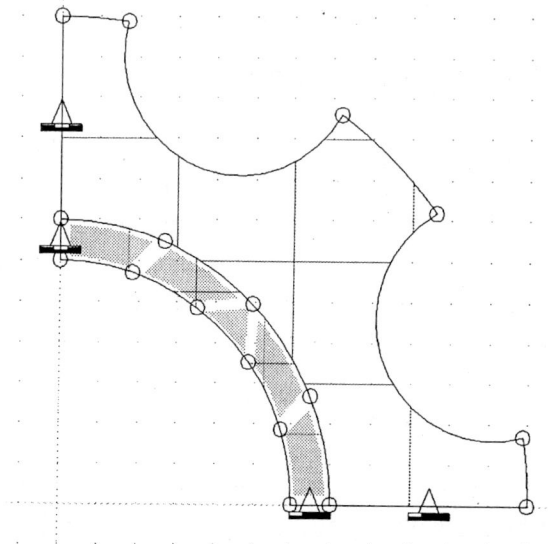

Figure 27 Elements created on inner surface using AutoGEM

Now create elements on the outer surface:

Surface

pick on outer surface. The mesh will appear
something like Figure 28.

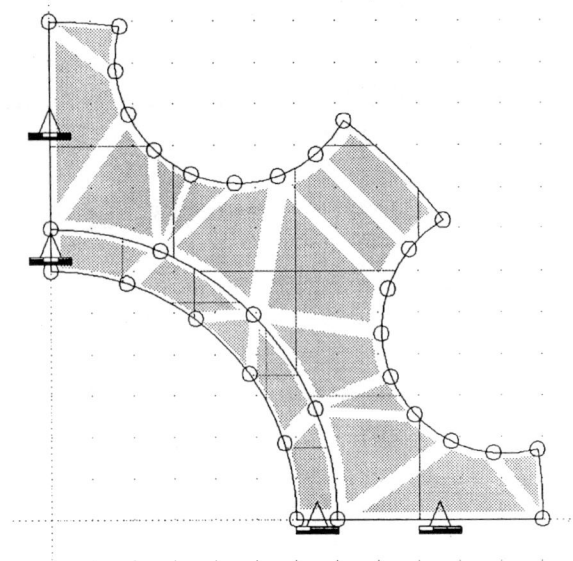

Figure 28 Elements created on outer surface
using AutoGEM

Now we can apply the pressure load:

Model > Loads > Pressure > Edge

Create a *New* load set **presload** and name the load **pres500**. Select the button under Edges and
click on the inner edges of the inner elements. Middle click. Enter a magnitude of *500*. *Accept*.
You may want to adjust the arrows:

Display > Settings

Using the Loads pulldown list select "*Head Touching*". Also turn on Display Load Magnitudes
and set the precision to *1*.

Applying a Temperature Load

For something a little different, we will apply a temperature load to the model. In Pro/M
Structure, all we can do is apply a uniform ("global") temperature to the entire model. Using
Pro/M Thermal, we could compute a temperature distribution through the model subject to
specified thermal constraints, then apply this temperature distribution to the model in Structure.
By itself, in Structure, the temperature we specify is the difference in global temperature from a
reference temperature (nominally 0), for which we assume the model is unstressed[3].

Loads > Temperature > Global

The temperature load will be contained in the same load set as the pressure, *presload*. (We will
introduce the use of multiple load sets a bit later in the tutorial.) Call the load **temp100** and enter

---

[3] It is also possible to define material properties that are functions of temperature.

a model temperature of **100**. This sets the change in temperature from the rest state (reference temperature of 0). A small symbol appears on the model to indicate that a temperature load has been applied, see Figure 29. The model is now complete.

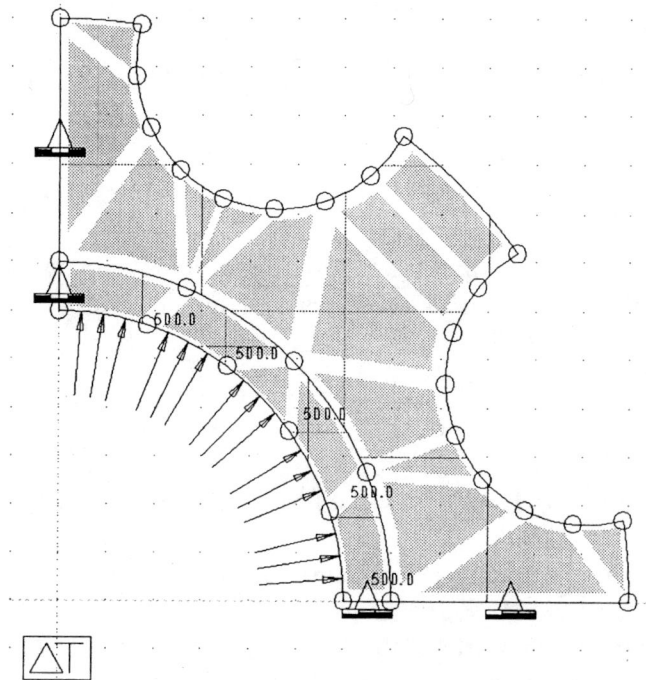

Figure 29 Pressure and temperature loads applied

Defining the Analysis

Quick Check

As usual, we always do a Quick Check to make sure that there are no modeling errors.

> ### *Main > Analyses*

Create a new static analysis **heatx**, check that **symedges**, and **preload** are selected, and set the convergence method to *QuickCheck*.

> ### *Run > Settings*

Select the directories for output and temporary files. Accept.

> ### *Start*

Accept error detection as usual. If you haven't saved it already, you will be asked to provide a model name - enter *"heatex"*. The analysis design study starts. Open the *Summary* window and look for other error/warning messages. Note that the total mass is 8.89e-4 lbf-s^2/in per inch of length along the exchanger (about 0.344 lb/in by weight) for the quarter model.

Multi-Pass Adaptive

Assuming there were no errors in the QuickCheck, go back to

Analyses > heatx > Edit

Change to a *Multi-Pass Adaptive* analysis with *5%* on *Lcl Disp & Lcl SE & Global RMS Stress* with a polynomial order maximum *9*.

Run > Start

Delete the previous files. Open the *Summary* window. The analysis run converges in 3 passes with an edge order 3. The maximum Von Mises stress is about 14,700 psi.

Initial Design Results

We'll create the usual two windows to show the Von Mises stress and deformation:

Main > Results > Create > [vmfringe]

Get the output directory *heatx*. Enter a title of the new window, and set up the definition to show a fringe plot of the Von Mises stress. Accept. Then *Copy* the window definition to a second window called *deform*. Review the new window in order to change the title, quantity **Displacement**, and type **Animation**. Accept and *Show* both windows.

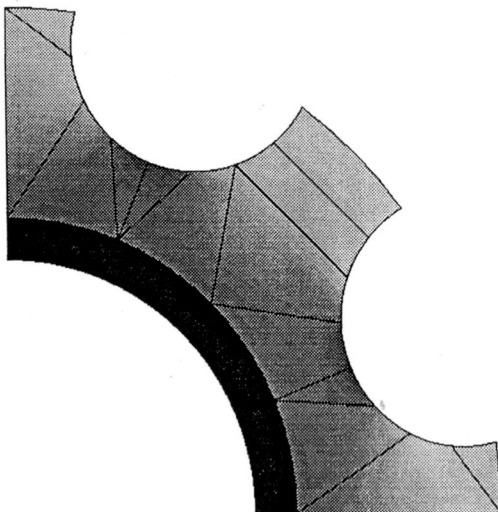

Von Mises Stress

Figure 30 Von Mises stress in original model

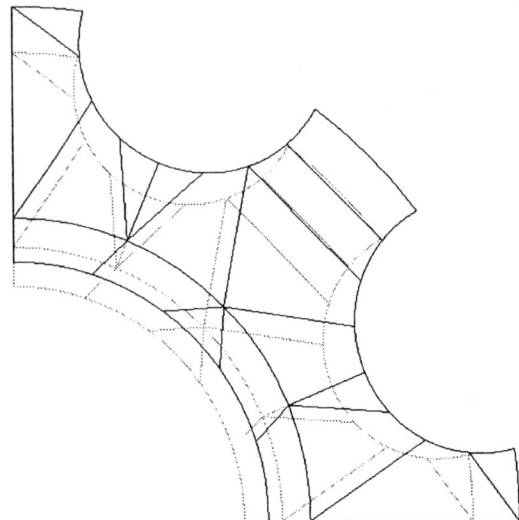

Deformation

Figure 31 Deformation of original model

The stress in the inner magnesium appears to be very uniform (all the same fringe color). Use Dynamic Query to examine the value and variation. The coefficient of thermal expansion of magnesium is greater than aluminum, so much of the load felt by the aluminum is coming from the expanding core of magnesium[4]. In the deformation window, check that the symmetric constraints are implemented properly (do an animation).

Before we proceed with the optimization, change the convergence on the multi-pass adaptive analysis to 1%.

Setting up the Design Variables

Now set up the design variables:

Model > Design Variables > Radius

Click on middle arc between the magnesium and the aluminum, then middle click. Enter a parameter name *"radius1"* and set start and end values to *1.55* and *1.85*. Accept and enter a description. Do a *Shape Review* or *Animate* to see the effects on the mesh. No problem here. Select

Radius

and click on *both* the fin cut arcs, then middle click. Name the parameter *radius2*, and set start and end values of *0.4* and *1.0*. Enter a description and accept. The design variable symbol will show up on only one of the arcs (see Figure 32).

Do a shape review or animation with both *radius1* and *radius2* turned on. See Figures 33 and 34. There doesn't seem to be any problem with the mesh throughout the changes in geometry. Notice that some of the mesh elements get very distorted during the geometry changes. This variation could not be accomplished with h-elements without remeshing completely. It would also be a cause for concern here if our basic analysis was not converging so quickly (at such a low edge order).

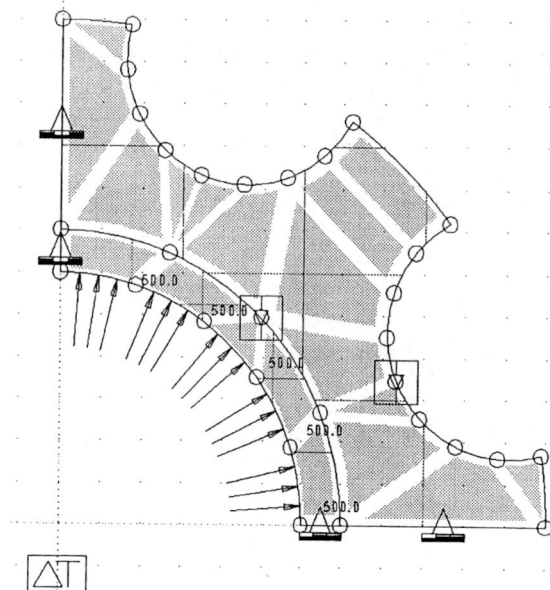

Figure 32 Design variables defined

---

[4] You can check this out later by coming back and changing the temperature to a smaller value, or deleting it entirely.

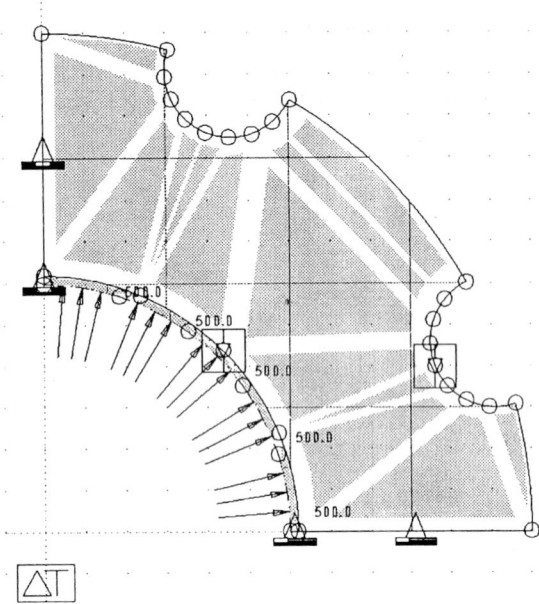

Figure 33 Design variables set to minimum

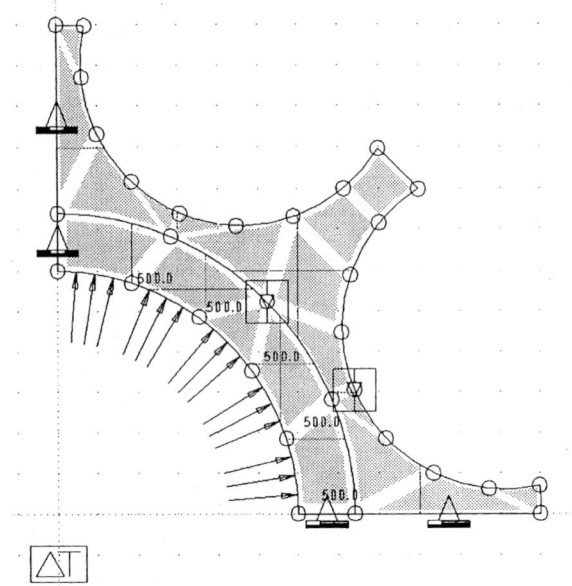

Figure 34 Design variables set to maximum

Setting up the Optimization Design Study

We now set up the definition of the optimization design study:

Main > Design Study

Enter name **heatxopt,** a description, and select Type *Optimization.*

Set the goal to minimize total mass. Set a limit on Von Mises stress using

Create

select *max_stress_vm* and enter a limit **14,000** (note that the initial design violates this).

Select parameters to optimize as **radius1** and **radius2**. Set the search limits from minimum to maximum. Set an optimization convergence of 1%. You can keep both *Regenerate Elements* and *Repeat P-loop Convergence* turned on. It may be that the distortion of the elements may cause some convergence problems. You can come back later with this turned off to see if there is any effect on the results, other than an expected reduction in execution time. The completed definition window is shown in Figure 35.

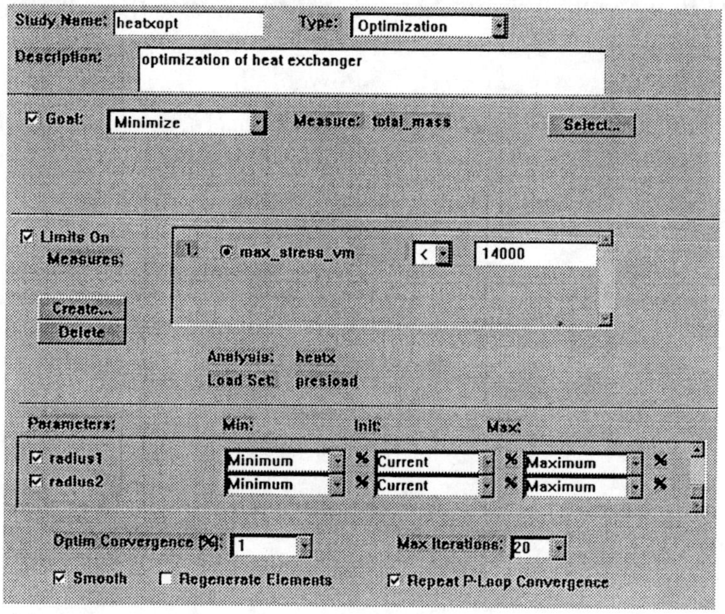

Figure 35 Setting design study options for the heat exchanger

We can now run the optimization.

Run > Settings

These should be the same as before.

Start

You will get a warning about elements that cannot be deleted (on the inner surface) if the mesh must be regenerated. Why is this? We can proceed with **Confirm**. Accept error detection. Open the summary window. The initial value of *radius1* is 66.7% and of *radius2* is 58.3%. The initial mass is 8.89e-4 lbf-s^2/in/in. Note the default optimization convergence tolerance is 1%. The first analysis discovers the stress violation, finds feasible values, and proceeds to do several iterations. The run converges at *radius1* 6% and *radius2* 73%, with a goal (mass) of 8.30e-4 lbf-s^2/in/in. The total mass has been reduced by 18% from the initial design.

Optimization Results

Set up a result window to show the shape history:

Results > Create > [shaphist]

Get the directory **heatxopt** that contains optimization results. Enter a title "*Shape History*". Select **Quantity(Shape History)**, check **Save Model**, and select a name for the final model **heatxbst**.

Copy window **shaphist** to new windows **vmhist** and **mass**. Review the definitions of those two windows to show quantity *Measure* and select *max_stress_vm* and *total_mass*. These will be plotted against optimization pass. Also copy the *vmhist* window to **vmbst** and change the window definition to show *Quantity(Stress)*, title *"Von Mises Stress (optimum)"* and set up a fringe plot. Observe that the final results for the optimum design are immediately available - we didn't have to save and reload the final design and perform an analysis on it.

Show the shape history result window. Step through the history, or start the animation. Some of the intermediate model geometry is shown in the figures below.

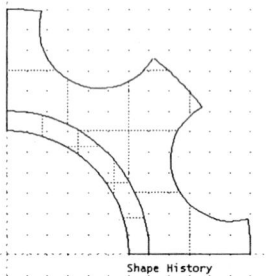

Figure 36 Shape history - original model

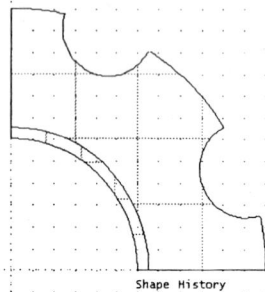

Figure 37 Shape history - iteration #1

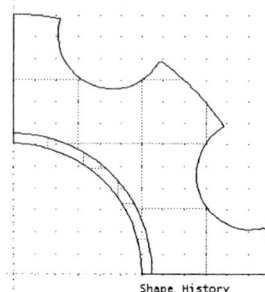

Figure 38 Shape history - intermediate

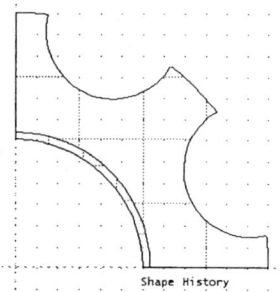

Figure 39 Shape history - final optimized geometry

The final geometry is shown in Figures 40 and 41.

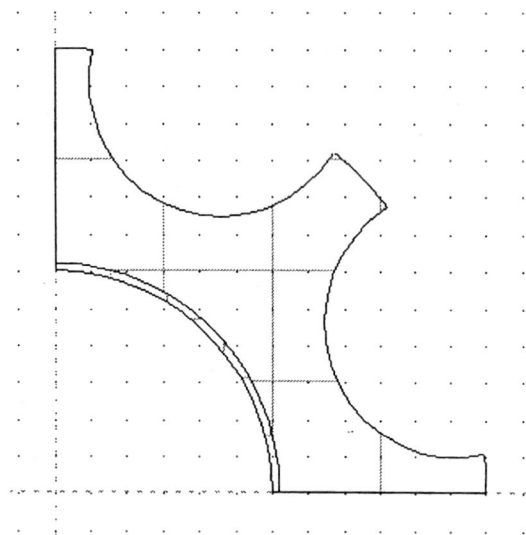

Figure 40 Final optimized geometry

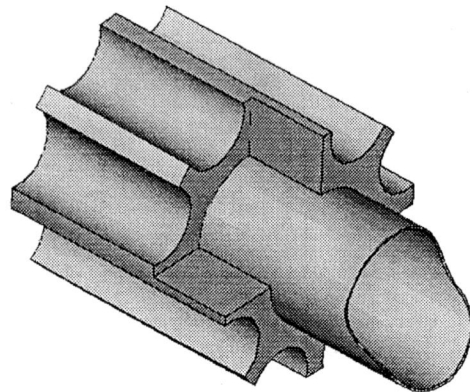

Figure 41 Image of the optimized geometry (cutaway view)

Now select and show the windows **vmhist** and **mass**. See Figure 42. Note that there may be something peculiar about the mass history graph. The final mass in the Summary window may not agree with the value shown on the graph.

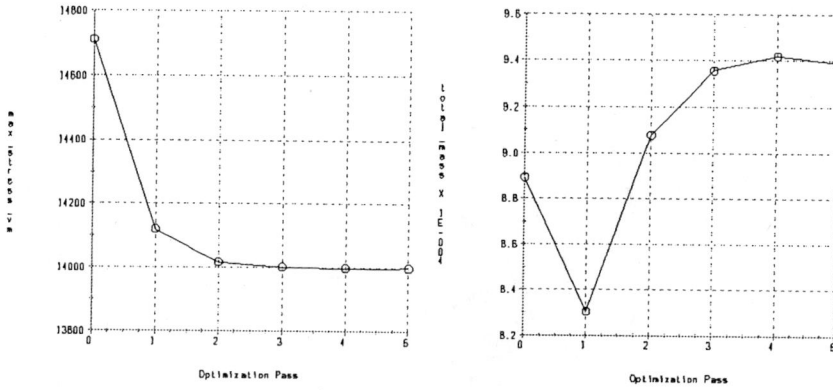

Figure 42 History of measures (Von Mises and mass) during optimization

Finally, select and show the Von Mises stress fringe plot **vmbst**. To see the variation in the stress a little better, edit the legend for the fringe colors so that the maximum value is 14,000 and the minimum value is 13,000.

Von Mises Stress (optimum)

Figure 43 Von Mises stress in optimized model (modified fringe legend)

For interest sake, repeat the optimization with a somewhat higher value for the maximum Von Mises stress, say 16,000 psi. With a higher allowed stress, you might expect Pro/M to reduce the amount of aluminum and increase the amount of magnesium (which is lighter) in the model. The result of this optimization is shown in Figure 44. As expected, the inner core of magnesium is considerably thicker than before:

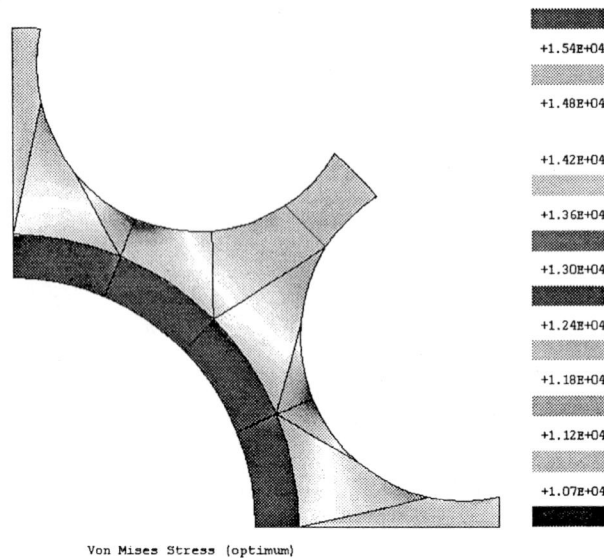

Von Mises Stress (optimum)

Figure 44 Model optimized for maximum Von Mises stress = 16,000 psi

Summary

This completes our introductory look at optimization using Pro/M Structure. As you have seen, it is quite easy to set up, although you do have to have a good idea of your search limits prior to running the program. If your search limits are too wide, you can expect to have problems with the mesh. Pro/M does give you the option of completely regenerating the mesh during the optimization (but remember that if any elements have loads or constraints attached, they will not be deleted during remeshing). You should remember that if remeshing is performed, Pro/M will use the current settings in AutoGEM, so these need to be set up first. You therefore need a pretty good understanding of what the AutoGEM options will do. You also need to have a good idea of the effects of mesh regeneration and convergence behavior.

In the next chapter, we will finally get around to looking at some simple three dimensional models. We will start in that chapter using simple plate and shell elements in 3D, introducing a number of new geometry and view commands as we go.

Questions for Review

1.   How can you find out the following information about a model: radius of an arc, length of a line segment, area of a surface, distance between two points, material assigned to an

element, magnitude and type of a load, constraint details.

2. When you specify a translation, does the reference point have to be part of the entity being translated? What other information is required?

3. What information is required to rotate an entity?

4. How could you make a circular (polar) array of circles, say 6 circles equally spaced?

5. What options are available in the *Snap* menu?

6. When you delete all the elements in a model, what is "left behind"?

7. What should you always do after creating one or more design variables?

8. How do you convert from Pro/M "mass" units into more familiar engineering units like lb or kg?

9. What is the purpose of the *Regenerate Elements* option in optimization? When would you want to use this option?

10. What is the purpose of the *Repeat P-loop Convergence* option in optimization? When would you want to use this option?

11. What search algorithm does Pro/M use in optimization?

12. What is the *shape history*, and how do you obtain it?

13. How can you plot the variation in a measure during the optimization?

14. How do you save the final optimized design?

15. Is it possible to create overlapping surfaces? How does Pro/M respond if you try to do this?

16. For what conditions (what type of model) should "plane strain" be specified/used?

17. In the second example, why did we create 4 elements on the interior surface? What happens if we use the AutoGEM defaults? (Try doing that and then creating the elements on the outer surface.)

18. How can you find out the radius of an arc or circle?

19. How can you find out the material assigned to an element? Does this depend on how the property was assigned?

20. What is meant by an *association*?

21. What information is required to translate an entity?

22. What is the difference between **Shape Review** and **Shape Animate**? What are these used for?

23. What information is required to set up an optimization design study?

24. What do the options *Regenerate Elements* and *Repeat P-loop Convergence* in an optimization design study?

25. How can you save the final optimized model?

26. How do you create geometry by snapping to the grid points, that is, how do you turn on the snap function?

27. What is special about the **Trim** command when used with closed curves?

28. What is the difference between the commands for Rotate and Translate with and without copying the entity to the new location?

29. Can multiple copies be made at the same time?

30. How would you create a polar array of circles, for example, bolt holes in a flange?

31. When creating a surface from edge geometry, what is the significance of the magenta edges?

32. In a plane strain model, why is it necessary to create the elements before a pressure load can be applied?

Exercises

1.   Repeat the optimization of the heat exchanger, using the default settings for AutoGEM. Delete the existing elements and mesh both surfaces at the same time. You will have to re-apply the pressure load. Review the optimization design study and turn Regenerate Elements off, but leave Repeat P-loop Convergence on. What are the results (total mass, radius1, radius2, maximum stress)? Comments?

2.   Set up an optimization for the centrifuge model of Chapter 5. The objective is to find the minimum mass without exceeding a stress of 20.0 MPa. The design variables are the thickness of the shells (*thick5* and *thick8*) and the location of the inner vertical support. How much was the mass reduction from the initial design? Show this in a graph.

3.   Continue the optimization of the previous question adding the following factors: The exterior of the centrifuge is an evacuated chamber (to reduce air friction) while the inside of the centrifuge is atmospheric pressure (101 kPa) as shown in the figure below. In addition, we cannot allow the maximum horizontal or vertical deflection anywhere to exceed 0.015 mm. Find the thickness of the shells and the location of the vertical support that will result in the minimum inertia about the Y-axis. For the optimized design, which constraints are active?

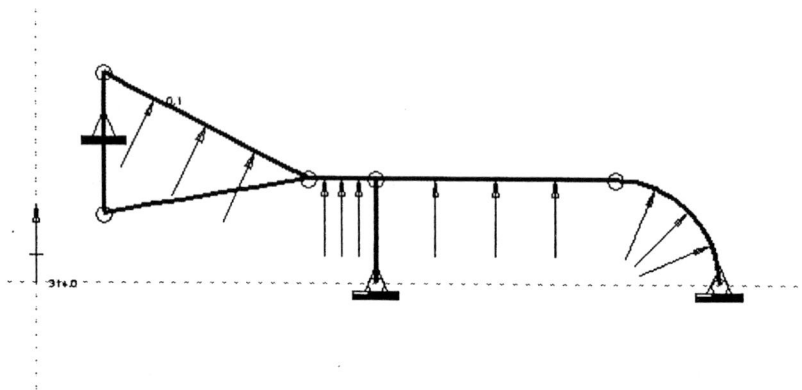

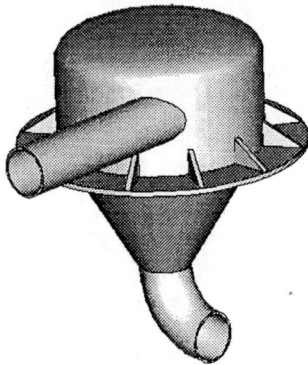

Synopsis:

Creating shell models in 3D; controlling the 3D view; a cantilevered C-channel beam; geometry commands for creating and manipulating surfaces in 3D; extruding and revolving curves to create elements

Overview of this Lesson

In this lesson we will produce our first three dimensional models, starting with a very simple model (a cantilever beam), using shell elements. This will serve to introduce the viewing controls available for 3D models. We will also use a new method to create surfaces and shell elements by extruding a curve. We will experiment a bit with different ways to create the shell elements, and see the rationale why this might be necessary. The second 3D model (shown above) is considerably more complex and will also be composed of shell elements created automatically using AutoGEM, but will require a number of new geometry creation tools that we haven't seen before.

Example #1 - Cantilever Beam

The problem is to compute the maximum bending stress and deflection at the tip of a simple cantilever beam, shown in Figure 1, subjected to a vertical load[1]. The steel beam is a standard 6" channel section. The web thickness is 0.2" and the flange thickness[2] is 0.3125". The beam is 36

---

[1] This problem was suggested by Charles Knight's book <u>The Finite Element Method in Mechanical Design</u>, PWS-Kent, pp. 221-224.

[2] Note that in a real channel section, the flange thickness varies transversely - see a structures or mechanical design reference book - and inside edges where the flange meets the web are filleted. We are assuming a constant thickness and sharp corners here.

inches long and loaded with a uniform vertical load of 2400 lb across the upper flange at the tip.

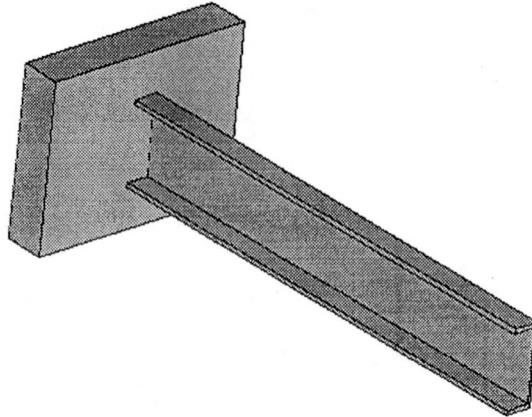

Figure 1 The cantilevered channel section beam

Start up MECHANICA or if it is already open, select

> *File > New*

The Model

Setting Up the Cross Section

We'll start by setting up the display options and creating a couple of reference lines:

> *Display > Master Visibilities > All On > Accept*
> *Main > Geometry > Curve*
> *Construction Geom > Horizontal > Snap(Point) > [0 0]*
> *Construction Geom > Vertical > Snap(Point) > [0 0]*

Now create a curve in the XY plane that defines the C-shaped cross section. This is the default *working plane* when you are in 3D. Other working planes can be selected (YZ, and XZ).

> *Curve > Line > Point Chain > Snap(Point)*

Enter the coordinate pairs (without the parantheses) of the points (see Figure 2): *(0, 0)*, *(1.92, 0)*, *(1.92, 6)*, *(0, 6)*. Note that we don't need to give a Z value - if omitted, it is assumed to be zero. Hit enter twice when completed. Some of the lines are probably off your screen, so select

> *View > Fit > Done*

and you should see the curve shown in Figure 2 (coordinates have been added for reference).

Figure with coordinate points:

(0, 6.0)   (1.92, 6.0)

(0, 0)   (1.92, 0)

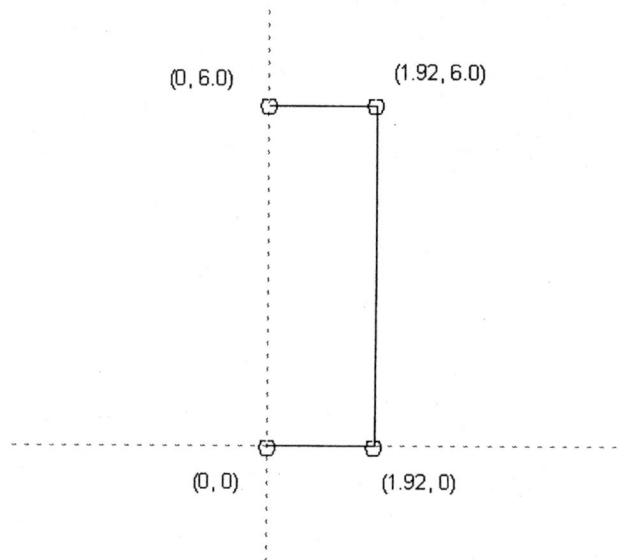

Figure 2 Cross section of beam

Extruding a Surface

We will create surfaces by extruding the C-shaped section along the Z-axis for a distance of 36 inches.

Geometry > Surface > Extruded > All

Middle click and read the prompt in the message window. To define the extrusion, we give a translation vector start and end point. With *Snap(Point)* selected, enter the coordinates of the start point as (*0, 0*) and the end point as (*0, 0, 36*). Accept the defaults for scale factor *<1>*, twist *<0>*, and number of copies *<1>* and press enter one last time. The 3D surfaces have now been created, but because of our view direction, we don't see them yet. Let's explore the tools for controlling our view direction.

Dynamic View Controls in 3D

There are three methods for you to change your point of view of the model. The first of these (the easiest) will be familiar to users of Pro/ENGINEER. The other two methods are unique to MECHANICA. Each method has advantages and disadvantages, and you should become familiar with all three.

Using CTRL + Mouse Buttons

These are the familiar view controls as used in Pro/ENGINEER. While holding down the Ctrl key on the keyboard, each of the three mouse buttons has a special function as follows:

CTRL-middle	Rotate
CTRL-right	Translate

CTRL-left   Zoom/Scale

Try these out now and see if you can produce the image shown in Figure 3. Depending on your graphics card, some of the edges might be clipped. To see the entire model, select *View > Fit | Done*.

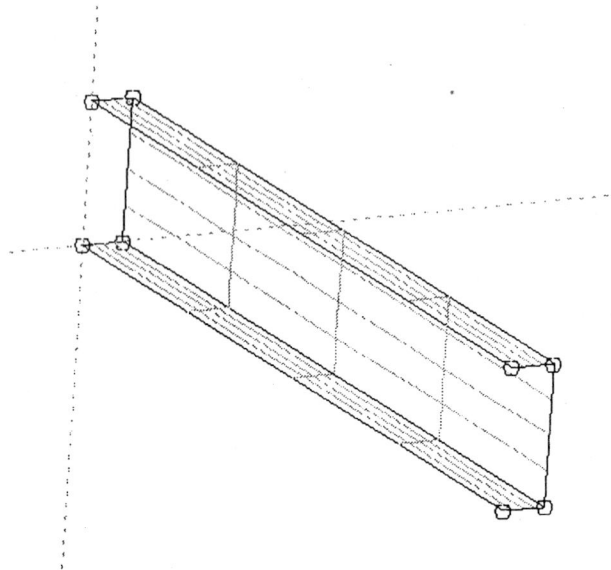

Figure 3 Surfaces created by extruding the cross section

One of the problems with using the dynamic spin control (CTRL-middle) is that, when you are deep within a MECHANICA menu (for example, doing an entity selection, the middle mouse button is interpreted as the Enter key. This can inadvertently close the command or back you out of the menu. The solution to this is to use one of the next two methods.

Using Function Keys

The same view controls are available using the function keys. For these, press the function key once to put you in dynamic view control mode. Pressing the left mouse button and dragging will accomplish the control. You can press and release the left button as often as you wish while staying in the same mode. Pressing any other button will exit the mode.

F2   Rotate
F3   Translate
F4   Zoom/Scale

Using the VIEW menu

We have seen the *View* menu before; for reference it is shown again in Figure 4. The buttons down the left side allow you to go immediately to previously defined views (top, front, right,

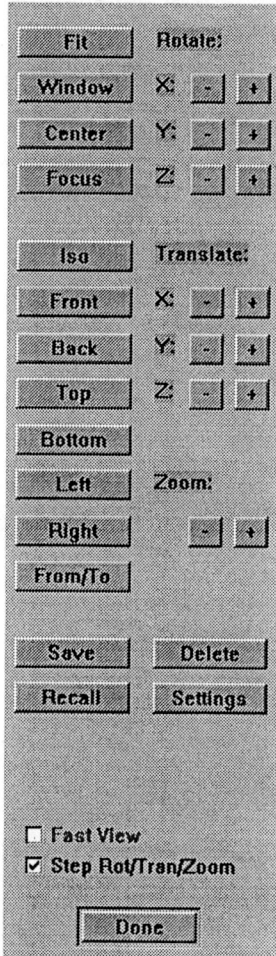

Figure 4 The *View* menu

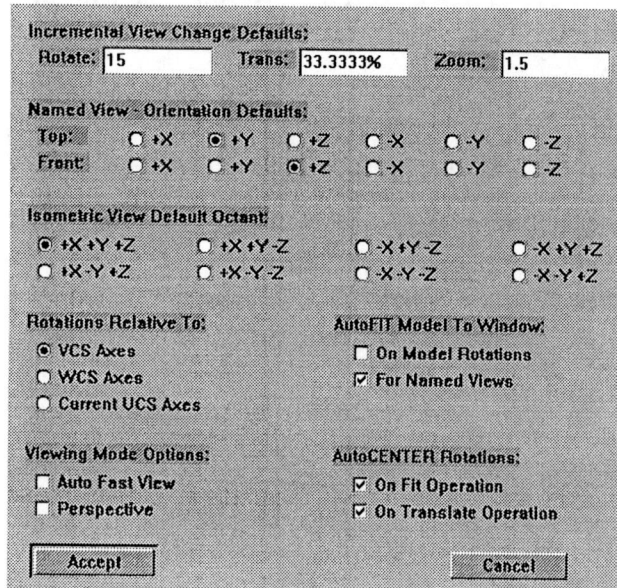

Figure 5 *Settings* for the *VIEW* menu

isometric, and so on). The buttons on the right allow you to rotate and translate relative to any of the X, Y, or Z axes of either the screen (the View Coordinate System, VCS) or the model (World Coordinate System, WCS). These buttons, labeled +/-, will modify the view incrementally with each press. The current increment size and other options can be modified by pressing the *Settings* button, which brings up the window shown in Figure 5. The increments are specified in the boxes at the top. The orientation of the named views is selected immediately below. Selection of the rotation axes (VCS or WCS) is on the left. Let's experiment with these: select *WCS Axes*, return to the view menu, select *Center > Snap(Point)* and click on the point at the origin (where the reference lines cross). Now use the +/- buttons in the **View** menu. This may be a useful way to get to a specific desired orientation more precisely than using the mouse functions described above.

Go back into the *Settings* window and turn on *Perspective*. Try to obtain the image shown in Figure 6 at the right. This may take some experimentation using the *Fit* and *+/-* translation and rotation commands. When you are finished, return the settings to the VCS axes and turn perspective off.

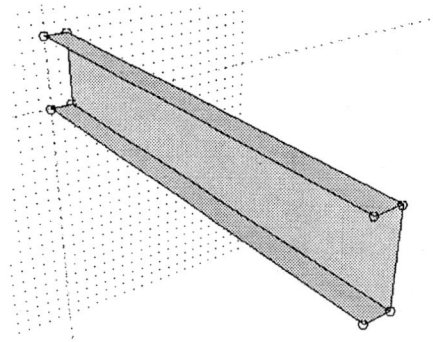

Model A

Figure 6 Perspective view of model

We are now going to look at a couple of variations for setting up this model. We will first try to create the model using the basic procedures we have used before, that is, creating elements on surfaces using AutoGEM. We will try a couple of variations of this, neither of which will be particularly effective in this case. This will motivate us to use a completely new method to create elements in the second version of the model.

To start, we need to define the model type (this is actually the default):

Main > Model > 3D

Creating Elements using AutoGEM

Carry out the usual procedure to create elements from a surface:

Elements > AutoGEM > Surface > All

and middle click. The default AutoGEM settings will create 3 quad elements as shown in Figure 7. The shell elements are shaded in green if you use

Display > Settings > Display Type(Flat Shade) | Shade(Elements) | Accept

Note that the maximum aspect ratio of the elements (on the flanges) is 18.8.

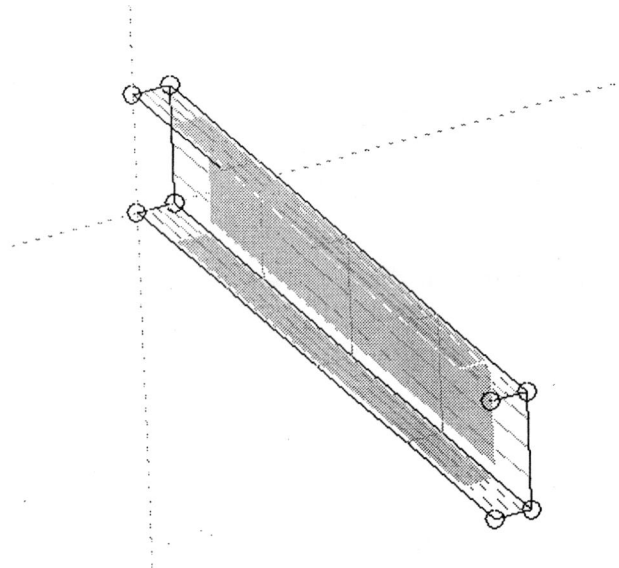

Figure 7 Shell elements created with default AutoGEM settings

Now we must go through the usual routine of defining the remaining model parameters.

Model > Properties > Material

Move **STEEL_IPS** to the right pane. Now select

> *Assign > Shell > All >* (middle click) *> Close*
> *Properties > Shell Property > Shell*

Click on the bottom and top flange elements, then middle click. Enter a property name *"flange"* and specify a thickness of *0.3125* inches. Accept the dialog. Then select

> *Shell*

and click on the web element, then middle click. Select the *New Set* button, give a property name of *"web"* and specify a thickness of *0.20* inches.

Set up the constraints at the fixed end of the beam:

> *Model > Constraints > Curve*

Create a *New* constraint set called **fixedend**. Name the constraint **fixedend** as well and select the three original curves in the XY plane; middle click. Leave all translational and rotational degrees of freedom fixed. Accept the dialog.

Apply a uniform load:

> *Model > Loads > Curve*

Create a *New* load set **endload** and name the load **endload**. Select the edge of the top flange at the end of the beam. Enter a component FY of *-2400. Accept* the dialog.

The model is now complete. You might want to change *"tail touching"* to *"head touching"* in the *Display > Settings* menu, also set Display Load Magnitudes Precision to *1*. The final model should appear as shown in Figure 8.

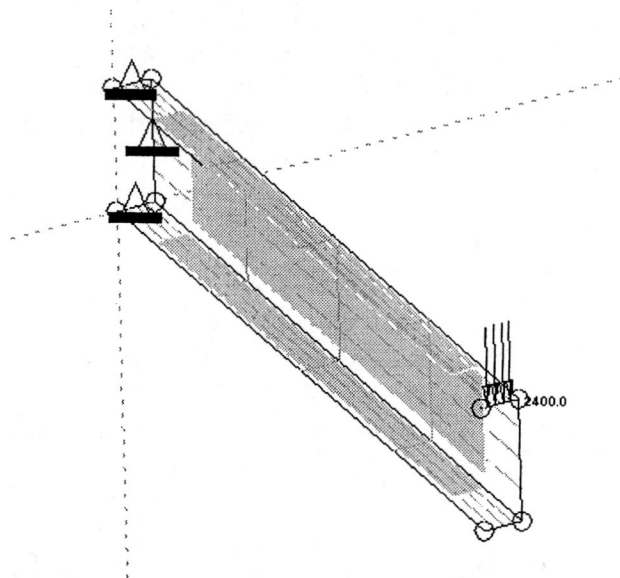

Figure 8 Completed model

Analysis and Results

We will proceed in the usual manner, starting with a Quick Check and moving on to an adaptively converged solution. Select

> *Main > Analyses*

Create a *New* static analysis name **pbeam**. Make sure the constraint set **fixedend** and load set **endload** (only) are highlighted and set **QuickCheck**. *Accept* the dialog.

> *Run > Settings*

Set up your preferred temporary and output file locations.

> *Start*

Accept error detection. A message window about shell alignment opens. This refers to the direction of the assumed outward normals to the shells. This would be important if we were applying a pressure load, and is not critical for this model so select *No*. If you have not already saved the model, you will be asked for a name of the model file, enter "*pbeam*". Open the *Summary* window. There should be no errors, but only a warning about convergence not being checked. Note that the maximum value of Sigma_ZZ (the normal bending stress) is about 43,000 psi although this number, of course, should not be trusted!

Assuming there were no errors in the QuickCheck, modify the analysis to perform a multi-pass adaptive analysis.

> *Analyses > Edit*

You might note that *Single Pass Adaptive* is available for this model. This is a type of analysis somewhere in the middle between a QuickCheck and MultiPass. A first pass is made using order 3 elements. From the estimated error, Pro/M computes the edge order required for a "good" solution, and immediately performs that solution, then quits. This might be useful if you are confident in the convergence obtained, and you want to speed up the computation. For our purposes, use *Multi-Pass Adaptive* as usual, with *5%* convergence on *Lcl Disp & Lcl SE & Global RMS Stress*. Set a maximum polynomial order of *9*. Now we are ready to:

> *Run > Start*

Delete the existing output files and open the *Summary* window. Note that the model does not converge in 9 passes. Meanwhile, the maximum bending stress sigma_ZZ has increased (in magnitude) to about 50,000 psi. This really doesn't mean very much without assured convergence. In order to obtain that, we need to go back and remesh the model with smaller elements.

Modifying the Mesh with AutoGEM

First, we need to delete the existing elements:

> ***Edit > Delete > Entity > Shells > All***

Middle click twice. Change the AutoGEM settings using

> ***Model > Elements > AutoGEM > Settings > Define/Review***

change the maximum aspect ratio from 30 to **5**. Now select

> ***Surface > All***

and middle click. This time, AutoGEM produces 25 tri and 5 quad elements with a maximum aspect ratio of 5.0. The mesh will look something like Figure 9. Remember that the loads and constraints have been applied to the geometry, but you will have to assign the material and shell (thickness) properties to the elements before this model is ready to run. You can see the advantage of assigning these properties to the underlying geometry and surfaces. Do that now - it will be easier than selecting individual elements anyway. A multipass run should converge on pass 8 with a maximum stress sigma_ZZ of around -49,000 psi. Meanwhile, this isn't a particularly pleasing mesh aesthetically, and contains more elements than are required for this model[3]. Furthermore, this gives an opportunity to find out about another way to create elements.

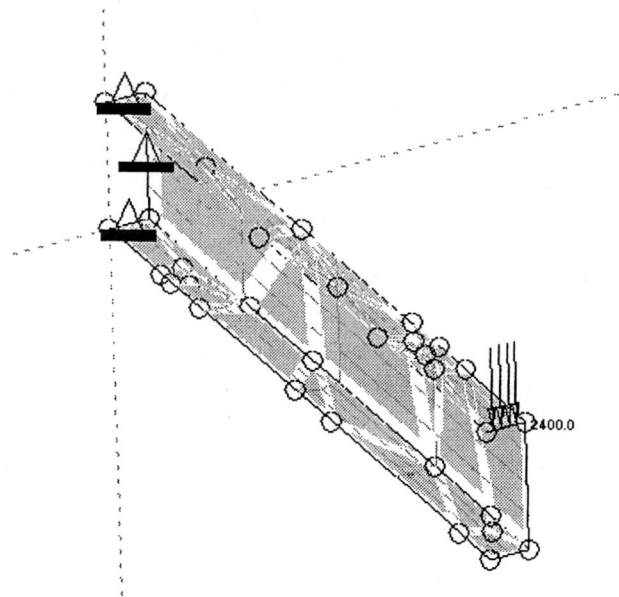

Figure 9 Shell element mesh created with
AutoGEM using aspect ratio 5

---

[3] When you have some time, try using AutoGEM with a maximum aspect ratio of 2 for this model. It will create well almost 300 elements! If you try this and it is taking too long, you can interrupt AutoGEM with the Esc key on the keyboard.

Before proceeding on the next version of this model, we have to delete most of the existing one:

> *Edit > Delete > Entities > Shells > All (middle click)*
> *Surfaces > All (middle click)*
> *Load > All (middle click)*
> *Curves > All > Deselect*

Click on the original three curves and middle click twice. These curves are all that should be present for the model geometry.

> *Points > All*

Note that you cannot delete the points associated with the three initial curves that define the beam section.

For the following, it will be handy to hide the constraints for a minute:

> *Display > Master Visibilities*

and turn off the constraints.

Model B

In this second version of the model, we will create the elements directly by extruding a curve. The same operation can be performed by rotating a curve. This will produce a more regular element pattern than, for example, AutoGEM.

Extruding Shell Elements

To create the elements shown in Figure 10 below (note there are 6 elements along the length of the beam):

> *Main > Model > Elements*
> *Extrude > Curve > All*

then middle click and read the prompt. Just as we did for the extruded surface, we specify the start (*0, 0*) and end points (*0, 0, 6*) (☞ note the Z value here is 6) of a translation vector, a scale factor (default *<1>*), twist (default *<0>*), and number of copies, *6* in our case.

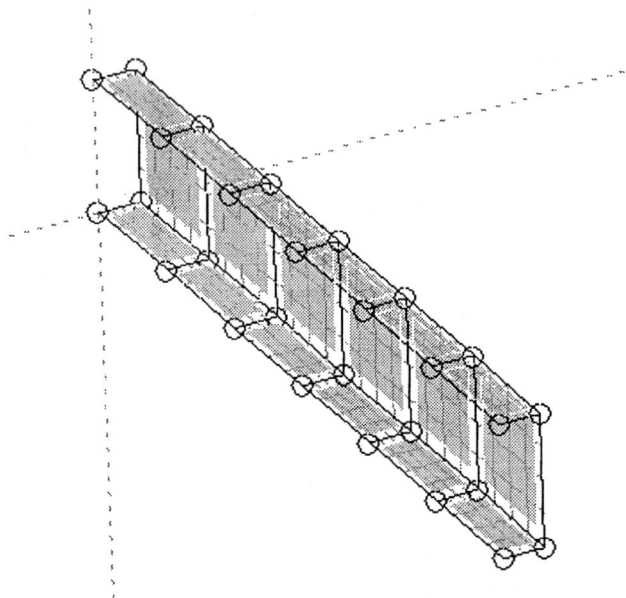

Figure 10 Shell elements created by extruding the section curves

We can turn on the constraint display again:

> ***Display > Master Visibilities***

and check constraints back on.

Since these are all new elements, we need to specify all the remaining model parameters:

> ***Model > Properties > Material***
> ***Assign > Shell > All > (middle click) > Close***
> ***Properties > Shell Property > Shell***

Click on the 6 elements along each of the top and bottom flanges. Middle click. Select the existing property set name "*flange*".

> ***Shell Property > Shell***

click on the 6 elements in the web. Middle click. Use the existing set "*web*".

> ***Model > Loads > Curve***

In the existing load set **endload**, create a load called **endload** and select the top edge at the end of the beam. Enter a value for FY of *-2400*.

Our new model is now complete and should appear as shown in Figure 11.

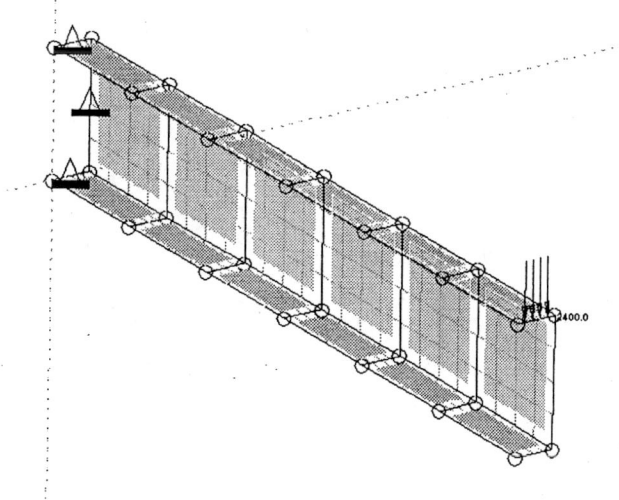

Figure 11 Completed model

Analysis and Results

Since we deleted the previous load and created a new one, we should make sure the analysis parameters are set properly:

Main > Analyses

The analysis **pbeam** should still be selected. *Edit* it and change back to a **QuickCheck**. Make sure the constraint and load sets are selected.

Run > Settings

These should be unchanged from before.

Start

Delete the existing files and open the *Summary* window. No errors are reported so we can change the analysis to an adaptive one:

Analyses > Edit

change to *Multi-Pass Adaptive*, 5% on *Lcl Disp & Lcl SE & Global RMS Stress* with a maximum polynomial order of *9*. Then,

Run > Start

Delete output files. Open the *Summary* window. Convergence is obtained on the 6th pass. The maximum value of the bending stress sigma_ZZ is about 54,500 psi. Notice in the Measures list that values for max_beam_bending, etc, are given as zero. These measures refer only to beam elements, which we will meet a little later in the tutorial.

Set up a result window to show a fringe plot of the bending stress:

Results > Create > [sigmaZZ]

Get the output directory *pbeam\\.* Enter a title "*Bending Stress - sigma-ZZ*", select Quantity **Stress** and **ZZ** in the pull-down list. Select a fringe plot. Copy this window definition to a new window called *defY*. *Review* this window and change the quantity to *Displacement*, change to **Component** and check the **Y** box. Change the display type to *Query*. Copy this window to a third window called *defX*. Review this window and change the title and displacement component to *X*. Finally, create a window to show the deformation animation.

Show the stress window *sigmaZZ*. Use the dynamic view controls to rotate/translate/ scale. The fringe plot is shown in Figure 12 below. Note that the stress is largest at top (in tension) and bottom (in compression) of the beam, as predicted by simple beam theory. However, this stress varies across the width of the flange. Recall that in simple beam theory the bending stress is a function only of the distance from the neutral axis provided that the cross section is symmetric about the plane of loading. This is not the case with our C-section. The theoretical analysis for our beam involves consideration of the shear center of the beam section.

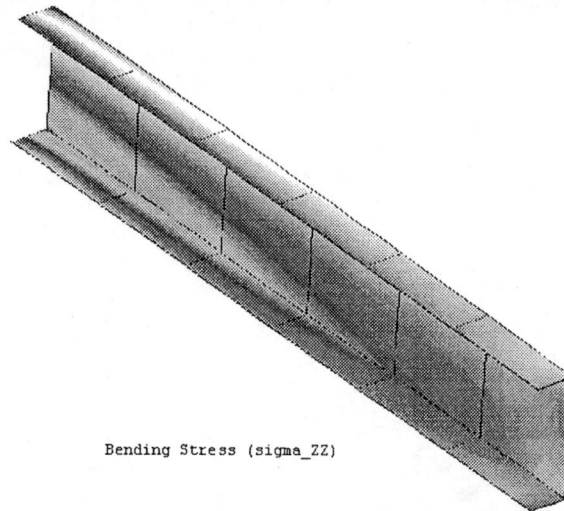

Bending Stress (sigma_ZZ)

Figure 12 Bending stress (σ_{ZZ}) in the cantilever beam

Show the deformed shape (Figure 13) and note the twist in the beam. This is what is not included in simple beam theory, and also explains why the stress is about 3 times larger than predicted by that theory.

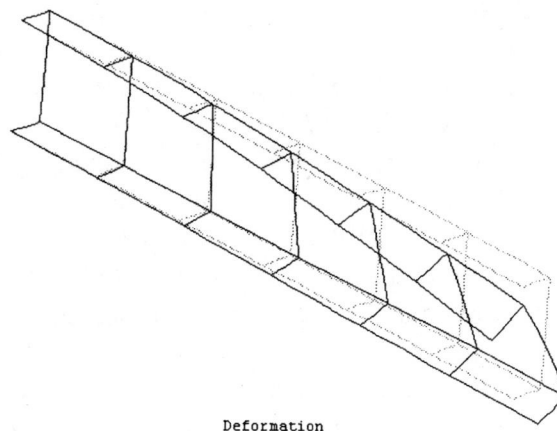

Deformation

Figure 13 Deformation of the beam under load

Show the windows **defX** and **defY**. In each window, select *Controls > Query* and pick on the top and bottom corners of the beam at the free end. This will report the deflections in the X and Y directions, respectively, at these points. It is interesting to note that at these points the lateral deflection (X) is about twice the magnitude of the vertical deflection (Y), due to the twisting of the beam.

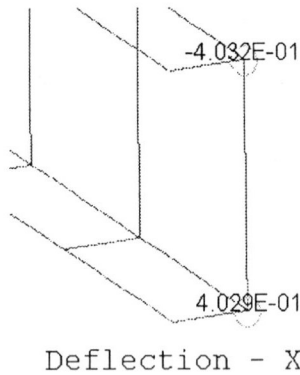

Deflection - X

Figure 14 X-displacement of nodes on the beam

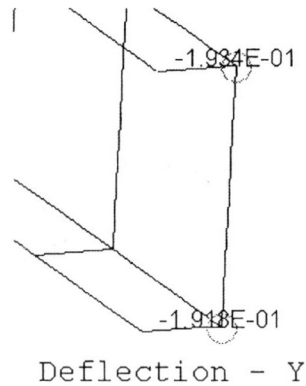

Deflection - Y

Figure 15 Y-displacement of nodes on the beam

For comparison sake, the results reported in Knight's book using an h-code model with 504 quad elements are: maximum bending stress ±54.1 ksi, defY -0.184", defX 0.376". These are within a few per cent of the results obtained here.

We are finished with this model, so you can close it out.

Example #2 - The Cyclone

Our second example of a 3D shell model is based on a simplified cyclone separator, shown in Figure 16. A cut-away view is shown in Figure 17. Because the model is not axisymmetric, we cannot use the methods of Chapter 5. A fluid enters via the horizontal pipe to the top cylindrical portion of the cyclone approximately tangent to the outer wall. As the fluid circulates around the wall of the cylinder, centrifugal force will cause a separation of materials with different densities in the fluid stream. The mechanism for extracting the separated material is not included in this model. The heavier material fluid stream leaves by the bottom exit (called the underflow) through the pipe elbow. The lighter material fluid stream usually leaves through an axial hole at the top of the cyclone (overflow), that is not shown in this model. The cyclone is supported by the circumferential ring around the bottom of the cylinder, and support flanges (not shown) on the end of the inlet and outlet pipes.

We will create a model of the cyclone using 3D shell elements. A number of new geometric construction techniques are introduced here. Since working in 3D is quite a bit more complex than in 2D (largely because of the difficulty of visualizing the geometry), you will have to be quite careful going through these steps. You would be advised to read ahead before attempting any of the new commands.

Figure 17 The cyclone - cut-away view

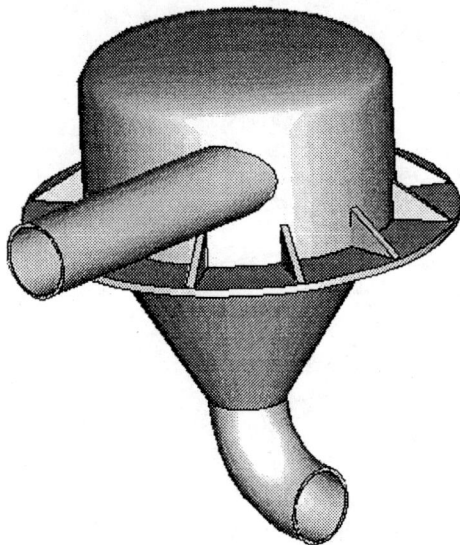

Figure 16 The cyclone

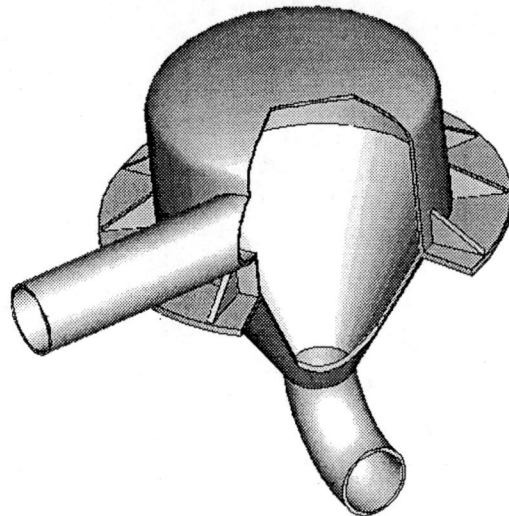

The Model

Start up Pro/M as usual, and construct the horizontal and vertical construction lines. These will be useful references when you are looking at the 3D wireframe structure of the model.

> *Display > Master Visibilities > All On*

You can turn off the grid, since it won't be very useful in this exercise (although it can sometimes provide a useful visual cue).

> *Main > Geometry > Curve*
> *Construction Geom > Horizontal > Snap(Point) > [0 0]*
> *Construction Geom > Vertical > Snap(Point) > [0 0]*

The geometry and dimensions of the cyclone are shown in Figure 18. We will ignore the triangular gussets on the mounting rim, and create the remainder of the shell model using 6 surfaces. Two of these are surface primitives (cylinder and cone), one is an extruded circle (the inlet pipe), and the other three are revolved curves (a quadrant of an ellipse, a line, and a circle).

The model will be loaded using a vertical load representing the weight of fluid inside the cyclone and a small internal pressure.

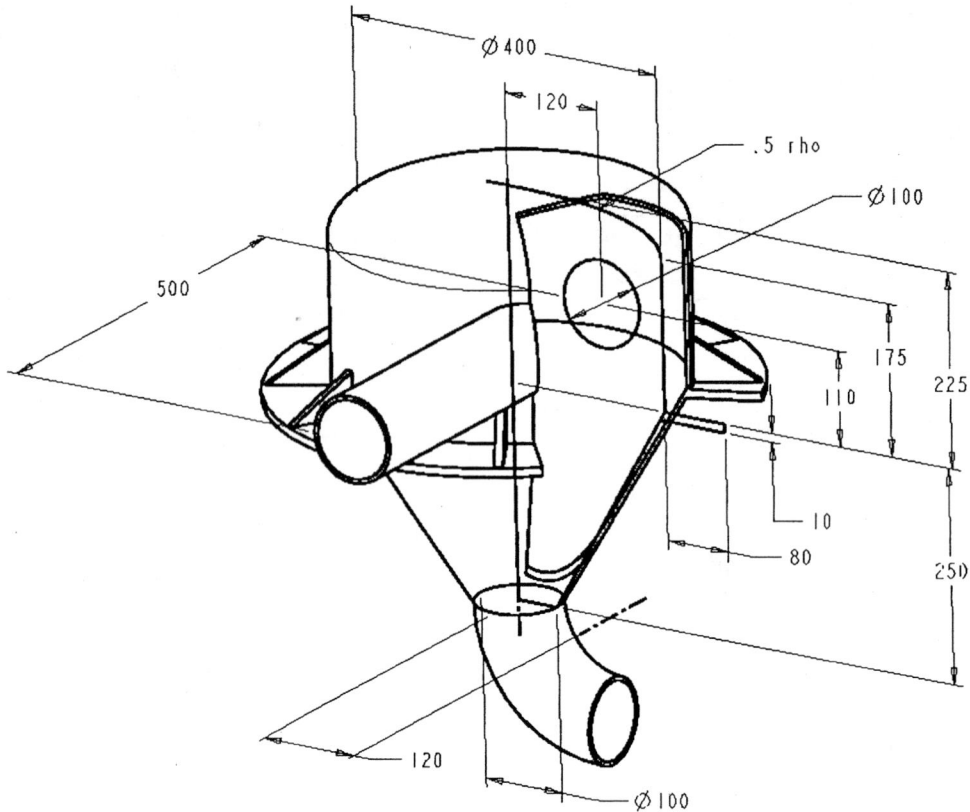

Figure 18 Geometry and dimensions of the cyclone (all dimensions in mm)

Creating 3D Surfaces

In the first part of this lesson, we created surfaces by extruding lines. Any curve can be extruded to form a surface. Pro/M also contains some commands to create types of surfaces directly without first creating a defining curve. We will use two of these primitives in this model.

● The Cylinder

We start by creating the cylindrical part of the body:

> *Geometry > Surface*
> *Cylinder > Snap(Point)*

The cylinder is defined by specifying the location of the center points on each end, and its radius. For our model, the bottom center point is at the origin, so enter (*0, 0, 0*) (without the parantheses). The top center point is at (*0, 175, 0*), and the radius is *200*. When the cylinder has been created, middle click. You will have to

> *View > Fit*

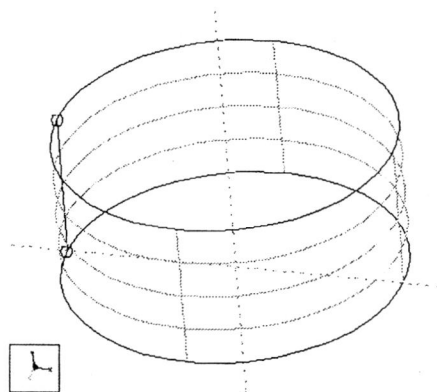

Figure 19 Cylindrical surface primitive

and use the view commands, or do a dynamic rotation and zoom, to get a good view of the cylinder as shown in Figure 19. Select **Done** in the **View** menu when you are through.

● The Cone

The wide part of the conical surface is on the bottom of the cylinder. The "top" of the cone is actually the narrow end at the bottom of the cyclone. Select

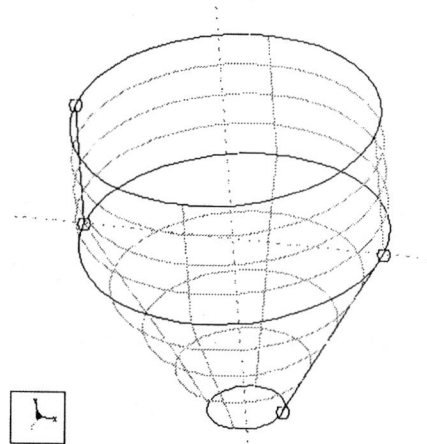

Figure 20 Cone surface primitive added to cylinder

Cone > Snap(Point)

and enter the following data:

center point of bottom	*0, 0, 0*
center point of top	*0, -250, 0*
radius of bottom	*200*
radius of top	*50*

then middle click or press enter. The cone should appear as shown in Figure 20.

● The Inlet Pipe

Construction of the inlet pipe is complicated by the intersection with the big cylinder. We have to trim the pipe to the cylindrical surface, and also punch a hole through that surface. Start by drawing a circle on the XY plane (at Z = 0) and extruding it parallel to the Z axis to form the pipe. See Figure 18 for the dimensions and locations of this circle.

Geometry > Curve > Circle
Radius-Center > [50] > [120 110 0]

Middle click twice. The circle is shown in Figure 21. Now, extrude the circle to form a surface:

Geometry > Surface > Extruded

Click on the circle, middle click. The translation vector for the extrusion does not have to be attached to the curve, as it was in the first part of this lesson. Here, enter the start of translation vector as (*0, 0, 0*) and the end of the vector as (*0, 0, 500*). Accept the defaults for scale *<1>*, twist *<0>* and number of copies *<1>*. Middle click. The surface should appear as shown in Figure 22.

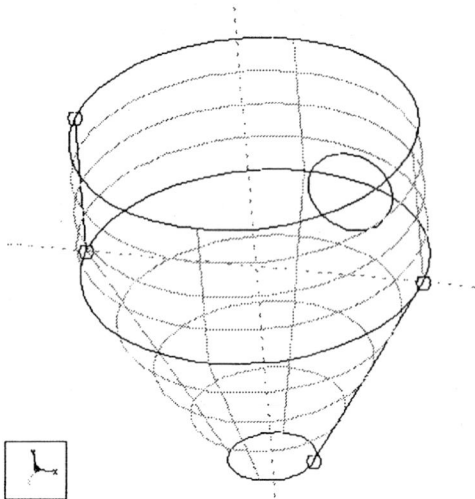

Figure 21 Circle to be extruded to form pipe

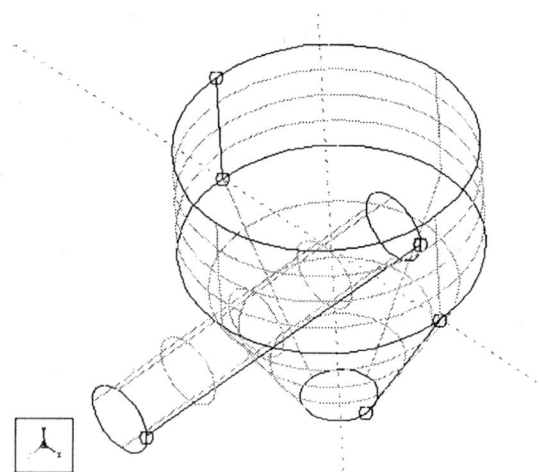

Figure 22 Extruded surface formed from circle

Editing 3D Surfaces

As you can see in Figure 22, the extruded pipe surface intersects the cylinder. We need to trim back these surfaces. First, we need to create a curve at the intersection of the two surfaces:

Geometry > Curve > Surf-Surf Intrsct

Click on the pipe surface, then on the cylinder surface. There may be multiple surfaces at each or both these pick points. If so, a window will open which allows you to cycle through the possible surfaces (using *Next*) until the one you want is highlighted in red. When this occurs, *Accept* the surface. A curve will be created at the intersection of these as shown at the right.

Now we need to trim back the pipe surface and punch a hole in the cylinder. Start with the pipe:

Edit > Geometry > Trim Surface

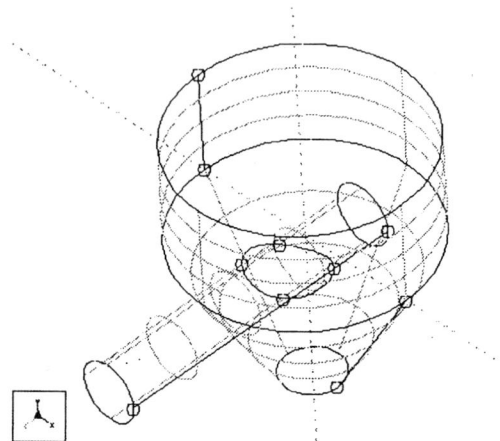

Figure 23 Intersection of pipe and cylinder surfaces

and click on the surface of the pipe. Read the prompt. The exterior edge we need is the outer circular end of the pipe, farthest from the cylinder. Pro/M finds a junction at the intersection curve we created above and highlights the two possible ways to leave the junction. Click on the intersection loop. Another junction is found that comes back to the start. Click on this edge. Read the message window. There are no interior loops, so middle click. The surface is trimmed back, and Pro/M asks if we want to trim the surface curves inside the big cylinder; accept the default (yes). The curves inside the cylinder are deleted as shown in Figure 24.

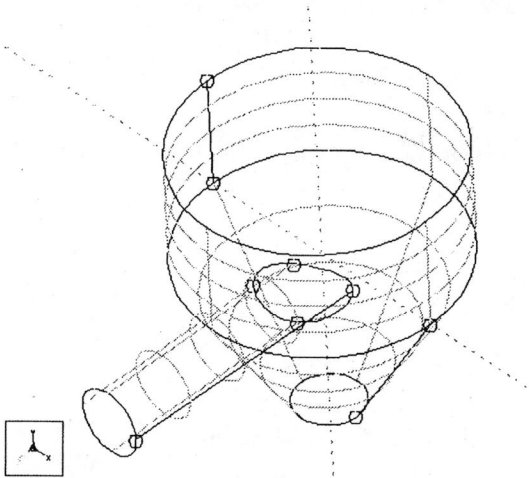

Figure 24 Pipe surface trimmed to cylinder

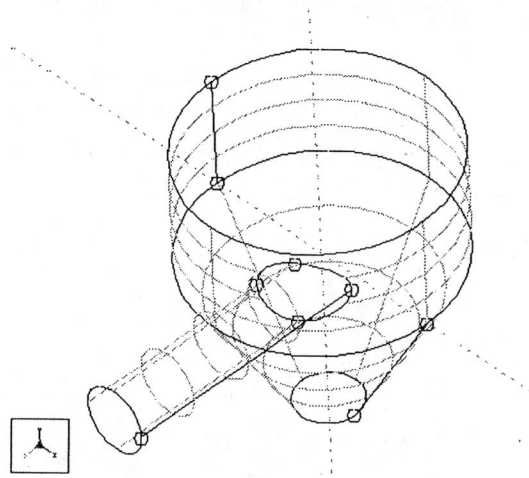

Figure 25 Cylinder surface trimmed to intersection curve

We need to punch a hole in the big cylinder surface. Pick that surface now. Read the message window and click on the top edge of the cylinder. Why are there no "junctions" found for this surface as there were for the inlet pipe? Read the message window again. The interior loop is the intersection curve with the pipe. Select this and then middle click. Trim the surface curves as before (there actually aren't any). Middle click again. We have now created a hole in the cylinder where the pipe joins the surface, Figure 25. You can see this better if you turn shading on for the surfaces using

Display > Settings > Display Type(Smooth) | Shade(Geometry) | Accept

Return to the unshaded display before continuing.

Revolved Surfaces

The remaining surfaces in the model are all obtained by revolving curves. This involves specifying the curve and the revolve axis.

● The Elliptical Top

We'll create an ellipse, trim it back to a single quadrant, and then revolve this around the Y axis. It will be useful for us to create a couple of points to locate the axes of the ellipse:

Geometry > Point > Single Points > Snap(Center)

Click on the edge at the top of the cylinder - the snap option finds the center of this arc (or circle). This new point will be the origin of the ellipse.

Snap(Point) > [0 225 0]

gives the point at the top of the cyclone. Now create the ellipse

Geometry > Curve > Ellipse > Cent-Axis Points > Snap(Point)

The ellipse center is at the top center of the cylinder, the end of the major axis is on the cylinder, and the end of the minor axis is at the top of the cyclone, as shown in Figure 26. Middle click.

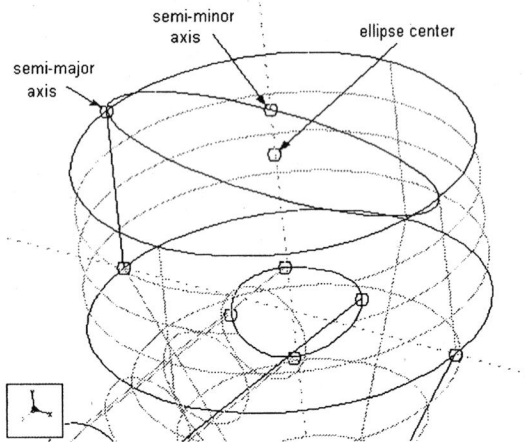

Figure 26 Constructing the elliptical top

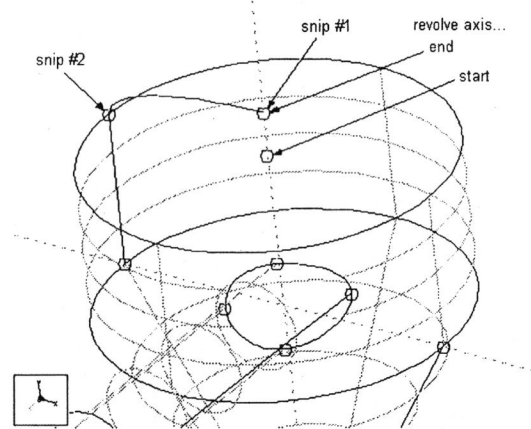

Figure 27 Splitting the ellipse and setting up the revolved surface

We want to remove all but one quadrant of the ellipse. We will use a new command for this,

Edit > Geometry > Split Curve

Click on the ellipse. Using *Split Snap(Point)*, click on the points at the ends of the major and minor axes as shown in Figure 27. We have divided the single ellipse curve into two separate curves and can delete the remaining portion of the ellipse

Edit > Delete > Entity > Curves

click on the larger portion of the ellipse and middle click. See Figure 27.

Now we will revolve the ellipse:

Geometry > Surface > Revolved

Click on the remaining quadrant of the ellipse and middle click. The revolve axis goes through the two points on the Y-axis construction line. Click

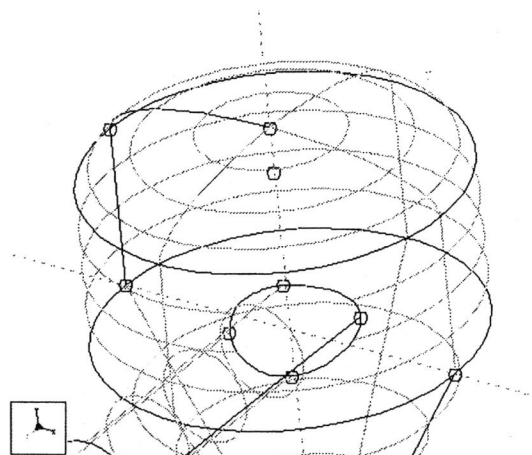

Figure 28 Top revolved surface complete

both points, and accept the default revolve angle of *360* degrees. The top surface of the cyclone is created as shown in Figure 28.

● The Elbow

The 90 degree elbow on the exit of the cyclone is created as another revolved curve. We have to be careful with the revolve axis here:

Geometry > Surface > Revolved

select the bottom circle on the cone. Middle click. We will specify the axis location by entering the start point coordinates as *120, -250, 0*. The axis is perpendicular to the current working plane (XY plane), so just hit enter. Give the revolve angle of *90* degrees.

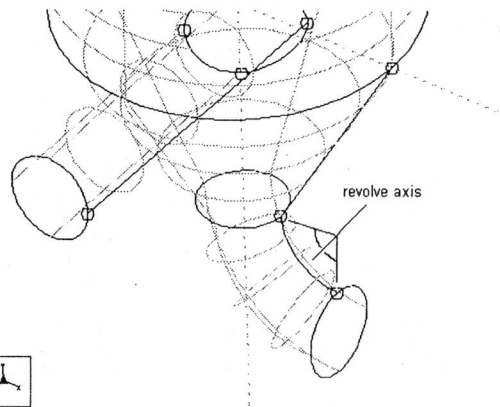

Figure 29 Revolving the bottom curve in the cone to form the exit elbow

● The Support Rim

The final surface is the ring around the circumference of the cylinder at its base. We'll create a straight line, then revolve it.

Geometry > Curve > Line > Two Points > Snap(Point)

Pick the point on the cylinder on the horizontal construction line. The end of the line is at (*280, 0, 0*). Middle click. The line is shown in Figure 30.

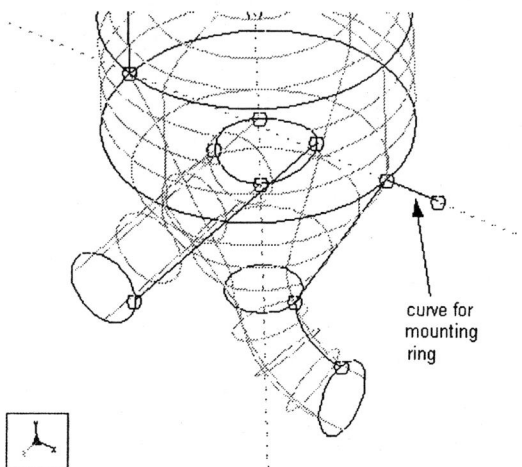

Figure 30 Constructing the curve to form the rim

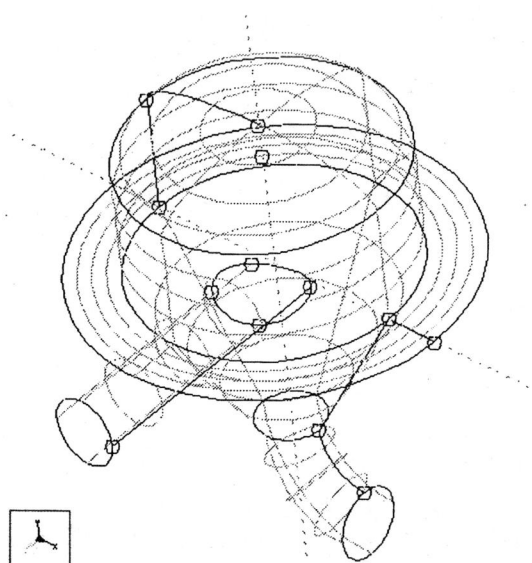

Figure 31 Mounting rim complete

Now revolve this segment

Geometry > Surface > Revolved

select the line segment and middle click. The revolve axis can be designated using the start point at (*0, 0, 0*) and end point at (*0, 100, 0*). The rotation angle is *360* degrees. See Figure 31.

A shaded view of the model with all the surfaces completed is shown in Figure 32.

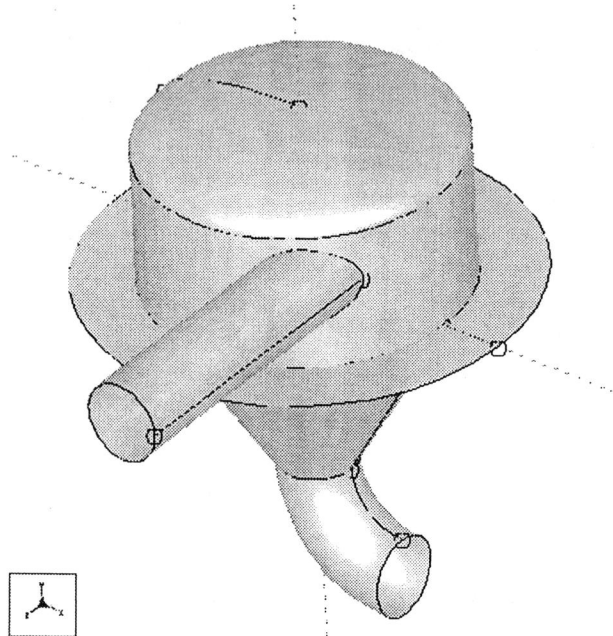

Figure 32 The completed 3D surface model

Completing the Model

We are now ready to complete the definition of the model: material, shell properties, constraints, loads, and so on. This should be pretty routine by now, so we'll go over this quickly.

Main > Model > 3D
Properties > Material

Move SS_mmNS to the right pane. Now select

Assign > Surface > All

Middle click and *Close*. All the shells will have the same thickness (5mm) except for the mounting rim (10mm). Note the use of the deselect command here:

Properties > Shell Property > Surface > All > Deselect

click on the mounting ring to remove it from the selection set and then middle click. Enter a property set name "*thick5*", a description, and enter a value of *5* for thickness.

Surface

Select the mounting ring by itself, then

New Set

Enter a new name "*thick10*", a description, and specify a thickness of *10*.

We will constrain the model by fixing all the free edges:

Model > Constraints > Curve

Create a *New* constraint set **fixededges**. Select the outer edge of the mounting ring, and the curves at the ends of the inlet and exit pipe. Middle click. Set all the translations to fixed, and all the rotations to free.

We are going to apply a vertical load to the conical surface (due to the weight of fluid in the cyclone body), plus an internal pressure on all surfaces.

Model > Loads > Surface

Create a *New* load set called **loads**. Call the first load in this set **weight**. Select the surface of the cone and middle click. Accept the defaults of *total load*, *uniform*, and enter a component FY of -*500* (about 110 lb). The load will appear on the surface as shown in Figure 33.

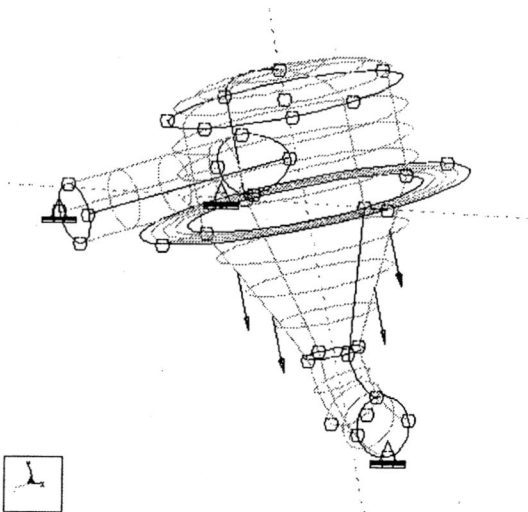

Figure 33 Constraints on edges and vertical load on the cone

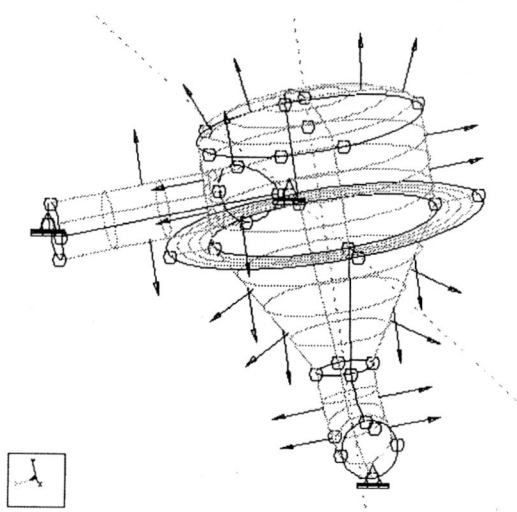

Figure 34 Internal pressure load applied

Now apply a pressure load to all surfaces except the mounting ring:

Pressure > Surface

Name the load **presload** (in load set **loads**). Select the button under Surfaces and pick

All > Deselect

Click on the mounting ring and middle click. Read the message about surface normals and accept *Yes* to see the directions of the normals. No surface normals should need to be flipped. Enter a magnitude of *0.02* (about 3 psi). The pressure load arrows will appear on the model. You should spin the model around to make sure that the surface normals are correct (that is, the pressure is acting outward everywhere), and that there is no pressure acting on the mounting ring. See Figure 34.

We will create elements using AutoGEM:

Model > Elements > AutoGEM

Make sure you are using the default settings and select

Surface > All

Middle click. AutoGEM creates 45 tri and 24 quad elements[4]. Use

Display > Settings

to set up smooth shading, and shrink the elements.

This completes the creation of our model, which should appear as shown in Figure 35.

---

[4] This is considerably more than the number of elements created by AutoGEM in Release 20 of MECHANICA, which was 16 tri and 24 quad elements for this same geometry. Changes are made in the AutoGEM algorithm in almost every release.

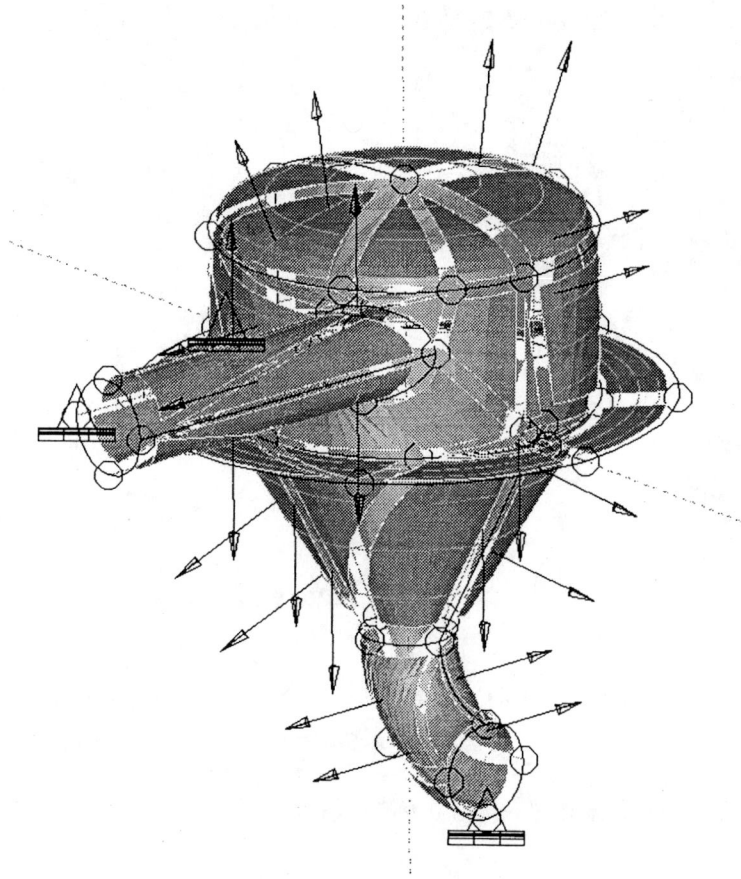

Figure 35 The completed model ready for analysis

Analysis and Results

Set up a *QuickCheck* static analysis called **cyclone** and run it, accepting error detection (don't forget to set up the directories for temporary and output files). If you haven't saved the model yet, you will get a chance to do that here. Call the model *cyclone*. Open the *Summary* window and look for any warning or error messages.

If all goes well, change the analysis to a *Multi-Pass Adaptive*, with *5%* convergence on *Lcl Disp & Lcl SE & Global RMS Stress*. Set the polynomial edge order maximum to *9*. When you run the analysis, delete the existing output files. The multi-pass run does *not* converge in 9 passes, so we should probably come back and remesh with slightly tighter AutoGEM settings to get a finer mesh. Before we do that, let's see what results we have now.

Create the usual result windows: Von Mises stress fringe plot, deformation animation, measures (maximum Von Mises stress, strain energy, maximum displacement Y), and P-level fringe plot. These are shown in Figures 36 through 41 below.

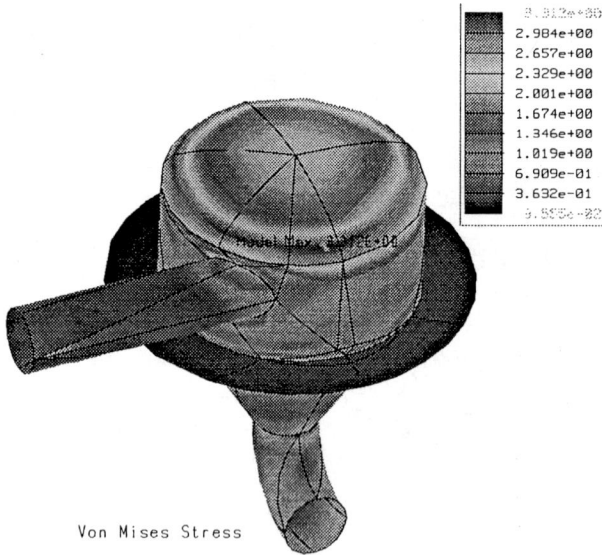

Figure 36 Von Mises stress fringe plot

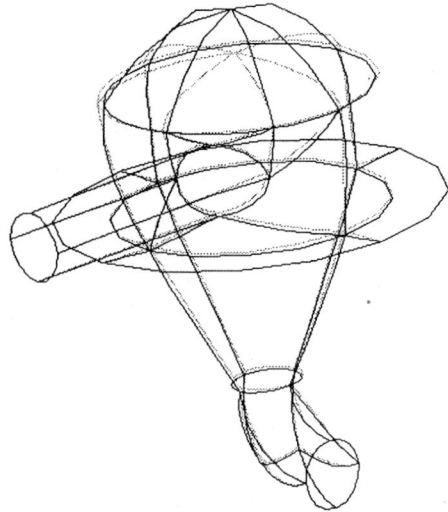

Figure 37 Deformed shape

Note the symmetry of the stress distribution on the top of the cyclone, despite the proximity to the inlet pipe in one region. In the deformation wireframe, we should look for the constrained curves to see if we have set the constraints properly. The three plots showing the convergence history of the multipass run should look similar to Figures 38 - 40.

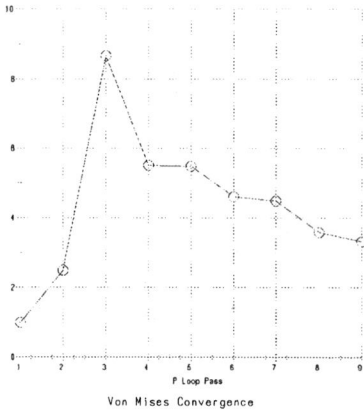

Figure 38 Convergence of Von Mises stress

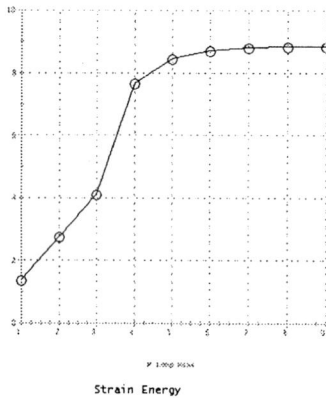

Figure 39 Convergence of strain energy

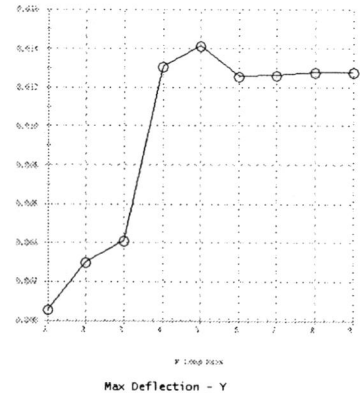

Figure 40 Convergence of displacement in Y direction

The convergence plots indicate the analysis was pretty close to converging on the 9th pass. It might be beneficial to remesh the model, so that convergence will occur at a lower order. This might even reduce the total execution time.

Finally, the P-level fringe plot is shown at the right. Note that the minimum P-level is 2 (one of the rim edges), the maximum P-level is 9 which occurs on most edges of the cylinder and cone. As mentioned previously, this is grounds for concern and you might like to remesh this model with a finer mesh to obtain convergence using a lower maximum p-level.

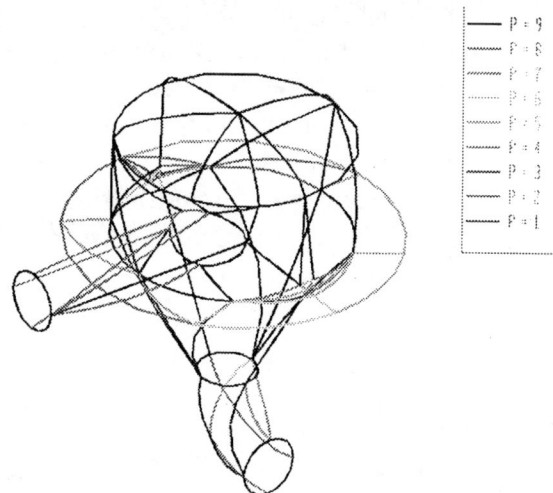

This completes this part of the lesson. As an exercise, you might like to add the gusset plates between the mounting rim and the cylinder.

Figure 41 P-levels in multi-pass adaptive run (minimum 2, maximum 9)

Summary

We have seen a number of new tools for creating geometry in three dimensions. These include extruding and revolving curves to create surfaces, creation of surface primitives, tools for editing surfaces. To make full use of these, you should experiment with them in the exercises given below.

One of the major difficulties when dealing with 3D is visualization of the model. Pro/M offers useful tools for the display and manipulation of the model and you should also experiment with these until they become quite comfortable to use.

Questions for Review

1.   What is the default working plane in 3D?
2.   What information is required to define a translation vector for an extrusion?
3.   In addition to the translation direction and distance, what options are available when extruding a curve to make a surface?
4.   Can you extrude more than one curve at a time?
5.   What are the three 3D view functions available with the mouse buttons? What are the corresponding function keys for these functions? What is the difference between the two methods?
6.   What are the axis directions for the View Coordinate System VCS?
7.   How can you get a perspective view of the model?
8.   How do you change the increment size for rotation in the View menu?
9.   How do you set up rotations and translations of the view with respect to the World

Coordinate System WCS?

10.   What is our first remedy to a static analysis design study that will not converge in the maximum number of passes?

11.   What advantage might there be to directly creating elements by extruding curves rather than using AutoGEM?

12.   When elements are extruded from a curve, a surface is created at the same time. Is this a single surface, or a segmented surface for each element? How can you find out?

13.   An extruded curve forms a _____. What do extruded points and surfaces form?

14.   What is meant by a surface primitive?

15.   Is the Cone surface restricted to right circular cones? What data is required to create a cone?

16.   Where is the command for finding the intersection of two surfaces?

17.   What is the difference between the **Trim** and **Split** commands?

Exercises

1.   A U-shaped steel beam is cantilevered out from a wall and carries the loads shown in the left figure. The beam is a C-channel with dimensions given on the right. Find the magnitude and location of the maximum Von Mises stress, and the maximum displacement.

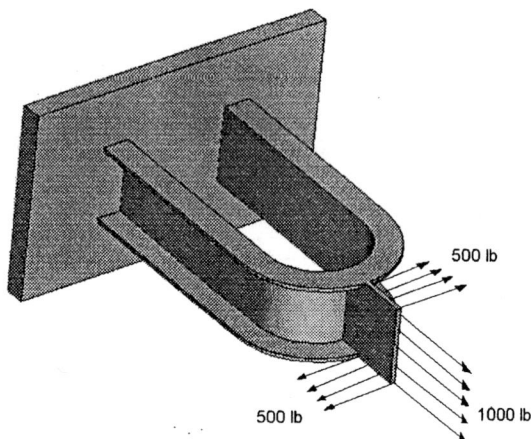

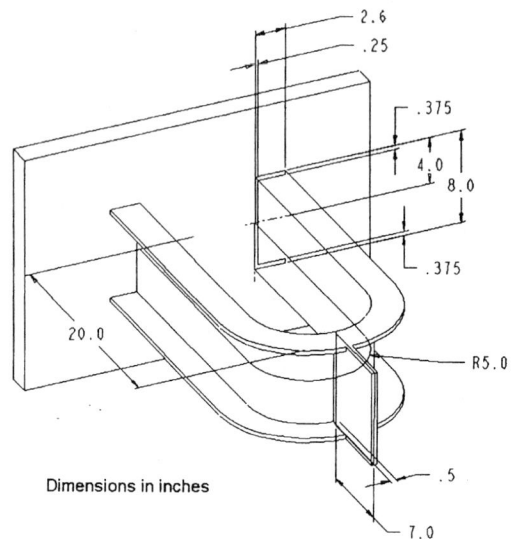

2. A mounting bracket is shown in the figure at the right. The bracket is made of aluminum and carries the loads indicated. The bracket is fixed to the wall using the two holes on the back plate. Find the maximum Von Mises stress and the maximum deflection. Dimensions are given in the figure on the next page.

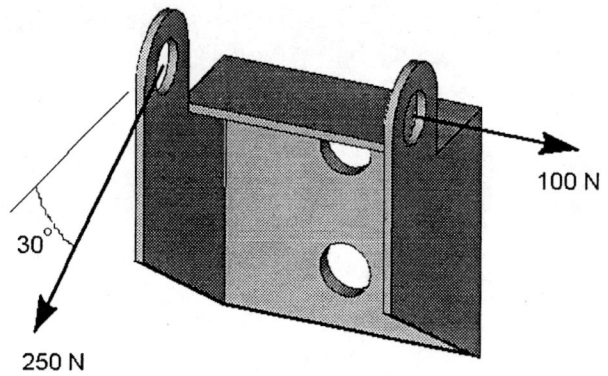

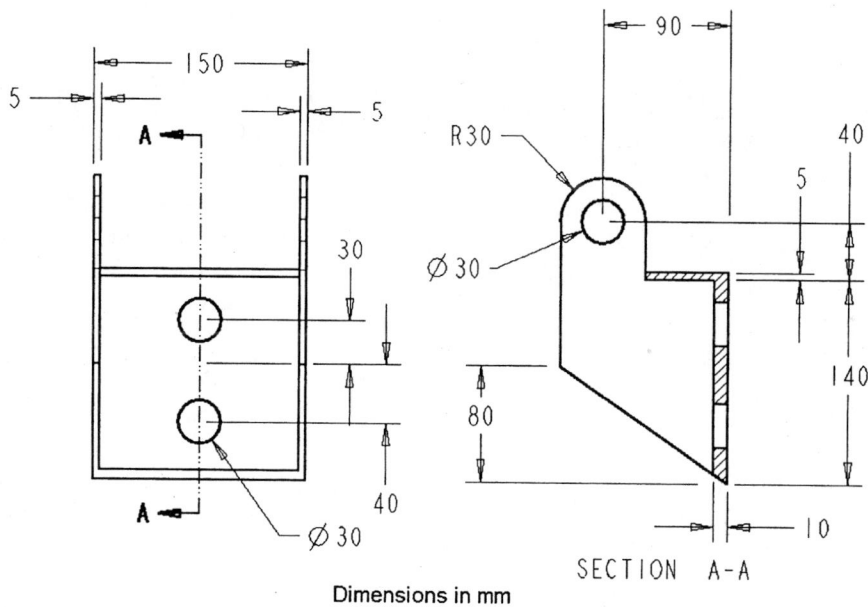

100 N

30°

250 N

150

5

5

A

30

40

A

Ø 30

90

R30

Ø 30

40

5

80

140

10

SECTION A-A

Dimensions in mm

This page left blank.

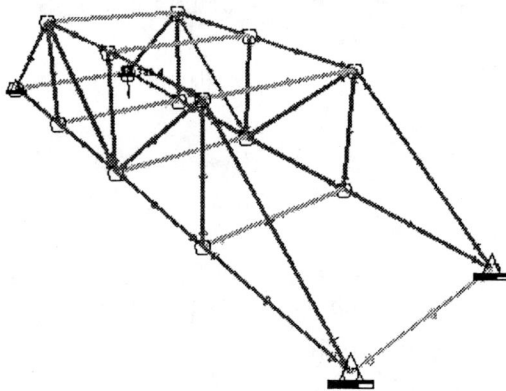

Chapter 8 :

Beams and Frames

Synopsis:

Beam elements in 1D, 2D, and 3D problems; beam coordinate systems, sections, and orientation; distributed loads; beam releases; shear and bending moment diagrams; trusses and frames; gravity load; groups of entities

Overview of this Lesson

Beams are fundamental structural elements. This lesson introduces the main concepts required to model isolated beams and beam elements as components of frames and trusses. The difficult subject of beam coordinate systems is introduced with sufficient depth to handle problems with simple symmetric beam cross sections. Beam orientation in 3D requires a solid understanding of these coordinate systems.

Three example problems are used to illustrate the Pro/M commands. The first is a simple cantilever beam (a diving board) with a tip load. New results windows are created to show the shear and bending moment diagrams for each beam element. The second example is a more complicated continuous indeterminate beam. This introduces distributed loads and the use of beam releases. The final example is in three parts: a simple 2D frame, a 2D truss, and a 3D frame. These illustrate more ideas in beam orientation, beam releases, and gravity load. In the final model, the loading caused by a specified displacement of a constraint is used to model the settling foundation beneath one corner of the 3D frame.

Beam Coordinate Systems

One of the potentially confusing issues arising in the use of beam elements is their orientation with respect to the World Coordinate System, WCS. This is particularly true for curved beams, and beams whose cross sections are asymmetrical about their centroid in at least one lateral direction (such as channels and angles) and/or are offset from the underlying geometric curves.

For the most general case, this orientation is described/defined using up to three coordinate systems. For this lesson, we only need to worry about two of these - the BACS and the BSCS[1].

The Beam Action Coordinate System BACS

On the screen, beam elements are represented (usually) as thick green lines. Beams are associated either with geometry curves or connecting two (or more) points defined in the WCS. We will deal only with straight beams in this lesson. For these, the underlying curve or points will define the X-axis of the beam's BACS (see Figure 1). The beam's local Y- and Z-axes are perpendicular to the beam. The orientation (relative to the WCS), ie. rotation of the beam around its local X-axis, is defined by specifying the direction that the BACS Y-axis is pointing. The components of this vector are given in the WCS. Some simple examples showing the specification of the BACS Y-Axis using vector components are shown in Figure 2. This definition is accessed through the Properties menu.

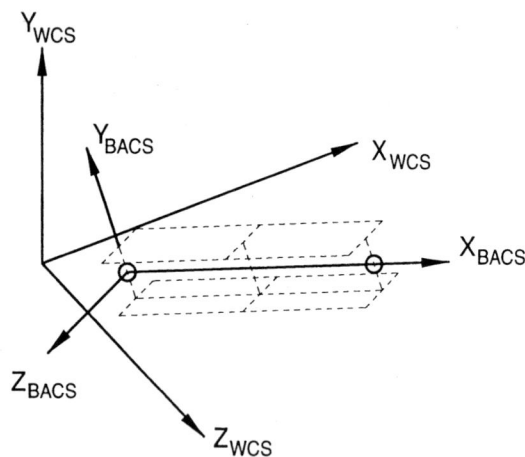

Figure 1 The BACS axes

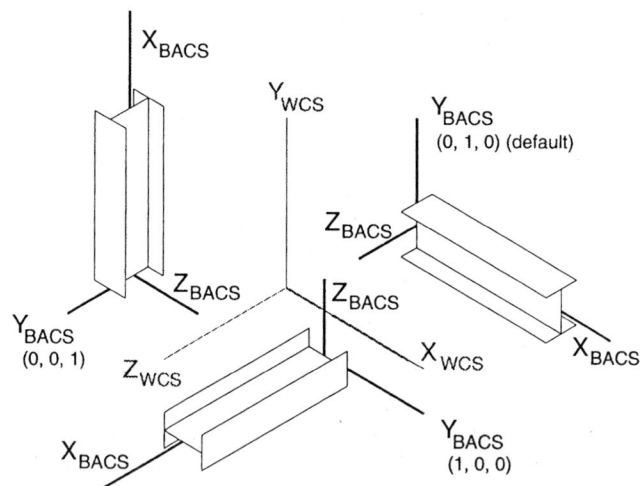

Figure 2 Illustrating BACS Y-Axis Orientation

The Beam Shape Coordinate System BSCS

The beam cross sectional shape and position are defined relative to the BSCS. The standard cross sections built in to Pro/M are shown in Figure 3. The shape is defined in the BSCS YZ plane. For most standard shapes, the origin of the BSCS coincides with the centroid of the section. The X-axis of the BSCS (coming out of the page in Figure 3) is always parallel to the X-axis of the BACS, that is, along the beam. The BSCS origin (or its shear center) is defined by offsets DY and DZ measured from the origin of the BACS. See Figure 4. The orientation of the BSCS is determined by the angle theta specified in the Beam Orientation property window.

The BSCS is parallel to the BACS if theta is zero. In addition, if the offsets DY and DZ are zero, then the BSCS coincides with the BACS. This will be the case in all the examples used in this

---

[1] The third system is the BCPCS (Beam Centroidal Principal Coordinate System). See the on-line help for further information on this system.

lesson.

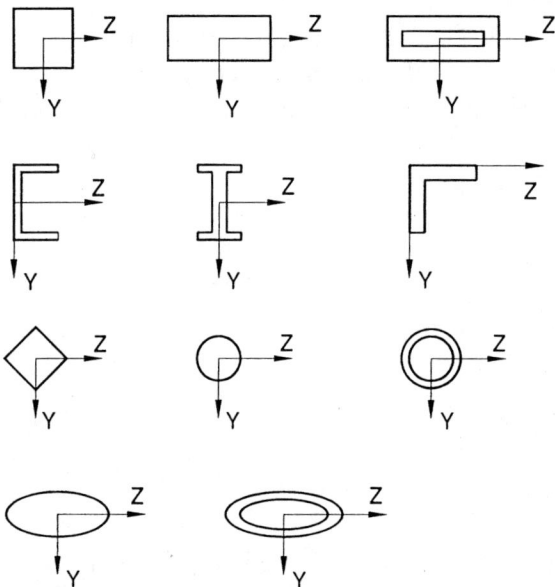

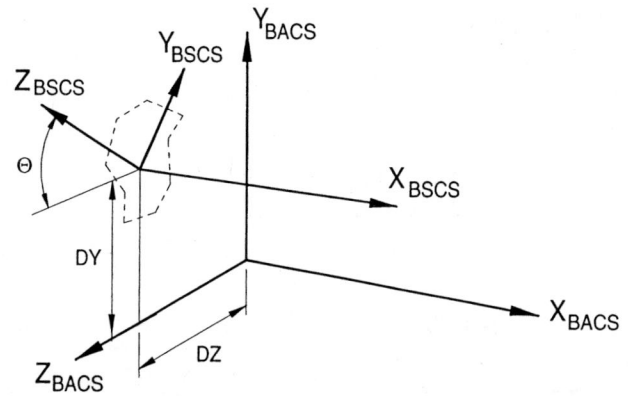

Figure 4 Definition of the BSCS axes relative to BACS. The frames coincide when theta, DY, and DZ are all 0

Figure 3 Standard Beam Section Shapes defined in the BSCS axes

When a beam cross section and orientation are specified, the combined properties will appear as an icon in true scale at several locations along the beam element. This serves as a visual cue to the size and orientation of the beam. Some examples are shown in Figure 5. These icons also indicate the directions of the BSCS Y- and Z-axes. The Y-axis is an open V (the Y axis is upward in Figure 5), while the tip of the Z-axis is an open arrowhead.

Now, this all seems pretty complicated, and indeed it is. Fortunately, in most cases, the Pro/M defaults are exactly what is required and you can do a lot of modeling knowing only the bare essentials.

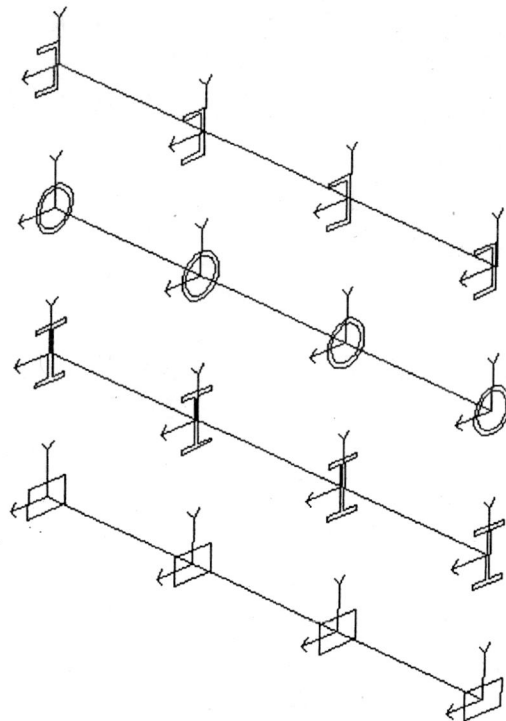

Figure 5 Beam elements with section icons

Example #1 - Basic Concepts

Our first example is a simple beam similar to a diving board. This will introduce some of the concepts involved in using beam elements. Before we proceed with the model, set up Pro/MECHANICA in the usual way, and specify a grid spacing of 12 inches:

> *Display > Master Visibilities > All On | Grid | Accept*
> *Display > Settings > Grid Spacing > [12]*
> *Main > Geometry > Curve*
> *Construction Geom > Horizontal > Snap(Point) > [0 0]*
> *Construction Geom > Vertical > Snap(Point) > [0 0]*

Zoom out until you can see the entire grid in the right half plane.

The Model

The model is shown in Figure 6. The cross section is a hollow rectangle, 24 inches wide and 2 inches high, with a wall thickness of 0.125 inch. The beam is cantilevered out from the wall, and rests on a simple support 10' from the wall, with an overhang of 6'. The material is aluminum and a downward vertical load of 200 lb is applied at the tip. This is a static load, and we will calculate the bending moment and stress, and static deflection, as if someone was just standing at the tip, not bouncing up and down. Note that this problem is statically indeterminate - that is, the simple methods of statics cannot be applied because of an extra unknown in the reactions. Nonetheless, analytical methods[2] could be used to solve for the bending stress and deflection at the tip.

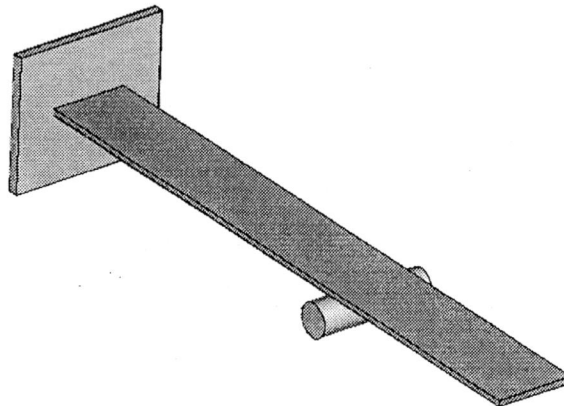

Figure 6 The diving board model - a simple indeterminate beam

---

[2] See the *singularity method* discussed in most mechanical design textbooks.

Geometry

The beam will be created along the WCS X-axis, which is the horizontal construction line.

Utility > Display Coordinates
Geometry > Point > Single Points > Snap(Grid)

Click on the grid to create points at (*0, 0*), (*120, 0*), and (*192, 0*). Middle click.

Beam Elements

We will create two beam elements directly from the points:

Main > Model > 3D
Elements > Beam > Element Snap(Point)

Each element is created by clicking on the end points. Thus, click on the left end and the middle point to create the first element. Then click on the middle point and the right end to create the second. The beam elements will appear as thick green lines. Middle click.

Beam Properties

Specify the material:

Model > Properties > Material

Move the material **AL2014_IPS** to the right pane. Then select

Assign > Beam > All

and middle click twice.

Now we have to specify the beam section and orientation.

Beam Section
Beam > All

and middle click.

Beam Section

The beam section properties window comes up. Enter the data as shown in the figure at the right. Note the section type is "*Hollow Rect*". Other sections available for selection in this window are

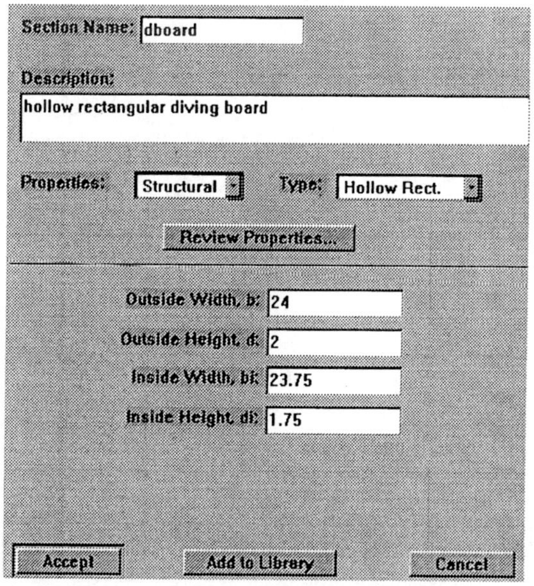

Figure 7 Section properties window

shown in Figure 3. When this is selected, enter the dimensions of the cross section as shown in the figure and accept the dialog.

You will notice on the screen that some schematic symbols have appeared. See Figure 8. If you spin the view a bit, you will see these better. Compare the Y-axis direction of the BACS with the WCS icon in the lower left corner. (The BACS Y-axis is shown in Figure 3.) We'll have to change the orientation of this beam.

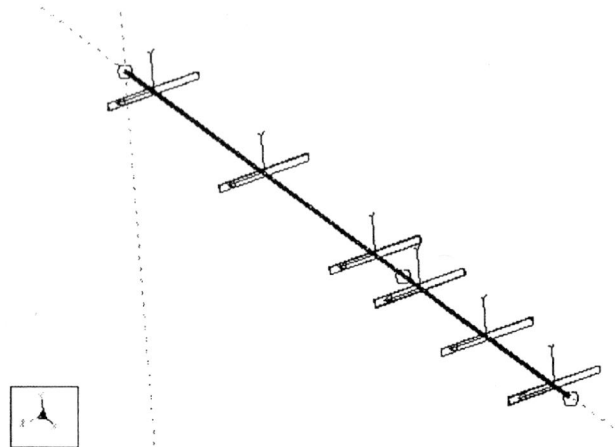

Figure 8 Model with beam sections and orientation defined

Beam Orientation

The Y-axis of the section is pointing in the WCS Z-direction by default. We need to change this. Note that even if the direction was correct, Pro/M requires that we explicitly define this orientation (perhaps to make sure we know what we are doing!):

Properties > Beam Orientation > Beam > All

We will see the beam orientation window as shown below.

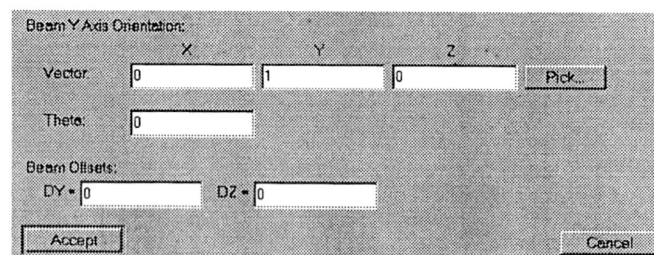

Figure 9 Beam orientation window

Note that the default orientation vector is (0, 0, 1) which signifies the WCS Z-axis. Change this vector to (**0, 1, 0**). Note also that the defaults for Theta and the Offsets are all zero - this is just what we want. Accept the dialog. The model should now look like Figure 8.

Completing the Model

The rest of the model creation is pretty routine.

Constraints

Model > Constraints > Point

Create a *New* constraint set **fixed**. Name the first constraint **wall** and select the left point on the beam, middle click. Leave all the constraints fixed for this cantilevered end. Accept the dialog and move on to the other constraint:

Point

Name this constraint **roller** (still in constraint set **fixed**). Select on the middle support on the beam. At this constraint we want to simulate a roller, so free the rotation constraint around the Z-axis and also free the translation in the X direction.

Loads

We'll apply a single point load on the tip:

Model > Loads > Point

Create a *New* load set **vloads** and select the point at the right end; middle click. Enter a value Y component force of *-200*. Note that the load direction is relative to the WCS.

This completes the model, which should now appear as Figure 10.

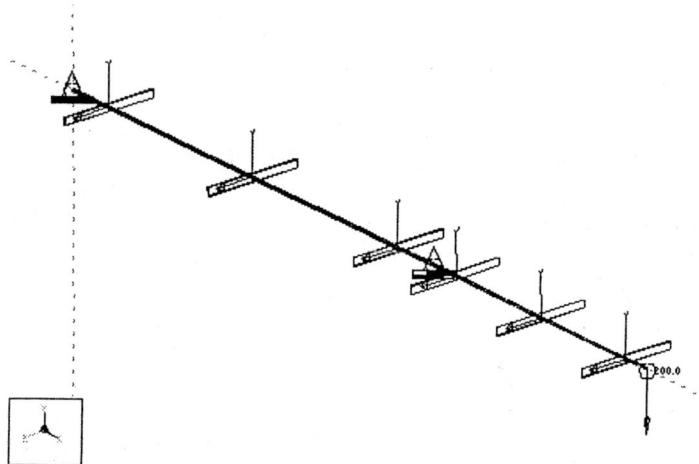

Figure 10 Model completely defined

Analysis and Results

Performing the analysis involves the usual steps:

> *Main > Analyses*

Create a *New* static analysis called **dboard**. Make sure the constraint and load sets are highlighted and set the convergence method *QuickCheck*.

> *Run > Settings*

Set up the usual locations for temporary and output files. Then accept the dialog and

> *Start*

If you haven't saved the model yet, do so now, using the name **dboard**. Open the *Summary* window and check for errors. Assuming there are none, then select

> *Analyses > Edit*

and change to a *Multi-Pass Adaptive*. Set a 1% convergence criterion. You can set the maximum polynomial order to *9*, although we will find that beam models converge much quicker than this.

> *Run > Start*

Delete the existing output files. Open the *Summary* window. The run converges on the 2nd pass, with zero error. What order polynomial was used? The maximum bending stress **max_beam_bending** is 2,670 psi, and the maximum displacement in the Y direction -0.998 inch.

Shear and Moment Diagrams

We will create the usual result windows for stress and deformation, with one slight difference:

> *Results > Create > [bending]*

Get the output directory "*dboard*". In the result window definition, enter a title "*Bending stress*". Under Quantity, select *Stress* and in the pull-down list select *Beam Bending*. Create a fringe plot.

Copy this window to another called **deform** and change the definition to produce a displacement animation.

The bending stress figure is not reproduced here. It shows the maximum stress occurs at the roller support. The deformed shape of the diving board is shown in Figure 11. Note that the slope at the left end is zero, as it should be for a cantilevered support.

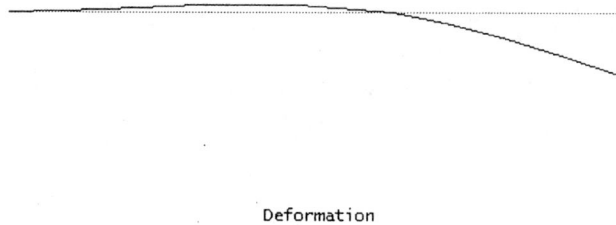

Deformation

Figure 11 Deformed shape of the diving board

Now for some new forms of result windows: the shear and bending moment diagrams. These are created separately for each beam element. *All forces and moments in these diagrams are computed relative to the BACS.* Copy one of the existing windows to a new one called *"beam1"*. Change the definition so that Quantity is **Shear and Moment**, and deselect all options except **Vy** and **Mz** as shown in Figure 12. Pick the **Select** button and click on the left beam. Middle click. Note that the highlighted element end point will be on the left end of the graphs.

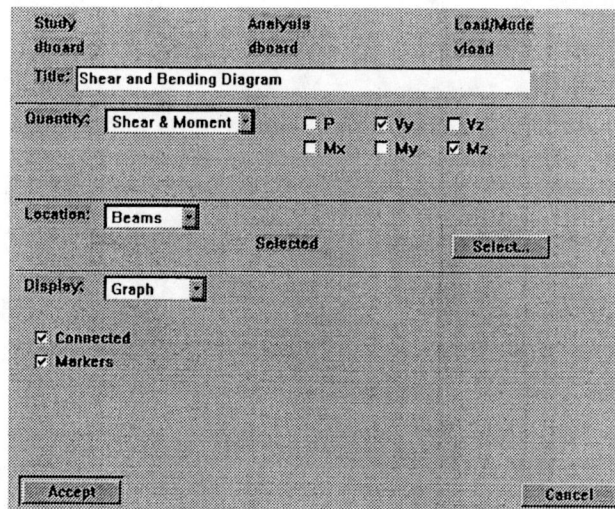

Figure 12 Result window definition for shear and bending moment diagrams

Copy this window definition to another called *"beam2"*. Review this definition and change the selected element to the one on the right. Note the location of the origin of the graph.

In the Show window, highlight the *beam1* and *beam2* definitions only, and select *Show*. We get the combined shear and bending moment diagrams for the two beam elements (note that the horizontal and vertical scales may be different.) shown in Figure 13.

IMPORTANT POINT: From your knowledge of simple beam theory, what sign convention does Pro/M use for shear and bending moment?

What happens to these graphs if we reverse the direction of the BACS Y-axis using the beam orientation property?

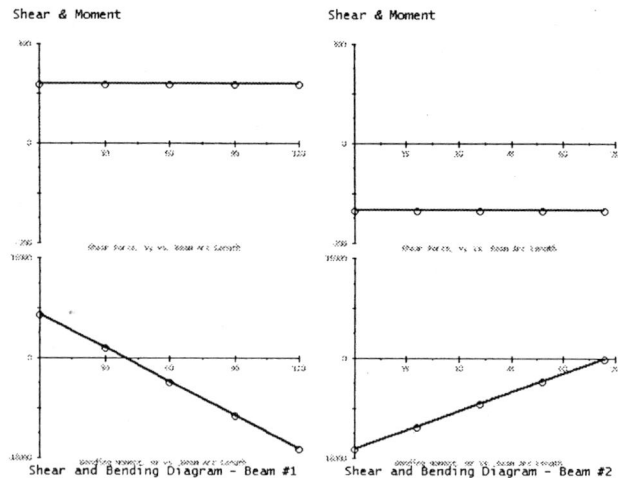

Figure 13 Shear and bending moment diagrams for the two elements

Finding the Support Reactions

Copy the *bending* result window to a new window called *Yreact*. Review this and under Quantity select *Force*, *Reaction*, and set the direction to *Y*. Change Location to *Points* and check *Use All*. Set the Display Precision to *3* and under GEM Subset check the box beside *Points*. See the figure at the right for the completed window definition.

Copy the *Yreact* window definition to a new one called *Zmom*. Change the Quantity to *Moment*, and direction *Z*.

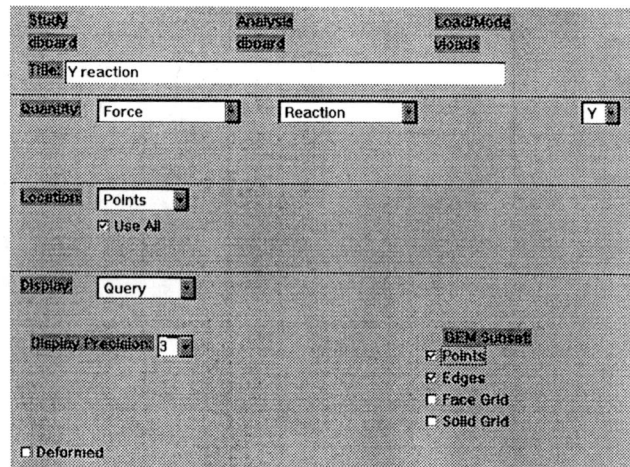

Figure 14 Result window definition for showing the support reactions

Highlight the two new window definitions in the Show column and select *Show*. Here are some new commands for dealing with these windows. Use the pull-down menu command

Windows > Resize_Move

to reshape the result windows from a left/right layout to a top/bottom layout. Follow the prompts in the message window to do this. See Figure 15 for the desired final layout.

Now select Controls, click in the top window, then Query and pick on the two support points. Repeat for the bottom window. This will display the reactions at these points.

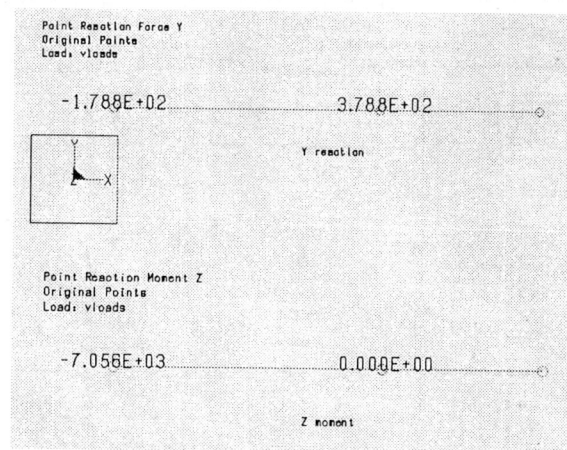

Figure 15 Support reactions

Changing the Constraint

We'll change the constraint on the left end to a pinned joint instead of cantilever

Edit > Constraint

Click on the constraint at the left end. Change Z rotation constraint from fixed to **Free**. Run the Multi-Pass Adaptive analysis again. The maximum displacement in the Y direction is now -1.17 inch, so it has increased a bit from the previous case. The maximum bending stress is the same (Why? Is this a general result?).

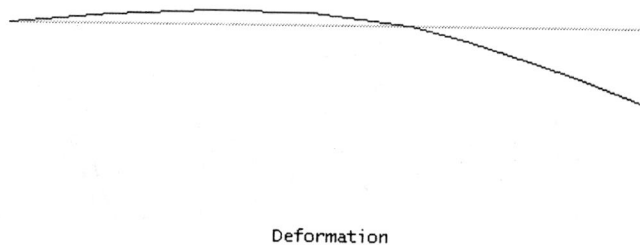

Deformation

Figure 16 Deformed shape of the diving board with pinned left end (RotZ free)

The deformation change from the previous case is not very pronounced. With a pinned end, the beam is free to rotate and should have a non-zero slope at the left end. You might like to increase the scale for the deformation to better see the differences from the previous constraint case.

The new shear and bending moment diagrams are shown in Figure 17. Note that the bending moment goes to zero at the left support, as it should.

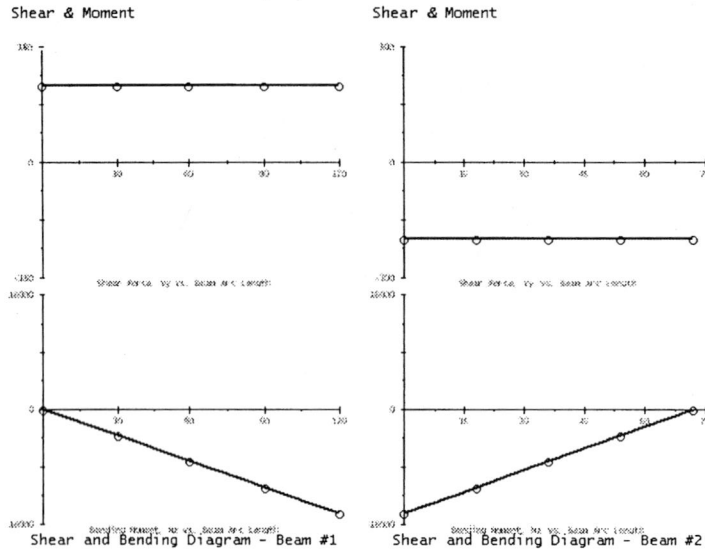

Figure 17 Shear and moment diagrams for model with pinned left end

Now on to the second example...

Example #2 - Distributed Loads, Beam Releases

This example is a bit more complicated and will introduce the use of distributed loads and beam releases. Before we proceed with the model, set up Pro/MECHANICA in the usual way, and specify a grid spacing of 0.2:

> *Display > Master Visibilities > All On | Grid | Accept*
> *Display > Settings > Grid Spacing > [0.2]*
> *Main > Geometry > Curve*
> *Construction Geom > Horizontal > Snap(Point) > [0 0]*
> *Construction Geom > Vertical > Snap(Point) > [0 0]*
> *Utility > Display Coordinates*

Pan and zoom the window so that you see from X = 0 out to X = 3 comfortably.

The Model

A drawing of the model is shown in Figure 18. We will use SI units: lengths in meters, force in Newtons. The steel beam cross section is an I-beam. To accommodate the distributed loads, and to provide sites for beam releases in the second part of the example, the model is divided into 4 beam elements. The origin of the WCS XY system is at the left end.

IMPORTANT NOTE: This beam violates the MECHANICA guidelines for use of beam elements. This guideline is that the *ratio of a beam element length to its largest cross section dimension (its aspect ratio) should be greater than 10:1*, that is, the beam element should be long and slender. This is a normal assumption even for simple beam theory. In short, stubby beam elements, shear takes on an important role not accounted for in long slender beams. We are using this beam here strictly for demonstration purposes.

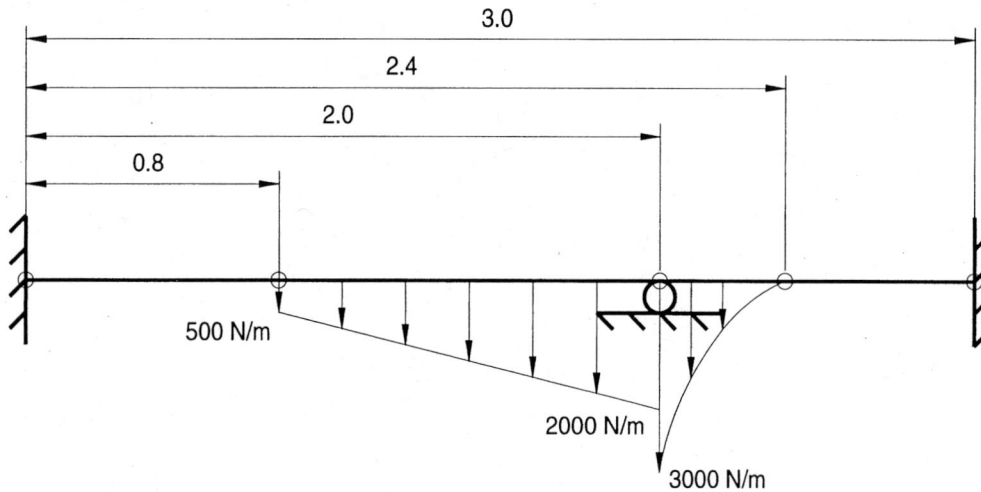

Figure 18 Indeterminate beam with distributed loads (dimensions in meters)

Beam Elements

We will create the four elements directly, without first creating points.

> *Main > Model > 3D*
> *Elements > Beam > Element Snap(Grid)*

Create four elements between the following points (*0, 0*), (*0.8, 0*), (*2.0, 0*), (*2.4, 0*), (*3.0, 0*).

Beam Material

> *Model > Properties > Material*

Move **STEEL_MNS** to the right pane. Then select

> *Assign > Beam > All*

Middle click twice.

Beam Sections

> *Beam Section > Beam > All*

Middle click. Enter a section name, **ibeam** and select the Section type "**I-Beam**" and enter the following values:

flange width	*0.1*
flange thickness	*0.015*
web height	*0.10*
web thickness	*0.01*

The section icons appear on the beam. You might like to spin the view to see these clearly.

Beam Orientation

Properties > Beam Orientation > Beam > All

Change the orientation vector to (**0, 1, 0**). Accept this dialog.

Completing the Model

Constraints

The beam left and right ends are fixed (cantilever) and the middle support is a roller. These are all point constraints, with the main difference being whether we allow rotation about the Z axis.

Model > Constraints
Point

Create a *New* constraint set **supports**. Name the first constraint **wall**. Select the far left and right points and middle click. Leave all the degrees of freedom as fixed. *Accept* the dialog.

Point

Name this constraint **roller** and select the middle point (third from left). This is the roller support so free the X translation and Z rotation.

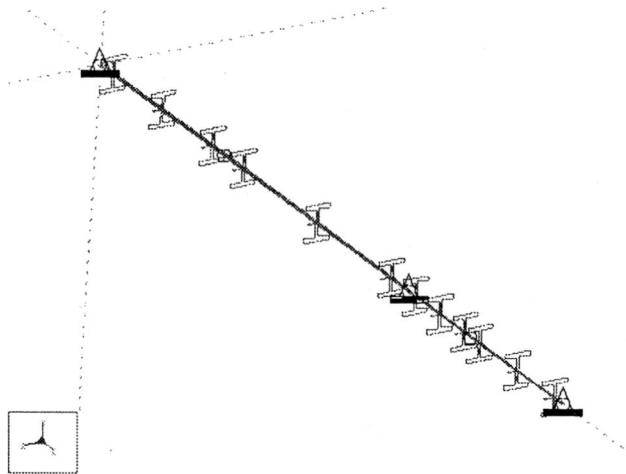

Figure 19 Beam with properties and constraints

The model should now appear as shown in Figure 19.

Distributed Loads

Pro/M can define distributed loads on beam elements using either built in functions (linear, quadratic, cubic, quartic) or specially defined user functions. We have two distributed loads in our model.

Model > Loads > Beam

Create a *New* load set **vloads**. Name the first load **linear**. Select the button under Beams and click on the second element from the left. In the **Distribution** pull-down list pick *Force Per Unit Length* and in the next list, pick *Interpolated over Entity*. Select the *Define* button. The interpolation window opens as shown at the right. Also note the magenta X's which appear on the model; if you look closely you will see that these points are numbered 1 and 2. We are going to create a linearly interpolated load, so we just set values at each end of the element and Pro/M will interpolate along the element. The values we enter in the interpolation window are scale factors that apply to the load components entered in the previous window. Enter the values shown in Figure 20.

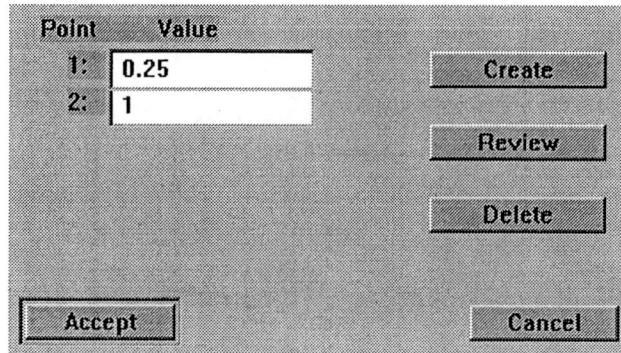

Figure 20 The Interpolation window for distributed loads

Accept this dialog. Back in the **Force/Moment** definition window, enter a value of FY of *-2000*. Select the *Preview* button, to see the direction of the load and the shape of the interpolation function. It should appear as shown in Figure 21. *Accept* the dialog. The shape of the displayed load function will change.

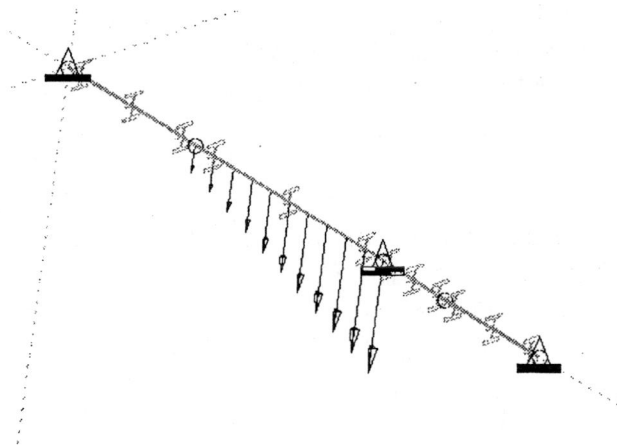

Now for the second load:

Loads > Beam

Figure 21 Linearly distributed load assigned

Name this load **quadratic** (still in load set **vloads**). Select the next element along the beam. Once again, select *Force Per Unit Length* and *Interpolated Over Entity* and select the *Define button*. Since this is a quadratic distribution, we need to create another point. Click the *Add* button to set up an intermediate point along the element. In the Snap menu, select *Midpoint*, and click on the element. Middle click. You may have to zoom in to see a small magenta number 3 beside the new X icon. Enter the values for the three points as follows:

point 1   *1.0*
point 2   *0*
point 3   *0.25*

Accept the dialog. In the **Force/Moment** window enter a value of FY of *-3000*. Click on the

Preview button to see the defined interpolation function as shown in Figure 22. *Accept* the dialog. Once again, the displayed shape of the load function changes.

To review the two loads, select

Edit > Load

Click on any of the load arrows. Follow the prompts to get the load definition window and then select Preview. This will show the actual distribution shape. Repeat this for the other load.

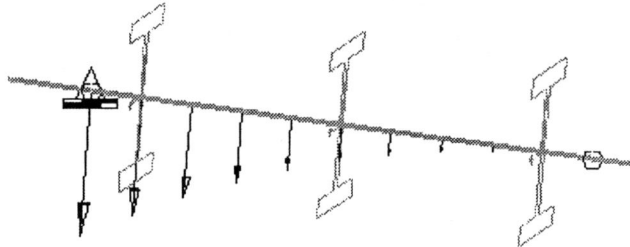

Figure 22 A quadratic distribution with 3 points

Analysis and Results

Main > Analyses

Create a New static analysis called **cbeam.** Make sure the constraint and load sets (**supports** and **vloads**) are highlighted. Select a *Quick Check* and accept.

Run > Settings

Set up the desired output and temporary directories. Then accept the dialog and *Start*. If you haven't saved the model yet, you can provide a name for it, like "*cbeam*". Open the *Summary* window and look for errors. Assuming there are none, set up a *Multi-Pass Analysis* with a 1% convergence. In the analysis definition window, select the *Output* tab and beside **Plotting Grid** enter the value *10* - this will give us smoother curves in the result windows. *Run* the model. In the *Summary* window you will see that convergence is obtained on pass 3. The maximum displacement in the Y direction -2.44e-5 m, and the maximum bending stress is 1.26 MPa.

Shear and Moment Diagrams

We will create windows showing the deformation of the beam, and the shear and bending moment diagrams for each element.

Results > Create > [deform]

Get the output directory **cbeam**. Enter a window title "*Deformation*" and set up an animation of the displacement. The maximum deformation will look like Figure 21. As usual, compare this with the anticipated result, and pay close attention to the constraints. The slope of the deformed beam looks like it is zero at each cantilevered end, and the deflection at the middle support is zero, as expected.

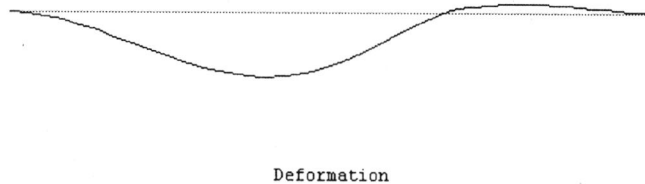

Deformation

Figure 23 Beam deformation

Now set up four new result windows (***beam1***, ***beam2***, ...) to show the shear and bending moment diagrams for each element. For each of these, select **Quantity(Shear and Moment)**, check *Vy* and *Mz*, set up an appropriate title, and use the select button to identify which element to use in each window. Pay close attention to which end of the element will be placed at the left side of the graphs - this is highlighted in magenta when you pick the element. When all four windows have been defined, *Show* them. They will appear as shown in Figure 24, which has been reformated for presentation here. Note that the vertical and horizontal scales in each window are different. Nonetheless, we can look for things like continuity of bending moment along the beam, bending moment in the beam at each end, discontinuity in shear at the middle support, and so on.

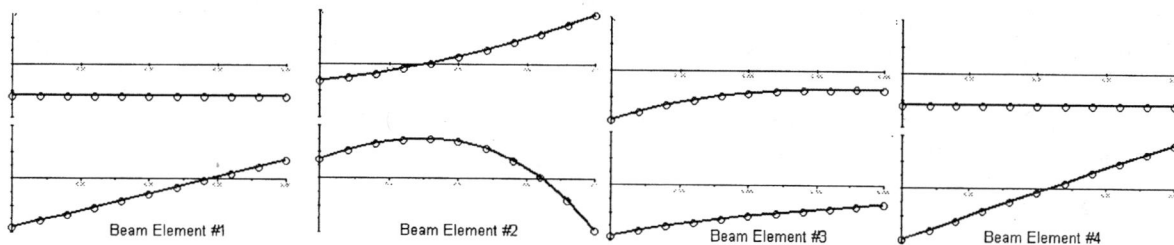

Figure 24 Shear (top) and bending moment (bottom)) diagrams for each element

Beam Releases

A beam release is used to change the type of connection between adjacent beam elements. For a normal (unreleased) connection, all six components of force and bending moment in one element are carried through the connection to the next element. This results in continuity of these parameters along the beam (except at constraints or point loads). In this lesson, we will look at two cases where we want to interrupt this continuity using beam releases. In the present example, we will modify the model so that the beam is hinged at the second and fourth points. A hinge parallel to the Z axis of the element means that no bending moment can be transmitted through the connection. For static equilibrium of the beam on either side of the hinge, this requires that the bending moment be zero at the hinge.

To demonstrate this with the current beam, first we'll modify the loads a bit:

Edit > Delete > Entity > Loads

and click on the quadratic load to the right of the middle support. Middle click twice.

Edit > Load

Click on the linear load. Increase the magnitude of FY to **-4000**.

Run a Multi-Pass analysis of this. In the ***Summary*** window note the maximum bending stress is 2.5 MPa and the maximum Y displacement is -5.0e-5 m. The deformed shape looks like Figure 25.

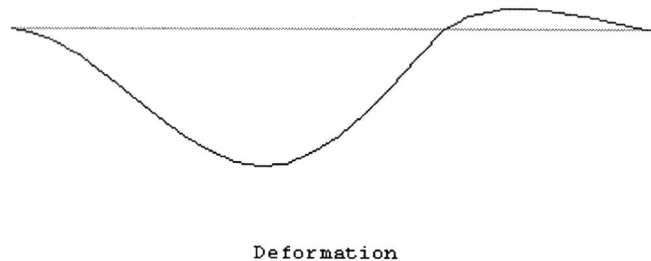

Deformation

Figure 25 Deformation of beam before beam releases applied

Note the continuity (smoothness of curvature) of the deformed shape. The shear and bending moments look like Figure 26. Note the non-zero bending moments at the connections between the first and second element, and between the third and fourth element.

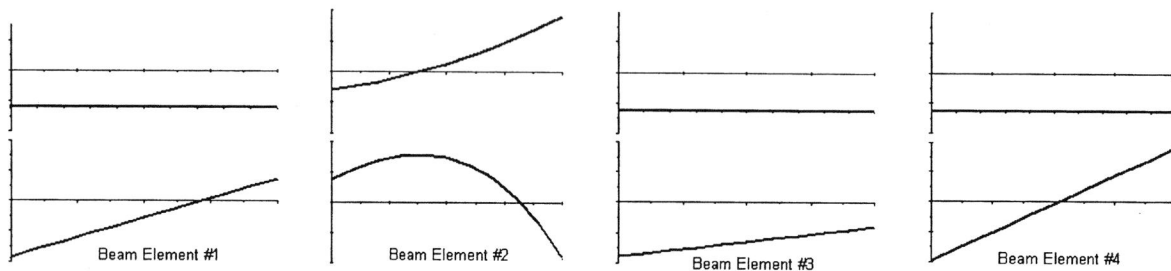

Beam Element #1   Beam Element #2   Beam Element #3   Beam Element #4

Figure 26 Shear and moment diagrams before beam releases applied

Setting Releases

We will release two points:

Model > Properties > Beam Releases

Click on the farthest right beam element and middle click. The element highlights. Read the prompt in the message window and click on the left end of the element (the 4th point along the beam). In the **Beam Release** window that opens (Figure 27), free the rotation in the Z direction as shown. Accept the dialog. A small circle around the beam element close to the release point appears to indicate the release. We do not need to release the connecting element.

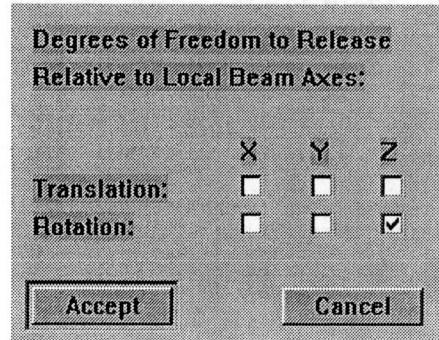

Figure 27 Defining beam releases

Now click on the first beam element, middle click, and select the second point along the beam. Release the Rotation Z degree of freedom on this point as well. The locations where beam releases are applied are indicated on the model by small circles around the element just beside the element end point, as shown in Figure 28.

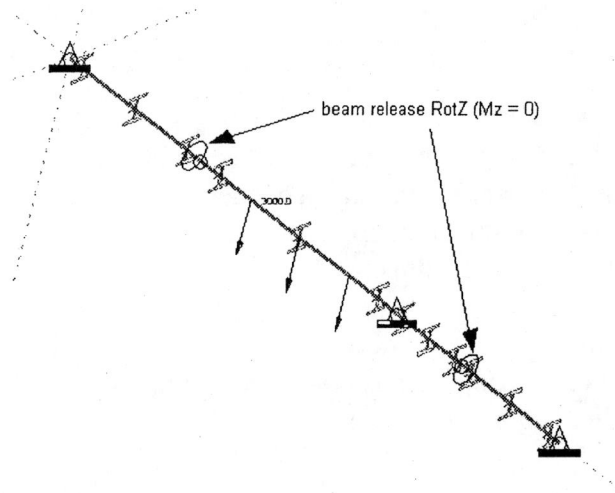

Figure 28 Icons showing location of beam releases

Results

With the new beam releases, rerun the multipass adaptive analysis:

Main > Run > Start

Delete the output files. Open the *Summary* window and note that maximum bending moment is now 4.59 MPa and the maximum Y displacement is -8.33e-5m. The deformed shape of the beam with releases is shown in Figure 29. Note the abrupt changes in slope at the points of the beam releases.

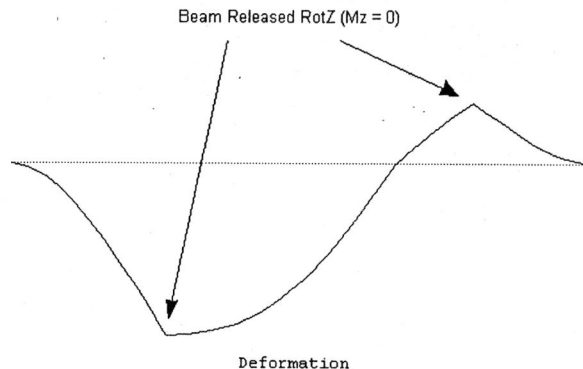

Figure 29 Deformation of beam with releases

Now **Show** the shear and bending moment diagrams. Observe that the shear is non-zero and continuous between these released connections, and the moment has indeed become zero.

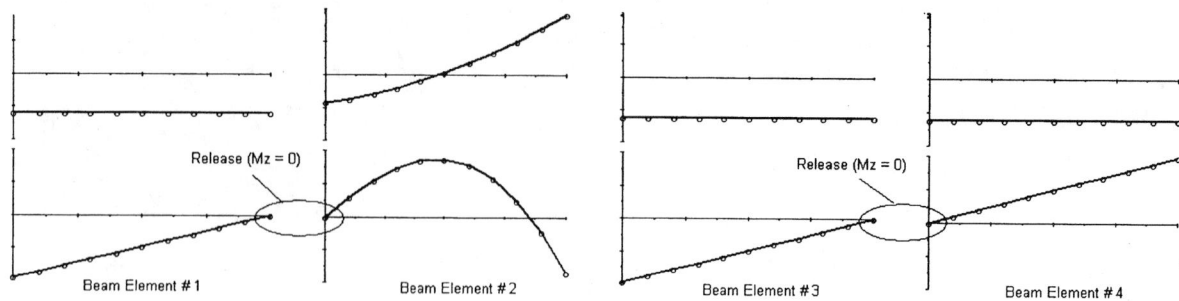

Figure 30 Shear and moment diagrams with beam releases

Some other cases where beam releases will come in handy are in modeling trusses (no moment of any kind transmitted through a connection) as we will see in the next example, an expansion joint (no axial load transmitted), or a connection like a dovetail (all forces and moments transmitted except shear in one direction).

Note that in both of our beam examples, we have used loading only in the XY plane. This was for simplicity only, and is not a restriction in Pro/M. We can apply loads in any direction, including applied moments.

Example #3 - Frames and Trusses

The Model

The two previous models have been relatively simple one dimensional beams. Beams, of course, can be combined to formed complex 2D and 3D structures. In this section, we will investigate how to create frames and trusses based on the geometry shown in Figure 31. The material is steel and the beam section is a hollow circular pipe with an outside diameter of 3" and a wall thickness of 0.25". This shape will make specification of the beam orientation a bit easier. We will start off with a 2D frame.

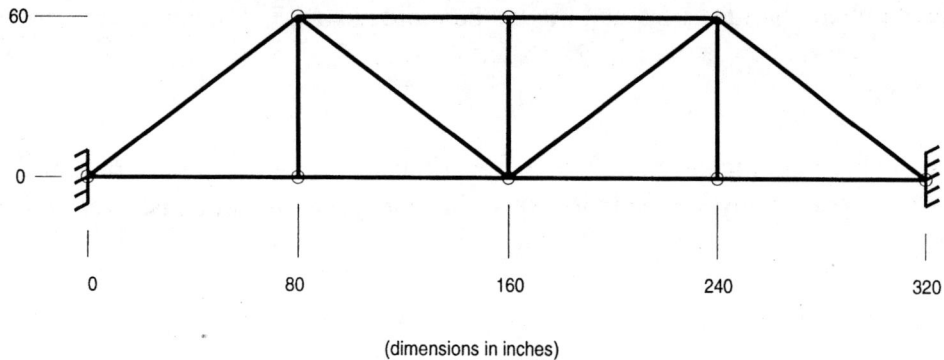

Figure 31 Frame/truss geometry

Set up the Pro/M environment in the usual way. A grid spacing of *20* will be handy here.

Beam Elements

Create the beam elements directly, without underlying geometry:

> *Main > Model > 3D*
> *Elements > Beam > Element Snap(Grid)*

and create elements according to Figure 31. Each beam element connects two nodes in the frame - there are 13 elements in all.

Beam Materials

Assign the material to the elements with

> *Model > Properties > Material*

Move **STEEL_IPS** to the right pane and select

> *Assign > Beam > All*

Middle click twice.

Beam Section

Set up the beam cross-sectional shape, a hollow circle with a 3.0" OD and 2.5" ID:

> *Properties > Beam Section > Beam > All*

and middle click. Enter a set name *"hcirc"* and select a **Hollow Circle** section from the pull down list. Set the outside radius as *1.5* and the inside radius of *1.25*.

Beam Orientation

Zoom in on the beam section icons and observe the orientation of the Y and Z axes of the BSCS. Remember that orientation must be explicitly specified for all beam elements, even if the default is satisfactory:

> ***Properties > Beam Orientation > Beam > All***

Middle click and accept the default orientation (0, 0, 1).

This model geometry will be common for three different problems (Models A, B, and C) treated below.

Model A - 2D Frame

Completing the Model

Loads

Apply a uniform load to one of the elements:

> ***Model > Loads > Beam***

Create a *New* load set called **vload**. Select the third element across the bottom. Middle click. Set a total, uniform load of Fy = *-1000*. Use *Display > Settings* to turn on the display of load magnitude.

Constraints

We will constrain the two end points of the model using pins:

> ***Model > Constraints***
> ***Point***

Create a *New* constraint set called **fixed**. Select the two points at the extreme left and right ends of the frame. Middle click. Set the Z rotation to **Free** to simulate pinned connections with the ground. Accept the dialog.

The model should now appear as shown in Figure 32.

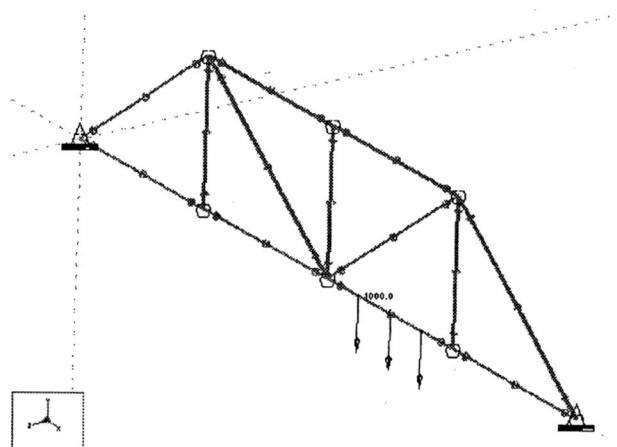

Figure 32 The completed 2D frame (Model A)

Analysis and Results

Set up a static analysis called **frame**. The constraint and load sets (**fixed** and **vload**) should be highlighted. Select a **Quick Check** analysis. **Run** the analysis (don't forget the **Settings**). You may be asked to enter a model name ("*frame*") to save the file. Check the **Summary** for errors and warnings. If all goes well, change the analysis to a **Multi-Pass Adaptive**, 1% convergence. Set a Plotting Grid of **10**, and rerun. Open the **Summary** window. The run converges in 3 pass. The maximum bending stress id 4467 psi, the maximum tensile stress is -501 psi. There is no torsion on any elements. The maximum displacement in the Y direction is -0.043 inch.

Create a result window showing a displacement animation. The maximum deformation should look like Figure 33. Note the continuity of slope of each beam through each connection. Also, each beam shows some bending.

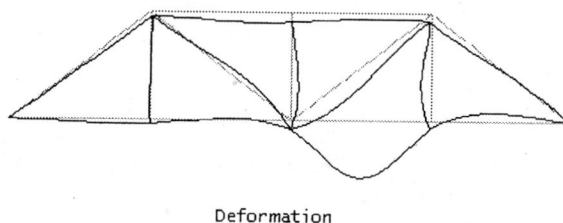

Deformation

Figure 33 Deflection of the 2D Frame

Create four windows to show **Stress - Beam Bending, Stress - Beam Tensile, Stress - Beam Torsional**, and **Stress - Beam Total**. Show these four windows. These are not reproduced here. What you should note are the relative proportions of the various contributions to the total stress. The maximum bending stress is 4467 psi, the maximum and minimum tensile stress are 310 psi and -501 psi, respectively. The torsional stress is zero everywhere. Thus the total stress is composed almost entirely of bending stress.

Model B - 2D Truss

In a classical truss model, elements can carry only an axial load (tension or compression) and loads must be applied only at the joints. In Pro/M, lateral loads can be applied to any element, and we only require that the bending moment vanish at the joints. For a 2D truss, we only need to worry about moments about the Z axes. We can set this up easily using *beam releases*. We want to release RotZ on the end of every element. Pro/M will not let us set releases on elements that already have a point constraint or point load attached, so we will first delete the constraints:

Edit > Delete > Entity > Constraints > All

and middle click twice.

Beam Releases

To set the beam releases:

Model > Properties > Beam Releases > All

and middle click. If all beams are selected, Pro/M automatically puts releases at both ends of each beam. Carefully read the window that opens. Check the release ***Rotation Y*** (this is the Y axis of the BACS). Accept the dialog. The frame with releases is shown in Figure 34.

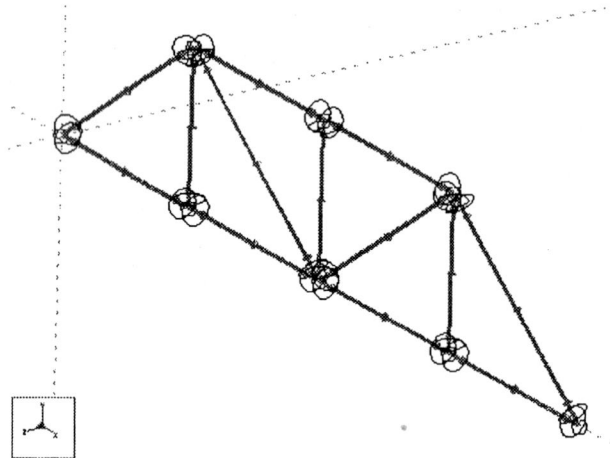

Figure 34 Beam releases applied to all elements to form the 2D truss model

Completing the Model

We need to redefine the constraints, since these were deleted to create the beam releases.

Constraints

Model > Constraints > Point

select the same two points as before. In the constraint definition, free the rotation around Z (note that this is relative to the WCS).

This completes our creation of the 2D truss model, see Figure 35.

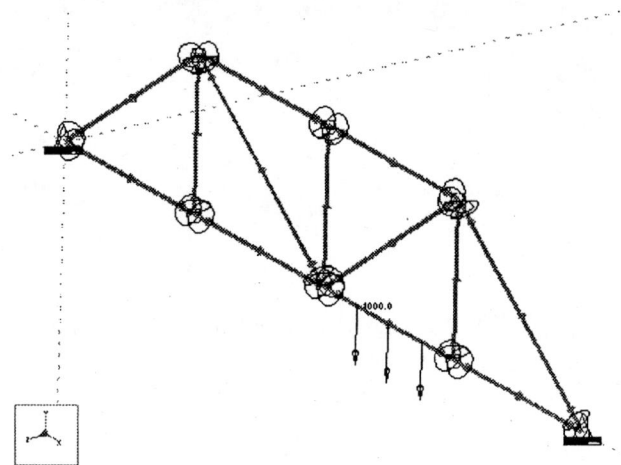

Figure 35 Truss model complete (Model B)

Analysis and Results

Since we have deleted the old constraint set, we need to update the analysis definition:

> *Main > Analyses > Edit*

and make sure the new constraint and load sets are selected.

> *Main > Run > Start*

Accept error checking. You will get a message about points not being attached to elements at the location of the constraints. We must delete the release on at least one element going into the constrained points. Do this using:

> *Edit > Delete > Property > Beam Releases*

and select the upper diagonal beam elements at each end of the frame. Removing the releases on these elements will not affect the results because all elements they connect to are still released.

Now go to *Run > Start* again. Delete the output files and open the *Summary* window. Convergence is obtained on pass 3 with a maximum bending stress of 7286 psi, a maximum tensile stress of -482 pis. The torsional stress is zero everywhere. The maximum Y displacement is -0.118 inch.

The deformed shape is shown in Figure 36. Note the bending in the loaded beam, while the other beams are all straight. If you look at the bending stress window, you will see that only the one element has any bending stresses.

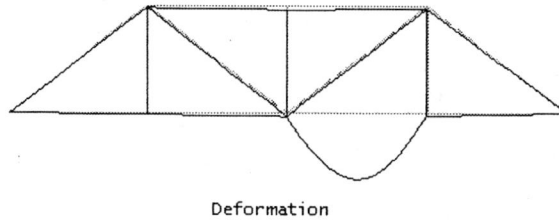

Deformation

Figure 36 Deformation of truss with uniform load
on one element

Let's go back and modify the existing load to convert it to *-500* lb point loads on each end node
of the same element. Many FEA packages for trusses only allow point loads at the nodes. Delete
all the existing loads and constraints. Reapply beam releases to all beam elements (freeing the Y
rotation). Now create constraints (free the rotation about Z) at the end points, and two point
loads at each end of the third element on the bottom of the truss. Let's see what problems we
might have, using a command we haven't used before:

Model > Model Check

We evidently have some trouble here. Delete the releases on the end diagonal elements and the
third element between the loaded points using

Edit > Delete > Properties > Beam Releases

and clicking on the elements. Middle click and select

Model > Model Check

again. It appears that this has solved the problem. The model should appear as in Figure 37.

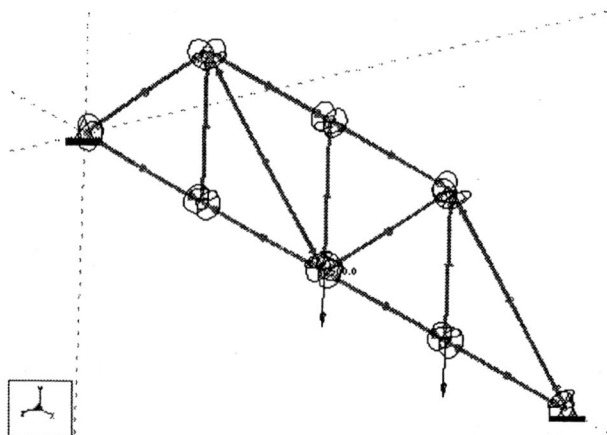

Figure 37 Uniform load replaced by two point loads

Check the analysis to make sure the new load set is being used. Rerun the analysis. In the *Summary* window, note the maximum bending stress is essentially zero (6e-12), the maximum tensile stress is -482 psi, torsion is zero. The maximum Y displacement is -0.0067 in. The deformation looks like this...

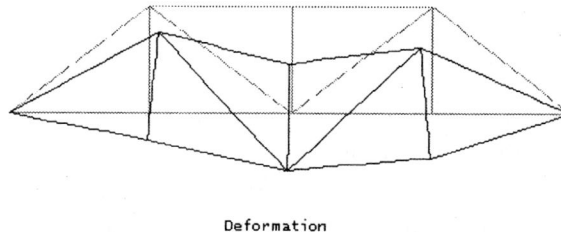

Deformation

Figure 38 Deformation of truss with point loads.
No bending in any element

Observe that all elements remain straight. This is a consequence of requiring zero bending moment on the end of each beam, and no lateral loading. Each beam element is then a two-force member, with the force being axial. Create new stress windows, and note that none of the elements have bending or torsional stresses. You should also be able to identify which elements in the truss are zero force members.

Model C - 3D Frame

We'll take the existing 2D frame and copy it to form another side of a 3D frame. We are eventually going to do something a bit different here: apply a displacement constraint to model a slumping foundation below one of the frame supports. First, get rid of the beam releases and existing loads:

> *Edit > Delete > Property > Beam Releases > All .. middle click twice*
> *Edit > Delete > Entity > Loads > All .. middle click twice*

Modifying the Model

Translated Copy

> *Edit > Translate*

Check the *Copy* box and select

> *Beams > All*

Middle click and select *Snap(Point)*. For the start location enter (*0, 0, 0*). For the end location enter (*0, 0, 80*). The number of copies is *1*. Middle click. The beams are translated and copied, taking all their properties (material, section, orientation) with them.

We now need to create some new elements to connect the two sides of the frame.

Model > Elements > Beam > Snap(Point)

Create the 8 elements (5 on the bottom and 3 on the top) to connect the two sides of the frame. Middle click when finished. To apply properties to these 8 new elements, here is a new tool....

Creating Groups

We will assign the 8 new beam elements to a special group. Beside the *View* command at the top of the screen, select the *Group* button. The groups window (Figure 39) appears. In this window, select *Create*, and enter a group name "*crossbeams*" and a description. Change the color to orange (or your choice), and accept the dialog. Then *Add > Beams* and click on the 8 new elements. Middle click twice.

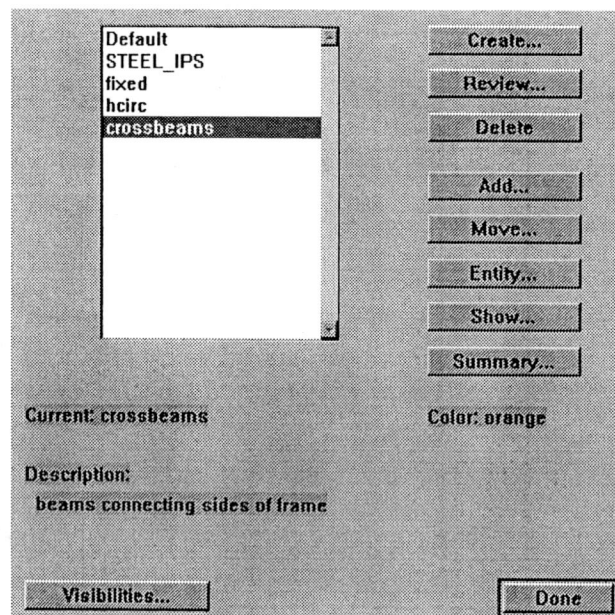

Figure 39 The *Groups* window

You might like to explore the other buttons in the Groups window, then select *Done*. Now select

Display > Group Visibilities

and deselect the *Default* group. *Accept*. The new elements will show in orange. It will now be very easy to assign properties to members of this group. At the end of each of the following two command strings (some middle clicks required), accept all dialog boxes:

Model > Properties > Material
Assign > Beam > Group > crossbeams | Accept > (middle click twice)
Properties > Beam Section
Beam > Group > crossbeams | Accept > (middle click) *> hcirc | Accept*

The orientation property will be a little different:

> ***Properties > Beam Orientation***
> ***Beam > Group > crossbeams | Accept >*** (middle click)

For these lateral beams we need the BACS Y-axis to point in the WCS Y-direction. Thus, set the Y Axis Orientation to (*0, 1, 0*) and accept the dialog.

Completing the Model

Constraints

We will initially set constraints on all of the corners the same as before:

> ***Model > Constraints > Point***

In the constraint set **fixed**, select the end corners and free the rotation around Z (note this is relative to the WCS).

Gravity Load

To get a feel for the effect of gravity on this frame:

> ***Model > Loads > Gravity***

Create a *New* load set **gload**. Set the y-component to *-386.4* (remember we are using inches). A symbol appears at the origin indicating the direction of gravity in the model[3]. See Figure 40 at the right (note that this is a perspective view, which makes interpretation of wireframe models a lot easier). You can just make out the gravity arrow at the far back corner.

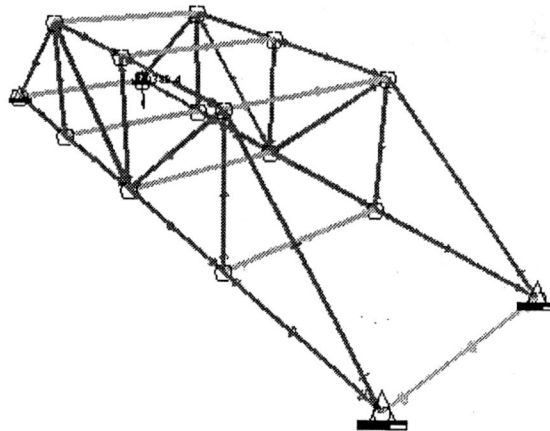

Figure 40 Perspective view of complete 3D frame (Model C) with gravity load

---

[3] Of course gravity acts on every element, not just the corner!

Analysis and Results

> *Main > Analyses > Edit*

Select the load set **gload** (only) and constraint set **fixed**. Accept the dialog and run the analysis.

> *Run > Start*

Delete output files and open the *Summary* window. Convergence is on the 3rd pass. Note the maximum bending stress is 448 psi, maximum tensile stress is -294 psi, maximum torsion stress is 9.2 psi, and the maximum Y displacement is -0.0064 in.

The deformed shape is shown below. You may have to recreate the *deform* window we set up before since we have changed the model since then. Each element sags a bit under gravity. The animation of this looks like the frame is melting!

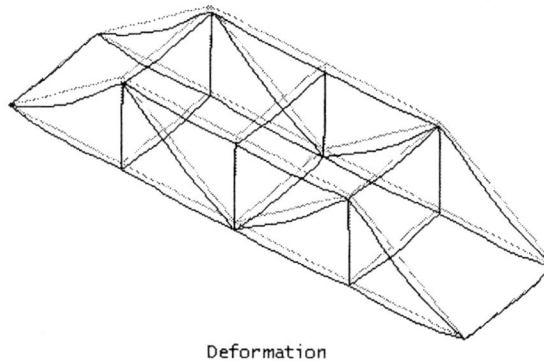

Deformation

Figure 41 Deformation of Model C under gravity load

Displacement Constraint

Now we will modify the constraint at one corner to simulate a settling foundation for the frame. This represents a forced displacement in the Y direction for the constraint.

> *Edit > Constraint*

Click on the front, right corner point constraint. Change TransY from fixed to *Prescribed*, and enter a value of *-0.5*. Middle click twice.

> *Run > Start*

Delete the output files and open the *Summary*. The maximum bending stress is now a whopping 20,457 psi. The maximum tensile stress is -457 psi, maximum torsion stress is -783, and the maximum Y displacement is at the constraint, -0.50 inch. The deformation looks like the following figure. You will have to change the scale factor for the deformation display. Note the curvature in the crossbeam at the end of the frame and recall that we have set RotX to *fixed* on both end constraints. You might like to free this constraint and run the analysis again to see what happens.

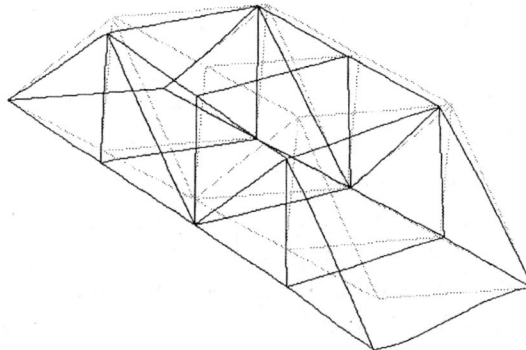

Deformation

Figure 42 Deformation of Model C with displaced support on front corner

In the stress windows, you will note that the bending stress is very low in all elements except the crossbeam entering the displaced point. You might like to edit all the constraints to free rotations around all axes to see what happens.

As an added exercise, you might like to try to apply beam releases to convert this model to a truss. Before you do that, select *View > Right* and *View > Top* and figure out what problems you might encounter with a truss model!

Summary

This has been a busy lesson and we have covered a lot of material. Beam models can be the simplest in terms of geometry, but possibly the most difficult to set up in terms of modeling parameters required. The most difficult of these parameters, particularly in 3D, are related to the problem of determining beam orientation. In addition, we have not dealt with asymmetric beams, like channels or angles, or curved beams. Before you try that, you should consult the Pro/M documentation and study the sections on the BSCS (Beam Shape Coordinate System) and the BCPCS (Beam Centroidal Principle Coordinate System). The idea of beam releases is also probably a new concept, and their use in modeling will require some additional study.

In the next chapter, we will cover the final topic in stress analysis - solid models. Before you go on to that, you are encouraged to try some of the exercises below.

Questions for Review

1.   What does BACS stand for?
2.   How is the X-axis of the BACS determined?
3.   How are the Y- and Z-axes of the BACS determined? That is, what is the relation of the BACS to the WCS?
4.   When a load is applied to a beam, in what coordinate system are its components specified?
5.   What is the BSCS? What parameters are used to define it? Relative to what?
6.   What standard beam sections are available in Pro/M?
7.   What command can you use to determine the direction of an element's X and Y directions?
8.   In our diving board problem, how would you model the case of a person standing on one of the corners at the tip of the board? Discuss both loads and constraints for this scenario.
9.   Find out if and where Pro/M writes any data to a file associated with the shear and moment diagrams.
10.   What is the Pro/M general guideline for the beam element geometry?
11.   Is it possible to create a single distributed load that spans several elements?
12.   Is it possible to have two or more distributed loads acting on the same element, say in different planes (e.g. a linear distributed load in the XY plane, and a quadratic load in the XZ plane)?
13.   Is it possible to have both point loads and distributed loads acting on the same element?
14.   Can a point load act in the center of an element?
15.   Can you think of a way to model a tapered beam?
16.   What sign convention does Pro/M use to draw shear and bending moment diagrams? Is this the same one you usually use?
17.   What is the purpose of a beam release, and how is it applied?
18.   What is the coordinate system used to define beam releases?
19.   Assume there are two collinear beam elements that meet at a point. Describe the physical situation that would result in the following beam releases for one of the elements at that point:

	Translation Released			Rotation Released		
	X	Y	Z	X	Y	Z
Case 1	✔					
Case 2					✔	✔
Case 3				✔		
Case 4				✔	✔	✔
Case 5		✔				✔

20.   What is the basic difference between a frame and a truss? How does this complicate the model?
21.   How do you create a group? What can you use groups for?

Exercises

1.   For the beam and loading shown below, find the maximum bending stress. Plot the shear and bending moment diagrams for each element. Redo the problem assuming pinned ends. The cross section is a hollow rectangle, 4" high and 3" wide with a wall thickness of 0.25". The material is steel.

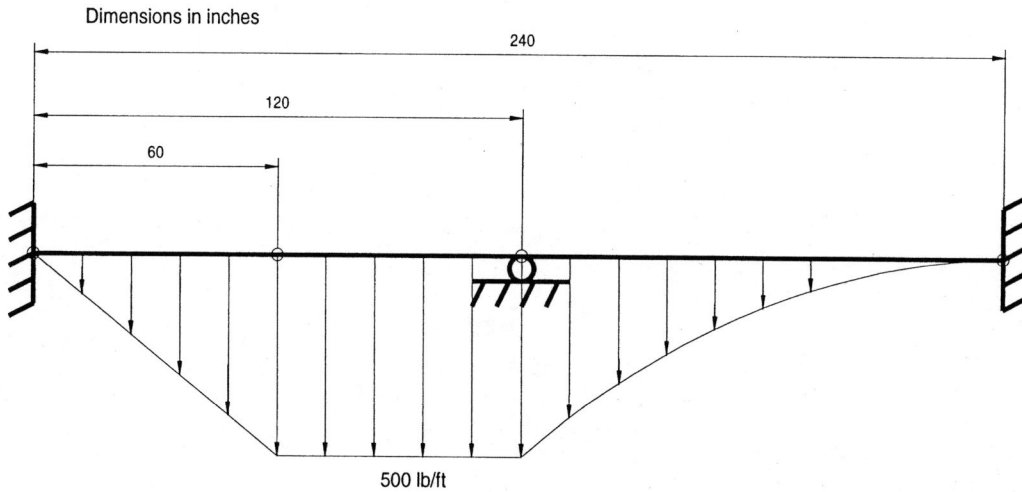

Dimensions in inches

240

120

60

500 lb/ft

2.   A transmission tower is shown below (2D model only). During a hurricane, the loads on the tower caused by the cables are deflected 30° from the vertical. First using a frame model, find the maximum stress and deflection in the tower. Then, convert to a truss model and report the same quantities. The steel cross section is a hollow circle, OD 8.0 cm, with a wall thickness of 5.0 mm. Are any members in danger of buckling?

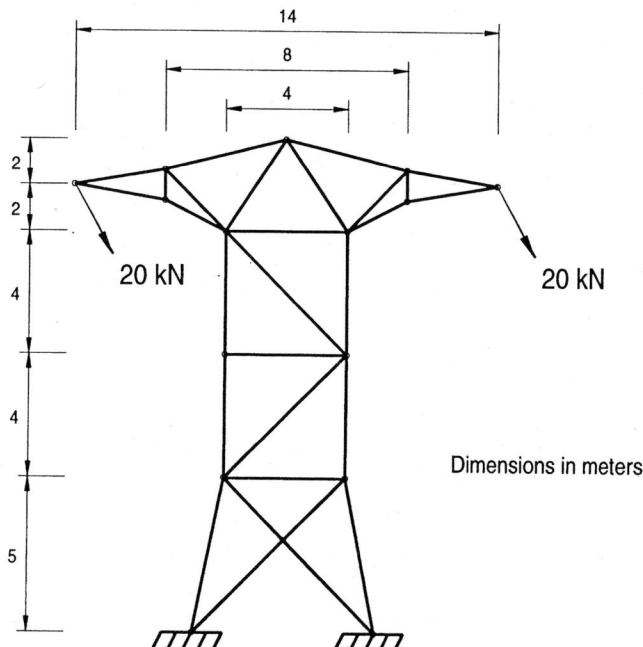

14

8

4

2

2

20 kN

4

20 kN

4

Dimensions in meters

5

This page left blank.

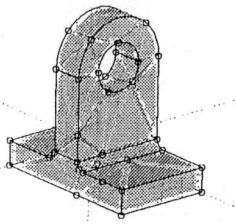

Chapter 9 :

Solid Models

Synopsis:

Creating solid models using manual, semi-automatic, and fully automatic methods; solid element types; extruding surfaces contain shell elements; extruding multiple curves simultaneously; setting up new coordinate systems

Overview of this Lesson

In this final chapter dealing with independent mode, we will look at the creation of solid elements for modeling parts for which the simpler elements and models (plane stress, plane strain, beams, etc.) are not applicable. General 3D solid models are quite difficult to make and there are enumerable ways to do it. We will use a single simple part and use three different methods to create the model to expose you to a number of approaches. The first is a fully manual method for creating individual elements and the mesh. The second approach is semi-automatic, using AutoGEM to do some of the element creation steps. In the third version, we will use AutoGEM to create the entire solid element mesh. Other than creation of the geometry and mesh, the other modeling procedures are the same as we have seen many times before, so these are not given in great detail. We will introduce a new command for creating a *User Coordinate System* (UCS) that will make some of the geometry creation a bit easier.

Modeling with 3D Solids

Solid Element Types

Pro/MECHANICA uses three different solid model elements, illustrated in Figure 1. These are 6-sided bricks, 5-sided wedges, and 4-sided tetrahedrons ("tets"). The surfaces and edges of these elements do not have to be planar or straight. As you can imagine, there are some restrictions on the allowed geometries of individual elements, although these are not excessively severe. For example, the interior angle between faces of an element where they meet at an edge cannot be outside the range from 0 to 175 degrees. These rules are embedded in the mesh generator AutoGEM, and will not normally cause problems. If you do any manual mesh generation, you may have to beware of these (consult the Pro/M documentation for further details).

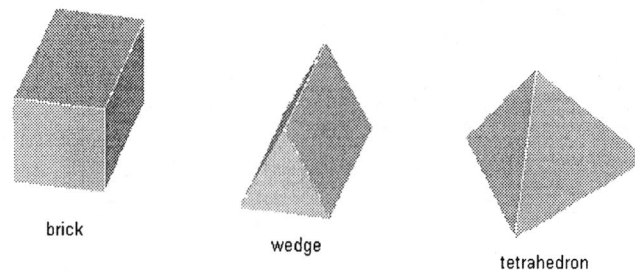

brick

wedge

tetrahedron

Figure 1 Solid elements in Pro/MECHANICA

Solid Model Construction

There is a lot of flexibility in how we can create a mesh for a solid model. The available methods span the range from purely manual to purely automatic (and transparent). Generally, solid models of even moderately complex parts will not be feasible using manual methods. If you are using Pro/M in conjunction with a solid modeling CAD program, like Pro/ENGINEER (in *integrated* mode), then you may never even see the mesh. However, cases may arise when you require stricter control over the mesh, or there are special requirements of the mesh which cannot be met by the automatic mesher. In these cases, you may have to create some (or all) of the mesh using methods discussed in this lesson.

Just for interest, in this lesson we will look at the full range of mesh generation, from manual to automatic, for the same part geometry. As in the previous chapters, we will use Pro/M as a stand-alone program, without exploring its use in integrated mode with Pro/ENGINEER which is covered in the next chapter.

Basically, there are three different levels of mesh construction: manual, semi-automatic, and automatic. We will explore all three of these in this lesson.

Element Creation Methods

Manual

To create each element manually, we can use a combination of geometric primitives (points, edges, and surfaces). Some of these possibilities are illustrated in the figure at the right. For example, two non-intersecting curves can be selected to identify a quadrilateral face, and selecting two non-intersecting quadrilateral faces will produce a brick element. We can also extrude a surface[1] to form a brick or wedge (depending on the shape of the surface). We can revolve a surface to form a curved brick, wedge, or even tet element (the shape depends on the initial shape of the surface and whether one edge of the surface touches the rotation axis). The possibilities are unlimited! To illustrate the method, our first version of the part model in this lesson will be constructed manually.

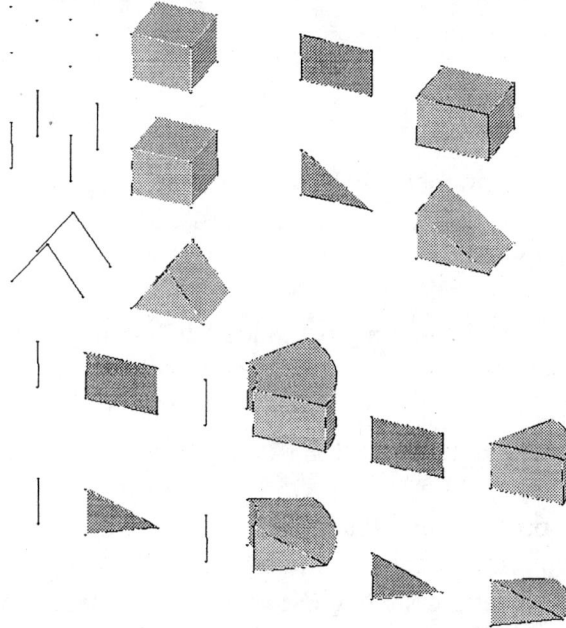

Figure 2 Some methods for creating solid elements

Automatic

The automatic mesh generator AutoGEM will create a mesh of solid elements (usually tets) from any solid volume, even ones with interior voids. Volumes can be created by extruding or revolving surfaces or using volume primitives (cones, cylinders, and so on). The only restriction is that the volume must represent a valid solid. For users of Pro/ENGINEER, this is not a great concern since Pro/E will only create valid solids. If volumes are created manually and combined to form the part, you will have to be careful about trimming and/or deleting interior surfaces formed by the individual volumes. There can be no cracks at the edges or where surfaces meet. Also, Pro/M does not automatically "join" volumes together in the same way that, for example, a union of solid primitives is performed in solid modeling CAD packages. If you run Pro/M in integrated mode with Pro/E, then AutoGEM will do all the mesh generation for you, and in fact, you will never even see the mesh.

We will use AutoGEM to create the solid mesh in the third variation of this lesson's model.

---

[1] Actually, we extrude or revolve a shell element associated with the surface, then delete the shell.

Semi-Automatic

If you don't like the mesh produced by AutoGEM, or require special care in some parts of the model, you can use a combination of AutoGEM and manual methods. You are, of course, allowed to delete any individual elements created by AutoGEM, and create your own to fill the same volume. We will perform a semi-automatic mesh generation in the second version of the part model in this lesson.

Imported Models

We have mentioned the use of Pro/M in integrated mode with Pro/ENGINEER. This is probably the easiest way to deal with 3D solids. Keep in mind, however, the discussion in chapter 1 about the difference between CAD and FEA models.

Pro/M is also able to import models in a number of formats (IGES and DXF, to name a few).

Applying Loads and Constraints

Solid models require the same special treatment of loads and constraints as we have seen before. In general, avoid point and line loads and constraints that can lead to theoretically infinite local stresses, or be prepared to use excluded elements. We have seen that AutoGEM picks up on this modeling error and will automatically create small elements at point loads or constraints. Re-entrant corners can also sometimes cause problems with convergence.

With that brief introduction to solid models, let's proceed with our first example.

The Model Geometry

The part we will study in this lesson is a simple bracket, shown in Figure 1 below. The material is aluminum. Dimensions (in inches) of the part are shown in Figure 2. The part is supported on the end faces of the base and carries a load applied to the inside surface of the hole. The load is directed so that symmetry of the model is not available.

Figure 3 The bracket model

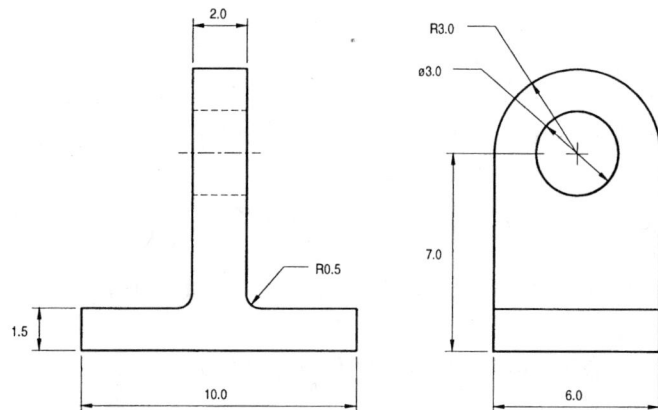

Figure 4 Bracket geometry

Set up our working environment:

> *Display > Master Visibilities > All On | Grid | Accept*
> *Display > Settings*
> > *Display Type(Flat Shade)*
> > *Shade(Elements)*
> > *Shrink All Elements | 0.2*
> > *Grid Spacing | 0.5*
> > *Accept*
> *Utility > Display Coordinates*
> *Main > Geometry > Curve*
> *Construction Geom > Horizontal > Snap(Point) > [0 0]*
> *Construction Geom > Vertical > Snap(Point) > [0 0]*

Pan and zoom the display to see the upper right quadrant out to x = 10.

Model A

For this version of the model, we will see how to construct solid elements by extruding shell elements associated with surfaces. This method of model construction is not quite at the lowest level, since we will be doing some extrusion to duplicate elements. Manual methods of element creation give us the most control over the shape and layout of the grid. However, as we will see, the process is still quite laborious.

Our plan of attack is to first create the base of the bracket, up to and including the fillets. Then we will create the vertical support with the hole. In order to create extruded (or revolved) solid elements, we must create shell elements associated with a planar surface. So, for each of the base and support, we first need to create surfaces and shells along one planar surface.

The Base

Geometry and Surfaces

Start by creating the vertical edges shown in Figure 5 below:

Curve > Line > Two Points > Snap(Grid)

The vertical lines are 1.5 inches long, positioned at x = 0, 2.0, 3.5, 6.5, 8.0, and 10. The horizontal line is from (4,2) to (6,2). Complete with the triangle.

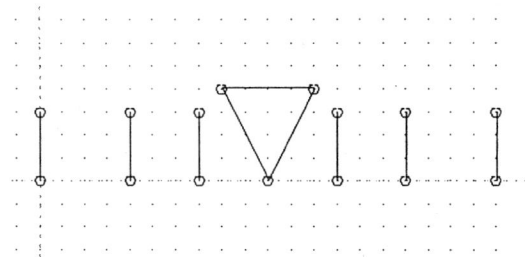

Figure 5 Creating the base - step 1

Continue by connecting the tops and bottoms of all the vertical edges. Note that each horizontal curve is made up of shorter line segments connecting the vertical lines.

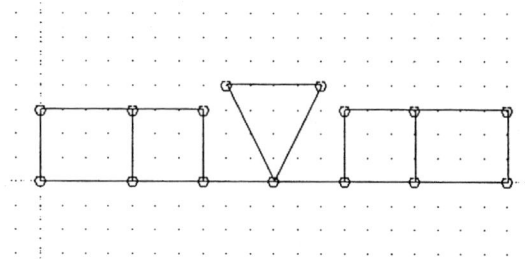

Figure 6 Creating the base - step 2

When these edges are completed, middle click. Now create the arcs for the fillet.

Curve > Arc
Start-Center-End > Snap(Grid)

Note that arcs are created counterclockwise. Create the arcs shown in Figure 7. Each has a radius of 0.5 (the grid spacing).

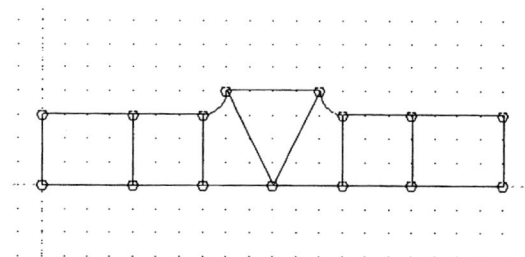

Figure 7 Creating the base - step 3

Creating the Surfaces

The requirement for surfaces is based on what we want to do two steps from now. When we create solid elements by extrusion, the base geometry must consist of shell elements associated with surface(s). Thus, we need to first create surfaces, then shell elements on those surfaces. The base geometry consists of seven polygons (6 quadrilaterals and 1 triangle). We will define a surface on each polygon:

Geometry > Surface > Planar

Select the edge on the far left. It highlights up to a junction. Select the branch that will go around the rectangle to eventually return to the initial edge. Once the rectangle is closed, read the prompt (it is asking you to identify interior edges - there are none), and middle click. Continue with the remaining elements. The figure at the right shows the first surface completed, and the second under construction. Middle click when all seven surfaces have been defined.

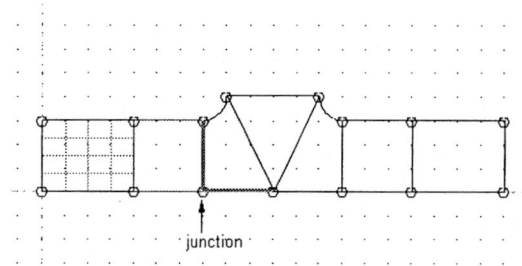

Figure 8 Creating planar surfaces

Creating Shell Elements

Now we need to create a shell element on each of the surfaces.

Main > Model > 3D
Elements > Shell > Element Snap(Quad) | Curve

Select curves on opposite sides of each individual quad surface. One element will be created for each pair of curves. There are 6 quad elements. For the triangular element select

Element Snap(Tri) | Point

and click on the three vertices. The completed shell mesh looks like the figure below.

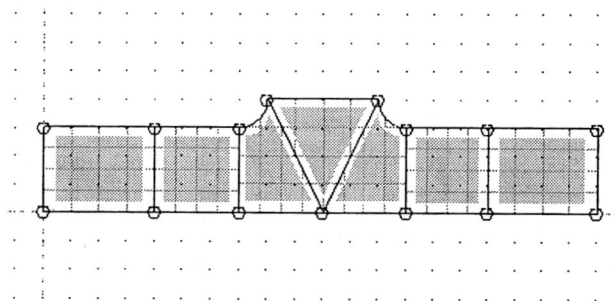

Figure 9 Shell elements completed

Extruding the Solid Elements

Spin the view a bit, note that shell elements are actually green. We are going to extrude in the direction of the WCS Z-axis. The extrusion will ultimately produce 4 elements in this direction from each original shell element. These will be a mix of brick and wedge elements. To extrude the elements:

Model > Elements > Extrude > Surface > All

Middle click. The start of the translation vector is at the origin, so select **Snap(Point)** and click on the origin at the point where the construction lines cross. The end of the translation vector for the first row of elements is (*0, 0, 1.5*). Accept the defaults for scale *<1>*, twist *<0>*, and enter the number of copies *4*. When shell elements are extruded, the initial shell can be kept in the database (for example if you also wanted to extrude in the other direction). This results in a sort of laminated shell/solid element, which we don't want here. Delete the initial shell by accepting the next default *<y>*. A total of 28 blue elements will be created as shown in Figure 10. This completes the construction of the base.

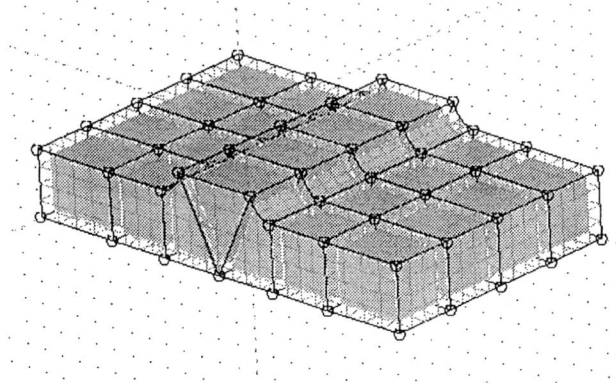

Figure 10 Base solid elements completed

The Upright

We'll use the same general procedure to make the elements for the vertical part. A slight change in procedure will involve specifying a new working plane.

Geometry and Surfaces

Start by extruding four edges from the top of the fillet to create several small vertical surfaces. See Figure 11.

Main > Geometry > Surface > Extruded

Click on the four edges at the top of the fillet on the right hand side of the upright (see the figure below). Middle click. The start of the translation vector is at the top of the fillet on the XY plane (use **Snap(Point)**); the end of the translation vector is at (*6, 3.5*) (use **Snap(Grid)** and the coordinate display). Use scale *<1>*, twist *<0>*, and set the number of copies as *2*. The extruded surface is shown in Figure 11.

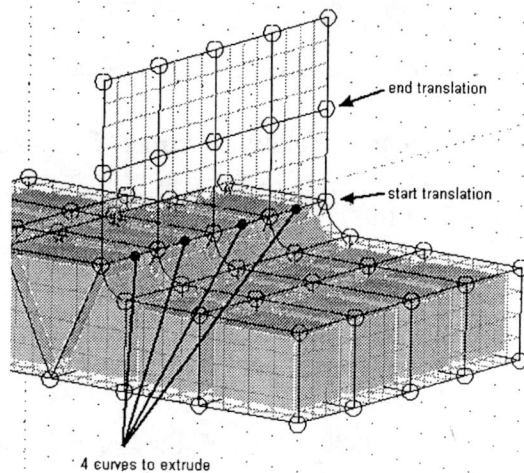

Figure 11 Creating extruded surface for upright

We need to extend one edge upwards to the height of the circle center. Select:

Geometry > Curve > Line > Two Points > Snap(Grid)

Click at the top corner of the surface on the XY plane (coordinates (*6, 5*)) and again at coordinates (*6, 7*). Middle click. We want to copy this curve to the front of the part.

Edit > Translate > ..check the Copy box.. > Curves

and select the vertical line. Middle click. Using *Snap(Point)*, pick the lower point on the line (the start point), and the top corner of the surface at the front of the part (the end point). Set the number of copies as *1* and middle click. See Figure 12.

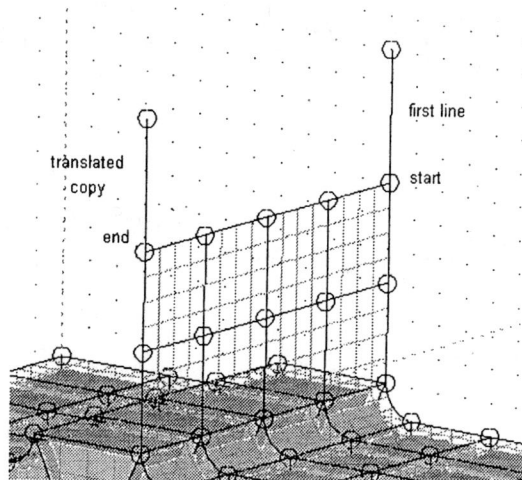

Figure 12 Completing geometry for upright

Changing the Working Plane

We want to draw the circular arcs in a plane parallel to the YZ plane:

Utility > Coordinate System > Working Plane > YZ | Accept

Note the grid rotates around to the left of the part. You might note the color scheme on the WCS coordinate system icon in the lower left corner. The current working plane axes are shown in red. Now we can create the top arc and hole for the circle

Geometry > Curve > Arc > Start-End-Radius > Snap(Point)

Click at the top of the line on the right (on the XY plane), the arc end is at the front, and enter a radius of *3*. Middle click.

Curve > Circle > Radius-Center

Enter the radius as *1.5* and using *Snap(Center)* click on the arc. Middle click twice. The geometry is shown in Figure 13.

In order to create the individual surfaces, we need to divide the arc and circle by creating more points along each entity:

Geometry > Point > Along Curve

Click on the arc and enter the number of points as *3*. By default, the new points are equally spaced. Do not middle click just yet.

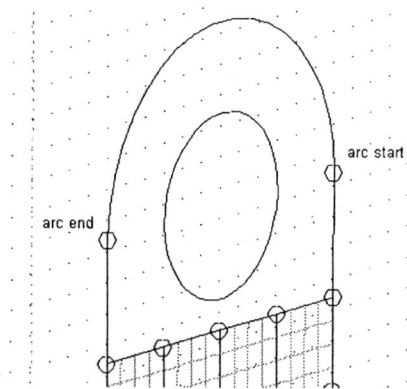

Figure 13 Drawing the arc and circle

To create the additional points on the circle, it will be handy if we are looking straight on the plane. While still in the Point menu, select

View > Right | Done

Now click on the circle and enter *8* points. We need to tell Pro/M where the first point should go. Use *Snap(Grid)* and click at the 3 o'clock position on the circle. Middle click. See Figure 14 for all the point locations.

While we are still in the right view, add line segments that connect all the dots on these new curves:

Geometry > Curve > Line > Two Points > Snap(Point)

With all the lines complete, as shown in Figure 14, we can make the surfaces the same way we did for the base:

Geometry > Surface > Planar

and work your way around the circle creating small surfaces.

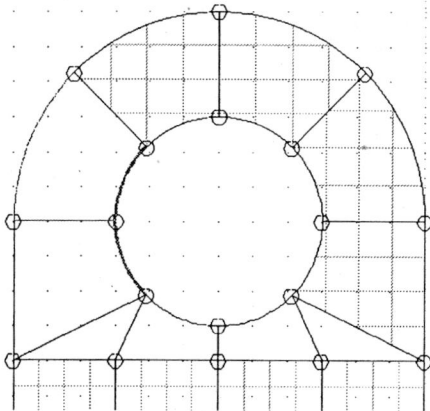

Figure 14 Creating planar surfaces

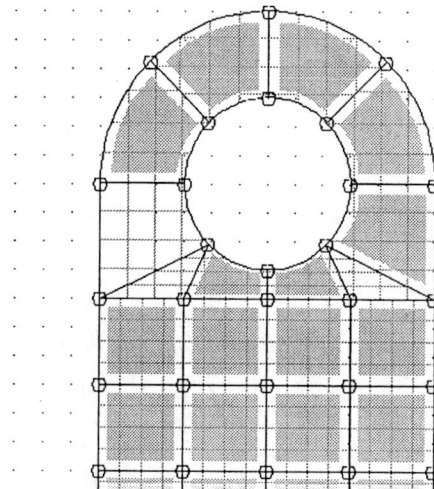

Figure 15 Creating shell elements

The next step is to create shell elements on each individual surface:

Main > Model > Elements > Shell > Element Snap(Quad) | Curve

and click on opposite edges of the quad surfaces. Figure 15 shows the shell elements under construction. Don't forget the eight elements on the vertical surface above the fillet.

For the two triangular elements, select

Element Snap(Tri) | Point

and click on the three vertices of each element.

Extruding the Solid Elements

Now we can extrude the surfaces carrying the shells:

Elements > Extrude > Surface

Hint: Keep the right view and zoom in on the display. Otherwise, Pro/M may keep opening a window asking you to select from a number of different possible surfaces at a pick point. You can also hold down the CTRL key and pick with the left mouse button to create a selection box around the desired surfaces.

When all the surfaces are selected, middle click. Now use *View > Isometric | Done* to rotate the model a bit. (If you use CTRL-middle, you will leave the command unfinished). The translation start point is one of the points on the top of the fillet, the end point is on the other fillet. Set scale *<1>*, twist *<0>*, and copies *1*. Delete the shells. This completes our element creation, and the model should look like Figure 16.

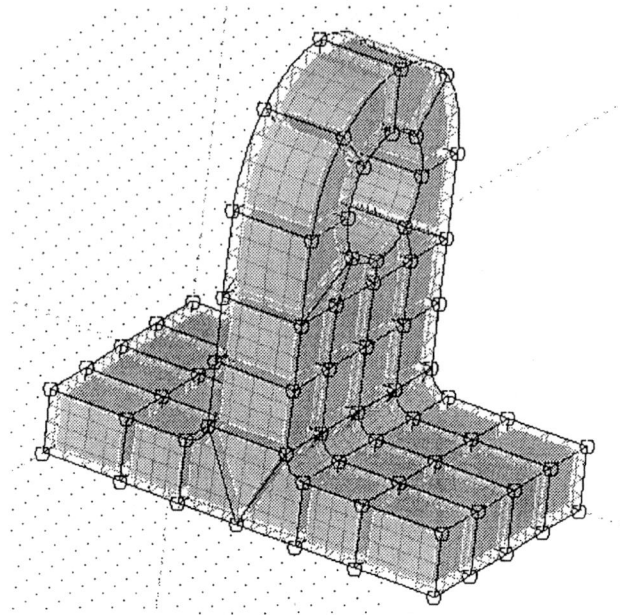

Figure 16 Completed solid element mesh

Now is a good time to save the model:

File > Save As > [brac1]

Completing the Model

Before we can run the model, we have to provide all the usual information: material, constraints, and loads. This should be getting pretty routine by now!

Material

Model > Properties > Material

Move the material **AL2014_IPS** to the right pane and select

Assign > Solid > All

Middle click twice.

Constraints

We will put constraints on the end faces of the elements. Assigning constraints directly to elements is not usually a good idea - we prefer to assign constraints for any elements to their associated geometry and/or surfaces. If necessary, we can constrain edge curves or points, but this can lead to convergence problems (unless we use excluded elements). We will assign to element faces here strictly for convenience, since it will be easier to pick element faces than surfaces.

Model > Constraints > Face

Create a *New* constraint set **fixedface**. We want to select the four right and four left faces. It will be necessary to spin the model to see all these surfaces. Once again, dynamic rotation (CTRL-middle) is not useful here since the middle mouse button will close out the command - use the *View* command and rotation buttons instead. Leave all degrees of freedom fixed. Rotations actually don't matter for solid elements anyway, since internally, the constraints are implemented at point nodes.

Loads

For the same reason as the constraints, we prefer to apply distributed loads over surfaces instead of line or point loads. Reorient the part so that you can see the surfaces on the inside top of the hole.

Model > Loads > Surface

Create a *New* load set **surfload**. Select the upper inside four surfaces of the hole and middle click. Set *Total Load, Uniform* with FX = *750,* FY = *1000,* FZ = *1500.* Accept the dialog. The model is now complete and ready for analysis.

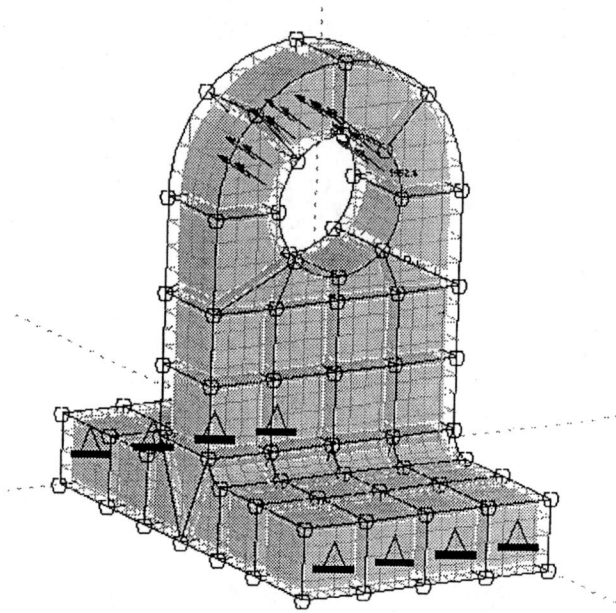

Figure 17 Completed model with loads and constraints

Analysis and Results

Go through the usual routine of performing a Quick Check and then a Multi-Pass Adaptive analysis as follows:

Main > Analyses > New

Enter an analysis name **brac1**, and make sure the constraint *fixedface* and load *surfload* are selected. The convergence method is a *Quick Check*. Accept the dialog.

Run > Settings

Set up your usual directories for temporary and output files. Then

Start

Accept error detection. Assuming no errors, open the *Summary* window. There should be no errors on the run. You might note the maximum Von Mises stress is 3222 psi, and the maximum displacement magnitude is 0.0071 inches. Close out the summary window and go back to

Analyses > Edit

Change to a *Multi-Pass Adaptive* method. In the interests of quick execution, use a *10%* convergence on *Lcl Disp & Lcl SE & Global RMS* stress, and set a polynomial maximum edge order of *6*. Accept the dialog and

Run > Start

In the *Summary* window, we see that convergence is obtained (within 10%) on pass 6 with a maximum Von Mises stress of 4064 psi and maximum displacement magnitude of 0.0074".

Create Result windows for the study **brac1** to show a fringe plot of the Von Mises stress, a deformation animation, and plots of two measures (*max_stress_vm* and *strain_energy*) to show the convergence behavior of the analysis. Show these windows - they should look like the figures below.

Note that the point of view in Figure 18 showing the Von Mises stress is from the back, left, top of the model (observe the WCS icon in the lower left corner). Use *Dynamic Query > View Max* to locate the maximum stress on the fillet.

The animated deformation Figure 19 agrees with our anticipated result - the support is pulled forward and to the right, and the base twists upward at the back.

The strain energy is converging nicely up to the 6th pass, with the Von Mises stress continuing to increase with each pass. When you have time (actually, this is an end-of-lesson exercise!), come back and re-run this model with a tighter convergence tolerance and higher polynomial limit.

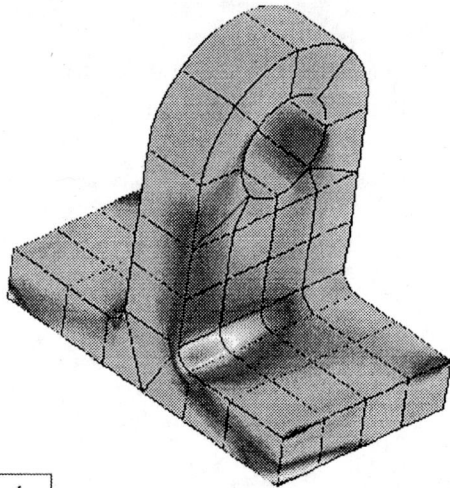

Von Mises Stress

Figure 18 Von Mises stress fringe plot

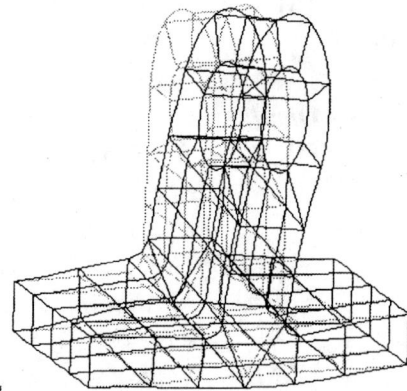

Deformation

Figure 19 Frame from the deformation animation

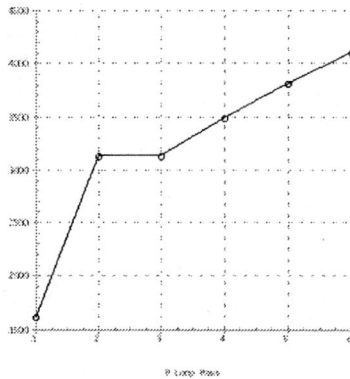

Von Mises Convergence

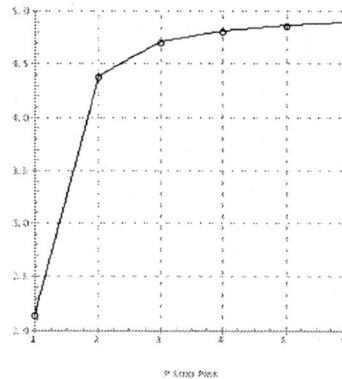

Strain Energy Convergence

Figure 20 Convergence behavior of Von Mises stress and model strain energy with loop pass

You might also create a result window to show the P-levels. This will show a minimum level of 3, and a maximum of 6. Most of the model is at levels 5 and 6.

Model B

For this version of the model, we will use AutoGEM to help create elements in a semi-automatic mode. Start Pro/M, or select *File > New* to start a new model. Then set up the environment in the usual way:

> *Display > Master Visibilities > All On | Grid | Accept*
> *Display > Settings*
> > *Display Type(Flat Shade)*
> > *Shade(Elements)*
> > *Shrink All Elements > 0.2*
> > *Grid Spacing > [0.5]*
> > *Accept*
> *Utility > Display Coordinates*
> *Main > Geometry > Curve*
> *Construction Geom > Horizontal > Snap(Point) > [0 0]*
> *Construction Geom > Vertical > Snap(Point) > [0 0]*

Zoom and pan until you can see the grid out to x = 10. We'll start by construction of the base, then we'll change the coordinate system and working plane to construct the upright.

The Base

Geometry

Create the base geometry according to the dimensions in Figure 4. Note that we don't need any of the interior vertical curves as we did in the previous model. See Figure 21.

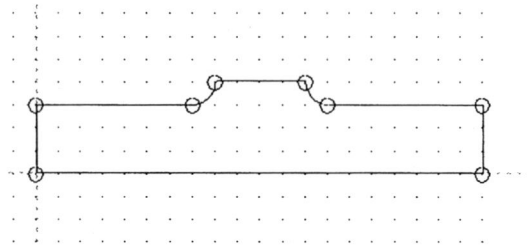

Figure 21 Base geometry for Model B

Add a point midway along the top edge between the fillet curves. The need for this point will be evident a bit later.

Now create a surface using these curves:

> *Geometry > Surface > Planar*

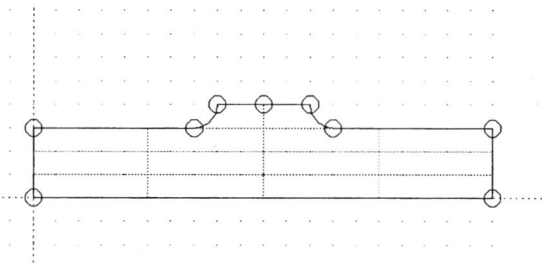

Figure 22 Surface created from outline curves

Click on any edge. The outer closed loop is found. There are no interior loops so middle click. See Figure 22.

Shell using AutoGEM

Here is where we do some automatic mesh generation to save some time. As in Model A, we want to extrude shell elements associated with a surface. In this case, we will use AutoGEM to create the shell elements.

Main > Model > 3D

We will change one setting in AutoGEM that involves the extra point we added above.

Elements > AutoGEM > Settings

Deselect the option **Move or Delete Existing Points**. If we do not do this, AutoGEM will delete this point since it is not required for a default mesh. Now select

Surface > All

and middle click. The default mesh will contain 4 quad elements. We anticipate that this may be too few elements (requiring a higher polynomial order). Let's create a finer mesh. Select *Undo* to delete the elements you just created.

Change the AutoGEM settings as follows, using the ***Define/Review*** button:

Edge Angle   *Minimum 20 Maximum 160*
Maximum Aspect Ratio   *5*

Once again, select ***Surface > All*** and middle click. This time, AutoGEM creates 3 triangle and 7 quad elements similar to that shown in Figure 23. The presence of quad elements is beneficial here, since these will become bricks after the shells are extruded in the next step.

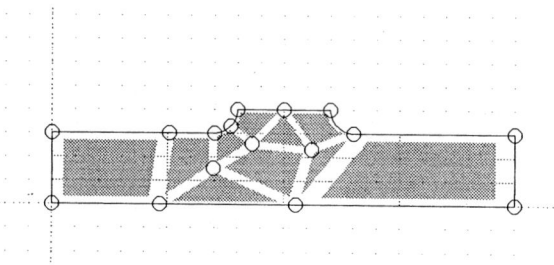

Figure 23 Shell elements created by AutoGEM

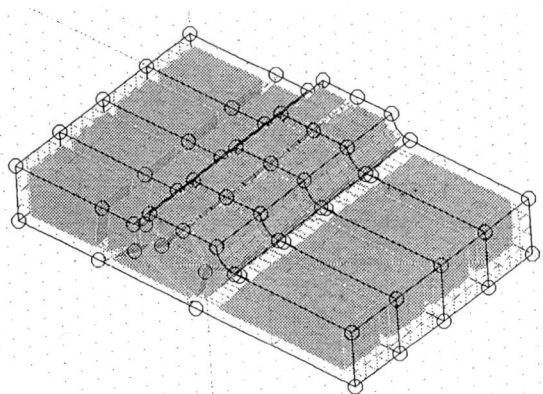

Figure 24 Solid elements created by extruding surface containing shell elements

Extrude Solids

Now we can extrude the shell elements to create solid elements.

Elements > Extrude > Surface

Click on the surface and middle click. The translation start point is at the origin. Use *Snap(Point)* and click on the point at the lower left in Figure 23. The translation end point is 1.5 inches along the Z-axis, at point (*0, 0, 1.5*). Accept the defaults for scale <1>, twist <0>, and enter the number of copies as *4*. Delete the shells. You should now have the mesh similar to that shown in Figure 24 on the previous page.

Changing the Coordinate System

To make it easier to create the geometry for the upright, we want to create a new working plane running along the top of the left fillet, and parallel to the WCS YZ plane.

Utility > Coordinate System > Cartesian

To place the new coordinate system, we need to specify three points: its origin, a point along the new X-axis, and a point along the new Y-axis. Using *Snap(Point)* click on the top of the left fillet at the back of the model (see Figure 25). The X-axis goes through the top of the other fillet; click on that point. Then set *Snap(Grid)* and click on a point vertically above the new origin to locate the Y-axis. When the system is created, select YZ as the new working plane. A new coordinate triad will appear with the current working plane axes highlighted in red.

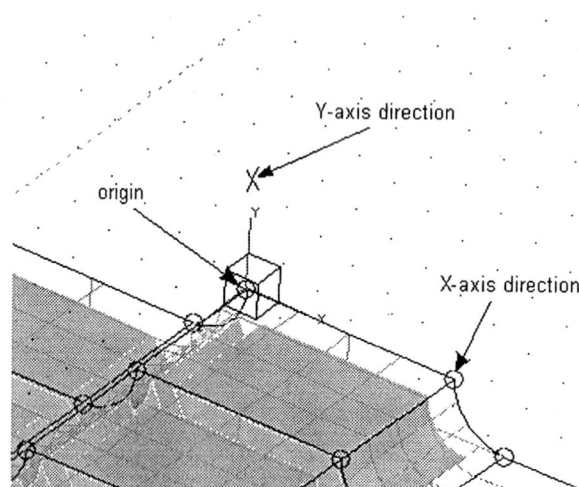

Figure 25 Setting up the new Cartesian coordinate system

The Upright

Geometry

Draw the geometry according to the dimensions in Figure 4 to produce the curves in Figure 26. To make this easier, you might like to reorient the view as follows:

View > Right | Done

While we are in right view, we want to add a couple of points on the circle to isolate the top surface of the hole from the bottom. The reason for this will be apparent when we apply loads. Notice that the coordinate display window is showing coordinate values in the new coordinate system, called the UCS (User Coordinate System).

Geometry > Point > Along Curve

Click on the circle and add **2** points. Use **Snap(Grid)** and click on the 3 o'clock position on the circle to set the start point.

We can now create the surface:

Geometry > Surface > Planar

Click on the arc. A closed loop is found immediately. Why were no junctions detected? Remember that we asked for a planar surface. Click on the circle (the interior loop) and middle click to create the surface shown in Figure 27.

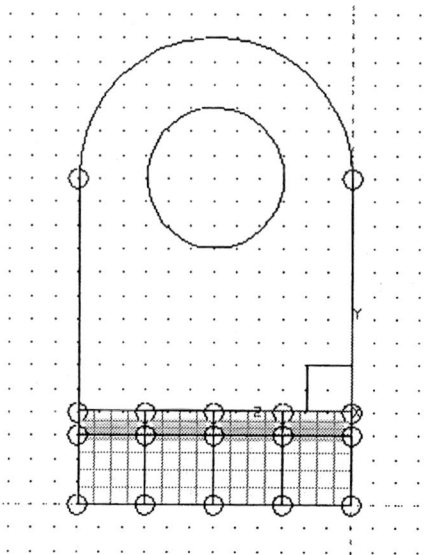

Figure 26 Geometry curves for upright

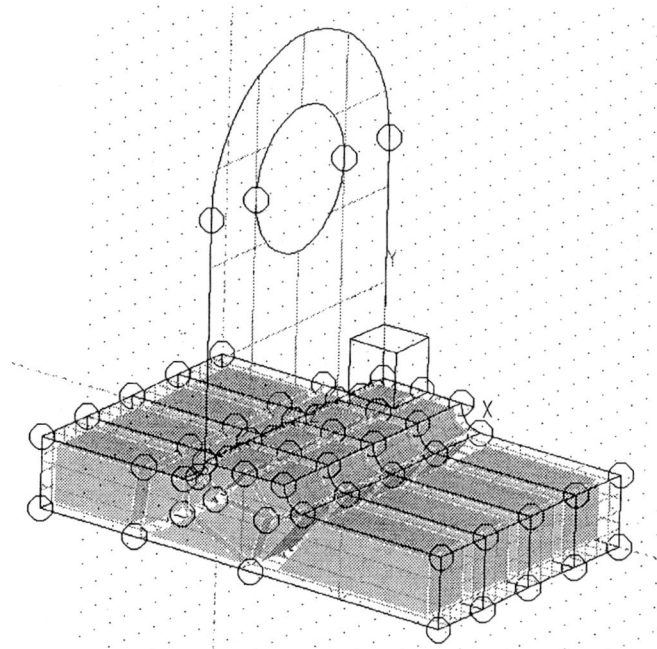

Figure 27 Surface created for upright

Shell using AutoGEM

Now we use AutoGEM again to create shell elements on this vertical surface.

> *Main > Model > Elements > AutoGEM*
> *Settings > Define/Review > Use Defaults | Accept > Accept*
> *Surface*

Click on the surface. AutoGEM creates 4 tri and 4 quad elements. Can you see why we needed the extra points on the circle? Also note that AutoGEM automatically used the existing points along the top of the fillet to create the four triangular shell element edges. This is necessary so that the final solid elements in the upright will share the same corner nodes as the mating elements in the base, ie. these elements must share common faces and nodes. This is also why we needed the extra point exactly midway along the top edge. Without defining the point at this location precisely, AutoGEM would have split the distance unequally. This would make it difficult to create the two rows of solid elements by extruding the vertical shells, which we do in the next step.

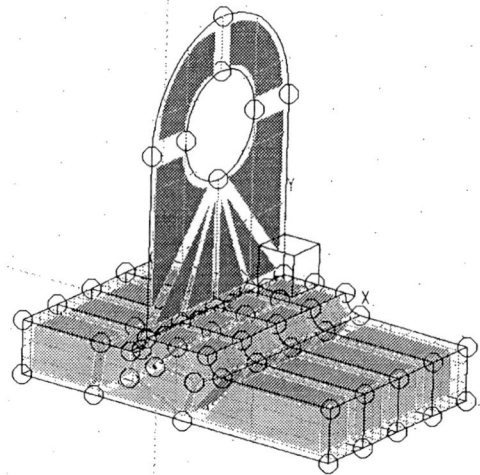

Figure 28 Shell elements created by AutoGEM

Extrude Solids

The shell elements are extruded to create solids. Note that there are two elements across the base between the fillets.

> *Elements > Extrude > Surface*

Pick on the upright surface and middle click. The translation start point is at the origin of the new coordinate system. Locate this using *Snap(Point)*. The translation end point is in the middle of the edge along the X-axis. Accept the defaults for scale *<1>*, twist *<0>*, and enter the number of copies as *2*. Delete the shells.

This completes the creation of the solid element mesh. Go to *View > Master Visibilities* and turn off the surface display. Then in *Display > Settings*, select *Points(Dot)* and deselect *Shrink All Elements*. The model will be shown as in Figure 29.

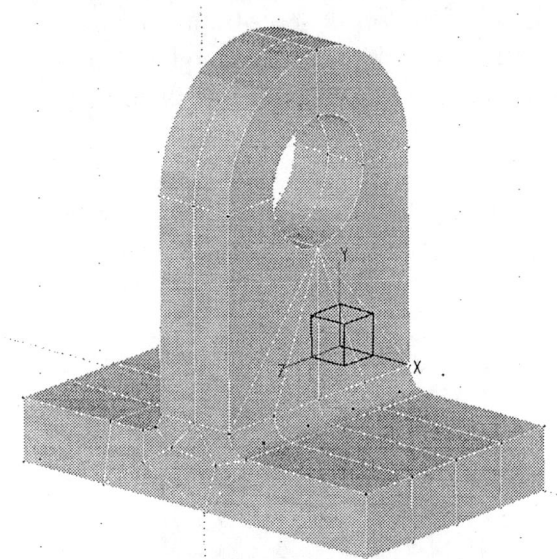

Figure 29 Solid elements created by
extruding surface of upright

Completing the Model

To complete the model, we need to supply material properties, loads, and constraints.

> *Model > Properties > Material*

Move the material **AL2014_IPS** to the right pane and select

> *Assign > Solid > All*

Middle click twice. Now apply the load:

> *Model > Loads*

We need to break one of our rules again by applying the load directly to the faces of the elements on the top inside of the hole, instead of the hole surface. (You might like to try applying the load to the surface to see the problem.) Spin the model if necessary to see these faces clearly. Then select

> *Face*

Create a *New* load set **faceload** and select the four inner faces at the top of the hole. Middle click. Set FX = *750,* FY = *1000,* FZ = *1500.* Make sure *Total Load* and *Uniform* are selected. Accept the dialog. The load arrows will appear.

> *Model > Constraints > Face*

Create a load set **fixedface** and, as before, set the constraints on the end faces. You may have to spin the view around to see the faces at each end of the model. When all eight faces are selected, middle click. Leave all the constraints as fixed and accept the dialog.

The model is now completed and is shown in Figure 30. There are 56 elements in this model, slightly more than in Model A which had 44.

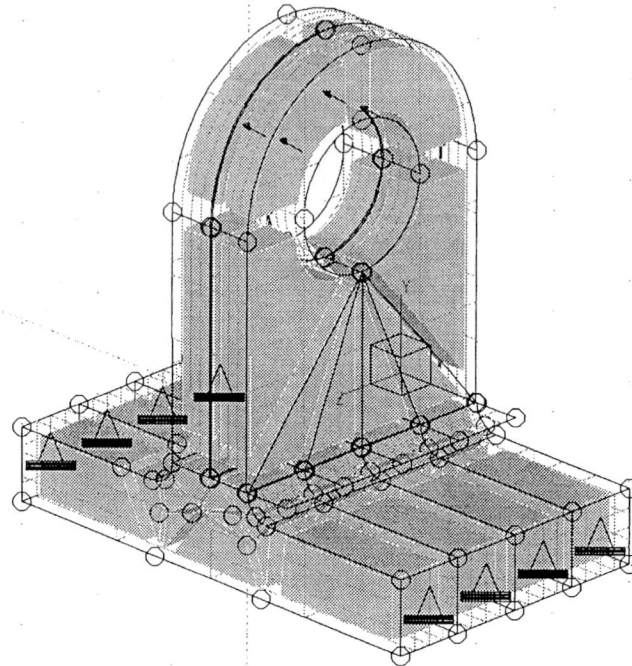

Figure 30 Model B completed

Analysis and Results

Go through the usual procedure of Quick Check and Multi-Pass Adaptive analyses. Call the analysis "*brac2*" and when/if required enter a name for the model "*brac2*". In the Multi-Pass Adaptive analysis, set the convergence to *10%* on *Lcl Disp & Lcl SE & Global RMS Stress*, and leave the polynomial order maximum set at *6*. As we will see, this is probably not a tight enough criterion for obtaining acceptable results, but will result in somewhat faster execution, which is OK for now.

The Multi-Pass Adaptive analysis convergences on the 6th pass, the same as before. In the *Summary* window, the maximum displacement magnitude is reported as 0.0074" (also about the same), but the maximum Von Mises stress is now about 4750 psi. The stress is quite a bit different from Model A, possibly due to our rather loose convergence criteria and low polynomial order.

Create and show the following result windows:

▸   Von Mises stress fringe plot

- ‣ deformation animation
- ‣ convergence history of Von Mises stress
- ‣ convergence history of strain energy
- ‣ P-level fringe plot

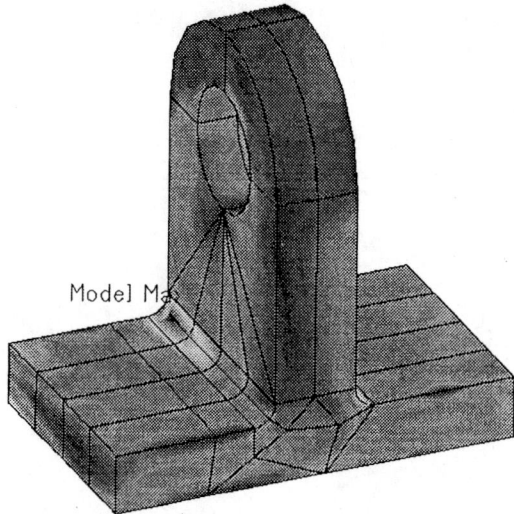

Figure 31 Von Mises stress (Model B)

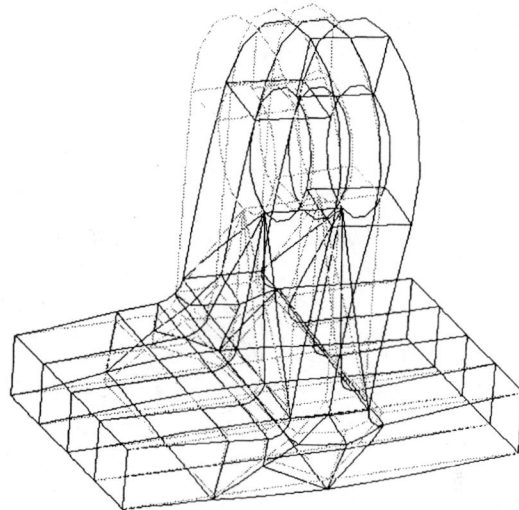

Figure 32 Deformation (Model B)

Note the maximum Von Mises stress occurs on the left fillet at the back of the model. The deformation agrees qualitatively with Model A, and our expectations. The convergence history plots are also similar to Model A.

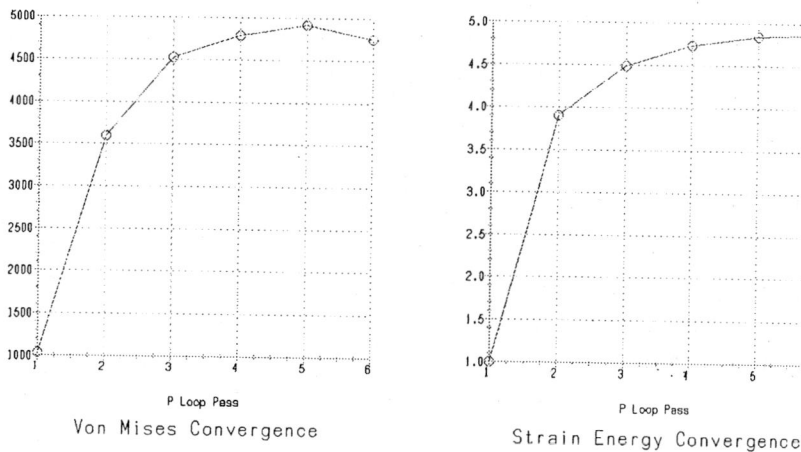

Von Mises Convergence

Strain Energy Convergence

Figure 33 Convergence history of Von Mises stress and strain energy (Model B)

In the P-level fringe plot, note the minimum polynomial order is 2 and the maximum order is 6. Virtually the entire model is at level 6. If we used a tighter convergence requirement (like 1%), we may have had problems with this mesh converging, even in 9 passes.

Model C

In this version of the model, we will create the entire mesh fully automatically using AutoGEM. As mentioned at the beginning of this chapter, AutoGEM can create a solid mesh only from a defined volume. Volumes can be created using primitives (cones, cylinders, etc) or, as we will do here, by specifying the enclosing surface(s). We have to be a bit careful here, since the volume representing our part can contain no open interior surfaces, that is, that do not enclose an interior volume or void.

Set up the working environment as usual:

> *Display > Master Visibilities > All On | Grid | Accept*
> *Display > Settings*
> > *Display Type(Flat Shade)*
> > *Shade(Elements)*
> > *Shrink All Elements | 0.2*
> > *Grid Spacing | 0.5*
> > *Accept*
> *Utility > Display Coordinates*
> *Main > Geometry > Curve*
> *Construction Geom > Horizontal > Snap(Point) > [0 0]*
> *Construction Geom > Vertical > Snap(Point) > [0 0]*

Pan and zoom the display to see the upper right quadrant out to x = 10.

Creating the Surfaces

The general procedure here is to create an outline curve and then extrude it to form a surface of the part. We will extrude one surface for the base and another two (including the hole) for the upright. We then have to fill in some missing surfaces manually.

Base Curves

The top, bottom, and end surfaces of the base can be created from a single set of curves. Create these as shown in the figure at the right using the dimensions in Figure 4 for reference. Note that the curve is open at the top across the two fillets.

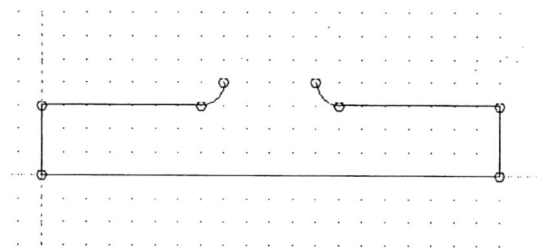

Changing the Coordinate System

Figure 34 Curves for base surfaces

To draw the curves for the upright, we need to create a new coordinate system and working plane:

Utility > Coordinate System > Cartesian

Indicate the origin using **Snap(Point)** and clicking on the top point on the left fillet. The X-axis is located on the top of the other fillet. The Y axis can be located using **Snap(Digitize)** and clicking anywhere above the model. The Y-axis will automatically be created perpendicular to the X-axis. The Z-axis is determined by the right hand rule. Select the **YZ** working plane. If the new coordinate system icon is not visible, make sure that

Display > Master Visibilities > UCS

is checked. Spin the model, and you should obtain the view shown in Figure 35.

To make construction of the upright curves easier, reorient the view using

View > Right | Done

Zoom out so that you can see sufficient space above the existing curves.

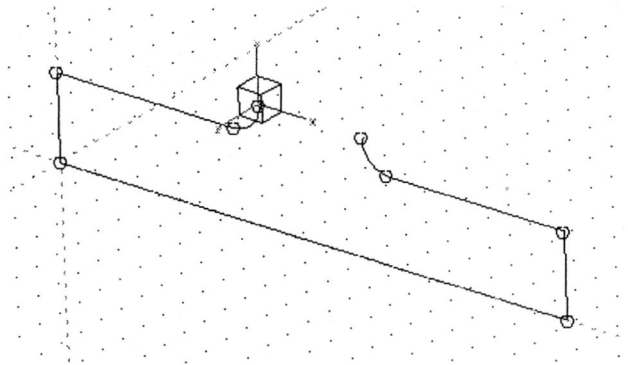

Figure 35 The second coordinate system (UCS)

Upright Curves

Draw the curves shown in Figure 36, using the dimensions in Figure 4. Note that the outer curve is open at the bottom. We do not want to create a surface here when this curve is extruded, since that surface would be inside the part. Spin the model to see both sets of curves as shown in Figure 37.

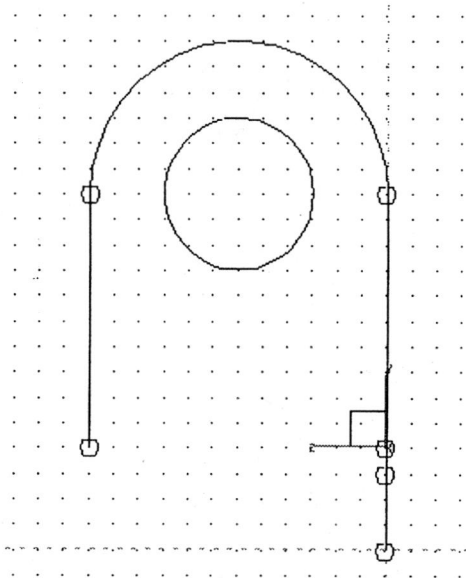

Figure 36 Defining curves for upright surfaces

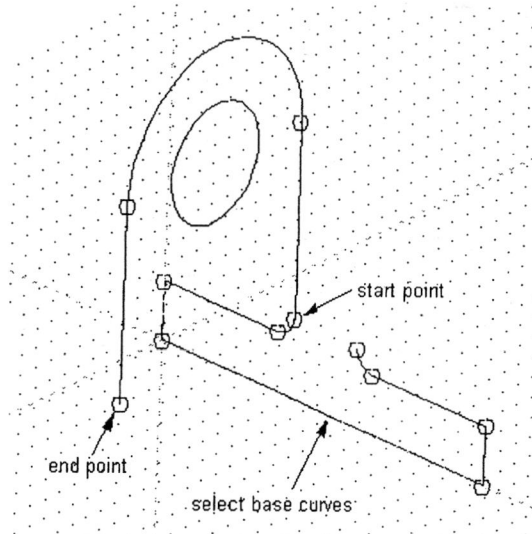

Figure 37 Preparing to extrude the base curves

Extrude the Base Surfaces

We are going to extrude the base curves in a direction parallel to the Z-axis.

Geometry > Surface > Extruded > All > Deselect

and click on the four curves on the upright.
Middle click. The translation start and end points
are indicated in Figure 37 above. Accept the
defaults for scale *<1>*, twist *<0>*, and number of
copies *<1>*. The resulting surfaces are shown in
Figure 38. Note that no surface was created across
the top of the fillets, as desired. Middle click.

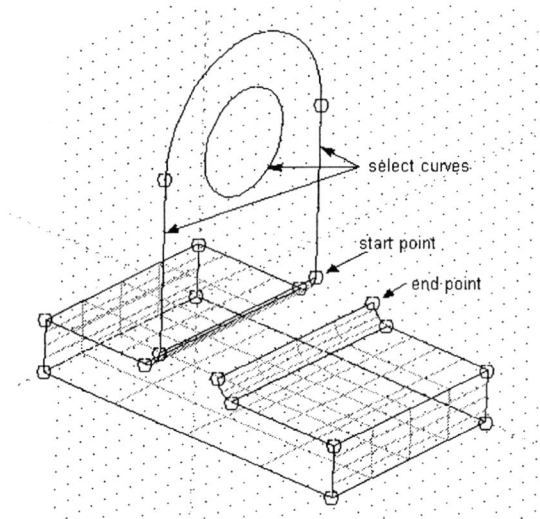

Figure 38 Extruding the upright curves

Extrude the Upright Surfaces

In the same way, extrude all the curves for the upright (see Figure 38):

Extruded

Click on the vertical lines and the arcs in the
upright geometry. Note there is no curve across the
bottom. The start and end points are indicated in
Figure 38. Accept the defaults for scale, twist, and
copies, then middle click. To get the image shown
in Figure 39, select

Display > Settings

and set *Flat Shade* and select *Geometry*.

Observe the missing surfaces.

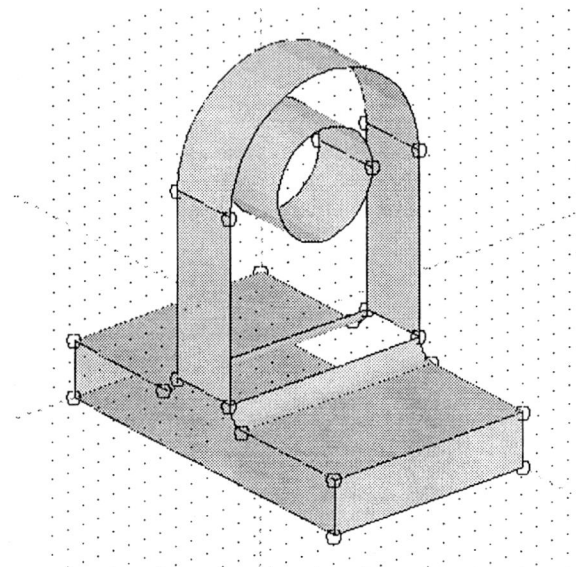

Figure 39 Extruded surfaces

Completing the Model Surfaces

We will define the missing model surfaces manually. While we are still in the Surface menu, select

Planar

Pick on one of the edges around the opening on the base at the front of the model. The curve will loop around until it meets a junction. Keep selecting the appropriate branch until the entire loop is created and highlighted in red. There are no interior loops so middle click. The surface is created.

Do the same for the back of the base and the two missing surfaces on the upright. For the missing surfaces of the upright, remember to indicate the circular edge of the hole as an interior loop.

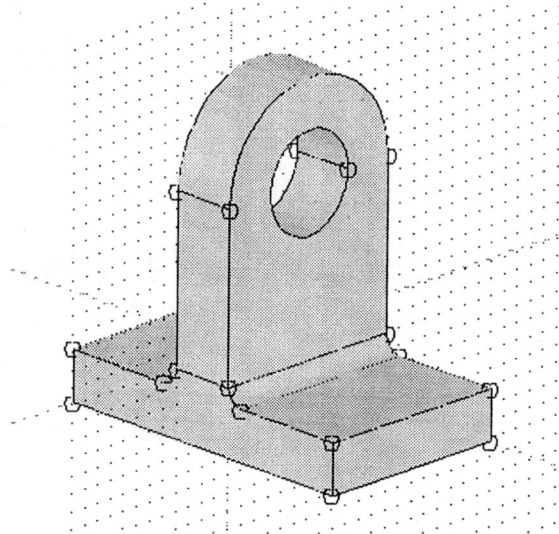

Figure 40 Surfaces of model complete

Creating the Model Volume

With the enclosing surfaces created, we can set up the model volume. This is a bit like creating a surface from a closed loop of curves. Here we create a volume from a closed set of surfaces.

Geometry > Volume > General

Click on any surface of the part. Pro/M locates all the exterior surfaces. There are no internal surfaces, so middle click and the volume will be created. There is no visibility or symbol for the created volume. Before we proceed, select *Display > Settings* and set *Shade(Elements)*.

Creating the Solid Mesh with AutoGEM

Now we will let AutoGEM do all the work:

> *Main > Model > 3D*
> *Elements > AutoGEM > Volume > All*

Middle click. Using the default settings AutoGEM creates 123 or so tetrahedral elements. The mesh is shown in Figure 41.

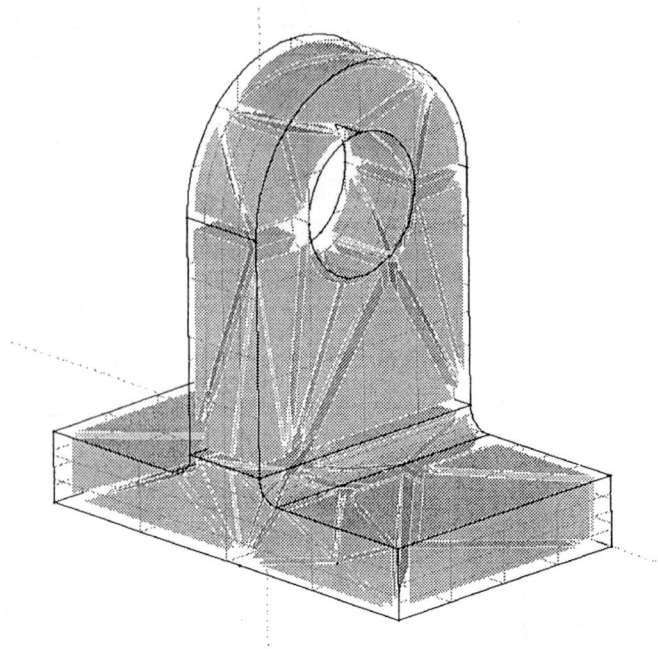

Figure 41 Solid mesh created by AutoGEM (about 120 tet elements)

Completing the Model

Complete the model by specifying the material (*AL2014_IPS*), and specifying loads and constraints. For the load ("*holeload*"), apply a Total, Uniform load (FX = *750*, FY = *1000*, FZ = *1500*) to the surface of the hole. It is not possible to isolate the upper surface of the hole (in this model), so the load is distributed uniformly around the entire hole surface. This means that it is pulling up on the lower hole surface - an interesting physical proposition! We can get away with this in this model because it should not greatly affect the stress distribution far from the hole[2]. The constraints ("*fixedsurf*") can be applied to the surfaces at either end of the base.

Save the model

> *File > Save As > [brac3]*

Analysis and Results

Once again (and finally for this part!) go through the usual procedure of Quick Check and Multi-Pass Adaptive analyses. Call the analysis "*brac3*". In the Multi-Pass Adaptive analysis, set the

---

[2] For something a bit more reasonable, check out the **Bearing** load type. This automatically distributes the load around the bearing surface, but cannot be used to provide a load parallel to the axis of the hole.

convergence to *10%* on *Lcl Disp & Lcl SE & Global RMS Stress*, and leave the polynomial order maximum set at *6*.

The Multi-Pass Adaptive analysis just meets the convergence requirement on the 5th pass. In the *Summary* window, the maximum displacement magnitude is reported as about 0.0061", and the maximum Von Mises stress is about 3900 psi. The stress is quite different from both Model A and Model B. The maximum displacement is also considerably different. The reason for this is not immediately obvious, but is probably related to our rather loose convergence criterion.

Create and show the following result windows:

▸ Von Mises stress fringe plot
▸ deformation animation
▸ convergence history of Von Mises
▸ convergence history of strain energy
▸ P-level fringe plot

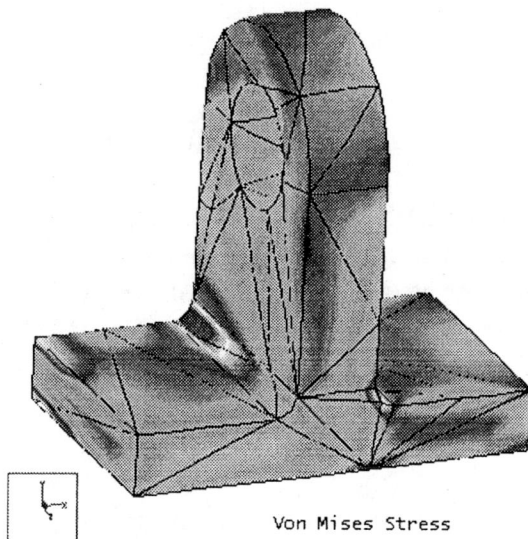

Von Mises Stress

Figure 42 Von Mises stress (Model C)

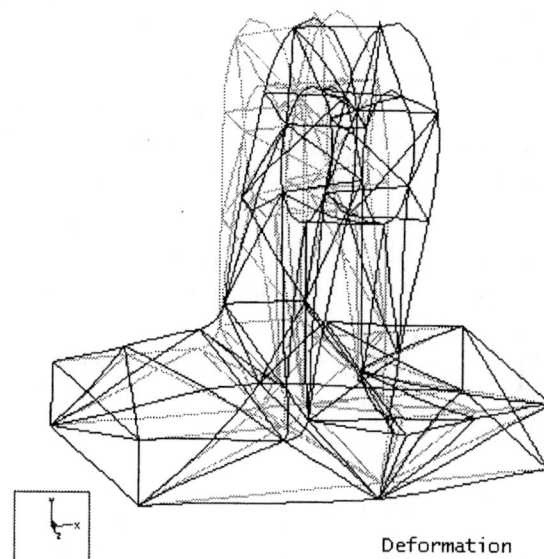

Deformation

Figure 43 Deformation (Model C)

The maximum Von Mises stress occurs in the same place as it did on Model B. You might like to study the stress pattern and values around the hole, since the load application is a bit different in Model C. Not much new is indicated in the deformation.

The convergence plots shown in Figure 44 are about as nice as you'd care to imagine. In particular, the Von Mises stress does not go through any of the spiky data we have seen before.

In the P-level fringe plot (not shown here), note the minimum level is 3 and the maximum level is 5. Virtually the entire model is order 5.

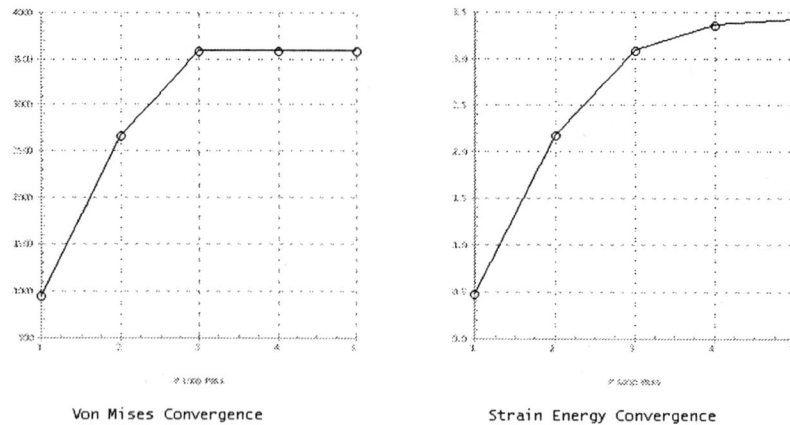

Von Mises Convergence   Strain Energy Convergence

Figure 44 Convergence behavior of Von Mises stress and model strain energy

Summary

In this chapter, we have seen how three different methods of analysis (in particular, the geometry of the mesh) can produce quite different results. In this case, this is partly due to our loose convergence requirements. Nonetheless, it is obvious that FEA results in and of themselves are not of much use without an understanding of how the model was created, how the analysis was performed, and how convergence was set up and monitored. The next time someone shows you some FEA results, ask them these questions! Or, when you are presenting *your* FEA results, be sure to supply this information. In particular, if you are using automatic mesh generation (for example in integrated mode covered in the next chapter), you should be concerned about how well the mesh will perform and the results it will yield.

Manual mesh creation is certainly laborious, but may sometimes be necessary to handle special or diabolical geometries, or to investigate the performance of the model. In general, such manual creation is performed by an FEA specialist dealing with "tricky" models. Meshing a complex geometry may require many hours of effort. Most users, if the quality of the results is especially critical, may be satisfied by changing the settings in AutoGEM in order to create a different mesh and re-running the analysis. This takes substantially less time.

As usual, there are some exercises at the end of this chapter for you to practice the methods we have covered.

Questions for Review

1. What are the three shapes of solid elements in Pro/MECHANICA?
2. What geometric primitives are required to create each type of solid element?
3. Are there any restrictions on the curvature of the edges of any solid element?
4. What form of geometric primitive does AutoGEM use to create solid elements?
5. For what reasons might you want to create the solid mesh manually?
6. What special considerations are required for applying loads and constraints to a solid model?
7. Can a surface be extruded directly to form solid elements? If not, what else is needed?
8. Is it possible to manually divide a brick element to create two wedges? To join two wedges to form a brick?
9. When shell elements are extruded to form solids, what is the final step in the process? What is this used for?
10. What is a UCS? What information is required to create one?
11. Is there a limit to how many UCS you can create?
12. What other types of UCS are available?
13. How could you specify a working plane at some angle to the WCS planes?
14. Is the direction of an extrusion restricted by the current choice of coordinate system or working plane?
15. Can you get AutoGEM to create brick or wedge elements?
16. In the AutoGEM settings area, what is meant by, and the difference between, edge angle and face angle?
17. See if you can find out how the aspect ratio of a solid element is determined.
18. Rerun the analyses for each model with a 1% convergence criterion and a maximum polynomial of 9. Compare the results in terms of accuracy, passes to convergence, and CPU time. Do you think you can generalize from these results?

Exercises

1.   Compute the maximum Von Mises stress and deflection in the steel hook shown in the figures below. Dimensions are in inches.

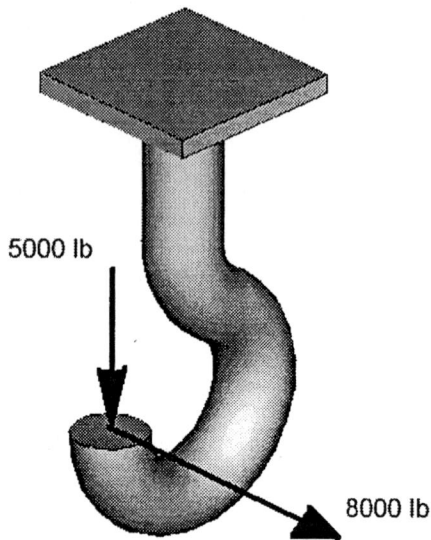

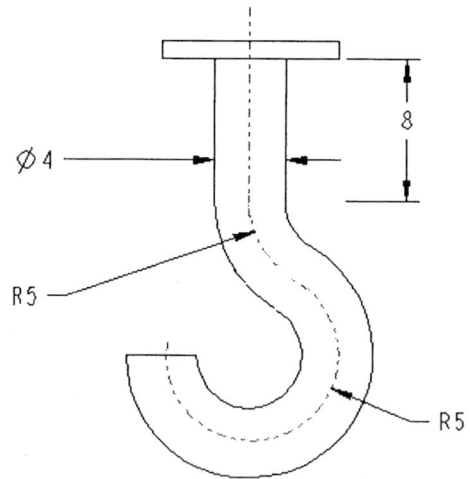

2.   Compute the maximum Von Mises stress and deflections in the directions of the loads on the end of the steel connecting rod. Dimensions are mm.

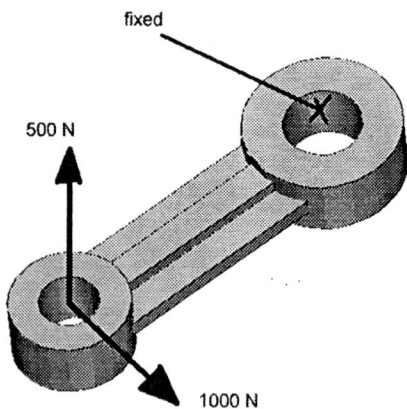

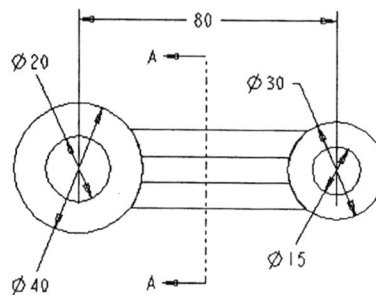

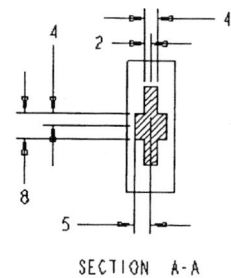

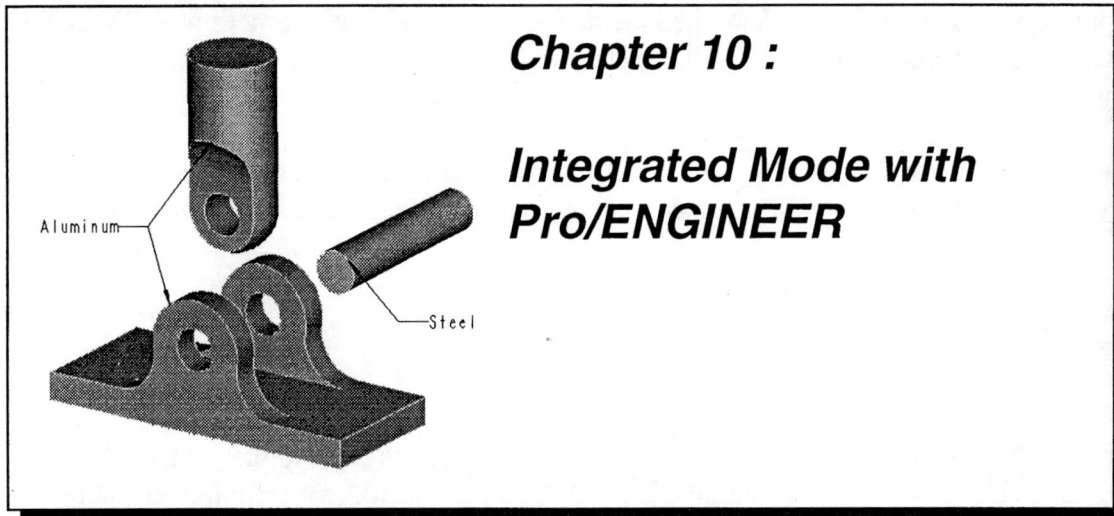

Chapter 10 :

Integrated Mode with Pro/ENGINEER

Synopsis:

Analysis of solid models created in Pro/ENGINEER; entering Mechanica from Pro/E; analysis features and the model tree; 3D solid models and 2D idealizations; cyclic symmetry; choosing design values for sensitivity studies and optimization; model idealizations (shell elements); contact models; analysis of assemblies.

Overview:

In the first section of this chapter, we will study the same solid model as Chapter 9, this time creating the part in Pro/E 2000i^2 and accessing Mechanica from the Pro/E interface. This is called "integrated mode." This is the most convenient way to treat solid models, but we will find that not all the functionality of Mechanica is available in this mode of operation. Once we are into Mechanica most of the menu picks and options will be familiar to you if you have completed the previous chapters. We will do the following:

- ♦   creating an FEA model from the Pro/E part
- ♦   examining the Mechanica model tree
- ♦   setting up and running an analysis
- ♦   design controls and specifying design parameters
- ♦   performing a sensitivity analysis
- ♦   optimization

In integrated mode, you will usually be treating solid models only. In Pro/E and Pro/M 2000i^2 you can now treat 2D (plane stress, plane strain, axisymmetric) problems using the (perhaps) more familiar geometry pre-processor in Pro/E (that is, Sketcher). Thus, in the second part of this chapter we will look at some common idealizations. We will have a quick look at 2D modeling in integrated mode. Another function in 2000i^2 is the ability to handle models with cyclic symmetry. This idealization will also be discussed with a couple of examples.

In the third part of this chapter, we will use shell elements as an idealization for a thin-walled 3D solid. Mechanica can automatically pair parallel surfaces to be modeled using shell elements, or you can create pairs manually.

Finally, we will look at the analysis of a simple assembly created in Pro/E. The mating surfaces between parts in the assembly are modeled as contact regions, which can separate when a load is applied to the assembly.

Analysis of a Solid Model

In this first part of the lesson, we will create a simple solid model in Pro/E and then launch Mechanica in integrated mode. This is without doubt the easiest way to treat solid models. You should remember, however, that the geometry required for the FEA may not be identical to the geometry of your part created in Pro/E. For example, minor cosmetic features may have to be suppressed in the Pro/E model, or else the Mechanica analysis may become impractical. This is called *defeaturing* the model. You can also exploit symmetry in the FEA model by cutting the Pro/E geometry along a plane of symmetry using a cut feature. Note that the entire FEA model must be symmetric, not just the geometry; the applied loads and constraints must also be symmetric for this to work properly.

Create the Model

See Figure 4 of Lesson 9. Call the new Pro/E part **bracket**. Make the features in the order shown in the figure at the right. These are:

♦   base: *Both Sides* blind protrusion off the FRONT datum plane
♦   support: *Both Sides* blind protrusion off the SIDE datum plane
♦   hole: create a datum axis and make a coaxial through-all hole
♦   fillets: create both fillets as the same feature

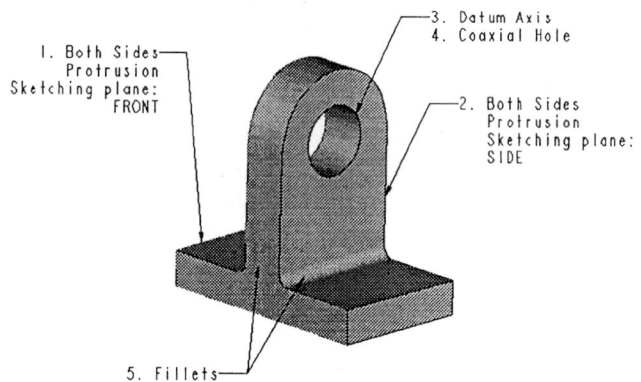

Figure 1 Part created with Pro/ENGINEER

These are important so that we can do the sensitivity and optimization later in this lesson.

Make sure your units are set up properly. In the PART menu in Pro/E, select

Set Up > Units

The window shown in Figure 2 will open. Make sure **Inch Pound Second (IPS)** is selected, press the *Set* button, and in the next window check the button **Interpret Existing Numbers (Same Dims)**.

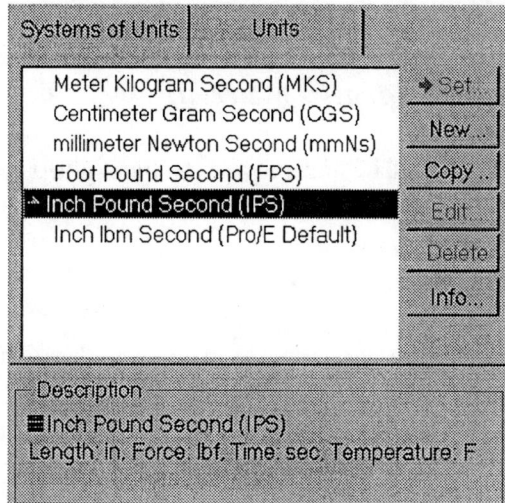

Select *OK* to accept the dialog.

Figure 2 Setting model units in Pro/E

Now call up Mechanica from the Pro/E pull-down menus:

Applications > Mechanica

A window may open up to remind you about using consistent units. The window can be disabled with an entry in the Mechanica configuration file *config.mech*. Disabling this window is probably not a good idea since you should always be very careful about units. Click *Continue*. The MECHANICA menu opens as shown in Figure 3. We will come back to the *Dsgn Controls* and *Settings* command a bit later. The *Configuration* command refers to the configuration file *config.mech* which operates in the same fashion as the Pro/E configuration file *config.pro*. The system will look for *config.mech* in a number of places, starting in the current working directory. You might like to come back and explore the contents of your current *config.mech* file, or set up your own file.

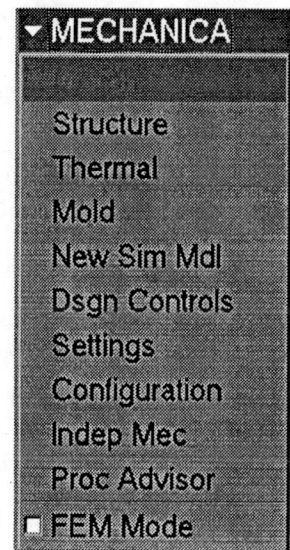

Figure 3
MECHANICA menu

For now, select

Structure

The familiar Mechanica commands open in a menu window. Using the Pro/E interface controls, turn off the display of all datum entities (planes, axes, points). The display will show a coordinate triad (the WCS) at the origin of the model. See Figure 4.

We now have to go through the usual FEA procedures of defining materials, setting up constraints and loads, defining the analysis, and so on.

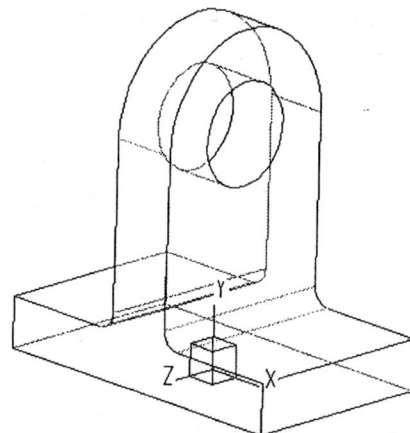

Figure 4 The model in Mechanica
(WCS shown automatically)

We start by selecting

> *Model > Materials*

Select **AL2014** and move it to the right pane. Note that Pro/E and Pro/M already know your units. Now select

> *Assign > Part*

Click on the part, middle-click, and then *Edit*. The next window shows you all the properties assigned to this material (note the units). Young's modulus should be 1.06E07 psi. We will need a mass density value for the optimization later. Select *OK > Close*.

In the STRC MODEL menu select

> *Constraints > Create > Surface*

For solid models, we always try to avoid point or edge constraints. Create a constraint named **fixedface** (in **ConstraintSet1**). Select the button under Surfaces and click on the two end surfaces of the base. You may have to rotate the model in the window, or use *Query Select*. Middle-click and leave all degrees of freedom as fixed (but remember that rotational constraints on solid elements are ignored). *Accept* the dialog. The model will now appear as shown in Figure 5. Note the symbols along the edges of the constrained surfaces. In the CONSTRNTS menu, select *Done/Return*.

Now select

> *Loads > Create > Surface*

Figure 5 Constraints applied

Enter a name like **surfload** (in **LoadSet1**) and select the surface of the hole. You may have to select twice to get both surfaces of the hole. Middle click. Make sure that **Distribution(Total Load)**, **Spatial Variation(Uniform)** are selected and enter the values FX = **750**, FY = **1000**, and FZ = **1500**. Note that this loading is asymmetric, which is why we have not used geometric symmetry to set up the model. Accept the dialog (Figure 6) and you should see the model shown in Figure 7. Spin the model to see the direction of the applied load.

This completes the setup of the model.

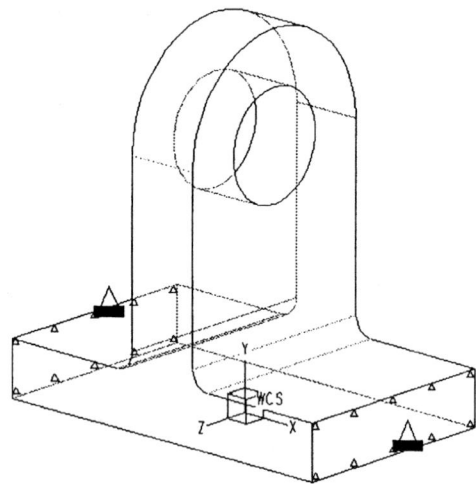

Name	
surfload	

Member of Set

| LoadSet1 | New... |

References
Surface(s)

⬆ Defined

Coordinate system

⬆ ☼ WCS

Distribution

| Total Load | |
| Uniform | |

Force		Moment	
Components		Components	
X	750	X	0
Y	1000	Y	0
Z	1500	Z	0

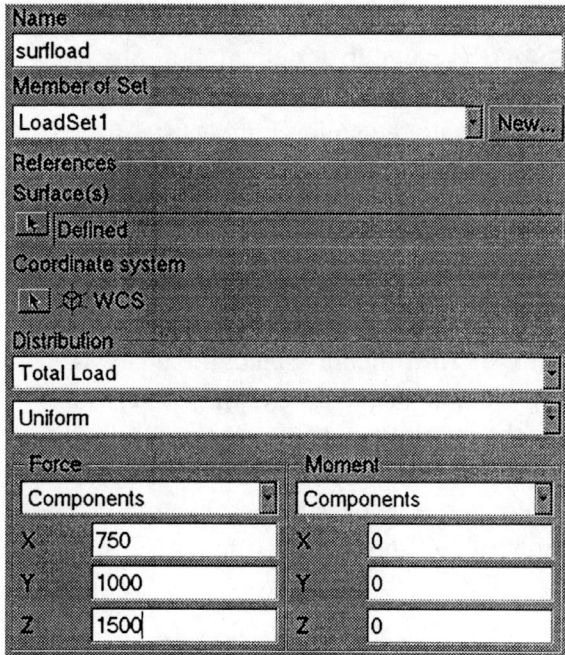

Figure 6 Load definition dialog window

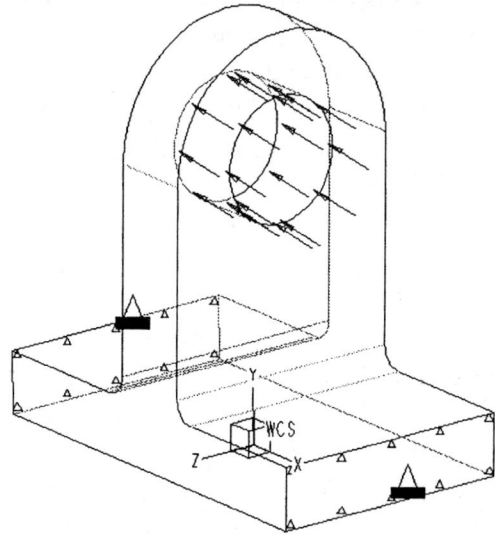

Figure 7 Model with constraints and load

Examining the Model Tree

Commands to edit and modify constraint and load definitions are most easily accessed from the model tree. Open the model tree for the part using

View > Model Tree

See Figure 8. Note the simulation features added at the bottom of the tree. Users of Pro/E will correctly anticipate that these model tree entities can be used to review, edit, and/or delete the various Mechanica entities by selecting them with the right mouse button. Try that now, but do not modify or delete any of the entities. These will only appear on the tree when you are in Mechanica. Once you return to Pro/E, the entities do not show up on the tree, although they are still defined for the model and contained in the part file.

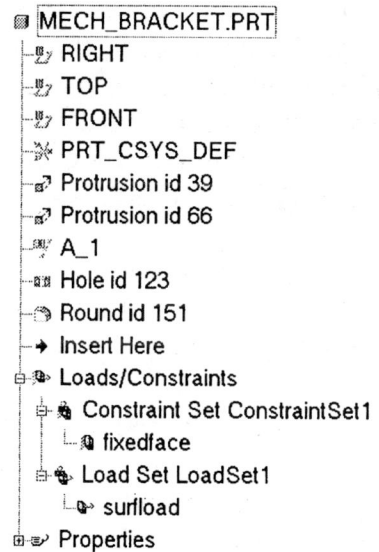

MECH_BRACKET.PRT
├ RIGHT
├ TOP
├ FRONT
├ PRT_CSYS_DEF
├ Protrusion id 39
├ Protrusion id 66
├ A_1
├ Hole id 123
├ Round id 151
├ Insert Here
├ Loads/Constraints
│ ├ Constraint Set ConstraintSet1
│ │ └ fixedface
│ └ Load Set LoadSet1
│   └ surfload
└ Properties

Figure 8 Model tree with simulation features

Running the Analysis

In the MEC STRUCT menu select

Analyses

Create a New static analysis named **brack1**. Make sure that the constraint and load sets are selected. For the convergence method, choose **QuickCheck** and *Accept* the dialog.

Go to the *Run* command in the MEC STRUCT menu and select the study **brack1**. You may want to check and/or change your **Settings**. Then press *Start*. Accept error detection as always on the first run of a model. The design study should start and you can follow progress by clicking the *Summary* button. AutoGEM will automatically create the solid elements (tets). After a few seconds the run should complete with (hopefully) no error messages.

Assuming no errors, select the *Analyses* command again. The analysis **brack1** should be highlighted, so just press the *Edit* button. Change the convergence method to *Multipass Adaptive*, using a **10%** convergence on **Lcl Disp & Lcl SE & Global RMS Stress** and a maximum polynomial order of **6**. *Accept* the dialog. Go to the *Run* menu. Select the analysis *brac1* and in the *Settings* window, check the box for using elements from an existing study, so that AutoGEM will not have to recreate the mesh. *Accept* the window and *Start* the analysis. You will be asked to remove the previous files created using the previous QuickCheck analysis. Open the *Summary* window. You should see the analysis converge on pass 5 or 6. The total mass of the model is 0.0446 (times g=386 in/sec^2 gives a weight of 17.2 pounds). Note the maximum Von Mises stress is about 4000 psi.

Create some result windows: in the MEC STRUCT window select *Results*. Create windows to show the Von Mises stress (fringe plot) and the deformation (animation). These windows are set up using exactly the same procedures described previously. The *Copy* and *Review* commands make it easy to set up new windows. One setting we have not paid much attention to is the *Feature Angle*. This controls whether or not the element edges will appear. The setting refers to the angle between element faces meeting along an edge. If this is less than the angle setting in the result window definition, then the edge does not show. If the Feature Angle (default 30 degrees) is high, then the entire mesh will be invisible. This has not been an issue in independent mode previously because the mesh is always visible in the graphics window. This is not true in integrated mode. To see the effect of this setting, leave the Feature Angle set to 30 in both of the result windows, but come back later and set it to 0.

Show the two result windows at the same time (see Figure 9). Notice that only the part edges are shown - no mesh (remember the feature angle setting)! Find out where the maximum stress is in the part.

Your Von Mises display may appear a bit murky. Select (in the SHOW CTL menu):

> *Controls* > [click on the VM window]

and deselect the **Shade** option.

To see the animation of the deformation, in the SHOW CTL menu, click

> *Controls* > [click on the deformation window] > *Start*

Use *Stop* to exit the animation.

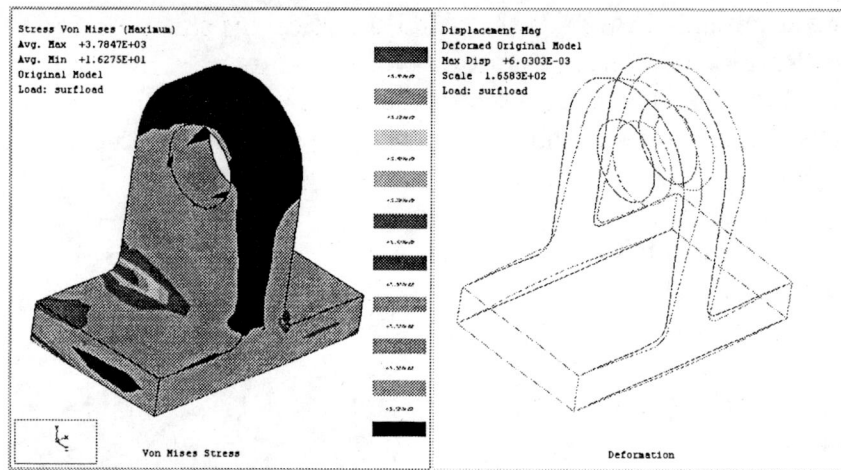

Figure 9 Von Mises stress (left) and deformation (right)

To illustrate an interesting visualization tool, select *Done/Return* and show the Von Mises window by itself. In **SHOW CTL**, select

CuttingSurfs > Create

to see the window shown in Figure 10.

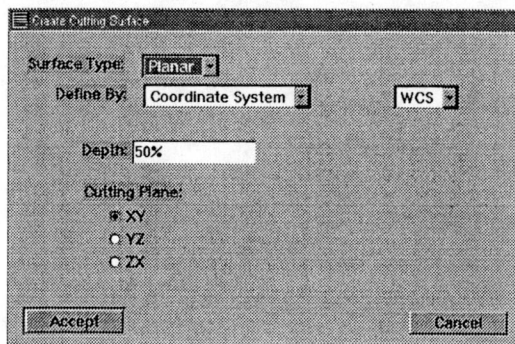

Figure 10 Creating a cutting plane

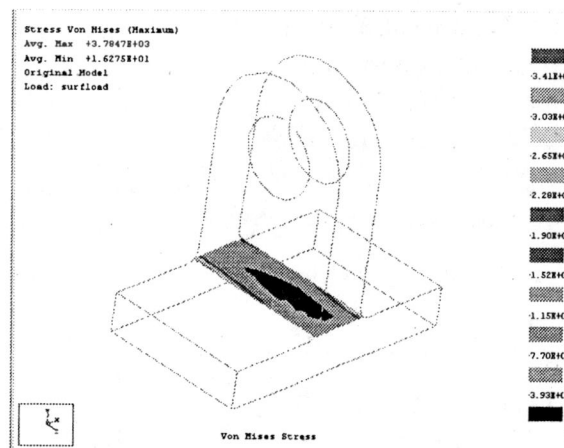

Figure 11 Von Mises stress on the cutting plane

In the **Depth** area, set a value of **1.6** (approximately through the part at the fillet), and select the **ZX** cutting plane (parallel to the base). *Accept* the dialog and in the **CUT SURF CTL** menu, select *Modify* and then *Dynamic*. Now, with the mouse pointer in the display window, dragging (with the left mouse button) the cursor up and down will move the cutting plane up and down in the part. Middle click to leave dynamic mode, then select *Cancel > Done*.

A *Capping Surface* is similar to the cutting surface, except that the model on only one side of the surface is also removed (in this case, above the cutting surface). Experiment with this command. Try setting the Capping Surface as XY (vertical surface parallel to the back of the model).

Here is another window definition we haven't seen before. Review the Von Mises result window definition. From the **Display** pull-down list, select **Contour** and check the option **Isosurfaces**. Set the Feature Angle to 30. Now show the window (Figure 12). This is displaying surfaces of constant stress level in the part.

Select **Done > Done/Return** to get back to the Result window dialog.

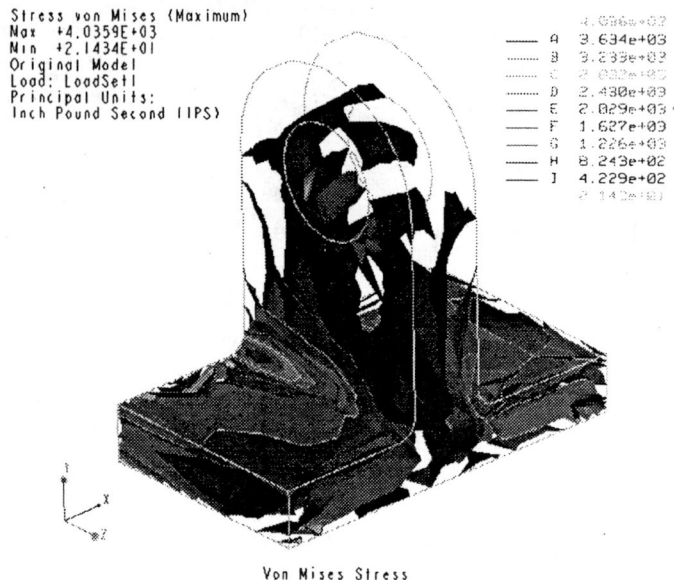

Figure 12 Isosurfaces of the Von Mises stress

Create two more result windows showing the convergence of Von Mises stress and total strain energy. In these window definitions use **Quantity(Measure)** and *Select* max_stress_vm or strain_energy. The display type is a Graph. Show both windows at the same time, as in Figure 13.

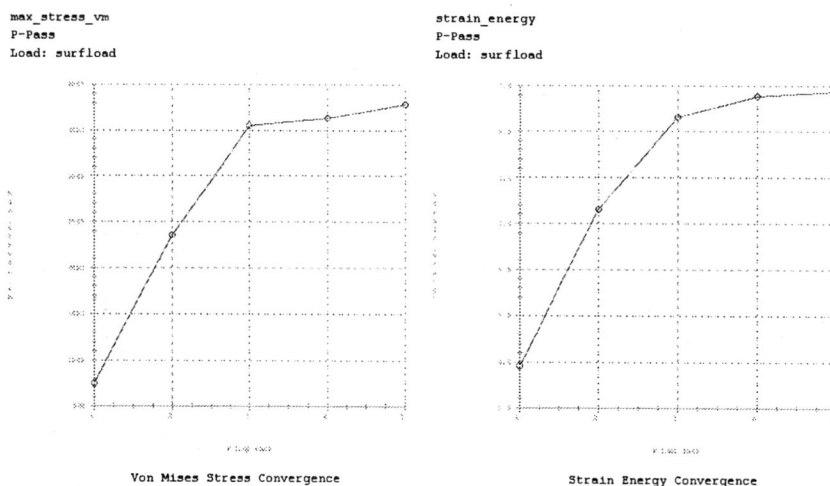

Figure 13 Convergence of Von Mises stress (left) and strain energy (right)

Sensitivity Study

We note that the maximum stress was on the left fillet at the rear of the part. We will set up a study to vary the radius of the fillet. In the MEC STRUCT menu select

> *Model > Dsgn Controls > Design Params > Create > Select*

Click on one of the fillets (assuming they are both in the same Pro/E feature). The fillet radius dimension will appear (see Figure 14). Click on the dimension value (currently 0.5) and the Design Parameter Definition window opens (Figure 15). The symbolic name for the dimension is listed (d18 in the figure, yours may be different). Enter a short description for the parameter and in the boxes at the bottom, enter minimum (0.25) and maximum (1.0) values to be used for the sensitivity study. Note that the current value is 0.5. Close the dialog window.

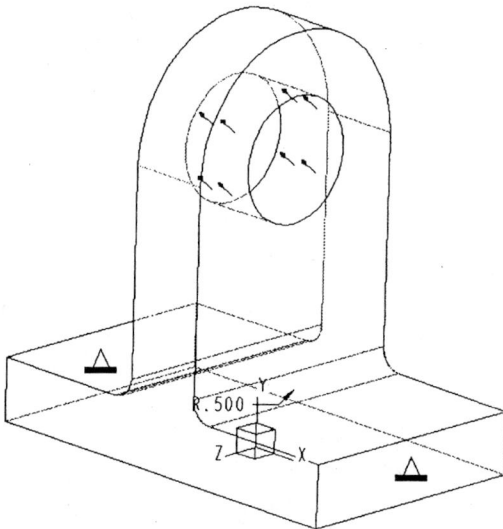

Figure 15 Defining the design parameter

Figure 14 Picking the fillet radius as design parameter

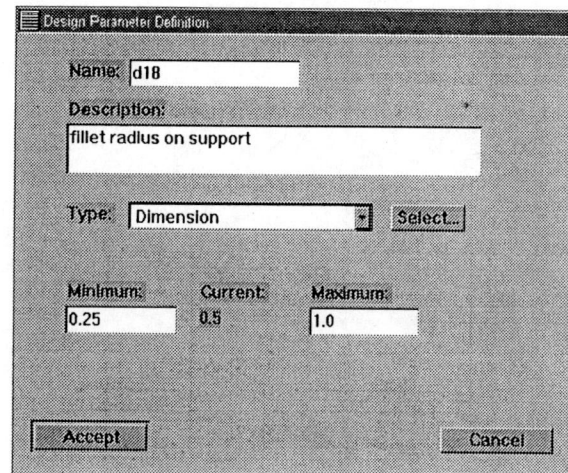

In the DSGN CONTROLS menu select *Shape Review*. Check the parameter (d18, or whatever your parameter name is). Select the minimum value of 0.25 and select the *Review* button. The part will be regenerated with the small fillet. Restore the part to it's original shape and select *Shape Review* again. Check the shape using the maximum value of the parameter. You can use *Shape Animate* to step through the entire range from minimum to maximum. This is useful if you have a number of parameters selected and you need to check if the part can be regenerated with different combinations of parameter values. This would obviously be necessary in order to create the mesh for different geometries that will arise in a sensitivity study, and later in an optimization. We will get to the **Optimize Hist** command later.

In the *Analyses* menu, select the current analysis **brack1** and change it to a **Single Pass Adaptive** convergence to speed up the work.

Now, in the MEC STRUCT menu, select

Design Studies

Create a new study called **bracket_sens**. The type we want is **Global Sensitivity** and the analysis is **brack1**. Select the parameter to be varied (d18, or whatever your parameter is called) between minimum and maximum values. Select **3** intervals. *Accept* the dialog, and select *Run*. In the **Run** window, select the design study **bracket_sens**. Check your *Settings* and *Start* the design study. The run will take a couple of minutes. Select *Summary* to watch the proceedings. When completed, select *Close*. In the MEC STRUCT window, select *Results* and create a couple of windows to show the variation of Von Mises stress and total mass using **Quantity(Measure)** and selecting the appropriate quantities. In the **Location** area of the result window definition, select the design variable d18 (or whatever your parameter is called). *Show* the windows, which should be similar to Figure 16.

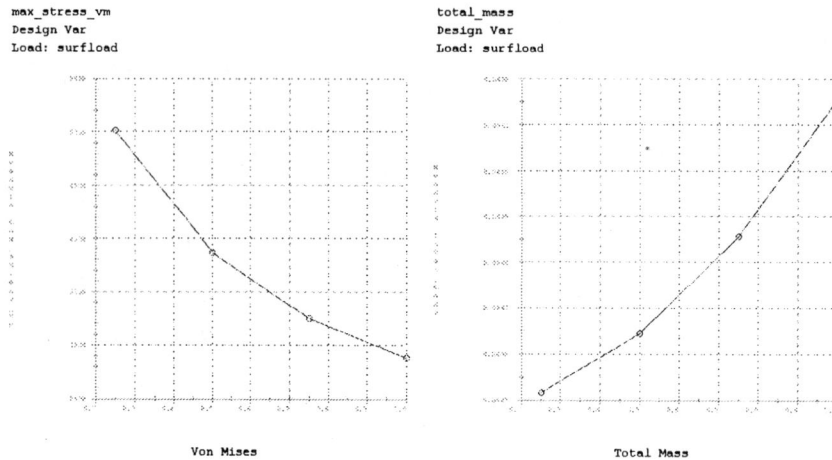

Figure 16 Sensitivity of Von Mises stress (left) and total mass (right) to the fillet radius

As we expect, as the fillet radius increases, the Von Mises stress will decrease but the part mass increases. In the next section, we will optimize the part geometry (including the plate thicknesses) to minimize the mass without exceed a given stress value.

Optimization

We want to minimize the weight of the bracket under the specified loads without exceeding a specified maximum Von Mises stress. We will pick another two design parameters as shown in Figures 17 and 18. These are the thickness of the base and support plates.

Starting in the MEC STRUCT menu, select

Model > Dsgn Controls > Design Params > Create > Select

Click on the base of the part. The dimensions will appear. Click on the height dimension (currently 1.5). Set minimum and maximum values of 1 and 2, respectively, for the design search space. Create another design parameter for the support thickness (currently 2). Set minimum value of 1 and maximum 3. Enter a description of the parameter, and *Accept* the dialog. We now have three design parameters defined. A shape review at the minimum and maximum values of all parameters results in the geometry shown in Figures 19 and 20.

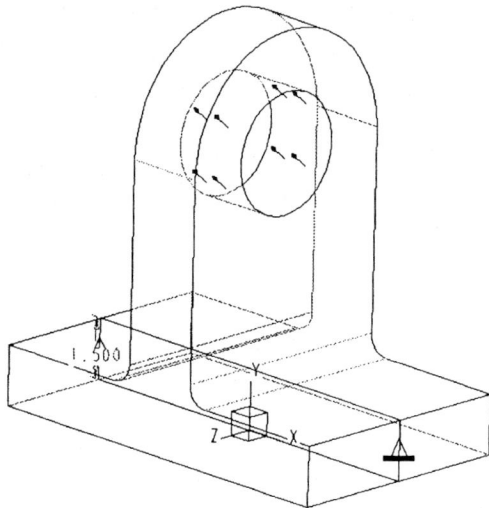

Figure 17 Choosing the base thickness as a design parameter

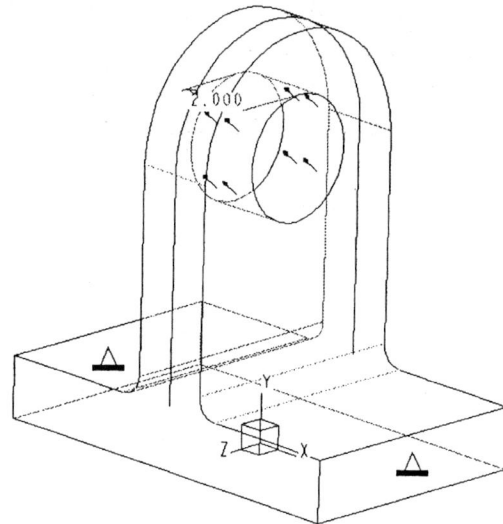

Figure 18 Choosing the support thickness as a design parameter

Figure 19 Geometry review with design parameters at minimum values

Figure 20 Geometry review with design parameters at maximum values

For the optimization, verify that the Analysis is set to a **Single Pass** adaptive convergence and that the constraint and load sets are selected.

Create a new design study called **bracket_opt**. Enter a description. The goal is to minimize the total mass. Create a limit on the maximum Von Mises stress and enter a value of **3500**. Check the three available design parameters for optimization. Examine the minimum and maximum values, and set the initial values of 0.5, 1.5, and 2. Set the optimization convergence to 5% with a maximum of 20 iterations. Leave the **Repeat P-loop convergence** off.

In the *Run* menu, make sure **bracket_opt** is selected. Make a note of the locations of the output files.

* * * NOTE: depending on your machine, the next step could take quite a while (1 hour on a Pentium 300MHz with 256M of RAM).

Start the optimization. If necessary, you can stop the analysis at any time and, as long as you don't delete or move files, restart it at a later time.

Go for coffee!

For this optimization, the final results should be approximately as follows:

- fillet radius 1.000"
- base thickness 1.42"
- support thickness 1.27"
- Goal: mass 0.0364 (about 14 pounds).

The achieved Von Mises stress on the final pass reported in the Summary window is about 3620 psi. This is a slight violation of our desired stress limit. We could get a better result by tightening up both the static analysis and optimization design study convergence criteria, at the expense of increased computer time.

The fringe plot of the Von Mises stress is shown in Figure 21. To create this, make sure you select the correct study **bracket_opt**.

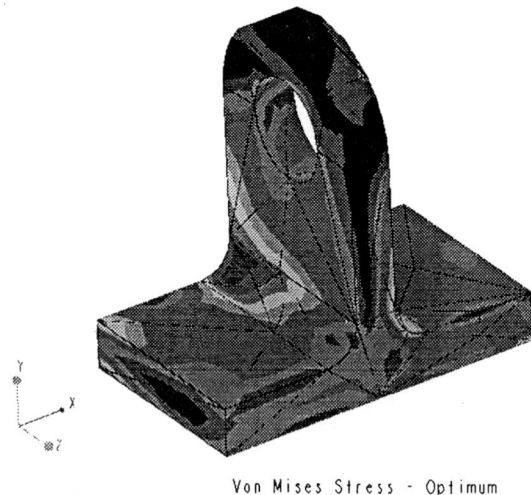

Von Mises Stress - Optimum

Figure 21 Von Mises stress in optimized part geometry

Create result windows to show the optimization history for the Von Mises stress and total mass. Use **Quantity(Measure)** and select **max_stress_vm** and **total_mass,** respectively, for these. The history plots are shown in Figure 22. Note that the Von Mises plot (on the left) indicates that the final geometry on iteration 7 actually achieved a maximum Von Mises stress of 3500.

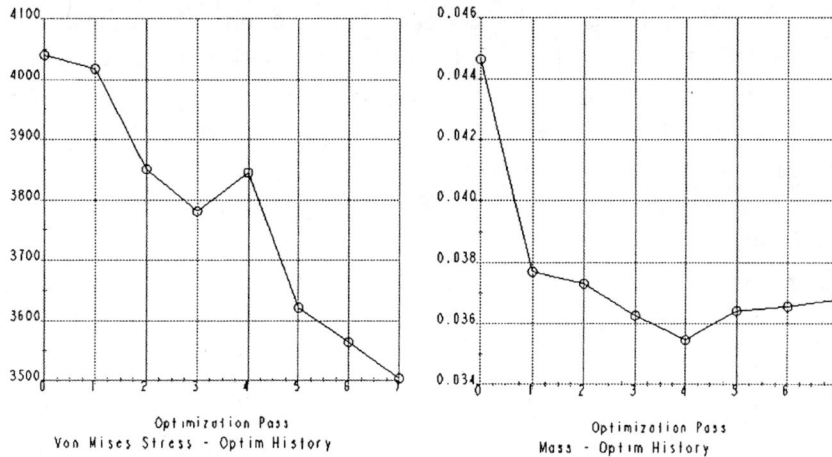

Figure 22 Optimization history of Von Mises stress (left) and total mass (right)

You can review the geometry changes that occurred during optimization. Change your Pro/E working directory to the directory where you stored the Mechanica results (using *File > Working Directory*). In the MECHANICA menu, select *Dsgn Controls > Optimize Hist > Search Study*. The study *bracket_opt* should appear in the listing. Check this and follow the prompts to see a series of shapes that occurred during the optimization. The figures below show the initial and final (optimized) shapes and the associated design parameters. At the end of the shape review, you are asked if you want to leave the model in its final shape. *Accept* the default (Yes).

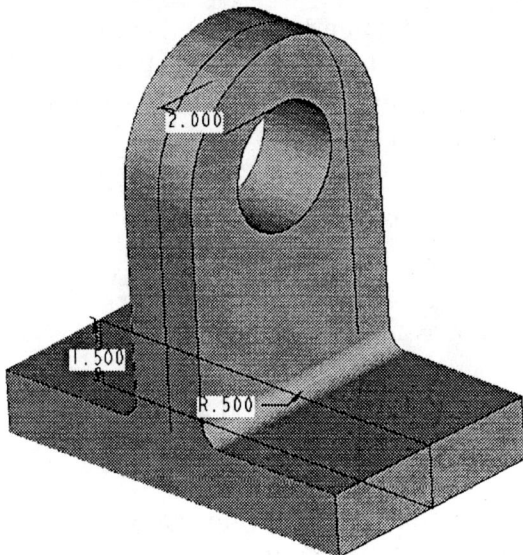

Figure 23 Design parameters - initial values

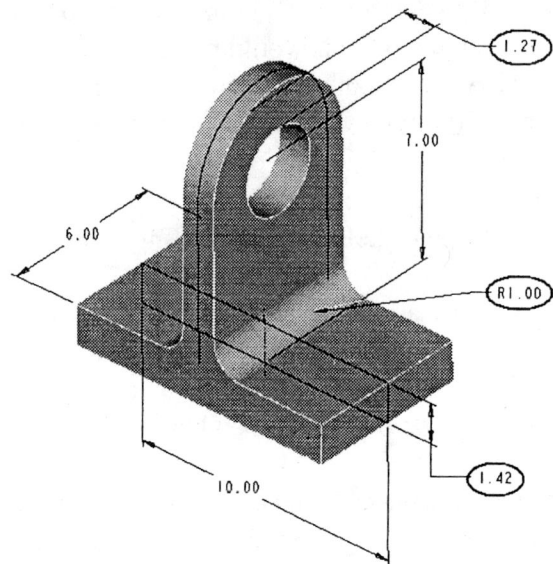

Figure 24 Design parameters - optimized design

Select *Quit* and return to the Pro/E window, using

Applications > Standard

Using the Pro/E *Modify* command, verify that the part now contains the optimized values for the design parameters. Use *File > Save As* to store the optimized part using a new file name.

The file containing all the intermediate values of the design parameters during optimization is stored in your results directory, and will be called *bracket_opt.dpi*. Extracting data from this file and plotting shows an interesting view of the optimization process (Figure 25).

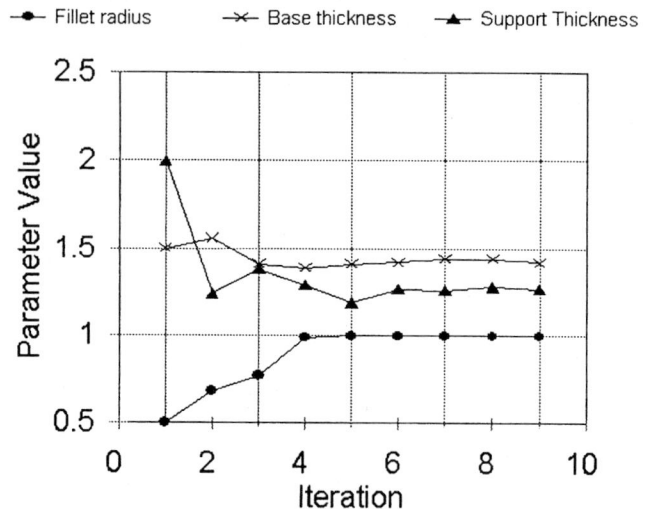

Figure 25 Behavior of design parameters through the optimization run

Limitations of Integrated Mode

It is clear that, since in integrated mode we are dealing with a solid Pro/E object, the default mode of operations uses only solid elements. This places quite a restriction on the types of models we can create. Of course it should be possible to analyze anything using solid models, but in many cases this would be impractical (for example a complicated 3D frame) and/or highly inefficient (for example an axisymmetric solid). Consider, for example, the analysis of a simple beam. Although this could be done using solid elements, it might take several dozen (or hundreds) to achieve the (desired) results that could be obtained with only a handful of beam elements. In the next section, we will see how idealizations can be used to set up different element types (shells, masses, springs, and beams).

We also saw above that the full set of AutoGEM settings is not available in integrated mode. You cannot exclude elements in integrated mode. Unless you are careful, you do not even see the FEA mesh. There are also some other differences. For example, in integrated mode you cannot plot the p-level of the elements.

A minor annoyance that occurs in integrated mode, if you have done the sensitivity study or optimization, is apparent if you go to your model and results directories. Quite a number of trail files are created there, essentially every time Pro/E is called upon to regenerate the model.

The reason why integrated mode is useful is the ease with which solid models can be created in Pro/E, and carried into Mechanica. Furthermore, when a Mechanica optimization is performed, the geometry is carried back into Pro/E. There is also only one interface to learn, in particular for creating geometry.

Launching Independent Mode

Given the limitations in integrated mode, the need may arise for some of the functions available only in independent mode, such as displaying the P-levels of the mesh. You can easily transfer to that mode by issuing the command

Indep Mec

in the MECHANICA menu.

Follow the prompts on the screen. You will end up with the bracket model in the stand-alone Mechanica interface. Note that the model is a volume only - you will have to create the solid elements from the volume. The loads, constraints, design parameters, and analysis definitions are all carried into independent Mechanica from Pro/E. You can do any modifications to the FEA model you want and/or use the *Results* command to create any form of result window. Geometric changes may be problematic since the model is no longer feature based or parametric. Remember, too, that any geometric changes will not be automatically carried back to Pro/E. Furthermore, if you run an analysis of the model in independent mode, you will not be able to read the part in Pro/E again. So, before launching into independent mode, you may want to make a second copy of the part file in some other directory.

Model Idealizations - 2D Models

As demonstrated in the previous section, the default element type used in integrated mode is a solid (usually a tetrahedron). It is possible to set up the model using some other types of elements by creating idealizations. With Pro/M 2000i^2 you can treat 2D problems in integrated mode. These include plane stress, plane strain, and axisymmetric problems. These idealizations are based on the geometry contained in the 3D Pro/E model. Primarily, the geometry of interest is a surface. Some restrictions and additional points need to be considered here. These are essentially the same concerns as we had in independent mode and are pretty self-evident:

1. The geometry for the FEA model must be coplanar.
2. The geometry must have an associated Cartesian coordinate system. This can be created in Mechanica.
3. The model must be in the XY plane of the coordinate system.
4. For axisymmetric models, the model must all be in the X>0 side of the coordinate system.

We'll examine this by revisiting an example presented earlier. This is the exercise at the end of Lesson 3, a plane stress problem, as discussed in Lesson 4.

2D Plane Stress Model

This example problem concerns the stress analysis in a thin flat plate. The model is created in Pro/E according to the dimensions repeated here in Figure 26. Note that the original problem used a plate thickness of 2mm. To illustrate a point with 2D plane stress modeling here, create the solid plate with a thickness of 10mm. Make the base feature using a one-sided protrusion off the Front datum plane. When the model has been created, use a cut feature along the symmetry plane to produce the solid geometry shown in Figure 27. Make sure your units are set to mmNs.

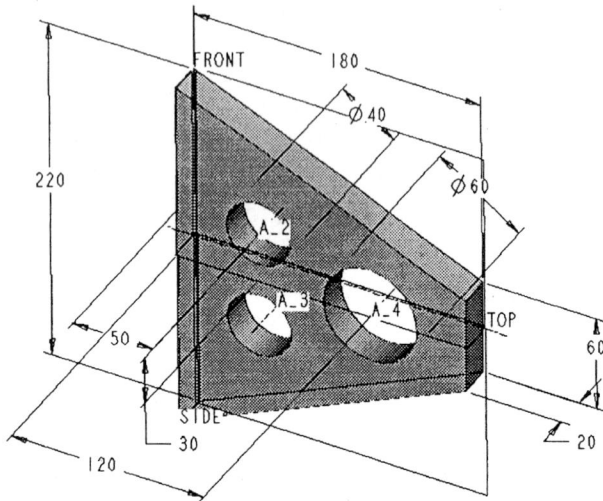

Figure 26 Thin plate model in Pro/E

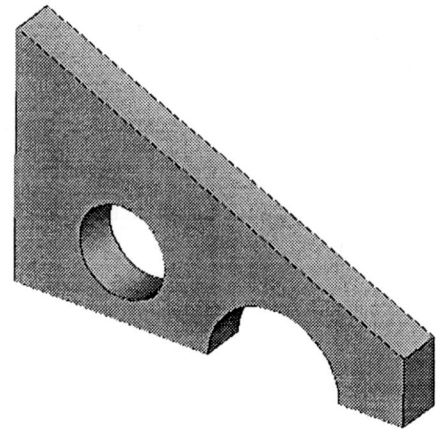

Figure 27 Half-plate solid model

Launch Mechanica using

> *Applications > Mechanica > Structure*

As mentioned previously, a 2D model must have an associated Cartesian coordinate system whose XY plane contains the surface geometry for the analysis. We'll create a coordinate system as a *Simulation Feature* here.

> *Model > Features*
> *Coord System > Create*
> *Pnt + 2 Axes | Cartesian | Done*

Click on the vertex at the front, left, bottom corner of the plate. To define the axes, pick first on the bottom front edge of the plate and finally on the left vertical edge. This creates a triad of vectors (2 yellow and 1 red) at the vertex. We specify which direction the red vector is pointing. Follow the prompts to set up the X and Y directions as shown in Figure 28. The coordinate system is created and appears on the model. Open up the model tree to see an entry for the feature there.

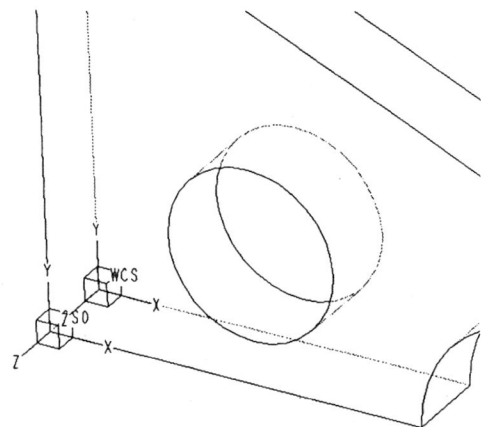

Figure 28 Creating the coordinate system

Now we can start setting up the plane stress model. Select

Model Type

This brings up the dialog box shown in Figure 29. Check the button beside **Plane Stress**. This activates the two buttons at the bottom of the window.

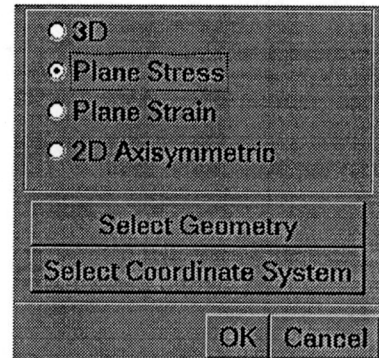

Select Geometry

We must now select the planar surface to be used in the 2D model. Click on the front face of the plate. It highlights in red. Middle click (or *Done Sel*) and the geometry will be highlighted in magenta. Now in the Model Type window, select

Select Coordinate System

Figure 29 Selecting the Model Type

and pick the coordinate system we created above. Select *OK*.

As you leave the Model Type window, a warning window will open up to let you know that if the model type is changed, all previously defined FEA modeling entities will be deleted (loads, constraints, materials, and so on). If that happens, you would have to create them again. Thus, be very careful about selecting the model type, since if you pick the wrong one and have to change it later, much of your work will be lost.

You can now apply loads, constraints, and material in the same way as we did in independent mode. Apply the constraints using *Edge/Curve* to the lower (symmetry) edge and the left vertical edge of the green modeling surface. Apply a horizontal load (500N) also using *Edge/Curve* to the right vertical edge. To have the load arrows going outward from the model, select

View > Simulation Display > Settings

and select **Tails Touching**. Finally, assign the material **AL2014** to the magenta surface.

The only variation with what we did in independent mode, and with what we will see a bit later with shell models, is how we specify the plate thickness. The command picks are non-obvious for this. For 2D plane stress models, we do this using the following (starting in the MEC STRUCT menu):

Model > Idealizations > Shells > New

This brings up the Shell Properties Definition window shown in Figure 30. Notice two things about this: we define the model thickness explicitly - it is not determined from the Pro/E model (which is 10mm thick). The Pro/E model is used only to determine the 2D geometry for plane stress models. Furthermore, we assign the material property to the shell instead of to the part.

Select the button under Surfaces and pick on the
model surface, then middle click. Enter a property
name and the thickness value **2**. The material is
selected from the pull-down list at the bottom.
Accept the dialog. Again, it is important to note
here that Mechanica does *NOT* pick up the plate
thickness from the 3D model in Pro/E. Recall that
our model has a thickness of 10mm. We will see
later that when we use a 3D shell idealization,
Mechanica will pick up the thickness from the
model. This does not happen in 2D!

Name
thick2

Surface(s)

Surface

Type

Simple

Thickness

2

Material

AL2014	More...

Figure 30 Defining shell property for plane
stress model

Our 2D plane stress model is now complete, and should appear as in Figure 31. Note the
additional symbols along the constrained edges. This helps you identify which curves have been
constrained. You can set up and run a **QuickCheck** analysis (with error checking) using the
AutoGEM defaults. The mesh consists of 2D plate elements. Review the analysis and change to
a **Multipass Adaptive** analysis with **5%** convergence, max edge order **9** (although we hope we
don't need that many). Run this analysis. The run should converge on pass 7 or 8. You should
compare the results obtained with those shown in Lesson 4. The Von Mises stress fringe is
shown in Figure 32 - note that this displays only a planar surface and not the entire 3D model.

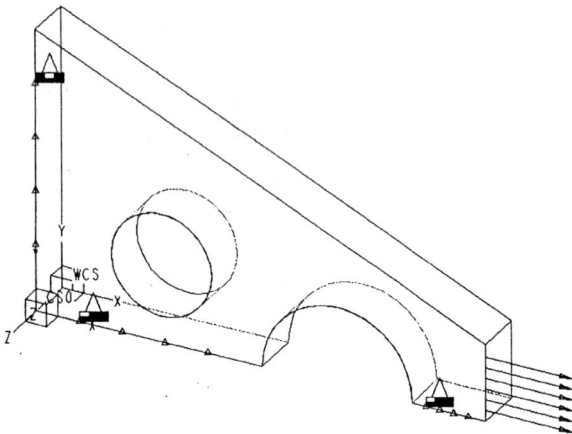

Figure 31 Completed Mechanica plane stress
model

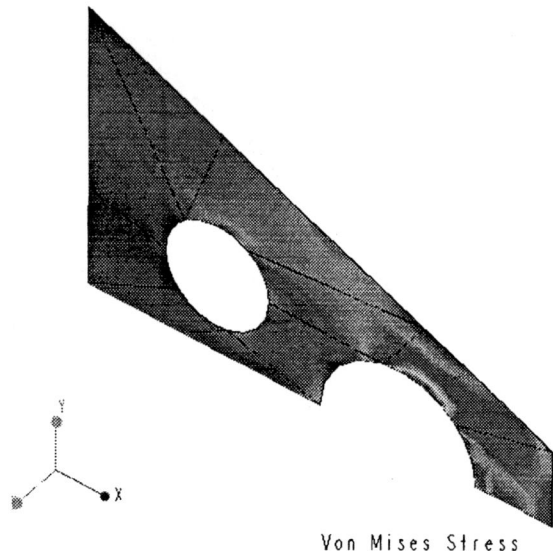

Von Mises Stress

Figure 32 Von Mises stress fringe for plane
stress model

Other 2D models (plane strain and axisymmetric) are created in a similar manner. There are
minor variations for these for specify material properties. Recall the restrictions on the geometry
mentioned at the beginning of this section. Also, sensitivity studies and optimization are carried

out in exactly the same way as previously presented. The advantage for 2D models, of course, is the speed with which that can be accomplished versus treating the model as a solid.

Cyclic Symmetry

An enhancement introduced in MECHANICA 2000i was a new kind of constraint that can be used for models that have cyclic symmetry. This is similar to axisymmetry in which the model is obtained by revolving a planar section (or curves defined on a plane) around an axis of revolution. Axisymmetric models are determined by 2D geometry and were covered in Lesson 6. In a model with cyclic symmetry, a 3D geometric shape is repeated identically an integer number of times around the axis. The geometry is not continuous (and therefore not truly axisymmetric), but cyclic. If the loading and constraints are also cyclic along with the geometry, then it makes sense that we should be able to analyze a single portion of the overall geometry. This is illustrated in Figures 33 and 34. The first figure shows a complete centrifugal fan impeller (somewhat simplified!). Because of symmetry about a horizontal plane, we can cut the fan in half, as seen in the second figure. If the loading is identical on all the blades (perhaps due to the applied air pressure and centrifugal load), we should be able to analyze a single blade by properly isolating it and applying constraints that capture the repetitive or cyclic symmetry. We will return to this model a bit later.

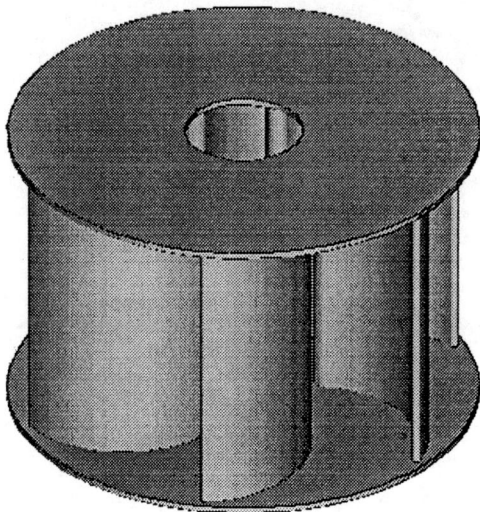

Figure 33 A centrifugal fan impeller   **Figure 34** Lower half of fan impeller

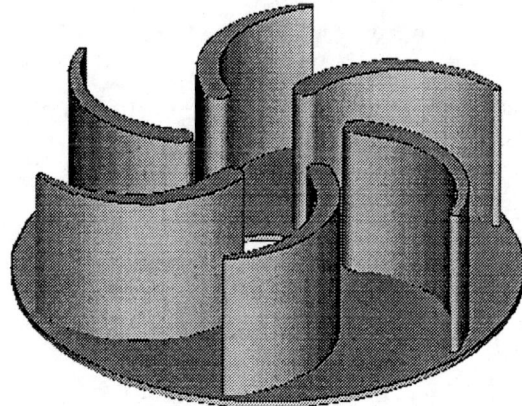

The major requirement for using cyclic symmetry is that the following items are all cyclic:
   ♦   geometry
   ♦   applied loads
   ♦   constraints
   ♦   material type and orientation
Pro/M will try to determine the axis for the cyclic symmetry automatically (as in the example following). If it cannot do this, you will be prompted to identify the axis yourself.

To demonstrate the procedure, we will revisit a model we dealt with earlier. This is the pressurized axisymmetric tank we treated using a 2D axisymmetric model. Note that the tank is fully axisymmetric, which is not required for cyclic symmetry. However this is a simple model to create and gives us a chance to compare results with another analysis method. The completed cyclic symmetry model is shown in Figure 35.

Model Geometry

In Pro/E, create a new solid model **axitank**. The units for this model are IPS. Create a 30° revolved protrusion off the red side of the FRONT datum. Align the axis of revolution with the SIDE datum and place the bottom of the sketch on the TOP datum. Dimensions are shown in Figure 4 of Lesson #5. Add an R0.5 round to the inner corner.

Transfer into MECHANICA with

> *Applications > Mechanica > Structure*

Cyclic Constraints

To define the constraints it will be necessary to have a cylindrical coordinate system at the origin of the datum planes. Create that now using

> *Model > Features > Coord System > Create*
> *2 Axes | Cylindrical | Done*

and use the procedures discussed earlier to create a cylindrical coordinate system as shown in Figure 35. Pick on the lower front edge (the **Theta = 0** axis) and the vertical edge on the axis (the **Z-axis**). Use the triad to specify directions. We must declare this as the current system using (in the **STRC MODEL** menu)

> *Current Csys*

Pick on the created cylindrical system (probably **CS0**). It will turn green.

The constraints on the two vertical faces of the model are cyclic. As our pie-shaped model is repeated (12 times) to form the upper half of the tank, the solution values on the two vertical faces must match up. Set up the cyclic constraint using

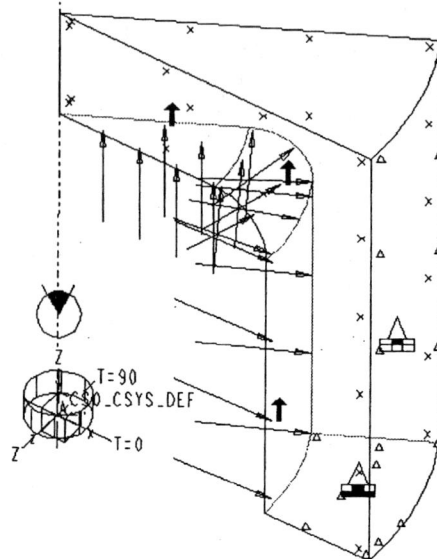

Figure 35 Completed cyclic symmetry model

> *Constraints > Create > Cyclic Symm*

Enter a constraint name **cyclic** (in ConstraintSet1). Under **References**, select the button below **First Side**, and pick on the front vertical face, then middle click. Now select the button below **Second Side** and pick on the back vertical face (use *Query Select*, or spin the model); middle click again. Notice that at the bottom of this dialog window, the **Axis** area is grayed out - Pro/M was able to determine automatically where the axis is located (intersection of the two planar surfaces). Accept the dialog. Constraint symbols (small x's) will appear on the two surfaces and the cyclic symmetry icon appears on the axis of the model as in Figure 35.

Completing the Model

We must also provide some additional constraints for the model. This is why we needed the new cylindrical coordinate system. Select

Create > Surface

Name the constraint **outer_face** (in ConstraintSet1). Select the button under **References** and pick on the outer curved face. The constraints to set here are: **FREE** the translation in R and Z, and **FIXED** for translation in Theta. Recall that rotational constraints are ignored for solid models.

We also need a constraint against vertical motion. Select *Surface* again and constrain the lower surface (on the XZ plane) as follows: **FREE** for the translation in R, and **FIXED** for translation in Theta and Z. Finally, constrain the edge along the axis against radial motion. Both of these constraints should be in ConstraintSet1.

Apply a pressure load (1000 psi) on the three inside surfaces of the tank. Put this in LoadSet1.

Finally use *Materials* to specify the material **STEEL** for the model. The model is complete and should now appear as shown in Figure 35.

Analysis and Results

Set up and run a **QuickCheck** analysis called **cyclic1**. Use ConstraintSet1 and LoadSet1 (that contains the 1000 psi pressure load). AutoGEM will create 12 solid elements. Assuming all goes well, change to a **Multi-Pass Adaptive** analysis with **5%** convergence and a maximum polynomial order 6. When you run this, open the *Summary* window. The analysis should converge on pass 6. Note the maximum Von Mises stress (about 4860 psi), and the maximum deflection $\Delta y_{max} = 0.000262$ in. Compare these to the results obtained in Lesson 5.

Create result windows showing a Von Mises stress fringe plot and a displacement animation. These are shown in Figures 36 and 37 below. Note the stress pattern on the side (cyclic) faces are identical and very similar to the axisymmetric model in Lesson 5, and is uniform around the axis of rotation along the round. In the deformation animation, the deformation is also as expected.

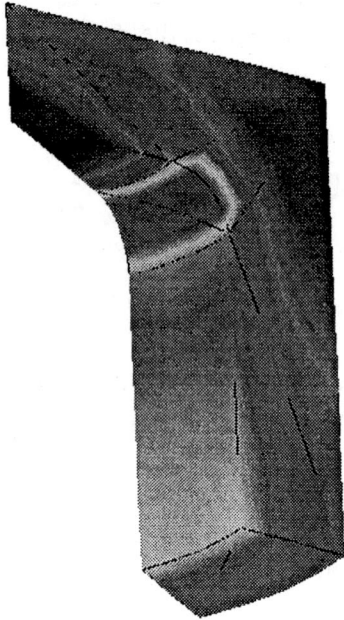

Von Mises Stress

Figure 36 Von Mises stress in cyclic model

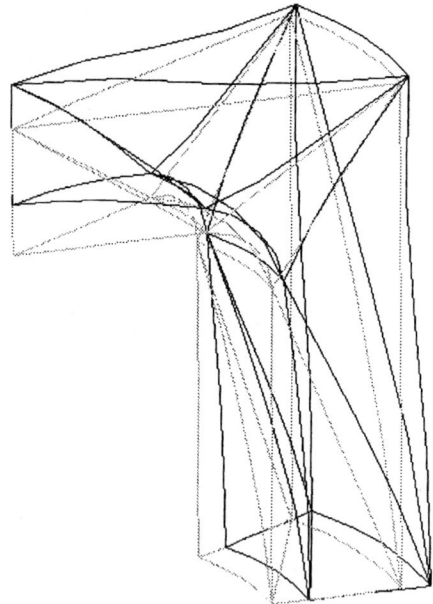

Deformation

Figure 37 Deformation of cyclic model

Create a couple of result windows showing the convergence of the Von Mises stress and the strain energy. These are shown in Figure 38 below. Pretty good convergence here.

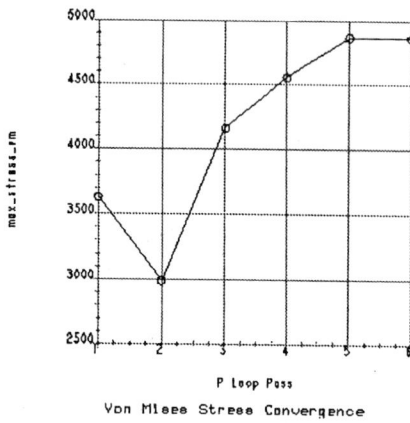

Von Mises Stress Convergence

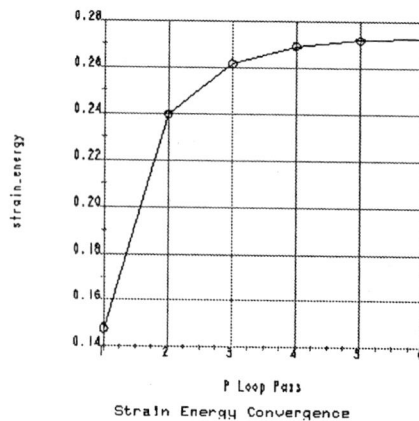

Strain Energy Convergence

Figure 38 Convergence of Von Mises stress and strain energy in the simple tank model with cyclic symmetry

Let's return to the example mentioned at the beginning of this section - the centrifugal fan problem. In Pro/E, we can isolate one of the blades using judicious cuts. Beware that the surfaces where cyclic constraints are to be applied must be identical shapes - the cyclic "instances" of the blade and end plate combination must fit together perfectly around the whole fan. The included angle between the cuts must be obtained as 360° divided by a whole number, in this case, 6. This is easy to set up in Pro/E if you use a datum curve to define the desired shape of the cut on the end plate and then create a rotated copy (around the central axis) of the datum curve. You then create the cut using the *Use Edge* option in Sketcher and picking the datum curves.

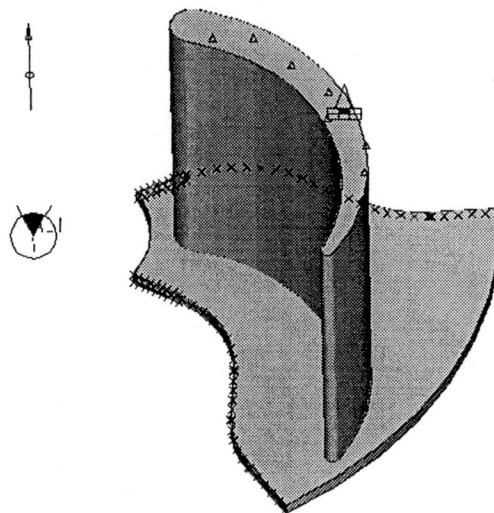

Figure 39 Cyclic symmetry model of fan blade

The resulting geometry and model is shown in Figure 39. The cyclic symmetry constraints are placed on the cut faces of the end plate. Depending on the geometry of the end plate cut, you may have to identify the cyclic symmetry axis for this geometry. The only other constraint is due to symmetry on the top surface of the blade in the model to prevent rigid body translation along the axis. The model is loaded with a centrifugal load (notice the symbol in the upper left corner of the figure) that appears on the axis of rotation of the fan.

Some results of running this model (389 solid elements) are shown in the figures below. Note the maximum stress levels are near the boundaries and at the junction of the blade trailing edge and the end plate, which is a reentrant corner. We might have expected this! This model would need some re-work before providing good results.

Von Mises Stress

Figure 40 Von Mises stress on centrifugal fan blade

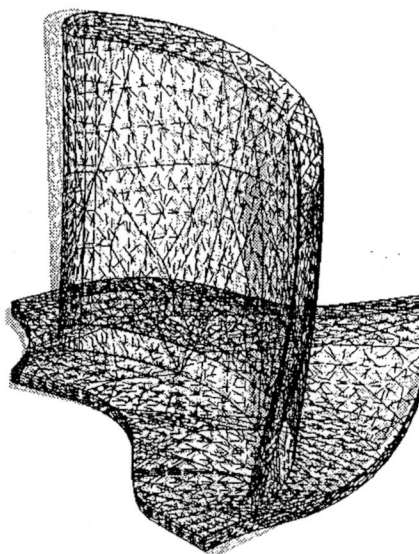

Figure 41 Deformation of fan blade and end plate

This concludes our discussion of cyclic symmetry. We will move on to some further idealizations possible in integrated mode - replacing thin-walled solids with shells.

Shell Models

In this section we will illustrate another type of idealization - using shell elements to represent thin-walled solids defined by pairs of parallel surfaces. We will see that in this case (unlike the 2D plane stress example), Mechanica reads the shell thicknesses directly from the Pro/E model. In the first example, the surface pairs forming the thin wall are determined automatically. In the second example, we will identify the pairs manually.

Model #1: A Pressurized Tank

We will analyze the small pressurized tank shown in Figure 42 (approximately in default orientation). The tank has a hemispherical shape on the bottom. Create this new part called **shelltank** making sure that you set up the units as mmNs. The dimensions (in mm) of the major features of the tank are shown in Figure 43. Note that the round dimensions are given in Figure 42. Use the *Shell* feature in Pro/E to create a wall of uniform thickness (1.0mm) throughout. To take advantage of symmetry, create a final vertical cut through the model to remove the front half of the model.

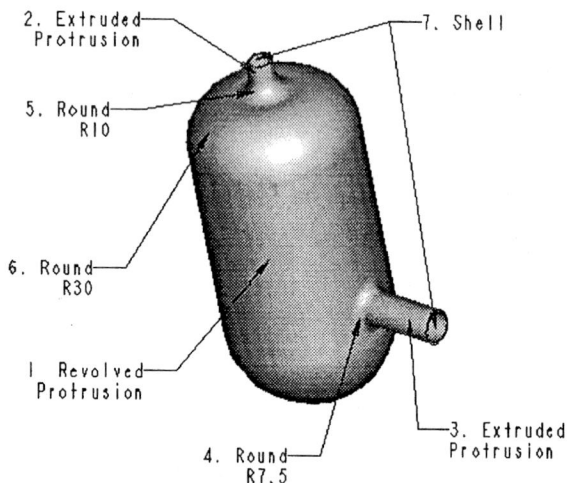

Figure 42 Pro/E features used to form tank

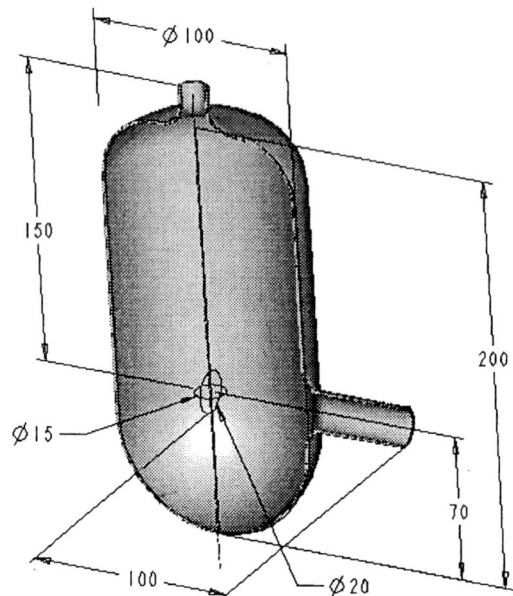

Figure 43 Tank dimensions

Defining the Shells

When the geometry is complete, select

Applications > Mechanica > Structure

Recall that the default model type is 3D, so we don't need to change that. Our first job is to define the shells in the model. These are idealizations, so select

Idealizations > Shells > Midsurfaces > Auto Detect

You will see red and yellow lines on the edges of the cut surface representing the edges of the paired surfaces. See Figure 44. Then click on

Compress > Shells Only > ShowCompress

This will show the midsurface (yellow highlight) between the two model surfaces that will be used to create the shell elements (Figure 45). Note that *Show Both* displays the shell edges in yellow and the original surface edges in green. The shells are created at the midsurfaces of the pairs.

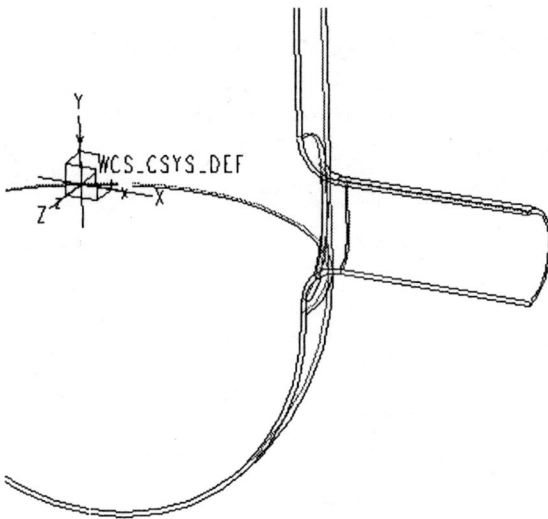

Figure 44 Automatically paired surfaces (closeup)

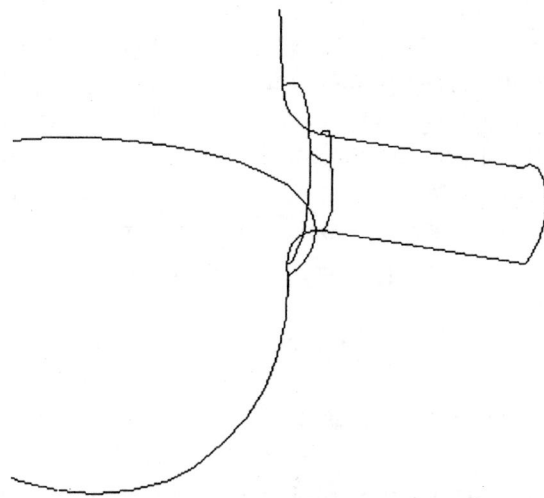

Figure 45 Compressed surfaces only (closeup)

Note in the **SHELLS** menu, there is a *Properties* command that lets you define the shell thickness. This property can then be assigned to surfaces. We will not do that here.

Go to the top MECHANICA menu and select *Settings*. Notice that the option **Use Pairs** is now checked. The next time you bring this model in from Pro/E, MECHANICA will automatically use the paired surfaces.

While you are in the Settings menu, make sure your AGEM settings are set to the default.

Assigning the Material

We now need to assign the usual materials, constraints, and loads to the model. Start with the material. In the **STRC MODEL** menu, select:

> *Materials*

Bring the material **SS** (a stainless steel) from the library into the model. Then select

> *Assign > Part*

Thus, material assignment is done in exactly the same way as for a solid model.

Assigning the Constraints

In 3D solid models, we normally apply constraints to surfaces. For the symmetry constraint in this model, that would be the thin surfaces created by the symmetry cut. However, those surfaces will disappear when the shell surface is created by compressing the surface pairs. Also, remember that, unlike solid elements, shell elements have rotational degrees of freedom. So, remember that:
- ♦ we must apply constraints to edges or curves, and
- ♦ we must keep rotation of those edges in mind.

In the **STRC MODEL** menu,

> *Constraints > Create > Edge/Curve*

Call the constraint **symedges** (member of ConstraintSet1). Select the button under Curves, and go around the outer edge of the solid model on the symmetry plane and pick all the edges of the tank. You may have to zoom in and use *Query Select* to do this. Each edge will highlight in blue when selected. When all edges are selected, middle click. Symmetry requires that the Z translation be **FIXED**. The X and Y translations are both **FREE**. Also because of symmetry, we need to set the X and Y rotations as **FIXED**, and **FREE** the rotation around Z. Think carefully about these constraints and how they arise from symmetry. Accept the dialog.

We will also constrain the edges of the side and top inlet/outlet pipes. Select

> *Create > Edge/Curve*

again. Name the constraint **sidepipe** (still in ConstraintSet1). Select the Curves button and pick the outer edge of the pipe coming out the side of the tank. Set all degrees of freedom to **FIXED** for this edge (no translation, no rotation). Repeat for the pipe leaving the top of the tank (call it **toppipe**). The constraints should appear as shown in Figure 46 (these are a bit of a jumble at the top of the model).

Assigning a Pressure Load

Now, in **STRC MODEL**, select

Loads > Create > Pressure

Name the load **presload**, in LoadSet1. Select the
button under Surfaces and click on all the interior
surfaces. Each surface will highlight in red as it is
selected. Don't forget the interior surfaces of the
rounds. You may have to spin the model to ensure
that all surfaces are picked. Then, middle click.
Enter a load magnitude of **0.1** (recall that our units
for pressure are MPa; our applied pressure is equal
to 100 kPa, about atmospheric pressure). Accept
the dialog. The model should now appear as
shown in Figure 46.

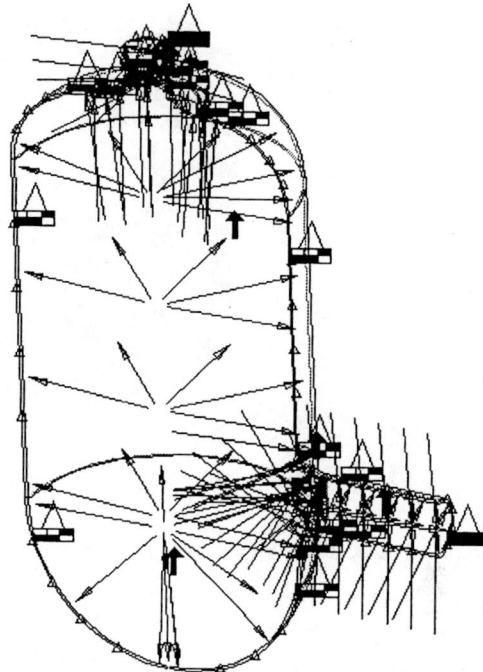

Figure 46 Completed model

Defining and Running the Analysis

We can now define the analysis

Analyses > New

Create a static analysis named **shelltank**. Make sure constraint and load sets are selected. Select
a **QuickCheck** convergence. Go to the ***Run*** menu, review the ***Settings***, and ***Start*** the analysis.
Always accept error detection for the first run of a new model. Open the ***Summary*** window. 51
shell elements are created. The maximum Von Mises stress is around 16.2 MPa. Assuming no
errors, change the analysis to a **Multi-Pass Adaptive** convergence (10% on **Local
Displacement, Local Strain Energy & Global RMS Stress**, max order 9) and rerun the
analysis. You can use the elements from the previous study. The run should converge on pass 7
with a maximum Von Mises stress of about 16.8 MPa.

Viewing the Results

Create some result windows for Von Mises stress and deformation animation. Set the Feature
Angle to zero in both of these. These are shown in Figure 47 below. Note the very large scale on
the deformation (>2000). Is the deformation consistent with your expectations? Locate the
position for the maximum stress. Observe the variation in size of the shell elements.

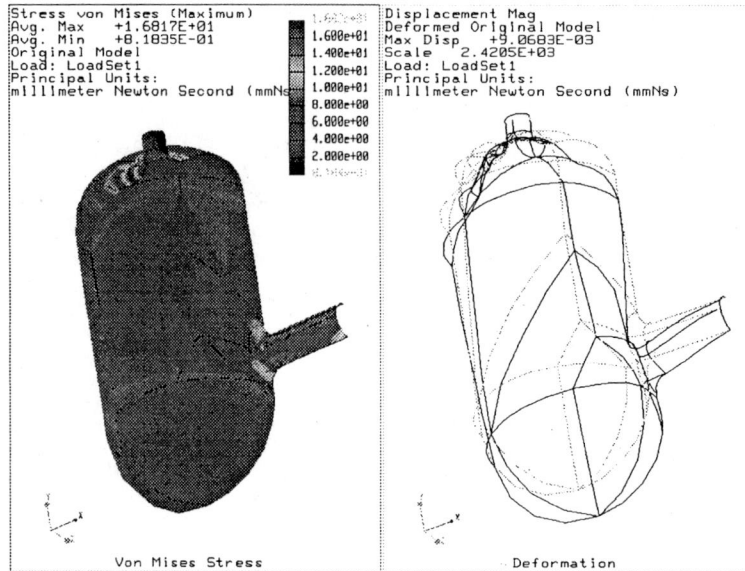

Figure 47 Von Mises stress (left) and deformation (right)

The convergence behavior for this model is shown in Figure 48. This is a pretty well-behaved model!

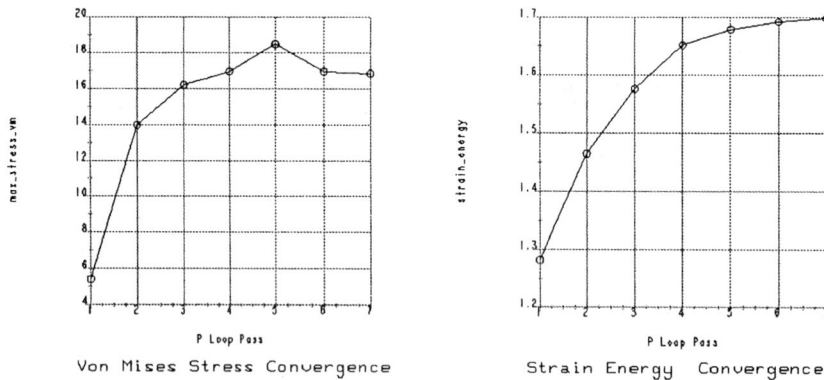

Figure 48 Convergence of Von Mises stress (left) and total strain energy (right)

Exploring the Model

You should spend some time exploring this model. Here are a few things to try:

1. In the *Settings > AGEM Settings* menu, there is an option for **Detailed Fillet Modeling**. Find out what this does and what effect it has on the results.
2. Back in Pro/E, change the radii of the rounds on the two pipes. How small can these be? What happens if you suppress the rounds altogether?
3. Modify the constraints on the side and top pipes. Remove all rotational constraints. For the side pipe, specify only translation in the X direction as fixed. For the top pipe, specify only translation in the Y direction as fixed. Coupled with the symmetry constraint (translation Z fixed), these are sufficient to remove all rigid body degrees of freedom. What effect does this have on the results?

Model #2: A Mounting Bracket

In this model, we will select the surface pairs manually. The model is one used as exercise #2 at the end of Chapter 7 - the mounting bracket shown for reference in Figure 49. In Chapter 7, we created surfaces and shell elements in independent mode. Here, the model is created in Pro/E and we will use an idealization of the solid to create shell elements.

Creating the Model

Create the model **bracket** according to the dimensions shown in Figure 50. Make sure your units are set to mmNs. The view of the part in Figure 49 is approximately in the default orientation. Note that there will be two different shell thicknesses (5mm and 10mm).

Figure 49 The mounting bracket model

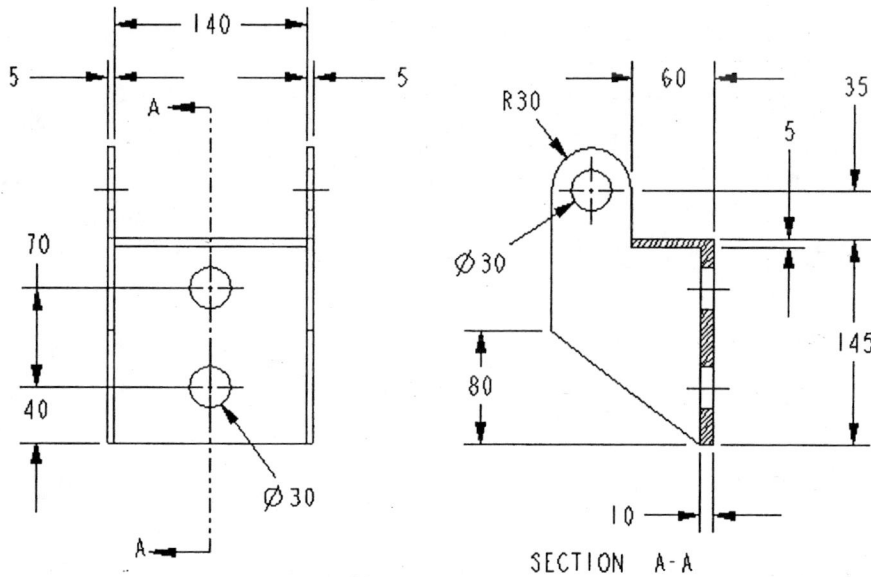

Figure 50 Dimensions (mm) of mounting bracket model

Defining Surface Pairs

When your Pro/E model is ready, launch MECHANICA with

>   ***Applications > Mechanica > Structure***
>   ***Model > Idealizations > Shells***
>   ***Midsurfaces > Create > Constant***

Pick the outer and inner surface of the vertical plate on the right side of the bracket, then middle click. The surfaces will highlight in red and yellow. Continue to pick pairs of parallel surfaces until all four pairs are selected. Then **Done Sel** and repaint your screen. Now select

> **Show > Select**

and pick on any surface. The paired surfaces will highlight. In the **MIDSURFACES** menu, select

> **Compress > Shells only**
> **ShowCompress**

The model will be replaced by the midplane surfaces as shown in Figure 51 highlighted in yellow.

Return to the MECHANICA menu, and check the **Settings**. **Use Pairs** is now checked.

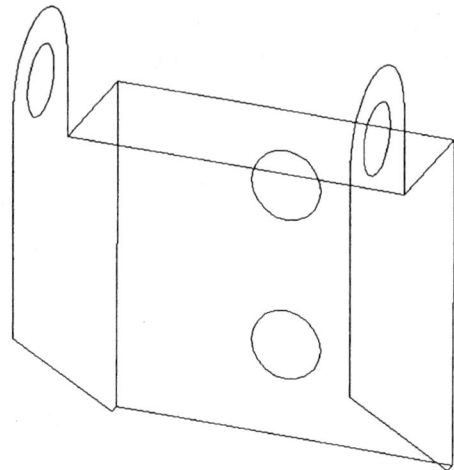

Figure 51 Compressed surfaces

Completing the Model

Assign the material AL2014 to the part:

> **Structure > Model > Materials**
> {move AL2014 to the model list}
> **Assign > Part**

Click on the part, middle click, and accept the dialog.

Now apply constraints. As before, we will apply these to edges.

> **Constraints > Create > Edge/Curve > New**

Create a new constraint set called **fixededges**. Name the constraint **holes**. Select the button under Curves and pick on the front edges of the two holes on the back plate of the bracket. They will highlight in blue. Middle click. Leave all translation degrees of freedom fixed, and the rotations free. Accept the dialog.

Now apply the loads:

> **Loads > Create > Edge/Curve > New**

Create a new load set called **holeloads**. Name the first load **right**. Select the button under Curves and pick on the edge of the hole on the right vertical plate. It will highlight in blue. Middle click. Select **Total**, and **Uniform** in the **Distribution** area and set the X component to **100**. Accept the dialog. Next, for the other hole:

Create > Edge/Curve

Name this load **left** (in load set **holeloads**). Select the edge of the hole on the left vertical plate. Select a **Total Load**, **Uniform** distribution. In the **Force** pull-down list, select **Dir Vector & Mag**. We want a force 30° below horizontal, so enter the vector components **(0, -0.5, 0.866)** in the X, Y, and Z directions, respectively. Enter a magnitude of **250**. See Figure 52. Accept the dialog.

Note that we applied the loads and constraints to edges, not surfaces (why?) and that we did not have to specify a shell property (thickness) - this is obtained from the Pro/E solid model.

Figure 52 Specifying a force by direction and magnitude

The model is now complete and should look like Figure 53. You can change the attachment of the load arrows using

> *View > Simulation Display Settings*

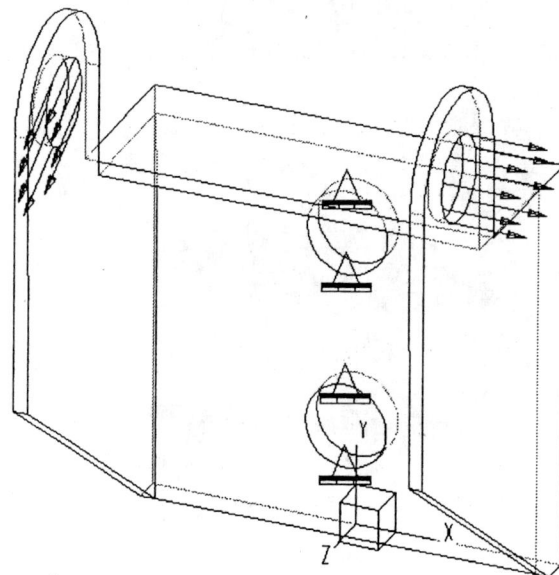

Figure 53 Mounting bracket model complete

Running the Model

Perform the usual analysis steps: set up and run a **QuickCheck** analysis. AutoGEM will create 58 shell elements. The maximum Von Mises stress is just over 100 MPa. *Edit* the analysis to run a **Multi-Pass Adaptive** analysis (5% convergence, maximum edge order 9). The multi-pass analysis does not converge on pass 9 - an indication that something is wrong. The maximum Von Mises stress has increased to 308 MPa which seems a little high (greater than the tensile strength?).

Create some result windows to show the Von
Mises stress and the deformation animation. The
deformation is shown in Figure 54. Note the scale
of the display. The maximum displacement is only
about one-half millimeter. This looks fairly
reasonable.

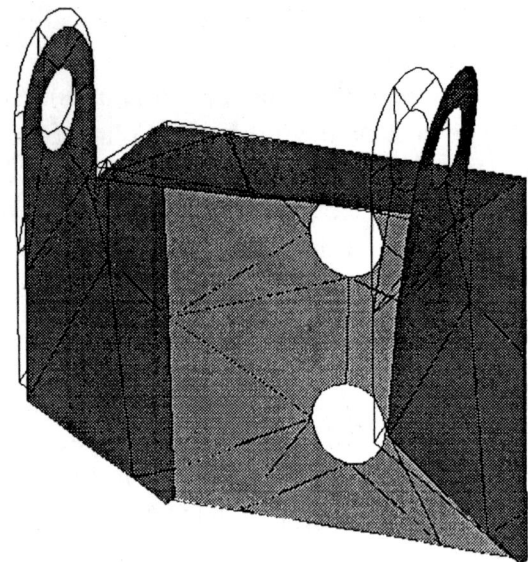

Now bring up the display of the Von Mises stress.
It first appears as in Figure 55. Almost the entire
model is shown in the lowest fringe color (below
26 MPa). There are two very small "hot spots" at
the corners of the vertical plates. Show the
location of the maximum Von Mises stress. It
occurs right at the top corner on the right plate. To
see the rest of the stress distribution in the part, we
need to redefine the stress levels assigned to the
colors in the legend.

Figure 54 Deformation of mounting bracket

In the SHOW CTL menu, select

Controls > Edit Legend

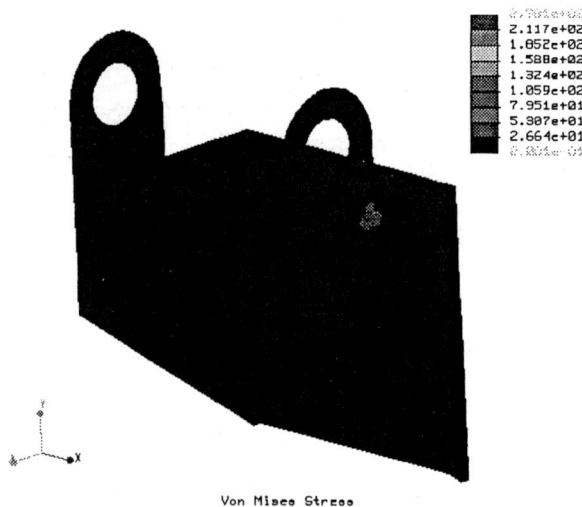

Figure 55 Von Mises stress fringe plot with
default legend

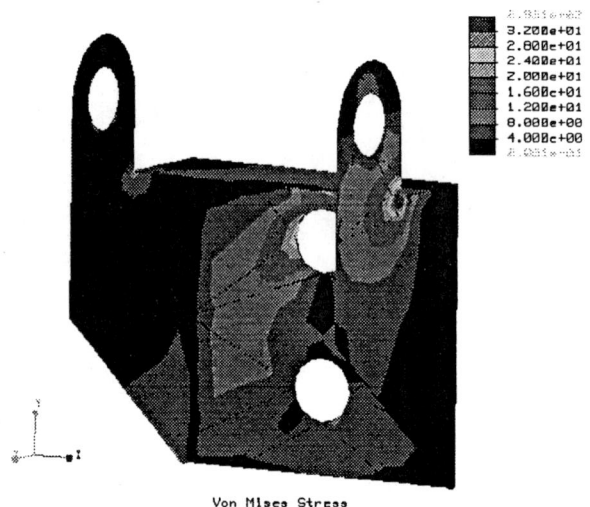

Figure 56 Von Mises stress fringe plot with
edited legend

Pick on the second from the bottom value in the legend (the lowest dark number). A dialog
window opens. Enter a value of **4**. Do not redistribute levels yet. Repeat *Edit Legend* and pick
on the number second from the top. Enter a value of **32**. This time, redistribute the levels. This
changes the fringe pattern on the part. See Figure 56. The legend is in multiples of 4. (You may
have noticed in the result window definition that the default legend has 8 levels - this setting is
adjustable there.) The "hot spots" are now much more visible, as well as the stress distribution
around the mounting holes.

Create windows to show the convergence history of the Von Mises stress and the total strain energy. These are shown in Figure 57. The Von Mises stress is increasing steadily with each pass with no sign of converging at all, while the strain energy does seem to be converging. This behavior indicates that there is a singularity at the reentrant corner. The p-code method in MECHANICA is not able to converge on this type of geometry, as it will continue to try to increase the polynomial order indefinitely in order to catch the (theoretically) infinite stress at the corner. This means that any results (especially the stress) reported right at the corner (and in the immediate vicinity) must be taken with a large grain of salt - it cannot be trusted at all!

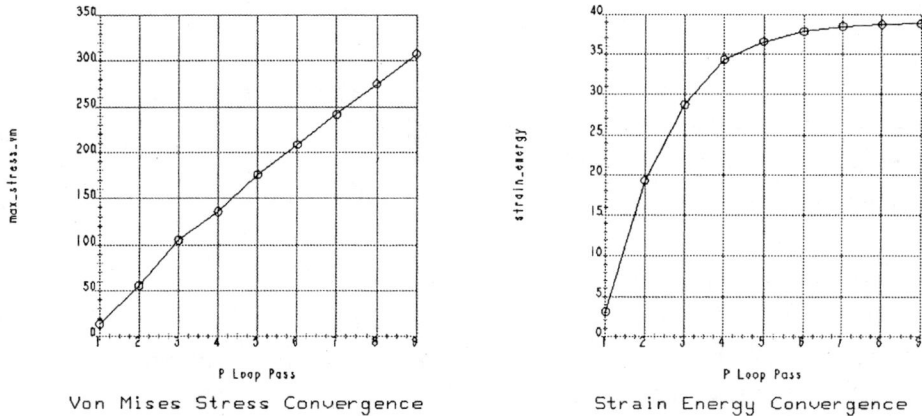

Figure 57 Convergence graphs of Von Mises stress (left) and strain energy (right)

Figure 58 below shows a closeup of the mesh created at the reentrant corner. AutoGEM actually creates several small elements at this corner. In independent mode, you can tell the program to ignore results on these elements (they are *excluded*) while it monitors convergence on the rest of the model. Unfortunately, this cannot be done in integrated mode. You must therefore be on the lookout for this type of behavior, especially with shell models.

In the *AGEM Settings* menu, you may have noticed an option called **Reentrant Corners**. By default, this is selected. Go to this menu and deselect the option. Rerun the analysis to see what happens to the mesh (see Figure 59) and the model results with this new mesh.

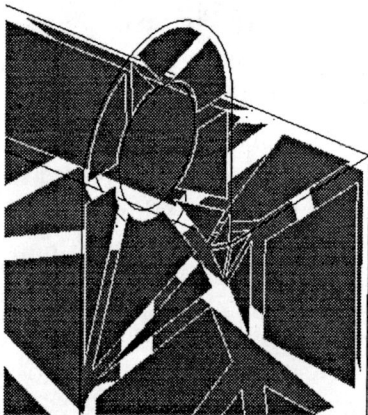

Figure 58 AGEM mesh with elements at reentrant corner

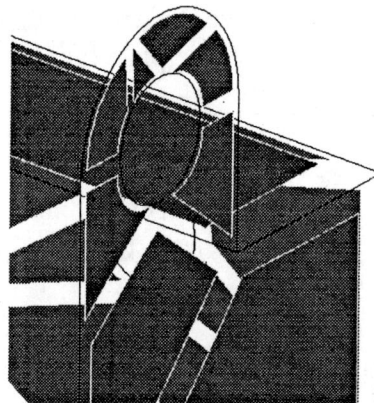

Figure 59 AGEM mesh with reentrant corner option turned off

Other Idealizations

So far, we have used a shell idealization for
thin-walled solids. In integrated mode, you can
also create idealizations for

- beams - defined on datum curves;
  sections and orientation defined as
  described in Chapter 8
- point masses - created on datum
  points (these can be created on the
  fly)
- linear springs - between datum
  points (also created on the fly) or
  between points and ground

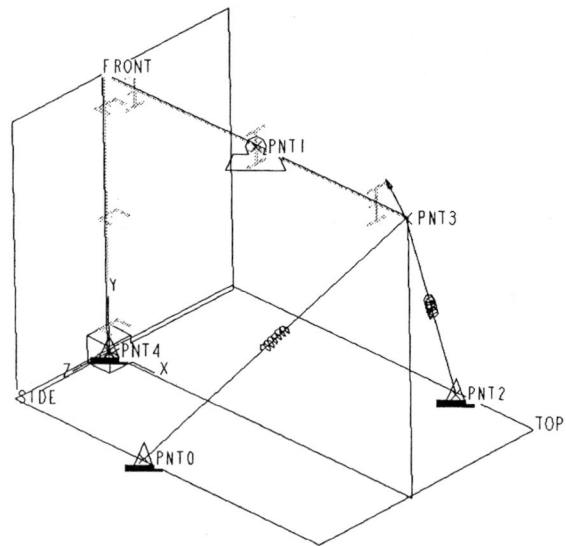

Figure 60 shows a "Rube Goldberg"-like model
that consists of two beams in an inverted L
shape. The different section shapes of the
beams are shown schematically. The upper

Figure 60 The "Rube Goldberg" model
showing other possible idealizations

beam has a point mass at its midpoint, and is attached to fixed datum points by springs. A
concentrated load is applied at the end of the upper beam. Since we have not dealt with masses or
springs previously in this tutorial, we will not do that now. Definition of springs is quite a bit
more complicated than indicated here. Full details are available in the on-line documentation.

Analysis of Assemblies in Integrated Mode

Pro/Engineer is noted for its ability to create and manage assemblies. These assemblies are
easily brought into MECHANICA for stress analysis. Be warned that (despite what we will see
here) analysis of assemblies requires very advanced modeling techniques and understanding.
One of the requirements for analysis of assemblies is the proper modeling of the contact between
adjacent parts. This will be illustrated using the simple assembly shown in Figure 61. This
consists of an aluminum base plate (approx. 24" X 10"), a steel pin (diameter 3"), and an
aluminum connector (diameter 6"). The holes in the lugs on the base plate and on the connector
are the same as the pin diameter. When assembled, an upward force is applied to the connector.
To take advantage of symmetry in the geometry and loads, a quarter model can be created in
Pro/E using a cut created in assembly mode. See Figure 62 (Note that this model is in the
positive quadrant - view is from top - left - rear; observe the coordinate systems in the figure).

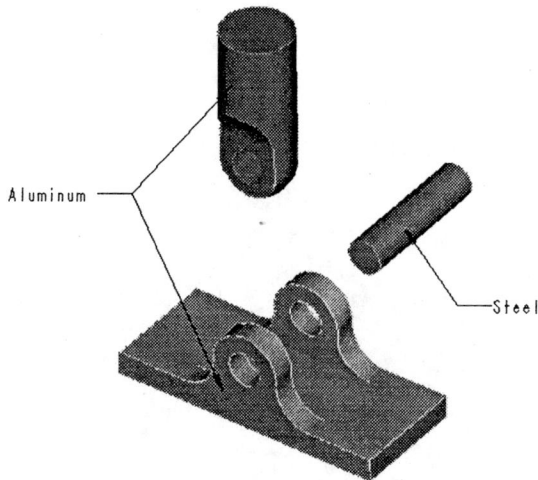

Figure 61 Pro/ENGINEER assembly (exploded)

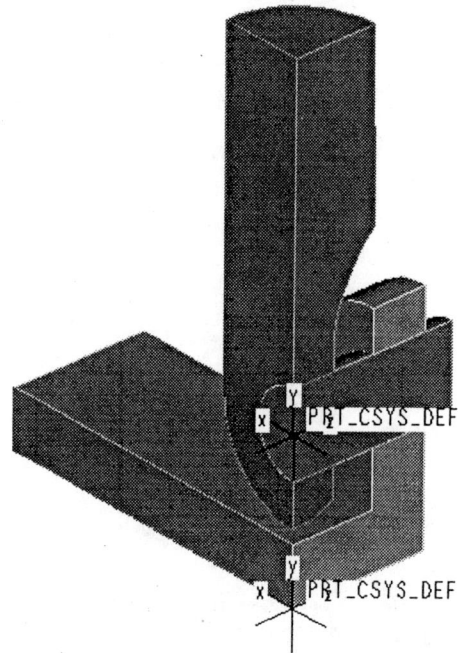

Figure 62 The FEA model

After you have created the parts, create an assembly in Pro/E. Make sure the units for each part and the assembly are consistent (IPS). When the quarter model is ready, bring it into Pro/M and assign materials to the parts. Select

> ***Applications > Mechanica > Structure > Model > Materials***

Bring the materials **AL2014** and **STEEL** into the model. Then, with AL2014 highlighted, select

> ***Assign > Part***

Click on the two aluminum parts; middle click. Select **STEEL** and assign this to the pin. Accept the dialog.

Constraints are applied to the two symmetry planes, and the lower surface. Start with

> ***Constraints > Create > Surface***

and apply appropriate constraints in ConstraintSet1 to the two cutting planes arising from symmetry. Name these **XYface** and **YZface**. These will involve fixing the translation perpendicular to the surface, and freeing the other two translations. Since the model will use solid elements, the rotational constraints don't matter. Note that surfaces of all three parts should be included in each constraint. Finally, apply a translational constraint to the bottom of the base to prevent rigid body motion perpendicular to that surface.

Now apply an upward load:

Loads > Create > Surface

Create a load on the top surface of the connector (**Uniform**, **Total Load**, **5000** lb upward). The model should appear as shown in Figure 63.

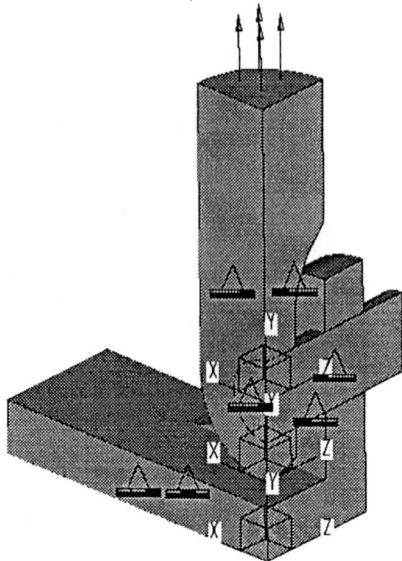

Figure 63 Model with constraints and loads

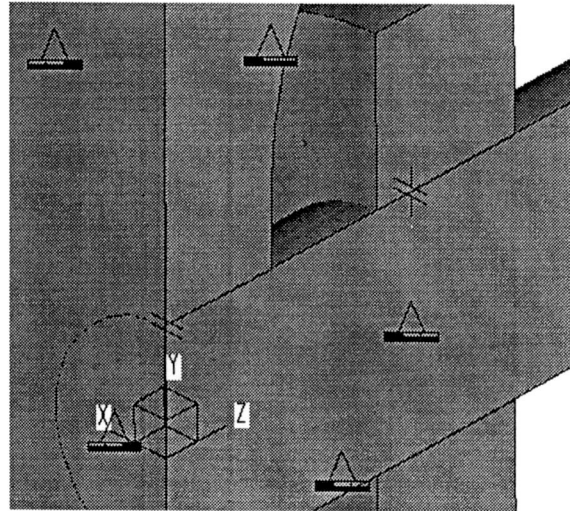

Figure 64 Contact regions defined between the pin and hole surfaces

Creating Contact Surfaces

If we perform an analysis of this model now, MECHANICA will "weld" the surface of the steel pin to the aluminum holes. This essentially creates a continuous solid whose material properties change as you cross the pin-hole surface. However, we know that because of the construction of the assembly and the applied load, as the load is applied, these surfaces might actually separate (create a gap). We can define contact surfaces that Pro/M can monitor for this - the surfaces are free to move apart (normal to the surface) to cause a gap to be created, but will not penetrate the other part. To create these contacts, in the **STRC MODEL** menu select

Contacts > Create > Part

and click on the cylindrical surface of the pin, then (using *Query Select*) click on the hole surface of the base part. A small contact region symbol will appear. Do the same where the pin passes through the hole on the connector. The two contact region symbols are shown in Figure 64. Use the *Review* command to confirm the surfaces are correct.

Set up and run a **QuickCheck** analysis called **contact1** to see if we have any errors in the model. At the bottom of the analysis definition window, we can set the number of **Load Intervals** to be used to apply the load. This is to account for the fact that the actual contact between surfaces in a complicated assembly may be made and broken as the load is applied. Furthermore, as contact is a non-linear problem, Pro/M must do some iteration here to determine the size/shape of the actual contacting regions. For now, use a single interval. (Come back later and try five equally spaced intervals and compare results.) ***Run*** the analysis. AutoGEM creates 187 or so solid elements. Assuming no errors, change the analysis to a **Multi-Pass Adaptive** analysis. The run should converge on pass 4 or 5. In the ***Summary*** window, note that the contact area and maximum pressure is given for the two contact regions.

Create result windows for the Von Mises stress and a deformation animation. Zoom in on the contact regions in the deformation window to observe the separation of the surfaces.

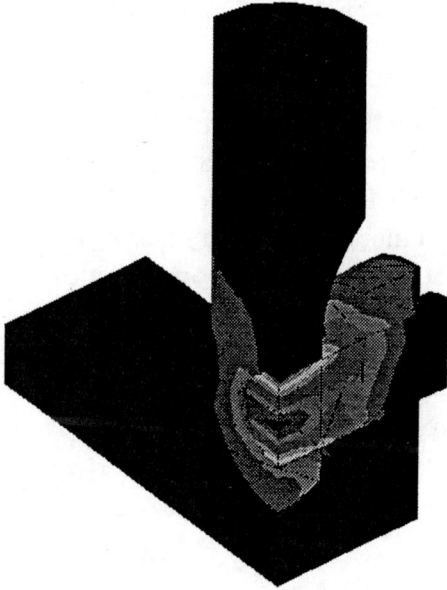

Figure 65 Von Mises stress fringe   **Figure 66** Deformed shape

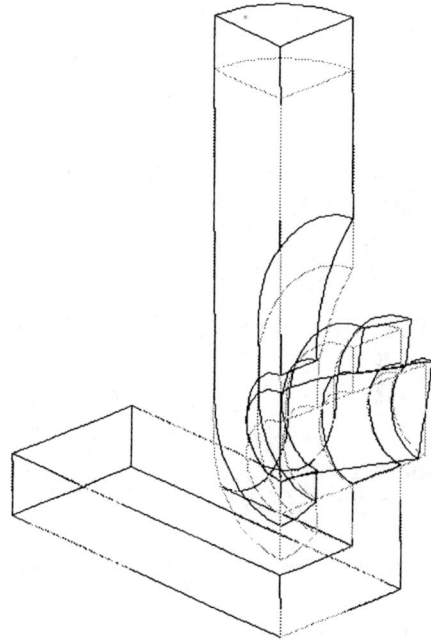

Create another result window showing the normal stress component in the direction of the load (the YY component). Check the option to show the model in the deformed shape. The result window is shown in Figure 67 (deformation scale is about 300). Note the gap that has been created around the pin, and the continuity of the normal stress where the surfaces remain in contact.

You might like to examine the stress on an XY cutting plane through the model.

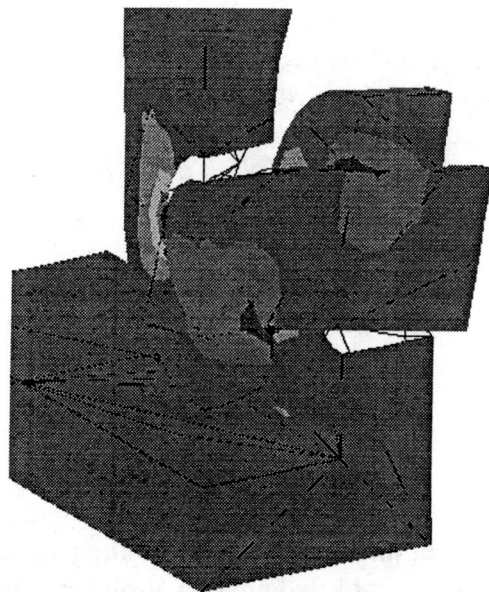

Figure 67 Normal stress (YY) contours

Summary

We have seen how to bring Pro/E models (parts and assemblies) into Mechanica running in integrated mode. The major Mechanica command menus are the same as independent mode. Some functionality of independent Mechanica is not present in integrated mode, such as control over excluded elements or certain result windows (p-levels, for example). Idealizations are available to handle thin-walled features using shell elements, as well as point masses, springs, and beams. You can also analyze 2D models (plane stress, plane strain, axisymmetric) using geometry created in Pro/E. Cyclic symmetry can also be exploited to simplify the FEA model for appropriate cases. In the analysis of assemblies, contact regions can be defined to handle the kinematic constraints between contacting surfaces.

The major advantage of integrated mode is the ease with which models can be created in Pro/ENGINEER. These geometry tools are superior to those in Mechanica, and also have the advantage that you don't need to learn a different set of commands for geometry creation. The Pro/E model, of course, is feature-based and parametric, while a model created in independent Mechanica is not. Furthermore, it is easy to set up sensitivity studies and design optimizations.

When using Pro/E to create solid models, remember the discussion of Lesson #1. The FEA model is not necessarily identical to the Pro/E CAD model. You may be able to defeature the part, and certainly use symmetry whenever you can, in order to produce an efficient as well as effective FEA model.

Conclusion

This completes this tutorial, and we have covered a lot of ground. Even so, we have not looked at many Pro/M commands, functions, or analysis types. It is hoped, however, that you are now comfortable enough using the program that you can experiment with these other capabilities on your own without getting lost. When you do try to do something new, you should set up a simple problem for which you already know the answer (either quantitatively or qualitatively) just to make sure your procedures are correct. Also, the on-line documentation is available to answer your questions about other aspects of Pro/MECHANICA. Your installation may also have installed an extensive set of verification examples that comes with the program.

In closing, it is useful to remind ourselves of some of the comments made in the first two chapters. First,

"Don't confuse convenience with intelligence."

Pro/M is undoubtedly a very powerful analysis tool. You should realize by now that, like all other FEA analysis tools, unless it is used properly, the results it produces can be suspect. Remember that in FEA we are finding an "approximate solution to an idealized mathematical model of a simplified physical problem." It is expecting a lot to hope for results that *exactly* match the solution found by nature! The most we should hope for are answers that are sufficiently accurate so as to be valuable.

Second, Pro/M is a huge program that will take many, many hours to master. As your knowledge and experience grows, applying your new skills in increasingly more complicated problems is an inviting prospect. However, when you start to feel the urge to rush off to your computer to tackle a new problem, remember the first goal of FEA is to

> *"Use the simplest model possible that will yield sufficiently reliable results of interest at the lowest computational cost."*

It may even be that your problem can be solved in other (cheaper and quicker) ways.

In short,

> *"Let FEA become a tool that extends your design capability, not define it."*

Good luck, and happy computing!

Questions for Review/Further Study

1. Where and how do you set up the units for the Mechanica model?
2. What degrees of freedom are associated with solid and shell elements?
3. How do you specify a part dimension as a design study for a sensitivity analysis?
4. How do you specify a Pro/E parameter as a Mechanica design variable?
5. Can you use Auto-Pairs for a model with thin walls of varying thickness?
6. How do you carry the optimized geometry determined in Mechanica back into Pro/E?
7. Can you create a model with mixed solid and shell elements?
8. Can you assign different material properties to different regions of the same part?
9. Is it possible to define anisotropic material properties in a solid model?
10. How are contact regions in an assembly created?
11. In a contact analysis, find out what the load increment setting does. When should it be used?
12. What other loads are available in integrated mode? Do these have any special requirements in the Pro/E model?

This page left blank.